Introduction to Law for Paralegals

ASPEN PUBLISHERS

Introduction to Law for Paralegals

Second Edition

NEAL R. BEVANS, J.D.

Western Piedmont Community College

Wolters Kluwer

Law & Business

AUSTIN   BOSTON   CHICAGO   NEW YORK   THE NETHERLANDS

© 2008 Neal R. Bevans

Published by Aspen Publishers. All Rights Reserved.

No part of this publication may be reproduced or transmitted in any form or by any means, electronic or mechanical, including photocopy, recording, or any information storage and retrieval system, without permission in writing from the publisher. Requests for permission to make copies of any part of this publication should be mailed to:

Aspen Publishers
Attn: Permissions Department
76 Ninth Avenue, 7th Floor
New York, NY 10011-5201

To contact Customer Care, e-mail customer.care@aspenpublishers.com, call 1-800-234-1660, fax 1-800-901-9075, or mail correspondence to:

Aspen Publishers
Attn: Order Department
PO Box 990
Frederick, MD 21705

Printed in the United States of America.

3 4 5 6 7 8 9 0

ISBN 978-0-7355-6920-1

Library of Congress Cataloging-in-Publication Data

Bevans, Neal R., 1961-
    Introduction to law for paralegals / Neal R. Bevans. — 2nd ed.
        p. cm.
Includes index.
ISBN 978-0-7355-6920-1
1. Law — United States. 2. Legal assistants — United States — Handbooks, manuals, etc. I. Title.

KF386.B45 2008
349.73 — dc22

2007033154

About Wolters Kluwer Law & Business

Wolters Kluwer Law & Business is a leading provider of research information and workflow solutions in key specialty areas. The strengths of the individual brands of Aspen Publishers, CCH, Kluwer Law International and Loislaw are aligned within Wolters Kluwer Law & Business to provide comprehensive, in-depth solutions and expert-authored content for the legal, professional and education markets.

CCH was founded in 1913 and has served more than four generations of business professionals and their clients. The CCH products in the Wolters Kluwer Law & Business group are highly regarded electronic and print resources for legal, securities, antitrust and trade regulation, government contracting, banking, pension, payroll, employment and labor, and healthcare reimbursement and compliance professionals.

Aspen Publishers is a leading information provider for attorneys, business professionals and law students. Written by preeminent authorities, Aspen products offer analytical and practical information in a range of specialty practice areas from securities law and intellectual property to mergers and acquisitions and pension/benefits. Aspen's trusted legal education resources provide professors and students with high-quality, up-to-date and effective resources for successful instruction and study in all areas of the law.

Kluwer Law International supplies the global business community with comprehensive English-language international legal information. Legal practitioners, corporate counsel and business executives around the world rely on the Kluwer Law International journals, loose-leafs, books and electronic products for authoritative information in many areas of international legal practice.

Loislaw is a premier provider of digitized legal content to small law firm practitioners of various specializations. Loislaw provides attorneys with the ability to quickly and efficiently find the necessary legal information they need, when and where they need it, by facilitating access to primary law as well as state-specific law, records, forms and treatises.

Wolters Kluwer Law & Business, a unit of Wolters Kluwer, is headquartered in New York and Riverwoods, Illinois. Wolters Kluwer is a leading multinational publisher and information services company.

For my wife, Deb,
the woman who makes it all possible

Summary of Contents

Contents

INTRODUCTION TO LAW

CHAPTER 1: AN INTRODUCTION TO LAW

CHAPTER 3: THE PARTICIPANTS IN THE LEGAL SYSTEM   **49**

CHAPTER 5: ETHICS   93

III. SPECIFIC TYPES OF LAW — 161

CHAPTER 8: PERSONAL INJURY LAW (TORTS) — 163

CHAPTER 13: WILLS AND TRUSTS   **281**

Preface

Introduction

This second edition of Introduction to Law for Paralegals provides an overview of the U.S. legal system and its participants, and an introduction to substantive law. The book presents these concepts by balancing theory with practice. As in the previous edition, the first few chapters introduce the student to the world of legal practice, from a discussion of the sources of law to legal research and the initial steps of bringing both civil and criminal actions. Later chapters examine specific areas of law in greater depth, while also focusing on the development of practical skills.

In this second edition, the author provides new cases and additional features, including updated web sites and questions keyed to the issues provided in the new case excerpts.

In addition to presenting a solid introduction to legal procedures and substantive issues, this text also emphasizes the richly rewarding life of a legal professional. Practical examples are included in each chapter, as well as profiles of legal professionals from judges to court reporters. Each chapter also profiles practicing paralegals from across the country. Their interview excerpts provide a window on the day-to-day practice of law that is rarely seen in any introductory text.

Features

This book was designed with the reader in mind. The text presents the material in a variety of methods to take advantage of different student learning styles. There is a strong visual element to the text with features such as "Issue at a Glance," a brief summary of an important issue raised in the chapter. Each chapter also contains a section discussing how to build practical skills.

Features found in the text include:

- **Chapter Objectives**
  Each chapter begins with clearly stated learning objectives to guide readers in their studies.

- **Issue at a Glance**
  Each chapter includes short synopses of issues discussed in the chapter, positioned adjacent to the material under discussion, not only as a way of

helping the reader synthesize important issues, but also as a visual marker for later study.

■ **Definitions**

As each new term is introduced, it is also defined for the student. These on-the-spot definitions provide a handy reference.

■ **Skills**

Each chapter contains not only discussions of the theoretical under-pinnings of law, but also practical examples to assist the student in building the skill sets needed to succeed in the legal field.

■ **Sample Cases**

Each chapter contains a case excerpt designed to emphasize some of the points raised in that chapter and to provide material for classroom discussions.

■ **Questions About the Case**

At the end of each case, a list of questions is provided to help students focus on the important aspects of the decision. These questions will facilitate classroom discussions.

■ **Chapter Summary**

Each chapter contains a concise summary of the major issues discussed. This feature helps readers focus on the important points raised in the chapter.

■ **Skills You Need in the Real World**

In keeping with the balance of theoretical discussion and practical examples, in the "Skills" section found at the conclusion of each chapter the author addresses how the student can learn a variety of important practical skills, from searching courthouse records to creating appellate brief banks.

■ **Profiling a Paralegal**

To help the reader make an emotional connection with the material under discussion, the author offers a profile of an individual paralegal in each chapter. These profiles are designed not only as a way to discuss practical aspects of the daily working life of paralegals, but also the essential role they play in modern legal practice.

■ **Ethical Discussion**

Ethics is a vital component of any legal text, but never more so than in an introductory text that will help lay the foundation for the reader's entire paralegal education and later professional life. To emphasize the important role that ethics plays in law, each chapter contains a separate ethical discussion in addition to the entire chapter devoted to this critical issue.

■ **Web Sites**

The Internet is becoming an increasingly vital link for students. The web sites at the end of each chapter will assist students in gathering more information about the chapter topics.

■ **Key Terms and Phrases**

A list of key terms and phrases used in each chapter will assist the student in mastering the concepts presented.

■ **Review Questions**

Extensive review questions test the student's comprehension of the issues under discussion. These review questions, coupled with the discussion questions, provide rich material for classroom discussions.

■ **Practical Applications**

While the review and discussion questions encourage dialogue about the topics in each chapter, the practical applications allow the student to put this theoretical knowledge to practical use and to make a stronger connection with the material, while building important skills.

■ **Non-Gender Specific Language**

In recognition of the impact of gender specific language, the author has adopted the following convention in the text: Each even-numbered chapter uses "he" in general discussions and examples, while the odd-numbered chapters use "she" for the same purposes.

Pedagogy

The following features are included in the text to accommodate different student learning styles:

■ Learning objectives stated at the beginning of each chapter
■ Terms and legal vocabulary set in bold and defined immediately for the student; also listed in the glossary for later reference
■ Many different visual aids that illustrate crucial points
■ Professional profiles to help the student make a personal connection with the material
■ Lesson plans in the instructor's manual that provide alternative presentations: for example, Lesson Plan A, which emphasizes practical applications, as opposed to Lesson Plan B, which emphasizes substantive law
■ End-of-chapter questions, activities, and assignments to hone the students' understanding
■ End-of-chapter ethical discussion
■ Web sites for further research and/or discussion

Instructor's Manual

The author has developed an extensive instructor's manual to accompany the text, which provides a wealth of resources for the instructor. The manual is also available on a CD, to help instructors make more efficient use of their time. Among the features in the instructor's manual are these:

- **Suggested Syllabi**
  Suggested syllabi are provided for various versions of an Introduction to Law courses, including alternate syllabi for instructors who emphasize theoretical over practical, or practical over theoretical.

- **Lesson Plans**
  The author provides several different lesson plans to help instructors who must present introductory courses in 6, 8,10,12, or 16 week formats.

- **Chapter Lecture Outline and Discussion**
  Each chapter is outlined for the instructor and annotations are added throughout the outline to provide additional discussion and classroom material for the instructor.

- **Additional Web Resources**
  The instructor's manual contains additional web sites to provide other resources for classroom discussion and assignments.

- **Additional Assignments**
  In addition to the chapter review and discussion questions in the book, extra assignments are provided in the instructor's manual.

- **Answers to Review Questions and Discussion Questions**
  The end-of-chapter review questions are answered in detail. The author also provides suggested answers for the discussion questions.

- **Test Bank**
  The test bank includes a variety of test questions:

  Essay questions (five per chapter)
  Short answer (ten per chapter)
  Multiple choice (twenty-five per chapter)
  True-False (ten per chapter)

- **Additional Features on Instructor's Manual CD:**
  Power Point Slides
  The author has prepared a power point presentation for each chapter of the text.

  Additional Cases
  Additional cases are provided for classroom discussion. These can be used in a variety of ways, including as lecture hand-outs and additional assignments.

Acknowledgments

The author would like to thank the following people for their assistance in preparing this book:

Betsy Kenny, Richard Mixter, Debra Holbrook, Lisa Mazzonetto, Pamela Tallent, John Purvis, Leah Laidley, Hon. Pamela South, Steven Ehlers, Keith Miles, Esq., Rena Harp, Mary Ann Shea, LNC, Jane Huffman, Hon. Mabel Lowman, Amanda Eury, April Gardin, Officer Marty McNeeley, Cherie Eddy, Leslie McKesson, Janice Johnson, Barry Stock, Darlene Burgess, Nina Neal, Esq., Tammy Atkins, Renee Collette, Lisa Dubs, Esq., Jean Jurasin, Officer David Cheek, Taura Hamilton, Donna Cooper, Cyndie Callaway, Esq., Sarah Roman, and Paula Barnes.

Introduction
to Law

I

An Introduction to Law

Chapter Learning Objectives

After completing this chapter, you should be able to:

- Discuss the definition and sources of law

- Explain the differences between civil and criminal law

- Describe the organization of the state and federal court systems

- Explain the basic hierarchy of the court systems ranging from the trial court to the various courts of appeal

- Explain the powers of the three branches of government

 **INTRODUCTION**

In this chapter, we focus on the basic foundations of U.S. law. In attempting to define what *law* is, we address a wide range of issues. This chapter also begins a discussion of the basic organization of the court system that is expanded in later chapters. Finally, we address the concepts of statutory law, case law, and common law and explain the crucial role played by each in the legal system.

 **WHAT IS THE LAW?**

When people use the term the **law,** they usually do not realize that this term encompasses a wide variety of topics. For instance, if you look up the word "law" in a legal dictionary (such as Ballentine's Legal Dictionary), you will see that the definition takes up nearly a page of written text. For legal professionals, the word *law* can encompass many different terms, depending on the circumstances of a case. For a prosecutor, the law refers to the criminal statutes that

Law
A rule or regulation that, if not followed, subjects the rule breaker to some form of sanction

3

make certain behavior illegal. For a civil attorney, "law" could refer to the rules of court or the rules governing civil procedure. The law could also refer to the decisions of the U.S. Supreme Court. Because the term is open to so many different interpretations, as a student of the law, you must understand how the law applies in different contexts. For purposes of introducing the topic of the study of law, we use a working definition that will slowly expand as we develop concepts in later chapters.

This working definition of the law covers areas as diverse as criminal statutes and rules of civil procedure. Before we develop any other concepts of what the law is and how it affects the legal system, we should first address some of the misconceptions that surround the study of law. Perhaps the biggest misconception has to do with the interplay of law and moral codes.

A. LAW AND MORALITY

Legal codes and moral codes operate independently of one another. Simply because something is legal does not mean that it is moral, and vice versa. It may be immoral to do many things that are not illegal to do. In this way, law and morality have very little to do with one another.

Example: Bill and Joe are at a casino. Joe begins to play with an eight-year-old girl who is there with her father. The girl's father is playing blackjack at a table across the room. Joe, who is eighteen years old, lures the little girl into the men's room, where he attacks her, savagely beating and raping her. While Joe is assaulting the girl, Bill walks into the men's room and clearly sees what Joe is doing. Bill does not attempt to stop the assault. Instead, he simply walks out of the men's room and leaves the casino. Later, the little girl's body is found in the men's room and the police focus on Joe when they review the casino surveillance tapes that show Joe and the little girl playing. When they ask Bill about what happened, he freely admits that Joe killed the girl and that he saw it happen.

Can Bill be prosecuted for his failure to stop the assault?

Answer: No. Criminal law does not, in most cases, provide any sanction against a person who fails to stop another person from committing a crime. While we would argue that Bill's actions are clearly immoral, they are not illegal. As you may have guessed, this factual scenario is based on a real case. Although the names have been changed, the result was the same. In the actual case, the witness who failed to stop the attack was not prosecuted. "Joe" was convicted and sentenced to life in prison, but "Bill" was never tried for any crime. Later, when we discuss criminal law, we explore this issue in greater depth, but it is important to remember that the standard of proof in criminal cases is very high. Many of the acts that we would consider to be immoral or improper are not necessarily illegal.

ISSUE AT A GLANCE

Although many laws are based on moral codes, in a strict sense, law and morality are independent of one another.

> If any one bring an accusation against a man, and the accused go to the river and leap into the river, if he sink in the river his accuser shall take possession of his house. But if the river prove that the accused is not guilty, and he escape unhurt, then he who had brought the accusation shall be put to death, while he who leaped into the river shall take possession of the house that had belonged to his accuser.
>
> If any one bring an accusation of any crime before the elders, and does not prove what he has charged, he shall, if it be a capital offense charged, be put to death.

FIGURE 1-1

Excerpt from the Code of Hammurabi

B. A SHORT HISTORY OF LAW

As long as there have been human societies, there have been rules. Prehistoric people did not leave written records of their laws, but they surely had some form of law. Stealing from a member of the tribe has always been against the rules in all communities (although stealing from other tribes often was not). With the advent of cities and greater sophistication in society, including the invention of writing, law came into greater prominence. In fact, many of the first writings discovered by archeologists center almost exclusively on two concerns: business and law. These two issues have been linked ever since. (Without law there is no way to enforce a contract.) As society evolved, laws became more extensive to deal with the wide variety of relationships between individuals. Eventually, the body of law was so diverse that almost every society sought some way of organizing it for ease of reference. Most of these societies **codified** their laws.

Codify
A systematic arrangement of the laws of a particular jurisdiction or area of law

One notable early attempt to codify the laws of human society, the Code of Hammurabi (1700 B.C.), stands out as a particularly well-organized, if somewhat drastic, series of laws.

Later, the Romans, who developed legal concepts to a complexity not seen again until the twentieth century, codified their laws in the Twelve Tables (450 B.C.), which set out all the basic laws of society (and the punishments for breaking them). Among Roman legal innovations were the concept of the condominium, wills, trusts, basic property law, and the creation of lawyers as a separate professional class.

All societies have created laws to control the behavior of their citizens.

 ISSUE AT A GLANCE

C. SOURCES OF LAW

There is a wide variety of sources of law. For instance, a state legislature may vote on a particular bill to make a certain action illegal. When this bill is signed by the state governor, it becomes a **statute.** A statute is binding on everyone inside the geographic limits of the state. Similarly, the United States Congress may also vote

Statute
A law that is enacted by the legislature and signed into existence by the executive branch

FIGURE 1-2

Excerpt from the
Twelve Tables

Table VIII: The Law of Torts

1. If any person had sung or composed against another person a song such as was causing slander or insult to another . . . he should be clubbed to death.

2. If a person has maimed another's limb, let there be retaliation in kind unless he makes agreement for compensation with him.

3. If he has broken or bruised a freemen's bone with his hand or a club, he shall undergo a penalty of 300 pieces; if a slave's, 150.

on a bill and send it to the President for signature. When he signs the bill, the federal statute becomes binding on everyone in the United States. There are also administrative rules and regulations that carry the same force as a statute. IRS regulations, for instance, although not statutes, carry as much weight as statutes. These administrative rules and regulations are covered in a later chapter. In discussing the sources of law, what is important is to understand that law can be found in many different places. To locate the law on a particular topic, you must first know and understand what type of law is involved in the case. In later chapters, we address the varied topics of criminal law, real estate law, and administrative law, among others. However, before moving on to those specialized areas of practice, we first address the various sources of law.

1. STATUTORY LAW

A statute is legislation that has been created by the legislature and signed into existence by the President (or the governor on the state level). Statutes can regulate a dizzying array of behavior, from crimes to agricultural practices. Legislatures enact new statutes every year and make changes to existing statutes. All these statutes are published in codes for ease of reference.

2. CASE LAW

In addition to statutory law, there is another, equally important, source of law: case law. Case law consists of the published decisions of appellate courts. These courts are empowered to interpret statutes and even, under certain circumstances, to invalidate a statute. We discuss case law in greater detail in the next chapter.

3. ADMINISTRATIVE RULES AND REGULATIONS

In addition to statutes and case law, there is another significant source of law: administrative rules and regulations. Federal and state agencies promulgate rules to enforce their areas of responsibility. These rules can be as important to a person as any statute. An agency, such as the Federal Emergency Management Agency or the Transportation Security Administration, can establish a rule that affects the entire nation.

 **DIFFERENT TYPES OF LAW**

In later chapters, we address legal topics as diverse as administrative law, real property law, and business law. But before we explore those legal topics, we can divide up the entire body of law into two general categories: criminal law and civil law.

Highlights

In 2001 plaintiffs in the 75 largest counties won just over half the 12,000 general civil cases at trial, with 442 or 4% awarded $1 million or more

FIGURE 1-3

Highlights of the American Court System*

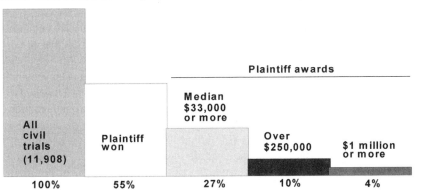

• During 2001 a jury decided almost 75% of the 12,000 tort, contract, and real property trials in the Nation's 75 largest counties. Judges adjudicated the remaining 24%. Tort cases (93%) were more likely than contract cases (43%) to be disposed of by jury trial.

• The 11,908 civil trials disposed of in 2001 represents a 47% decline from the 22,451 civil trials in these counties in 1992.

• In jury trials, the median award decreased from $65,000 in 1992 to $37,000 in 2001 in these counties.

• Two-thirds of disposed trials in 2001 involved tort claims, and about a third involved contractual issues.

• Overall, plaintiffs won in 55% of trials. Plaintiffs won more often in bench trials (65%) than in jury trials

(53%), and in contract trials (65%) more than in tort (52%) or real property trials (38%).

• An estimated $4 billion in compensatory and punitive damages were awarded to plaintiff winners in civil trials. Juries awarded $3.9 billion to plaintiff winners while judges awarded $368 million. The median total award for plaintiff winners in tort trials was $27,000 and in contract trials $45,000.

• Punitive damages, estimated at $1.2 billion, were awarded to 6% of plaintiff winners in trials. The median punitive damage award was $50,000.

• Plaintiffs prevailed in about a fourth (27%) of medical malpractice trials. Half of the 311 plaintiffs who successfully litigated a medical malpractice claim won at least $422,000, and in nearly a third of these cases, the award was $1 million or more.

*Bureau of Justice Statistics, U.S. Department of Justice. Civil Trail Cases and Verdicts in Large Counties, 2001.

Profiling a Paralegal

▶ Leah Laidley

 worked as a computer programs analyst for years before getting laid off and deciding to go back to school to become a paralegal. I went to work for a small firm almost as soon as I started my classes. I was surprised at how different a law office is from other types of offices. My biggest problem was that my "secretarial skills" — for want of a better term — weren't what they could have been. I had to learn some of the basics, like the right way to take a phone message. When I first started answering the phone, I'd just jot down the person's name and telephone number. When I handed it to the attorney, he'd say, "what's this about?" After that, I learned that you had to get more information. I had to learn how to type up letters and motions from a tape machine. The attorney I worked with just used a tape recorder. He'd dictate everything and I'd have to type it up from the tapes.

The firm I work for handles just about everything, although we concentrate on personal injury cases.

My particular specialty — learned through a lot of trial and error — is getting medical records. Contacts are everything when you're trying to get records. I think I was lucky when I first started doing it because I was honest with people. I'd call them up and say, "hey, I don't know what I'm doing. I'm new, so forgive me if I mess up." Once I got a name, like someone at the hospital records department, whenever I called back, I'd always ask for that person. I still do that. If I'm not sure about exactly what I'm doing when I call someone up, I'll just tell them. Most people are really friendly to you. Once I get the records ordered, I keep track of them. I get them all organized and filed so that the attorney can go through them later and get what he needs out of them. I'll sift through them all and find out exactly what insurance paid and what the client paid. I'll summarize all of this information for ease of reference and make sure that the attorney sees it.

A. CIVIL LAW VERSUS CRIMINAL LAW

Criminal law governs the area of arrest and prosecution of a person for committing a crime. Civil law governs areas as widely divergent as personal injury lawsuits, divorce, child custody, and administrative law, among many others.

To a legal professional, the differences between criminal law and civil law are profound. But to someone who is unfamiliar with the day-to-day practice of law, those differences might not be as obvious. Figure 1-4 highlights the main differences between civil and criminal law.

1. THE PARTIES

Governments bring criminal prosecutions against individuals. A private individual brings a civil lawsuit. The person who brings the civil lawsuit is referred to as a plaintiff. The person who is being sued is referred to as the defendant. When you see a case printed in a case law reporter, the first item listed is the **caption** (or the name) of the case. This is always given as the names of the parties involved. Civil cases are usually captioned *Plaintiff A v. Defendant B.* Because the government always brings criminal cases, the government is listed by name, not as a plaintiff. Criminal cases are captioned *Government (or State) v. Defendant.* The fact that the

Caption
The heading or title used in all legal pleadings

	Civil Law	Criminal Law	FIGURE 1-4
The Parties	Plaintiff — person who brings the suit Defendant — person against whom suit is brought	Government — entity that brings charge on behalf of citizens Defendant — person accused of a crime	
The Pleadings	Plaintiff begins lawsuit by filing a complaint	Government begins prosecution by filing an indictment (a/k/a accusation)	
The Rules	Rules of Civil Procedure (more relaxed rules about discovery and pleadings); few, if any, constitutional protections for defendant	Rules of Criminal Procedure (more strict rules about discovery and pleadings); numerous constitutional protections for defendant	
The Burden of Proof	Preponderance	Beyond a Reasonable Doubt	
The Verdict and Outcome	Liable Not Liable	Guilty Not Guilty	
	Monetary damages paid by liable party to other party	Defendant can be found guilty and sentenced to prison and/or fine; if found not guilty, defendant will be set free	

The Difference Between Civil Law and Criminal Law

person who is sued and the person who is accused of a crime are both termed *defendant* sometimes causes confusion. However, if you are ever in doubt about the kind of a case you are reading, the caption will normally give it away. (See Figure 1-5.)

A crime is a violation of a law. Crimes are usually based on statutes. We discuss statutes in much greater detail later in this book, but a word about them here is also appropriate. When a statute has been enacted by the legislature, it sets a standard by which a person's actions can be judged. In our previous example of Joe and Bill and the terrible crime that Joe committed, there was a specific statute that Joe violated. Criminal statutes cover behavior as diverse as rape, murder, shoplifting, and tax evasion. Civil actions, on the other hand, are usually not based on a statutory violation. Instead, they are based on property or financial losses. Rape and murder are examples of crimes; contract disputes and divorce are examples of civil actions.

2. THE PLEADINGS

The pleadings refer to the documents used in the case. In a civil case, the pleading that actually begins the suit is called a **complaint.** A complaint is drafted by the plaintiff's attorney and sets out the wrong suffered by the plaintiff and the reasons that the defendant should be forced to compensate the plaintiff for that wrong. A criminal case begins when the government charges a person with a crime through an indictment, information, or accusation.

Complaint
The pleading filed by the plaintiff and later served on the defendant; it sets out the details of the wrong suffered by the plaintiff and the reasons why the defendant is liable for those wrongs

FIGURE 1-5

Caption (or Style) of Civil & Criminal Cases (Used for All Pleadings in the Case)

STATE OF NEW YORK
COUNTY OF BURKE

SUPERIOR COURT OF BURKE COUNTY   FILE NUMBER: _____

YVONNE SMITH,   )
)
          Plaintiff,   )
)
          v.   )   COMPLAINT
)
)
CHARLES JONES,   )
)
          Defendant.   )
)
_____   )

The caption (or the style) of a criminal case is different:

STATE OF NEW YORK
COUNTY OF BURKE

SUPERIOR COURT OF BURKE COUNTY

STATE OF NEW YORK   )
)
)
          v.   )   ACCUSATION #03-CR-9087
)
)
)
JOHN DOE   )
          Defendant.   )
)
_____   )

3. THE RULES

When a defendant is charged with a crime, a host of constitutional protections are triggered, including the right to be presumed innocent, the right to a trial by jury, the right to an attorney, and many others. In addition, the procedural rules followed during the course of the criminal prosecution are different from those used in civil cases. The **discovery** rules, discussed in greater detail in a later chapter, are much more limited in criminal cases than they are in civil cases.

Discovery
The exchange of information between the sides involved in a suit

The parties to a civil case do not have as many protections (nor are the protections as necessary) as those available to a person accused of a crime. The Constitution gives people the right to bring a civil case, but has very little else to say about the issue. The discovery available to a civil litigant is much broader than what is available to the parties in a criminal case. Over the last few decades, court interpretations and the actual rules covering discovery have made the process more liberal. The parties to a civil case are not only permitted to learn as much about the other side's case as possible, they actually are encouraged to do so. Although there have been some reforms to criminal discovery in recent years, the information exchanged between the parties is much more limited than what is seen in civil cases.

4. THE BURDEN OF PROOF

When a party presents a case to the jury, there is a minimum threshold of evidence that the party must meet. This is called the **burden of proof** and it varies depending on the type of case. In most civil cases, such as divorce or contract disputes, the plaintiff's burden of proof is **preponderance of the evidence.** This means that the plaintiff must present enough proof in the trial for the jury to believe that the plaintiff's version of the case is more likely to be true than the defendant's version. In criminal cases, the burden of proof is beyond a **reasonable doubt.**

Burden of proof
The requirement that the party bringing the suit prove the allegations against the other party

Preponderance of the evidence
The proof required in a civil case; "more likely than not to be true"

5. DEFINING REASONABLE DOUBT

Commentators have been wrestling with the definition of reasonable doubt almost from the first moment it was used. In a criminal case, the government must present enough evidence so that the jurors will have no solid or reasonable objections to the government's version of the events. This is proof beyond a reasonable doubt and it is a higher standard of proof than that required in civil cases. Why would a criminal case have a higher standard of proof than a civil case? The founders of our legal system decided centuries ago that before a person would face imprisonment, fines, or even death, the proof required should be high. After all, taking away a person's liberty or life is a drastic step and should only be taken in the face of overwhelming evidence of guilt. On the other hand, the outcomes in a civil case are much less dire for the parties involved. No one is sentenced to prison, fines, or death as a result of a civil case. As a result, the standard of proof to bring such a case is commensurately lower.

Reasonable doubt
The proof required in a criminal case; not mere conjecture, but a doubt that would cause a reasonable person to have some hesitation in reaching a specific conclusion

One of the biggest differences between civil and criminal law is the burden of proof. In civil cases the burden is preponderance of the evidence; in criminal cases it is proof beyond a reasonable doubt.

ISSUE AT A GLANCE

6. THE VERDICT AND OUTCOME

In a civil trial, when the jurors decide that one party should pay damages to the other party, they find that party **liable** to the other side. In a criminal case, if the

Liable
A determination that one party has some obligation to another party, usually in the form of monetary payments (damages)

Guilty/Not Guilty
The verdict in a criminal case. Only authorized when the jury believes, beyond a reasonable doubt, that the defendant is guilty of the crime charged and that the government has proven that guilt

Damages
Monetary payments made in a civil case designed to compensate the plaintiff for an injury

jurors believe that the defendant is responsible for the crime charged, they find the defendant **guilty.** If, on the other hand, the jury does not believe that the defendant is guilty, the jury votes not guilty. In civil cases, once the jurors have decided the issue of liability, they then move on to **damages.** In cases in which they find no liability on the part of the defendant, they will decide that no damages should be awarded. However, in a criminal case, once the jurors have made a determination of guilt, their involvement in the case usually ends. Jurors do not decide on punishment; that is the judge's role. There is one important exception to this rule. In death penalty cases, once the jurors have decided that the defendant is guilty of the crime, some states require that they decide the separate issue of whether the defendant deserves death. However, in criminal cases, the jurors have no direct input as to the defendant's sentence. In cases in which the defendant is found not guilty, there is no further role for the jury or the judge: The defendant is released (assuming that she has no other charges pending against her).

INTRODUCTION TO THE VARIOUS BRANCHES OF GOVERNMENT

In the next few paragraphs we review the three branches of federal and state governments. The power of the government, and ultimately of the court system, flows from the interaction of these three branches. The Constitution forms the basis of this power.

A. THE CONSTITUTION

The United States Constitution took effect in 1789. It is the document that sets out the rights, duties, and responsibilities of the government and the citizens. Entire courses are taught exclusively on constitutional law, which we do not address in this text. Each state also has its own constitution. A state is free to expand on the rights promised to citizens in the federal Constitution, but is barred from removing or decreasing any of those rights.

1. THE ORGANIZATION OF THE FEDERAL GOVERNMENT

The federal government of the United States is based on a simple premise: that no one branch of government should have too much power. Each branch, therefore, has its own rights and powers that cannot be shared by the other branches.

a. Separation of Powers Among the Branches

The organization of the federal government is actually a model of efficiency and balance. Recognizing the dangers of vesting too much power in any one individual or institution, the Framers of the Constitution opted to divide up the powers and responsibilities of government. This division of power, called

Careers in the Law

▶ Judge

amela South didn't start out to become a judge, or even a lawyer. "I was in graduate school," she explained. "I was working on becoming an English professor. I had just gotten my master's degree and I was thinking about where to go to get a Ph.D. I was on track, but I didn't feel as though I'd made the right choice. I wanted to be involved in something; I wanted to make a difference somehow. Almost impulsively, I applied to law school. When I was accepted, I was surprised. I hadn't really thought about what I'd do if I got in. I quit my job at the university, said goodbye to my friends and moved. The decision quite literally changed my life. I enjoyed law school, although it was very difficult. When I graduated, I got a job in a small town law firm. I had only worked there about a year when I heard about an opening in the district attorney's office. I applied and was accepted. I wasn't sure if I'd like trial work. It turned out that I loved it. For six years, I was the assistant district attorney in charge of the child molestation team. We prosecuted people accused of molesting or otherwise hurting children. It was a job that I was very committed to, but it took a toll on me.

"When the chief magistrate approached me about coming to work for the magistrate court, I had to think about it for a long time. I loved my job as a prosecutor, but after so many years, I was ready for a change. I worked as a magistrate for about three years and then a position on the state court bench opened up. I was appointed by the governor two years ago and reelected this year.

"Sometimes, when I'm sitting on the bench, I still can't really believe it all. If I'd stayed in academia, I'd probably be teaching first-year English right now. Instead, I'm a judge. You have to pinch yourself sometimes."

---

separation of powers, forms the very core of the organization of the federal government. The U.S. Constitution divides the functions of government into three separate branches: the judicial, executive, and legislative.

> **Separation of powers**
> A provision of the U.S. Constitution that mandates that specific branches enjoy certain powers and that these powers cannot be shared or usurped by another branch

i. The Judicial Branch

This branch oversees the courts and is responsible for the fair administration of justice. The highest level of the judicial branch on the federal level is the U.S. Supreme Court. This court is responsible for interpreting the U.S. Constitution and is the highest court in the nation.

ii. The Executive Branch

This branch is responsible for running the day-to-day business of government and for enforcing the laws. The President of the United States holds the top executive position in the United States. Through the various agencies controlled by the President and his cabinet, he exercises considerable control over many aspects of law enforcement and other areas.

iii. The Legislative Branch

This branch creates laws. The United States Congress is divided into two houses, the House of Representatives and the United States Senate. These two bodies enact legislation.

ISSUE AT
A GLANCE

Government is divided into three branches: executive, legislative, and judicial.

2. STATE SYSTEMS

All state constitutions divide the functions of the state government in much the same way that the federal government does: three branches of government, each with some power over the other branches in a separation of powers scheme.

a. The Three Branches of State Government

On the state level, there is a judicial branch, an executive branch (headed by the state governor), and a legislative branch (the state legislature). Laws are created in much the same way as on the federal level and are passed on to the governor for signature. The governor also has veto power over a law, meaning that the governor can negate or vote against the law passed by the legislature. If the law is enacted, the state supreme court has the power to invalidate it by ruling that it violates either the U.S. Constitution or the state constitution. This system that permits one branch some control over the other branches is referred to as the **checks and balances** system.

Checks and balances
The right of one branch of government to oversee the actions of another branch of government. For instance, the U.S. Supreme Court is authorized to invalidate a statute created by the U.S. Congress

b. Variation Among the States

One of the biggest, and most understandable, mistakes made by a new legal professional is the assumption that the individual states are very similar in their approach to enacting laws and trying cases and in the procedures that they use in everyday legal activities. Nothing could be further from the truth. There is an amazing variety among the states in the ways that these activities are carried out. A trial in Florida might look very different from a trial in Alaska. Each state has its own rules and simply because a person has attended law school does not make her an expert in the procedures used in the various states. This is one of the reasons that each state regulates who is permitted to practice law within its boundaries.

ISSUE AT
A GLANCE

There are important procedural and substantive differences in the legal systems, rules, and regulations among all 50 states and the federal government.

BANNON v. SCHOOL DIST. OF PALM BEACH COUNTY
387 F.3d 1208 (C.A.11 (Fla.) 2004)

PER CURIAM:

Appellant Shelda Harris Bannon, on behalf of her daughter Sharah Harris, alleged that Appellees, School District of Palm Beach County and Principal Ed Harris, violated Sharah's First Amendment rights by compelling her to remove religious words and symbols from murals painted for a school beautification project. The district court granted summary judgment for Appellees because it concluded (1) Appellees never created a public forum, (2) the murals were school-sponsored speech, and, (3) Appellees' response was reasonably related to legitimate pedagogical objectives. We affirm.

I. BACKGROUND

This litigation concerns a school beautification project at a religiously diverse public school. While the school was undergoing long-term remodeling, students were prevented from walking into construction areas by dozens of large plywood panels in interior and exterior hallways. These panels were ugly, and would remain a part of the school for up to four years. To beautify the school, students were invited to paint murals on the panels. The school did not specifically prohibit students from expressing religious views. The school did, however, instruct students that their artwork could not be profane or offensive to anyone.

Sharah, a high school senior and member of the Fellowship of Christian Athletes (FCA), decided to participate in this beautification project. Although Sharah and her FCA colleagues planned to use verbal messages and religious symbols, they never gave Principal Harris or Cathy Roberts (the teacher supervising the beautification project) any notification or advance warning. No other student murals had verbal messages. On a Saturday afternoon, Sharah and other FCA students painted several murals with various religious messages and symbols.

Three of these murals were most notable. Sharah's first mural was next to the school's main office, had a crucifix in the background, and paraphrased John 3:16 as "Because He <<heart>>ed, He Gave." Sharah's second mural was only a few panels down from the office and read, "Jesus has time for you; do you have time for Him?" Sharah's FCA colleagues painted a third mural, located in a main hallway, that read, "God Loves You. What Part of Thou Shalt Not Didn't You Understand? God."

The following Monday morning, Principal Harris found a commotion on campus near Sharah's murals involving vocal students and teachers. Later that day, the murals received media attention in the form of phone calls, reporters from three television stations, and newspaper reporters. This publicity and controversy distracted the attention of students, teachers, and administrators from schoolwork, teaching, and administrative duties. As Principal Harris explained in his deposition, the expression in Sharah's murals interfered with the operation of the school,

> [b]ecause if it takes any time away from the productivity of the school in itself and the length of time that I had to spend on this, taking the principal's time, the assistant principal's time, the student's time away [from] the main focus of the school, . . . [so] the school was focusing more on the panels, overall, more so than [it] was focusing on the reason we were here.

Principal Harris did not expel, suspend, or otherwise punish Sharah for painting her murals. Instead, Principal Harris spoke about the murals with Ms. Roberts. Shortly thereafter, Ms. Roberts invited Sharah to step outside of class to speak privately. During this discussion, Ms. Roberts explained that although Sharah would need to paint over the overt religious words and sectarian symbols on all three murals, such as "Jesus," "God," and the crucifix, her other images and messages could remain. During her deposition, Sharah conceded this selective deletion was an attempt to keep her happy. Sharah repainted her murals and the FCA murals after school. Notably, Sharah was not the only student whose mural was edited. Principal Harris directed the removal of profanity, gang symbols, and satanic images from students' murals.

Appellant filed suit, but the district court granted summary judgment for Appellees on the First Amendment claims because it concluded Appellees did not create a public forum. Instead, the district court reasoned the beautification project fell "squarely in the category of school sponsored speech." Applying Hazelwood School District v. Kuhlmeier, 484 U.S. 260, 108 S. Ct. 562, 98 L. Ed. 2d 592 (1988), which governs school-sponsored expression, the district court held Principal Harris's restrictions were "reasonably related to the legitimate goals of disassociating the school from religious organizations and the endorsement of religious views and avoiding disruption to the learning environment from religious debate on the walls of the school." Appellant appealed.

DISCUSSION

Appellant first contends the district court erred because it did not subject the school's action to the First Amendment standards applicable in designated or limited public fora. Alternatively, even if the district court properly concluded Appellees did not create a public forum, Appellant contends the district court improperly applied Hazelwood, 484 U.S. at 273, 108 S. Ct. 562 (holding schools may restrict school-sponsored expression so long as the restriction is "reasonably related to legitimate pedagogical concerns"). Appellant maintains Hazelwood's standards do not apply when (1) the expression occurs during a non-curricular activity, or (2) the school's censorship of expression amounts to viewpoint discrimination. In lieu of applying Hazelwood, therefore, Appellant suggests the district court instead should have applied the rigorous standard of Tinker v. Des Moines Independent Community School District, 393 U.S. 503, 511, 89 S. Ct. 733, 21 L. Ed. 2d 731 (1969) (holding schools must tolerate pure student expression unless censorship is "necessary to avoid material and substantial interference with schoolwork or discipline").

Public Forum Analysis

For First Amendment purposes, there are three kinds of government property: (1) traditional public fora, (2) designated public fora, and (3) nonpublic fora. Perry Educ. Ass'n v. Perry Local Educators' Ass'n, 460 U.S. 37, 45-46, 103 S. Ct. 948, 74 L. Ed. 2d 794 (1983). In this instance, because the mural project was neither a traditional nor a designated public forum, it was a kind of nonpublic forum.

The mural project was not a traditional public forum. "[P]ublic schools do not possess all of the attributes of streets, parks, and other traditional public forums that time out of mind, have been used for purposes of assembly, communicating thoughts between citizens, and discussing public questions." Hazelwood, 484 U.S. at 267, 108 S. Ct. 562 (internal quotation marks and citations omitted).

Neither was the mural project a designated public forum. "The government does not create a public forum by inaction or by permitting limited discourse, but only by intentionally opening a nontraditional forum for public discourse." Id. (citations and internal quotation marks omitted). Indeed, a school creates a designated public forum only when "school authorities have by policy or practice opened those facilities for indiscriminate use by the general public, or by some segment of the public, such as student organizations." Id. (internal quotation marks and citations omitted). When a school retains editorial control over a forum, it has not created a designated public forum. See id. at 268, 108 S. Ct. 562 (concluding that a school newspaper was not a public forum because school authorities retained ultimate editorial control over production, publication, and content).

Far from "intentionally" opening a public forum for "indiscriminate use," Appellees merely solicited students to participate in a school beautification project. Appellees always retained editorial control over the murals in at least three ways. First, Principal Harris explicitly instructed students that none of the murals could be profane or offensive. Second, the mural project was supervised by Ms. Roberts, a faculty member. Finally, although Principal Harris told students to express themselves, he never said the murals were a forum for expressing their political or religious views. Thus, we conclude Sharah's expression did not occur in a traditional or designated public forum.

For these reasons, the district court correctly held Sharah's expression occurred in a nonpublic forum.

The real question is whether Sharah's expression occurred in the context of a curricular activity. In arguing Sharah's expression did not occur in the context of a curricular activity, Appellant underestimates how broadly the Hazelwood Court defined curricular activities. To be considered curricular, expressive activities need not occur in a "traditional classroom setting." *Hazelwood*, 484 U.S. at 271, 108 S. Ct. 562. Instead, expressive activities are curricular so long as they are merely (1) "supervised by faculty members," and (2) "designed to impart particular knowledge or skills to student participants and audiences." Id. In contrast to Appellant's position, *Hazelwood* never defined curricular activity in terms of whether student participation was required, earned grades or credit, occurred during regular school hours, or did not require a fee.

Here, even though Sharah did not paint her murals in a traditional classroom setting, her expression still occurred in the context of a curricular activity. The first prong is met because Principal Harris and Ms. Roberts were faculty members who supervised the beautification project. Likewise, the second prong is satisfied because the beautification project was designed to impart particular knowledge and skills to student participants and audiences; it allowed student participants to express themselves artistically, allowed student audiences to appreciate their fellow students' artwork, and promoted school spirit, among other things. Appellant's arguments that Sharah's expression did not occur in the context of a curricular activity — because students were not required to participate, they received no grade or credit for participation, the murals were painted on a Saturday outside of regular school hours, and students paid a small fee to participate — simply have no toehold in the relevant legal doctrines. They ignore how broadly the Supreme Court has defined school curricula for *Hazelwood*'s purposes. As such, Sharah's expression occurred in the context of a curricular activity.

Sharah's first mural (which included an image of a crucifix and the words "Because He <<heart>>ed, He Gave.", based on John 3:16) referred to Christ's crucifixion.

Sharah's second mural ("Jesus has time for you; do you have time for Him?") was a call for students to develop a personal relationship with Christ. The last mural by Sharah's colleagues ("God Loves you. What Part of Thou Shalt Not Didn't You Understand? God.") purported to be a message from God. These are obviously inherently religious messages, which cannot be recast as the discussion of secular topics from a religious perspective. Since the school did not permit any student in the context of a curricular activity to communicate such messages, it restricted speech on the basis of content, not viewpoint.

As explained earlier, a school's content-based censorship of school-sponsored student expression survives review under *Hazelwood* if it is reasonably related to legitimate pedagogical concerns. 484 U.S. at 273, 108 S. Ct. 562. Here, the district court correctly held that Appellees had a legitimate pedagogical concern in avoiding the disruption to the school's learning environment caused by Sharah's murals. Appellees' policy in prohibiting religious expression on its walls was reasonably related to this legitimate pedagogical concern because it ended the disruption.

CONCLUSION

For the foregoing reasons, we conclude Sharah's murals were school-sponsored expression in a nonpublic forum subject to restriction under *Hazelwood* because they occurred in the context of a curricular activity, and students, parents, and members of the public might reasonably believe them to bear the imprimatur of the school. We hold Appellees' censorship of Sharah's school-sponsored murals was a reasonable content-based restriction that was rationally related to the legitimate pedagogical concern of avoiding the religious controversy and debate generated by Sharah's murals.

AFFIRMED.

QUESTIONS ABOUT THE CASE

1 What are the basic contentions in this case?
2 Why is it significant that a school is not a "public forum"?
3 According to the court, what are the three types of public forums?
4 Does the school in this case represent an area traditionally associated with free speech?
5 Why is it important to consider whether or not Sharah's acitivity was curriculum based?

INTRODUCTION TO THE FEDERAL AND STATE COURT SYSTEMS

It is important for any legal professional to understand the organization of the various federal and state court systems. Attorneys often find themselves in different courts, which all have their own rules and guidelines. When taken as a whole, the federal and state court systems can be confusing, but we explore them as separate entities.

A. THE ORGANIZATION OF COURT SYSTEMS IN THE UNITED STATES

The organization of the court systems in the United States is based on a straightforward premise: The actions of one court can be reviewed (and changed) by another, higher court. Seen this way, the court system, whether on the state or federal level, is arranged as a pyramid. At the base of the pyramid are the various **trial courts.** These are the courts that most people are familiar with. Nightly television dramas feature the work of trial courts. This is where juries are empaneled, *where witnesses* testify, and where the drama of a trial is played out. However, there is another layer of the court system that is less well known, but just as important. This is the appellate level.

Trial court
The court that hears witness testimony, considers evidence, and reaches a verdict in civil and criminal cases

Example: Ted and Keisha are neighbors. Ted has been having trouble with his septic tank. It constantly overflows and a nasty discharge leaks from Ted's property on to Keisha's property. Keisha has three small children and because of the overflow she will not let them play in their own backyard. She has discussed the situation with Ted on several occasions, but he has refused to do anything about the problem. Keisha finally sues Ted, asking the court to order Ted to repair the septic tank and to pay Keisha damages for her inability to use her own property. The case goes to trial and Keisha wins. The jury awards her $12,000 for her loss of enjoyment in her property and the judge also orders Ted to repair the septic tank at his own expense within 30 days.

Ted is dissatisfied with the ruling. For one thing, he wanted to bring up evidence in the trial that part of the problem with his septic tank was the result of Keisha's actions. Ted alleges that when Keisha installed a deck in her backyard she sank a post in the ground that severed one of his septic drain lines. However, the trial judge refused to allow this testimony. Ted believes that the judge's decision was wrong. Instead of paying the $12,000 judgment and repairing the septic tank, Ted files an appeal in the state court of appeals.

The trial court is where a jury hears evidence presented by both sides in the suit. Witnesses testify on the stand and a judge presides to make rulings.

 ISSUE AT A GLANCE

---

1. COURTS OF APPEAL

When a case is appealed it is sent to an appellate court for review. An appellate court can review the case and is authorized to change the verdict, but only for specific reasons. If Ted can show that the trial court committed some legal error in his case that would allow the court of appeals to change the verdict. Ted must show that the trial judge's refusal to permit his evidence about Keisha's deck was a legal error and that the jury should have been allowed to hear it.

Most states and all federal jurisdictions have a court of appeals. This is the first level of appellate courts and where most people bring their appeals when they lose in the trial court. Courts of appeal do not retry cases. The losing party isn't given the opportunity of presenting new witnesses and evidence that was not heard in the original case. In fact, witnesses never testify in an appellate court and no jury is ever present. To a layperson, the activities in the appellate court would seem very dull. Instead of retrying the case, the parties appear before a bank of judges who listen to arguments and consider the written record of what transpired in the trial court. Appellate courts are not empowered to hear new testimony or consider newly discovered evidence. They focus on what happened in the trial court. If they believe that an error occurred, they are empowered to change the verdict, order a new trial, or take other actions.

In Ted's case, the appellate court agrees with him and reverses the trial court decision. However, the appellate process is not over. Keisha is now permitted to appeal this change in the verdict. However, the stakes are raised. If she wishes to appeal, she must bring her case in a higher court — the state supreme court.

2. THE SUPREME COURT

All states and all federal jurisdictions have a top court, although it doesn't always go by the name "supreme court." The highest court in the United States is the U.S. Supreme Court. Everyone has heard of this court. It is responsible for some of the significant changes in American society. The U.S. Supreme Court has made decisions in appellate cases that have affected millions of Americans, from those sitting on death row to women deciding whether to have an abortion. They make decisions in hundreds of appellate cases every year, although not all of them have such wide-ranging impact.

States also have their own supreme courts. In most cases, this court is called the state supreme court, but there are some states that refer to this court by another name. This court serves the same role on the state level that the U.S. Supreme Court serves on the federal level: It is the final authority on appellate issues in that jurisdiction.

Ted won his appeal in the state court of appeals. Now, Keisha wishes to appeal to the state supreme court. However, getting the state supreme court to accept an appeal is a difficult hurdle. If the court refuses to hear Keisha's appeal, the case is essentially over. On the other hand, if Keisha can convince the state supreme court that her case involves important state issues, the court may agree to hear her case.

Appealing a case to the state supreme court involves additional issues that we address in Chapter 7.

In New York, for example, the state's highest court is called Superior Court.

SKILLS YOU NEED IN THE REAL WORLD

INTRODUCTION TO PRACTICAL SKILLS

Throughout this book, we address theoretical issues, such as the organization of court systems, and the principles underlying specific areas of the law, such as criminal law, tort law, and other areas. However, a legal professional should also possess a full repertoire of practical skills. Each of the succeeding chapters of this book addresses practical skills, such as Internet legal research, organizing discovery, and photographing accident and crime scenes. You should acquire these skills along with your understanding of legal principles. Law is a balance between the theoretical and the practical and neither aspect should be neglected in your legal education.

CHAPTER SUMMARY

Law is a term that is difficult to define. Depending on the case involved, "law" could refer to a wide variety of legal concepts. As a basic concept, however, law refers to a rule that must be followed or a sanction will be imposed. Laws have been promulgated since villages, cities and states were first formed and they form the core of civilized societies. In discussing the concept of law, it is important to understand the organization of the state and federal court systems. All court systems are organized in a hierarchical structure, with trial courts at the bottom and appellate courts at the top. Once a trial occurs, the losing party has the right to appeal the loss to a higher court.

The sources of law are important to any discussion of the organization of the legal system in the United States. Statutory law refers to legislative bills that have been enacted by the executive branch of government. On the other hand, case law refers to the body of published opinions of appellate courts and the legal reasons on which they have based their decisions. Administrative rules are created by federal and state agencies and often carry the same weight as statutes.

ETHICS

Throughout this book, we address ethical concerns for paralegals. Although lawyers have had support staff since law as a profession first emerged, the arrival of a professional class of paralegals did not begin until the 1960s. The American Bar Association recognized the role of paralegals in 1967. As the number of paralegals has grown, their role has expanded. Today they are given broad responsibilities, but their training in the complex ethics of the legal field has often lagged behind their increased duties. With the founding of national organizations for paralegals and the creation of paralegal codes of ethics, the subject of the ethical duties of paralegals has begun to receive the attention it deserves. Throughout this text, the ethical duties of the paralegal are explored with just as much attention to detail as the practical duties. At the end of each chapter, the complicated role of the paralegal will be dissected and the ethical duty pinpointed. Paralegals are presented with ethical challenges every day and must be prepared to deal with them.

CHAPTER REVIEW QUESTIONS

1   Why is there a distinction between law and morality?
2   Explain how law has developed through history.
3   What are some of the sources of law?
4   What is case law? How is case law different from statutory law?
5   List and explain the important differences between criminal law and civil law.
6   What is the caption or style of a case?
7   List and explain the difference between proof to a preponderance of the evidence and proof beyond a reasonable doubt.
8   How does the burden of proof vary between civil and criminal cases?
9   How do the outcomes vary in civil and criminal cases?
10 Explain the concept of separation of powers.
11 List the three branches of government and explain their duties.
12 Give an example of an activity carried out by each of the three branches of government.
13 What is the function of the legislative branch of government?
14 Explain the hierarchical organization of the American court system.
15 Explain the various levels of the court system.
16 How is an appellate court different from a trial court?
17 Why is it important to have a balance between theoretical concepts and practical skills?
18 Why is the study of ethics important?

DISCUSSION QUESTIONS

1   Why do most states and the federal government have a three-tiered court system? Why is it necessary to have an intermediate appellate court and a final appellate court? Would it be more efficient to have only one appellate court? Why or why not?
2   Is our legal system too cumbersome? Is there a way to design a different system that still provides as many rights for the litigants?
3   Why is civil discovery more liberal than criminal discovery?
4   Are there any benefits to having several sources of law? For instance, some states have statutory law, administrative law, case law, and common law. Does this give the state wider experience to rely upon or simply cloud the issues?
5   Studies have shown that Americans are growing increasingly litigious. Why are more people likely to sue these days than, say, one hundred years ago?

PERSONALITY QUIZ

Is the legal field right for you? Take this personality quiz and see.

1   I enjoy problem solving.

0-strongly disagree   5-agree   10-strongly agree

Points: _____

2   I like challenging work that often forces me to stretch my abilities and talents.

0-strongly disagree   5-agree   10-strongly agree

Points: _____

3   I enjoy working with people.

0-strongly disagree   5-agree   10-strongly agree

Points: _____

4   I function well under deadlines.

0-strongly disagree   5-agree   10-strongly agree

Points: _____

5   I like to read.

0-strongly disagree   5-agree   10-strongly agree

Points: _____

Total Points: _____

If you scored between 30-50 points, you have many of the qualities that it takes to enter the legal field.

If you scored between 20-29 points, you might do well in the legal field, but you might do even better in a less demanding profession.

If you scored 19 or lower, the legal field is not a good choice for you.

PRACTICAL APPLICATIONS

1   Find out when the next trial is scheduled in your local courthouse. Trials (except juvenile hearings) are open to the public. Go in and

watch. What type of case is it? What are the issues involved? Who won and why?

2   Speak with a local attorney and/or paralegal. Ask this person what she likes about law as a profession. Also ask what she does not like about her profession. Does this person recommend the legal field? Why or why not?

3   Scan the weekly television listings to see how many law-related shows are on. Why are there so many? What is it about law that so many people find fascinating?

WEB SITES

The Federal Judiciary Home Page
http://www.uscourts.gov

The U.S. Supreme Court Home Page
http://www.supremecourtus.gov/opinions/opinions.html

Locating Specific U.S. Supreme Court Cases
http://www.findlaw.com/casecode/supreme.html

U.S. Supreme Court Media
http://www.oyez.org

Rules of the U.S. Supreme Court
http://www.law.cornell.edu/rules/supct/overview.html

The United States Constitution
http://www.gpoaccess.gov/constitution/browse.html

California Supreme Court
http://www.courtinfo.ca.gov/courts/supreme

Florida Supreme Court
http://www.floridasupremecourt.org

TERMS AND PHRASES

Burden of proof	Codify	Discovery
Caption	Complaint	Guilt
Checks and balances	Damages	Law
Liable	Reasonable doubt	Trial court
Preponderance of the evidence	Separation of powers	
	Statute	

SUGGESTIONS FOR FURTHER READING

There are several top-quality law periodicals available, including:

- *The American Bar Journal*
- *Legal Assistant Today*
- State bar journals
- State legal newspapers

Researching the Law

2

Chapter Learning Objectives

After completing this chapter, you should be able to:

- Explain the function of the appellate courts
- Describe the types of actions that an appellate court can take in a case on appeal
- List and describe the basic components of an appellate case
- Brief an appellate case
- Explain the conventions used in legal writing

 **INTRODUCTION TO LEGAL RESEARCH**

Legal research is different from any other type of research you may have done in the past. It has its own rules and procedures and a set of methods that is dramatically different from the type of research you might do to write a paper for an English class.

Here is an example of a typical research assignment for an English or history class: Write a paper on the first trip to the moon. How would you start?

Most of us would start with magazine articles or books about the first trip to the moon. From those you would find other articles and books and as you wrote your paper you would cite to all of these articles and books as authority for the statements that you make in the paper.

As you developed your material, you would provide some general, background information on how the space program developed, then go to the specifics of the mission that actually landed Neil Armstrong and Michael Collins on the moon in 1969. You might even throw in some anecdotes about weightlessness and the origins of the famous line, "That's one small step . . .".

Although this has the makings of a very good research paper for a history course, it would be a terrible legal research assignment.

First of all, the premise of legal research is different from other types of research. When you write a paper about the Apollo 11 landing, you provide general information to the reader. In legal research, you do not provide general information. In fact, you assume that the reader already has general knowledge and knows some basics about the legal system. Your reader already knows the difference between civil and criminal law, that direct evidence is different from circumstantial evidence, and so on. When you receive a legal research question, it is more likely to look like this:

"Our client was involved in a car wreck. He is the defendant and is being sued by another driver. The other driver says that our client ran the red light and struck her broadside. The other driver has a statement from a witness at the scene who claims to have heard our client admit to running the red light. Our client denies making the statement. The problem is that the witness who made this statement has since died. Is the other side still going to be able to use that statement?"

This is a very specific question and requires a very specific answer. You would not begin your written response to this question by explaining what a defendant is and how a civil suit is brought. That would be a waste of both your time and the reader's. Instead, you would address the specific question by telling the reader whether the statement can be used.

ISSUE AT A GLANCE   In legal research, specific questions require specific answers.

A. UNDERSTANDING THE NECESSITY OF LEGAL RESEARCH

Many people new to the legal profession are surprised to learn that legal professionals spend a great deal of time researching legal issues. People assume that paralegals and attorneys already know the law and have no further need to learn more about it. However, just the opposite is true. There are several important reasons why legal professionals carry out legal research throughout their careers.

Legal research is necessary because the body of law is so enormous that no one can know all aspects of any legal topic. The Western legal tradition stretches back to the time of ancient Rome. As you can imagine, the body of law that has accumulated over two millennia is enormous. The U.S. legal system is also based on England's system. The foundation for the English system stretches back for almost one thousand years. In addition to that body of law, there is also our legal tradition, established over two hundred years ago at the formation of the United States. When you add all that material together, you get a huge body of law covering everything from real property, torts, crimes, divorce, contracts, and an almost endless list of other issues.

Given the vast amount of cases, statutes, and common law, it is impossible for any single person to know and understand all areas of law. In fact, it is difficult to

FIGURE 2-1

Legal Research Is an Ethical
Requirement

Representations to Court.
By presenting to the court (whether by
signing, filing, submitting, or later
advocating) a pleading, written motion,
or other paper, an attorney or
un-represented party is certifying that
to the best of the person's knowledge,
information, and belief, formed after an
inquiry reasonable under the circumstances, — . . .
   (2) the claims, defenses, and other
legal contentions therein are warranted
by existing law or by a non-frivolous
argument for the extension, modification, or reversal of existing law or the
establishment of new law.[1]

master even a single area, such as criminal law or personal injury law. Conse-
quently, when a question comes up about a particular issue, a legal professional
must research it to understand exactly what the current state of law is on that
particular point.

New laws are created every year. If more than two thousand years of legal
tradition were not enough, there is an additional factor of new laws. Each state has
a legislature that is responsible for creating new laws on a wide variety of issues. The
United States Congress plays a similar role on the federal level. These bodies
produce thousands of pages of new laws every year. Once these laws are created,
they are just as binding as all the previously existing statutes.

Adequate legal research is an ethical requirement for attorneys. Although
many people do not realize this, proper legal research is an ethical requirement for
an attorney. For instance, under the Federal Rules of Civil Procedure, an attorney
must disclose unfavorable cases or statutes to the court. See Figure 2-1. When an
attorney fails to adequately research a legal issue and the client loses the case, the
client may have an action against the attorney for legal malpractice.

Legal research is often how one side wins a case. If the three previous reasons
are not enough, there is another reason legal research is so necessary: It's one of the
ways that you win.

So far, our discussion about legal research has proceeded from the basis that a
legal professional is studying the law in order to understand it. Although this is
true, the usual reason for conducting legal research is to convince a judge to rule in
your favor.

a. *Stare Decisis*

To have a solid grasp of the most important purpose of legal research, we must
examine one of the basic tenets of law: the importance of precedent. The principle
of *stare decisis* may be one of the most critical principles underlying the American
legal system.

Under *stare decisis,* a judge is bound by the precedent set in another case, even
if the judge doesn't like the ruling. *Stare decisis* explains why, as the composition of

Stare decisis
(Latin) "Standing by the
decision." The principle that
previously decided cases
stand as precedent for future
cases

[1] Fed. R. Civ. P. 11(b)(2). p. 52

Roe v. Wade *legalized abortion in the United States.* Miranda v. Arizona *created the famous "Miranda" rights heard on television police dramas every night and read by police officers to suspects thousands of times every day across the country. Both were cases decided by the U.S. Supreme Court.*

the U.S. Supreme Court changes over the years, controversial decisions such as *Roe v. Wade* or *Miranda v. Arizona* are not overturned.

The advantage of the principle *of stare decisis* is that it creates a certain amount of predictability in the court system. If a new case has similar issues and similar facts as a previously decided case, the court is bound to rule the same way as that previously decided case. This explains why legal research is so important.

Let's return to the example of the car wreck and the incriminating statement made by our client to a witness who has subsequently died. When researching this issue, you would search out cases that involved similar issues. For instance, you would review previous cases until you found some that involved the issue of using a dead witness's statement. How did the courts rule in those cases? Did they allow the statement to be used at trial? If so, were there any limitations placed on the use of that statement?

Suppose you find ten cases in which the court refused to allow the statement to be used. But you have also found three cases in which the court allowed the statement into evidence. Why this discrepancy? If *stare decisis* is the rule, shouldn't the courts have always ruled the same way? *Stare decisis* has two components, similar issues and similar facts. In those three cases in which the courts ruled differently, you will probably discover that there were facts that changed the ruling. Those cases might have involved statements made under different circumstances, such as sworn testimony on the witness stand. Your job as a legal researcher is to explain the circumstances of those rulings and attempt to predict how the court will rule in your case. This means that you must also examine the facts of all the cases and see which cases had facts closest to your own case. The interesting thing about legal research is that in the huge body of law that exists today, parties can almost always find some language, somewhere, that justifies their position.

 *Stare decisis:* **similar facts + similar issues = similar result.**

As you can see, legal research involves analysis not only of the law, but also of the facts. Later, we discuss where you go to find this information.

Stare decisis is not a system that is unique to law. People use the principle of *stare decisis* in arguments every day. We'll use a very common example to illustrate this point:

John has just turned 16. His older brother, Carl, is 18. When Carl turned 16 he was allowed to drive the family car on dates. He was also allowed to stay out until midnight on Fridays and Saturdays. John approaches his parents and makes the following argument:

"I'm 16 now, and I want the same privileges that you gave Carl. I want to drive the family car on dates and I want to stay out until midnight on weekends."

John's argument is that his "case" involves similar issues and similar facts as a previous decision. He argues that Carl's situation is a precedent for how his parents should act in his situation. Barring any other developments, fairness dictates that John's parents should rule the same way.

However, John's parents counter, "Yes, that's true. We did give Carl those privileges, but, unlike you, he hadn't been arrested for marijuana possession. You haven't demonstrated the same level of maturity as Carl, therefore you won't get the same privileges."

John's parents have ruled that his case is not the same as the previous situation. The facts are different and this justifies a different ruling.

Although somewhat simplified, this is exactly how a court rules on issues presented by attorneys. The attorneys will argue how their case is either exactly like a previously decided case (and that the judge should rule the same way) or that their case is somehow different (and that the judge should rule in a different way).

One of the purposes of legal research is to find a case, with similar facts, legal issues, or both, in which some other court ruled your way.

 ISSUE AT A GLANCE

B. RESEARCHING THE LAW IN BOOKS AND OTHER MEDIA

Now that we have discussed the main purposes of legal research, we devote some attention to identifying the various sources of law and how these figure into legal research. Among these sources are:

1   Case reporters
2   Statutes
3   Legal encyclopedias
4   Treatises
5   Online legal research

Profiling a Paralegal

▶ Pam Tallent

hen I decided to get a paralegal degree, I was already working full time. I knew that I'd have to do some of my homework during lunch breaks, so the first thing I did was run it by my boss. Both of the bosses that I've had while I've been in the paralegal program have been totally supportive. Their approach was, well, this will only make you better at what you're doing.

I take Internet courses through a local community college. During lunch, I'll log on to my course web site to take care of an assignment. If I have to do a paper or a project, I'll stay at work late to type it up, or to use our library for research. Our library has statutes and other books, and that's very helpful. I also asked an attorney across the street if I could use his library. He was very kind and told me that I could come over any time that I needed to. One semester, I spent nearly every lunch hour over there, reading and researching. It's amazing how friendly most people will be, if you explain your situation to them. They have just opened up their resources to me. It makes you realize how nice most of the people in the legal community are.

1. CASE REPORTERS

Affirm
The appellate court agrees with the verdict, or some ruling, entered in the lower court and votes to keep that decision in place

Reverse
To reverse a decision is to set it aside. An appellate court disagrees with the verdict, or some ruling, in the lower court, and overturns that decision

After a case is tried, the losing party usually has the right to appeal to a higher court. Appellate courts are courts of limited jurisdiction, meaning that they can only address certain issues and make certain rulings. When a party appeals a case, the appeal is not a new trial. Appellate courts do not retry cases. Instead, they review the record made in the trial court and consider the written briefs filed by the attorneys representing both parties. In most cases, an appellate court is limited to three possible decisions on an appeal: The court can **affirm, reverse,** or **remand** a case.

ISSUE AT A GLANCE

Appellate courts are courts of limited jurisdiction; they are limited in the types of decisions that they can make on appeal.

Remand
The appellate court requires additional information or an evidentiary hearing; it cannot conduct such a hearing itself, so it sends the case back to the trial court for the hearing, and then considers the appeal based on that hearing

Opinion
An appellate court's written explanation of the important facts and applicable law that justifies the court's decision and shows how the court followed the principle of *stare decisis*

Reporter
An annual edition containing all the published decisions of a particular court

Case law
The body of cases decided by judges who have interpreted statutes and prior cases

When an appellate court affirms a decision, it agrees with the lower court's decision in the case. If the decision is reversed, it means that the appellate court is changing the decision of the lower court. A remand directs the case back to the trial court for an additional hearing on some issue.

The appellate court's decision means that one party wins and the other party loses. To explain why it made a specific ruling, the appellate court publishes its decision in written form, called an **opinion.** Opinions are what legal researchers read to understand the current state of law on a particular topic. The court also writes out its opinion to show how it has followed the line of previously established cases on this issue.

When the court publishes an opinion in an individual case, this opinion and hundreds of others made by the appellate court that year are collected in book form. The book is called a **reporter.** Reporters are purchased by attorneys, government agencies, law libraries, and any other entity that wishes to have a collection of court opinions. The body of published decisions is known as **case law.**

a. U.S. Supreme Court

If you wanted to find a case decided by the U.S. Supreme Court, you would look in a U.S. Supreme Court Reporter. Suppose, for example, that you wanted to locate the famous *Miranda v. Arizona* case. This case is cited as *Miranda v. Arizona,* 384 U.S. 436 (1966). This cite provides information about how to locate the case. The first number (384) is the volume number. This tells you that you can locate the *Miranda* case by going to volume 384 of the U.S. Supreme Court Reporter. The next part of the cite, "U.S." is the abbreviation for the reporter. The second number (436) tells you that you will find the *Miranda* case on page 436 of volume 384 of the U.S. Supreme Court Reporter.

There are reporters for a vast array of other courts. For instance, there are reporters covering the various federal Courts of Appeal, federal District Court and federal Bankruptcy Court, among others. There are also reporters covering the state appellate courts.

Law can be found in statutes, case law, administrative rules and regulations, and so on.

ISSUE AT A GLANCE

2. STATUTES

When people speak of the "law," they are usually talking about statutes. On the state level, a statute is legislation that has been voted on by the state legislature and then passed to the governor for his or her signature. Once the governor signs this legislation, it becomes a statute and is binding on everyone in the state. There are statutes that govern how fast people can drive, what constitutes an assault, when a state taxpayer should pay taxes, and almost every other type of behavior.

On the federal level, we have the same procedure, although the names are different. The U.S. Congress votes on proposed legislation and passes it on to the President for signature. When the President signs the legislation it becomes binding on everyone in the United States.

For a legal researcher, statutes and case law are equally important. A statute is usually very brief and does not provide any explanations, making case law even more important because it provides an interpretation of the statute. For instance, consider the statute in Figure 2-2.

The statute in Figure 2-2 spells out incidents that can amount to assault in the third degree. However, the statute does not provide the answer to a question as simple as the following:

Jan playfully slaps Tom, her friend. Tom wants to bring charges against her for assault. Is such an action authorized under this statute?

To answer that question, a court must interpret the language of the statute and apply it to the facts of a particular case. This is why we say that for a legal researcher, case law and statutes are equally important. In this situation, if the only source of law we had was the statute, we would be hard pressed to answer Tom's question. However, this question has been brought up on appeal and a court has interpreted the statute to answer this specific question.

We have seen that court opinions are gathered together annually and published in books called reporters. The same process is also applied to statutes. Each year all the current state statutes are gathered together and published in

> ### Sidebar
>
> *The answer to Tom's question is no. Playful slaps should not be the basis of assault charges on this statute. The court's opinion that provides this answer can be found in* Matter of Shane T., *115 Misc.2d 161, 453 N.Y.S.2d 590 (1982), which is the case reporter for the State of New York's Court of Appeals.*

FIGURE 2-2

Assault in the Third Degree in New York State

A person is guilty of assault in the third degree when:

1. With intent to cause physical injury to another person, he causes such injury to such person or to a third person; or

2. He recklessly causes physical injury to another person; or

3. With criminal negligence, he causes physical injury to another person by means of a deadly weapon or a dangerous instrument.

Assault in the third degree is a class A misdemeanor.[2]

---

[2] N.Y. Penal Code §120.00. p. 61

Code
An organized, systematic collection of laws, rules, or regulations

a **code.** A code is a series of volumes containing statutes. There is a federal code that contains all the federal statutes and there are individual state codes.

3. LEGAL ENCYCLOPEDIAS

Legal publishers realized a long time ago that legal research is difficult and any product that could speed up the process would probably be in great demand in the legal field. Legal encyclopedias were developed to meet that need. A legal encyclopedia, such as *American Jurisprudence* or *Corpus Juris Secondum,* is a compendium of national case law and statutory law arranged by topic. These encyclopedias run to dozens of volumes and provide a good general reference for anyone researching a particular area of law. There are also state legal encyclopedias organized along the same lines. However, like any encyclopedia, legal encyclopedias were designed to provide general, if sometimes superficial information. They can provide guidance and background information and help guide a legal researcher to appropriate statutes or case law.

4. TREATISES

Some of the well-known national treatises include Corbin on Contracts *and* Prosser and Keeton on the Law of Torts.

Treatises are works on specialized topics of law. Written by eminent legal scholars, a treatise focuses on a narrow area of the law and explains it in detail. There are treatises for topics as diverse as real estate law and admiralty law. Treatises are a good resource when you are faced with a particularly difficult question of law and don't know where to start. The authors of legal treatises have explored their topic in minute detail and can often provide very good guidance.

Treatises and legal encyclopedias can help point a legal researcher in the right direction.

5. ONLINE LEGAL RESEARCH

Traditionally, legal research was always carried out using print media. Books were the source of law and the Internet was dismissed as nothing more than a curiosity. Online legal research is a relatively new phenomenon. Fifteen years ago, few Internet resources were available to a legal researcher. These days, between pay sites and free sites, a legal researcher can access the quality of sources that would have been unthinkable even five years ago. As a result, Internet-based research has come into its own. Cost has played a large part in that development. A private practitioner who wishes to have a complete library often finds that she can have access to vast resources online without having to purchase a single text. Online sources are constantly updated, where as books must be purchased annually.

Pay sites, such as Westlaw® or LexisNexis™, provide a wealth of information that would be prohibitively expensive to acquire in print form, assuming that someone had a library large enough to house it all. There is also a huge variety of free legal research sites on the Internet, although they vary considerably in quality. Free legal research sites do not have the scope of coverage found on the pay sites, although some of them are very impressive. Although free sites are improving constantly, your best bet with online research is still a pay site.

The two most extensive and well-known pay sites are LexisNexis and Westlaw.

a. LexisNexis

LexisNexis is a legal research site that allows a user to access cases, statutes, and other materials on both the state and federal level, as well as providing legal news and access to public records. Its "Courtlink" service provides access to more than a million federal and state court records through a single search interface. LexisNexis also provides a handy automatic alert system that notifies you through e-mail about new cases and other developments that could affect your recent research.

The "State Capital" service provides access to legislation from all 50 states, as well as pending bills, laws, state constitutions and proposed amendments, state rules and regulations, and even information about the state legislature.

b. Westlaw

Westlaw is the most widely used legal research pay site and it offers an amazing variety and scope for the legal researcher. Westlaw has a database containing cases and statutes from every state and federal jurisdiction as well as a huge selection of specialized areas, such as bankruptcy law, personal injury law, and commercial transactions.

Initially, Westlaw was a clunky, slow program that was not very user-friendly. In recent years, Westlaw has gone through some dramatic changes to improve the interface by making it more intuitive and to allow faster searches. However, it is still bogged down by its history. Search strings in Westlaw can often resemble a foreign language. However, Westlaw has worked hard to create natural language search engines and to slowly phase out some of the more bothersome features.

Among West's more popular services is its "KeySearch" feature that helps a researcher find cases and secondary sources using West's Key Numbering System. This system assigns a number to virtually every legal subject. "KeyCite" allows a researcher to confirm that the case or statute is still good law and has not been overturned by a new case.

c. Other Pay Sites: Loislaw

Loislaw™ is considered to be more basic than LexisNexis and Westlaw. You begin your search by selecting one of four choices. You can find a case or statute by citation, or you can search by key words, parties' names, or by parallel citation. It covers U.S. Supreme Court cases from 1778 to the present day. It also covers an impressive array of state and federal courts of appeal, but its coverage is not as extensive as LexisNexis or Westlaw. Other pay sites are listed in Figure 2-3.

FIGURE 2-3

Lesser-Known Pay Sites

**Fastcase
(www.fastcase.com)**

■ Allows legal research queries in
   natural language
■ Permits multiple citations
   look-ups
■ Allows searches to be based on date
   (or a range of dates), jurisdiction, and
   other fields

■ Has hyperlinked case citations
   throughout the research recovered

**VersusLaw
(www.versuslaw.com)**

■ Offers a multilevel approach, with a
   lower fee for access to few resources
   and a higher fee for access to more
   sites

READING APPELLATE DECISIONS

The best place to start a discussion of how to read and understand cases is to start with a sample case and break down its most obvious features. Later, we explore the actual language in the opinion to understand how, and more importantly, *why,* it was written the way that it was.

A. THE PARTS OF AN APPELLATE DECISION

The "style" or caption of
the case

MOBLEY v. STATE

218 Ga. App. 739, 463 S.E.2d 166 (1995)

The attorneys involved in
the case

Robert Greenwald, Lawrenceville, for appellant.
Daniel J. Porter, District Attorney, Phil Wiley, Neal R. Bevans, Assistant District Attorneys, Lawrenceville, For appellee.

The appellate judge who
wrote the opinion

BLACKBURN, Judge.

The court's decision

Following a jury trial, the appellant . . . (the rest of the case is omitted. The entire case, including the omitted language is presented later in this chapter).

Judgment affirmed.

The decision by the other
two members of the
appellate court

McMURRAY, P.J., and ANDREWS, J., concur.

1. THE STYLE OR CAPTION

When reading a case, the first item most people notice is the name of the parties involved. This is important information. It is called the style or sometimes the caption of the case. In the case example, we would say that the style is "Mobley versus State." The rest of the information provided, 218 Ga. App. 739, 463 S.E.2d 166 (1995), is the cite to the case. We can already glean some important information about this case before we've even had the chance to read it. For instance, most

FIGURE 2-4

Comparison of Pay Sites

Legal Research Site	Research Programs	Fee Charge (Yes/No)	Member Information	Free Services	Web URL (Address)
Westlaw	Cases, statutes, administrative regulations, updates of cases, KeyCiting and additional databases	Yes	Computer sign-on to website then registration for online use	WestWorks	www.Westlaw.com
Lexis Nexis	Cases, statutes, administrative regulations, updates of Shepardizing or KeyCiting and additional databases	Yes, but not all services	Computer sign-on to website then registration for online use	LexisOne	www.lexisnexis.com
Law Office Information Systems (LOIS)	State case law, rules, statutes, administration codes and federal materials for all 50 states	Yes, but fees are lower than most sites	Computer sign-on to website then registration for online use	None	www.loislaw.com
Versuslaw	Full text to case law in all 50 states and all federal courts	Yes, much lower than other sites	Computer sign-on to website then registration for online use	None	www.versuslaw.com
Findlaw	*Business resources, legal professionals, public & consumer resources*, Corporate Counsel, *Student Resources, Legal News and Commentary, Legal Market Center*	No	Go to website for online use	All services	www.findlaw.com
Public access to court electronic records	State and federal court records	Yes	Computer sign-on to website then registration for online use	None	www.uscourts.gov/PubAccess.html

criminal cases are captioned *"Individual v. State,"* or *"Individual v. People."* Because
this case is captioned *Mobley v. State*, it looks like it might be a criminal case. What
else can we learn about this case? We know that the case is from the state of
Georgia, because the case cite gives us the abbreviation for the State of Georgia
Court of Appeals Reporter. The second series of numbers, 463 S.E.2d 166, is same
case published in a different reporter. The *Mobley* case can also be found in the
South Eastern Regional reporter in volume 463, page 166. We also know that this
case was decided, although not necessarily tried, in 1995.

2. ATTORNEYS

Although a legal researcher usually does not need to know the identity of the attorneys involved in the case, there are times when this information can be helpful or
interesting.

3. THE APPELLATE JUDGE

The next item provided is the name of the judge who wrote the opinion. This
information can often be quite important, especially if you have an appeal pending
with the same judge. You can read the judge's other decisions and begin to learn
something about the judge's temperament and attitude.

4. THE BODY OF THE CASE

We discuss the body of the case later in the chapter. In the case example, the written portion of the opinion has been removed.

5. THE COURT'S DECISION

In the case example, we see that the court's decision in this case is "judgment
affirmed." Unfortunately, that decision does not tell us very much. We will
have to read the actual case to discover exactly what the lower court did. We
can say one thing for certain: Whatever the lower court did, the court of appeals
agrees with that decision.

6. CONCURRENCE OR DISSENT

The last part of an opinion lists the decisions of the other judges. In this case, both
"McMurray, P.J., and Andrews, J., concur." This means that both of these judges
agree with the opinion written by Judge Blackburn.

B. READING AND ANALYZING A CASE

Your ability to read and understand case opinions is absolutely essential to your
success as a legal professional. Although reading cases may, at first blush, seem
difficult and complicated, with a little perseverance you can easily build the skills

Careers in the Law

▶ Private Investigator

Steven Ehlers is a private investigator who works primarily with criminal defense attorneys. A former police officer, he now uses his talents to investigate cases for people charged with crimes. "When you work for criminal defense attorneys, especially those who do death penalty work, you have to beg for resources. The court doesn't always give you enough money to properly investigate the case, so you have to be creative. You have to learn how to talk to people and be persuasive. Whenever you find witnesses, they're always reluctant to testify. Say you've got a witness who's in prison, and he knows something about your case. What can you offer him? The prosecutor can offer him a deal on his sentence. The only thing we can offer him is a chance to explain his testimony in court because it's the fair thing to do to. Sometimes you find yourself working 18 hours a day on some cases just to get them ready for trial. You're constantly tracking down witnesses and records and trying to do the best possible job you can. But there are some advantages. A lot of police departments only have a couple of investigators. They are working dozens of cases at the same time. I can concentrate on one case and get to know that case better than anybody who works for the prosecution.

"When you're a private investigator, you spend a lot of time on the Internet, tracking people down. There are several very good sites where you can find a person's last known mailing address and other information. These days, anyone who is thinking about going into legal work should know how to do some rudimentary Internet investigation."

necessary to dissect any case, from a one-paragraph memorandum opinion to a full-blown 75-page U.S. Supreme Court decision.

Before we explore this chapter's sample case, there are several important points to examine. First of all, legal writing in general — and appellate decisions in particular — use their own conventions. Once you learn these conventions, you will find yourself moving through an appellate case with a minimum of difficulty. Secondly, reading appellate decisions is an acquired skill. We've all heard the old axiom, "you must learn to walk before you can run." This holds true with legal research as well. Finally, legal writing serves a different purpose than many other types of writing. It follows its own rules and has its own internal logic.

1. THE CONVENTIONS OF LEGAL WRITING

In the next few paragraphs, we discuss how to dissect an appellate case specifically, but the rules we develop could just as easily apply to a trial brief, a legal memorandum, or any other type of legal writing.

a. The IRAC Method of Legal Writing

One widely used convention of legal writing is the IRAC method. IRAC is an abbreviation for the system used to write most types of legal documents: Issue ☐ Rule ☐ Application ☐ Conclusion. Using this method, a person writing an appellate decision would first state the *issue* raised in the case, what the *rule* is under the facts, how that rule *applies* to these facts, and the *conclusion* that must be reached as a consequence.

We explore this method of writing by reading the *Mobley* case for content.

MOBLEY v. STATE
218 Ga. App. 739, 463 S.E.2d 166 (1995)

Robert Greenwald, Lawrenceville, for appellant.
Daniel J. Porter, District Attorney, Phil Wiley, Neal R. Bevans,
Assistant District Attorneys, Lawrenceville, for appellee.
BLACKBURN, Judge.

Here the court presents the factual background of the case

Following a jury trial, the appellant, Allan Mobley, Jr., was found guilty but mentally ill of one count each of burglary, aggravated assault upon a police officer, kidnapping with bodily injury, possession of a firearm during the commission of a felony, fleeing or attempting to elude a police officer, and reckless driving and three counts of kidnapping. The trial court denied Mobley's motion for new trial, and he now appeals. The charges arise out of circumstances in which April Daly, a former co-worker at a Gwinnett County movie theater, spurned Mobley's advances as he sought a romantic relationship with her. Obsessed with Daly and distraught, Mobley kidnapped her and three others at the theater, first holding the group at gunpoint for several hours and then taking Daly alone by gunpoint and driving to South Carolina, Florida, and Tennessee. After returning to Gwinnett County, Mobley, in a car which he forced Daly to drive, was pursued by the police in a high speed chase which ended when Daly lost control, flipped the vehicle, and rammed several police cars.

First issue on appeal

Application

The rule

1. Mobley first asserts that the trial court erred by improperly commenting upon his evidence and certain questions posed by his trial counsel. Mobley cites many such instances in the transcript; however, he does not argue, nor are we able to find, that he timely objected to such comments at trial. "A party can not during the trial ignore what

Conclusion

he thinks to be an injustice, take his chance on a favorable verdict, and complain later." *Johnson v. State*, 226 Ga. 511, 514, 175 S.E.2d 840 (1970). Accordingly, this enumeration of error presents nothing for review.

Second issue on appeal

2. Mobley next contends that the trial court erred by failing to recharge the jury on the issue of insanity. Specifically, Mobley argues that a request from the jury during deliberations asking for copies of the definitions of "insane" and "mentally ill" and a later question asking for a definition of "guilty but mentally ill" obligated the trial court to recharge its entire original charge on insanity to ensure the jury's understanding of the difference between not guilty by reason of insanity and guilty but mentally ill.

Over objection, the trial court recharged the jury as to the definition of "mentally ill" and "guilty but mentally ill," observing that "it may confuse the jury more than anything to give them a seven page charge when what they've asked for is a two paragraph charge." Before doing so, the trial court confirmed that the jury desired a recharge only as to the definition of "guilty but mentally ill." The recharge was given upon cautionary language advising the jury not to give it greater emphasis than the remainder of the charge.

The rule

"In determining whether the recharge contain[s] error, it is fundamental that we must look at not only the recharge but the original charge as well, as jury instructions must be read and considered as a whole in determining whether the charges contain error.

Where a charge as a whole substantially presents issues in such a way as is not likely to confuse the jury even though a portion of the charge may not be as clear and precise as could be desired, a reviewing court will not disturb a verdict amply authorized by the evidence." *Taylor v. State,* 195 Ga. App. 314, 315, 393 S.E.2d 690 (1990). Reviewing the recharge and the charge as a whole, we conclude that the complained of recharge would not mislead a jury of average intelligence. Also, we find the jury's verdict to be well supported by the evidence. Thus, we find no error.

Application

Conclusion

3. Mobley last enumerates that the trial court improperly put his character in issue by admitting testimony evidencing uncharged misconduct.

Third issue on appeal

Mobley first challenges the testimony given by Matthew C. Brown, one of the group he initially abducted at gunpoint insofar as it indicated that Mobley told him that he had purchased the gun used in the kidnapping from a drug dealer friend for $50. Mobley argues that he was prejudiced by the trial court's failure to give a curative instruction at the time of his objection. However, contrary to Mobley's argument, our review of the record indicates that the trial court instructed the jury that it was "to give no weight at all, to this witness' statement about the defendant's drug dealing friends, or that he knows what kind of friends he has. Disregard it, entirely." Mobley timely requested and received an appropriate curative instruction. "[W]e generally will not grant more appellate relief than that actually prayed for at trial." (Citations and punctuation omitted.) *Morrill v. State,* 216 Ga. App. 468, 474, 454 S.E.2d 796 (1995). We decline to do so here.

Mobley next challenges Daly's testimony that Mobley told her he had gotten his gun from a drug dealer, that he sexually assaulted her, and that he committed an armed robbery while they were in Tennessee during the course of her kidnapping. Mobley failed to object at trial to Daly's testimony concerning the weapon he used in the commission of the offense and her claim of sexual assault. We do not consider issues raised for the first time on appeal. *See Porado v. State,* 211 Ga. App. 728, 730, 440 S.E.2d 690 (1994). Any claim by Mobley of error to such testimony was waived.

The rule

Application

Mobley timely objected to Daly's testimony accusing him of armed robbery while they were in Tennessee; however, such offense occurred "during the commission of one of the offenses for which [Mobley] was indicted and was an integral part of the res gestae. Surrounding circumstances constituting part of the res gestae may always be shown to the jury along with the principal fact, and their admissibility is within the discretion of the trial court. Hence, acts and circumstances forming a part or continuation of the main transaction are admissible as res gestae and it does not matter that the act is another criminal offense. The fact that such part of the res gestae incidentally placed [Mobley's] character in issue does not render it inadmissible. A trial judge's determination that evidence offered as part of the res gestae is sufficiently informative and reliable as to warrant being considered will not be disturbed on appeal unless that determination is clearly erroneous." *Belcher v. State,* 201 Ga. App. 139, 140-141, 410 S.E.2d 344 (1991). In light of the foregoing, there is no basis for reversal upon the evidence complained of, and this enumeration of error is without merit.

Further discussion of the application

Conclusion

Judgment affirmed.

McMURRAY, P.J., and ANDREWS, J., concur.

As you can see from reading the *Mobley* case, appellate decisions are presented in a particular and unique way. Generally speaking, the IRAC method is used in almost all case opinions. The court states the issue, then follows it with the applicable rule. In the *Mobley* case, here is how the court sets up the first issue-rule application: "Mobley first asserts that the trial court erred by improperly commenting upon his evidence and certain questions posed by his trial counsel." The court then explains the rule in that state regarding this issue: When the defense fails to object during the trial, it has waived the issue on appeal. The application? The court refuses to consider this part of the appeal.

You can go through each issue raised in the case and apply the IRAC rule throughout the case. Sometimes, such as in second issue in the *Mobley* case, the court takes the items out of order. In the second issue, the court actually applies the rule before stating it. However, all of the basic elements are present.

2. LEGAL TERMINOLOGY

Before we leave our discussion of case opinions, we should address some of the terminology used by appellate courts. In Chapter 1, we discussed the terminology used in bringing a case to trial. We said, for instance, that in a civil case, the person who brings the suit is called a plaintiff and the person who is being sued is referred to as the defendant. On appeal, these terms change. The person who brings the appeal is called an **appellant.** The person who prevailed in the lower court, and who would like the decision to stand, is called the **appellee.** We also use the term *lower court.* The reason for this is simple: An appeal is always brought in a higher court, or a court with appellate jurisdiction that has the power to overturn the previous court's decision. As a result, the other court is called the lower court. When a case is on its first round of appeal, the lower court usually means the trial court. When the term *lower court* is used in the *Mobley* case, for example, the court is referring to the trial court in which Mobley was found guilty but mentally ill of the crimes of which he was accused. However, suppose that Mobley, after losing in the Georgia Court of Appeals, decided to appeal his case to the Georgia Supreme Court. If that court considered his appeal, the lower court would refer to the Court of Appeals.

Appellant
The person bringing the current appeal from an adverse ruling in the court below

Appellee
The person who won in the lower court

ISSUE AT A GLANCE   When a case goes up on appeal, the terms for the parties change from plaintiff and defendant to appellant and appellee.

3. BRIEFING CASES

Case brief
The process of writing out key elements and reasoning of the case so that you can refer to them later

A **case brief** is a summary, prepared by a legal professional, of the reasoning used by the appellate court to decide a legal issue. Briefing is useful for both attorneys and paralegals to understand the court's logic in reaching its decision. It helps you organize your thoughts about a case, and definitely helps you to understand the case better. Because courts are bound by *stare decisis,* a case brief can give the legal professional some sense of what the court may do in the future.

For instance, suppose that you were briefing the *Mobley* case? See Figure 2-5 for a sample case brief on the first issue in the case.

Question 1:	Did the trial court improp-
	erly comment on the
	evidence that Mobley
	raised during trial?
Answer:	No. The court ruled that
	Mobley failed to object;

therefore, the court never
considered the merits of
Mobley's argument.

Rule: When a party fails to object
at trial, the issue is waived
on appeal.

FIGURE 2-5

Case Brief of *Mobley v. State*

LEGAL WRITING

One of the purposes of understanding case opinions and the other aspects of legal reasoning is to be able to emulate it. For a legal professional, strong writing ability is absolutely essential. Communication and law go hand in hand, whether you are speaking with clients over the telephone, composing e-mail messages, or writing appellate briefs for the state supreme court. Having good writing skills can make or break your legal career. In the next few paragraphs, we discuss various types of legal writing and the significant role each plays in the day-to-day business of law.

A. MEMORANDUM OF LAW

A memorandum of law is a written discussion of a legal question. The memo often includes the researcher's opinion as to who will win in court. It objectively reports the law as it applies to the facts of the case. A legal memorandum is often as short as a single page and strives for objectivity. It is almost always reserved for members of the legal team and is not distributed to the judge or the other side in the litigation.

B. BRIEFS

When a case is appealed, appellate courts ordinarily require the lawyers to present their arguments to the court in writing. A brief (not be confused with a case brief) is a formal, written argument that discusses not only the facts of the case and the applicable law, but also seeks to advocate for the client. It attempts to persuade. The person to be persuaded is usually a judge or a justice of the appellate court.

C. BRIEFS VERSUS MEMORANDA

The brief is different than a memorandum of law. A memorandum of law is supposed to be objective. A brief is designed to advocate for one side over the other. In a brief, a lawyer argues his client's side of the case. As such, these two documents have a different appearance and are easy to tell apart.

Memoranda of law explain a topic; briefs argue a position based on facts and law.

SKILLS YOU NEED IN THE REAL WORLD

QUICK AND DIRTY RESEARCH

There will be times in your legal career when the speed with which you find the answer to a particular question is more important than your method. Here is where knowing some quick and dirty legal research techniques can really pay off.

When time is short and you need an answer fast, don't neglect the obvious. Has anyone else in the office ever researched this issue? Perhaps they have already prepared a memorandum on the precise topic. Check with fellow staffers and ask about their own recent research sessions. Never be too proud to ask for help. Your next stop in a quick and dirty research session is recent briefs.

RECENT APPELLATE BRIEFS

As we have learned in this chapter, a brief is a discussion of a legal question. Has the office prepared any briefs recently that deal with the same topic that you are about to research? If so, that brief would be a good place to start.

ONLINE LEGAL RESEARCH

Beyond office resources, there are also some quality Internet sites that should be considered. Try the free ones first. Go to www.aboutlaw.com or www.findlaw.com and type in your search question. An online site might point you in the right direction and save you a lot of time when it counts the most. Finally, don't be shy about asking for clarification (or ideas) from the person who is giving you the research assignment. Many times this person has a resource in mind already. See if this person can point you in the right direction to get a quick answer.

CHAPTER SUMMARY

Unlike other forms of research, the purpose of legal research is to locate cases or statutes that assist the client. When researching cases, the researcher seeks out cases containing similar facts and similar issues as the client's case. Legal research is designed to answer specific questions. General or background information is often useless in legal research. Mastering the skill of legal research is necessary because the body of law is vast and laws are constantly changing. Staying current on new developments in the law helps a legal professional better safeguard the client's interests.

Courts in the United States are bound by the principle of *stare decisis,* which requires judges to follow the principles set out in previously decided cases. The process of legal research involves reviewing the various sources of law. Law may be found in many different places, including statutes and case law. Statutes are legislative enactments that have been signed into existence by the executive branch of government. Case law, on the other hand, consists of the written decisions of appellate courts setting out their reasons for making a ruling in a particular case.

Legal writing differs from other types of writing in that it is very stylized and formal. Legal writing follows a set pattern of addressing the issues involved in a case, showing how those issues interact with the rule of law, and finally applying the rule to the case to reach a conclusion. Although legal research and writing is a skill that takes time to acquire, the effort pays huge dividends. Legal research and writing is the very core of the legal profession.

ETHICS: LEGAL RESEARCH AND ETHICS

When people use the term *ethics,* they usually have in mind situations such as the attorney-client privilege or the obligation of the legal team to act in the best interests of the client. Legal research is usually not very high on the list of ethical obligations, but it should be. Is there a connection between ethical obligations and legal research skills? Absolutely.

As part of its service, the legal team must provide the client with the best legal advice available. In the law, the best means the most up-to-date information possible. Although law is generally a slow-moving and conservative business, there are times when issues move very quickly. For instance, the U.S. Supreme Court could publish an opinion that immediately changes the legal landscape. Imagine the disastrous consequences to a client whose attorney is not aware that a recent case has changed the law. Suddenly, an action that was perfectly legitimate is now impermissible. Imposing an ethical requirement that attorneys bring their research as up to date as possible is one way of ensuring that the client receives the best possible service. Thorough legal research protects the client and also protects the firm from a claim of legal malpractice.

CHAPTER REVIEW QUESTIONS

1   What is the purpose of legal research?
2   List and explain four different reasons why a legal professional must carry out legal research.

3   Explain the principle of *stare decisis.*
4   What is a case reporter?
5   What are the three decisions that appellate courts may reach in a case?
6   Compare and contrast cases and statutes.
7   What is a code?
8   What are some examples of national legal encyclopedias?
9   Explain the types of Internet resources available to legal researchers.
10 What are some examples of online legal research pay sites?
11 How do online commercial legal research sites differ from free sites?
12 Explain the basic components of a reported case.
13 What is the "style" of a case?
14 What types of information can you learn from the identifying information at the beginning of a case?
15 Explain the IRAC method of analyzing legal writing.
16 How does one brief a case?
17 What is the difference between a legal memorandum and a brief?
18 What are some methods to carry out quick legal research?

DISCUSSION QUESTIONS

1   Are there too many levels of appellate courts in the United States? Why or why not?
2   Should the principle of *stare decisis* be abandoned? Why or why not?
3   Does the growing popularity of Internet-based research mean that printed legal research sources will become obsolete? Explain your answer.

PERSONALITY QUIZ

Would you be good at legal research? Take this personality quiz and see.

1   I am a detail-oriented person.

    0-strongly disagree   5-agree   10-strongly agree

                                                            Points: _____

2   I enjoy proofreading papers.

    0-strongly disagree   5-agree   10-strongly agree

                                                            Points: _____

3   I would rather write a paper than address a group.

    0-strongly disagree   5-agree   10-strongly agree

                                                            Points: _____

4   I like getting to the root of things.

0-strongly disagree   5-agree   10-strongly agree

Points: _____

5   One of my strongest characteristics is my drive to get things right.

0-strongly disagree   5-agree   10-strongly agree

Points: _____

Total Points: _____

If you scored between 30-50 points, you would probably enjoy and be good at legal research.

If you scored between 20-29 points, you might do well with legal research, but you would probably prefer to carry out some other activity.

If you scored 19 or lower, legal research is probably not your strong suit.

PRACTICAL APPLICATIONS

1   Locate the commonly accepted authorities (treatises) in your state on the subjects of real property law, wills and estates, commercial transactions, and corporations. Record the names of these authorities for later use.

2   Speak with veteran paralegals. Ask them about legal research and the methods that they use. Do they rely on the Internet or print media? Do they have any short cuts that they routinely use to speed up their research?

WEB SITES

LexisNexis
http://www.lexisnexis.com

Westlaw®
www.WestLaw.com

Loislaw
http://www.loislaw.com

The Virtual Chase (free legal research)
http://www.virtualchase.com

Legal Resource Links
http://www.legalresourcelinks.com

TERMS AND PHRASES

Affirm	Case Law	Reporter
Appellant	Code	Reverse
Appellee	Opinion	Stare decisis
Case brief	Remand	

The Participants in
the Legal System

3

Chapter Learning Objectives

After completing this chapter, you should be able to:

- Explain the role of judges in both civil and criminal cases

- Explain the difference between plaintiffs' attorneys and insurance defense attorneys

- Explain the role of the prosecutor and law enforcement officers in a criminal case

- Explain the role of the paralegal in the American legal system

- List and explain the roles of local government support personnel in the legal system

 **INTRODUCTION**

In this chapter we explore the many participants in the U.S. legal system, from paralegals to judges. We begin our discussion with the role played by judges.

 **JUDGES**

Judges play a critical role in our system. Most people know that judges preside at trials and make rulings on evidence. Judges are also responsible for keeping order in the court. A judge is empowered to hold unruly persons in **contempt,** which means that the judge can order the person to pay a fine or even spend a short period of time in jail. In criminal trials, when the jury finds a defendant guilty, it is usually the judge who sentences the defendant.

Contempt
A ruling that a person is in violation of a court order

Judges are required by their court rules and their own ethical code to be neutral and objective in all suits. Although the television-induced misconception is that a judge often sides with one party during a case, the reality is very different. A judge is not supposed to play favorites. To that end, a judge must not influence the jury to vote a certain way, or even to hint who the judge believes should win. Such an action would qualify as judicial error and be grounds for overturning the verdict on appeal.

Although there are many popular misconceptions about judges, it is certainly true that a judge occupies an important and influential position in the community. Judges have great responsibility placed on them and because many of them acquit themselves well under this burden, they enjoy enormous respect. Most judges also earn excellent salaries. The respect, power, and pay makes the position of a judge very desirable and many attorneys strive to become judges at some point in their careers.

A. QUALIFICATIONS

In most cases, judges are attorneys. In fact, most states require that any person seeking a judicial appointment already be a member in good standing of the state bar. This is true of almost all judicial positions. However, there are some judicial positions, in some states, that do not require the person to be a member of the state bar. For example, some states allow magistrates — judges who are empowered to issue warrants and to hear small claims suits — to be non-lawyers.

Judges are responsible for maintaining order in the court.
Judges can be appointed or elected to their positions.

B. ELECTED VERSUS APPOINTED JUDICIAL POSITIONS

States have varying approaches to selecting judges. In some states, judges are appointed by the governor or a special commission. In other states, judges run for election in the same way that mayors and state legislators do. This means that judges campaign like any other politician in order to be elected. However, judges usually run on a nonpartisan ticket. Judicial elections are still viewed as less political than other types of elections. Whether that perception is actually correct is another matter.

Recuse
To disqualify, such as when a judge removes herself from considering a case or is removed by another judge

C. RECUSAL

There are times when a judge will remove herself from a case. This is called **recusal.** A judge may recuse herself from the case when there is any appearance of a conflict of interest. For instance, suppose that one of the attorneys trying the case is a former law partner of the judge. In such a situation, even though the judge might believe that she could be fair and objective, the appearance of a conflict alone is enough to justify recusing herself and having another judge hear the case. Parties to a lawsuit can also bring a recusal motion against a sitting judge. For instance, a party might file a motion seeking to have a judge removed from the case because the judge has shown some bias or prejudice against the party or has an undisclosed conflict of interest. In such a situation, a different judge would hear the recusal motion. That judge would hold a hearing to consider evidence and to make a ruling as to whether the first judge should be removed from the case.

 **ATTORNEYS**

Whether a lawyer eventually works as a plaintiff's attorney, a prosecutor, a public defender, or any of the hundreds of other types of legal specialties available, the initial training is the same. In the next few sections, we concentrate on how a person becomes a lawyer and the impact that ethical rules can have on the lawyer's standing.

A. BECOMING A LAWYER

Paralegals are often interested in the process of becoming an attorney. Some plan on becoming attorneys themselves, while others simply want to have a better understanding of the attorneys with whom they will work. One of the best ways to understand the profession is to examine how a person becomes a lawyer in the first place. That process starts with law school.

1. LAW SCHOOL

Before a person is allowed to practice law, she must attend and successfully complete law school. When a student takes law classes on a full-time basis, it takes three years to complete the curriculum. There are part-time law schools, and even one Internet-based law school. Many successful and even famous attorneys have attended night law school while working at other professions. However, the vast majority of attorneys practicing today have attended a traditional, full-time law school.

To be admitted into a law school, an applicant must have a bachelor's degree in some discipline and have received a minimum score on the LSAT (Law School Admission Test). Most schools also require a minimum GPA in the applicant's bachelor's degree and some have additional requirements.

There have been several excellent books written about the law school experience, with *The Paper Chase* and *One L* leading the pack. Law school is very difficult and demanding. Classes center more on theory than practice, explaining a certain deficit that new attorneys often demonstrate: They know the theory behind a pleading, but they don't necessarily know where the pleading should be filed at the courthouse.

First-year law courses can be very intimidating. Professors often choose only one or two persons per class to answer questions and many times these answers must be given while the student is standing. By the time a student has completed three years of such courses, she is more than ready to leave school and try life in the real world. Unfortunately, one hurdle remains: the bar examination.

2. TAKING THE BAR EXAM

The bar examination is administered in different ways in different states, but no one could argue that the test is a mere formality. The examination often lasts for two days, consisting of both lengthy essay-style and multiple-choice questions. It is grueling and because passing the bar exam is absolutely essential to the life of a future attorney, law students spend hundreds, if not thousands, of hours preparing to take the exam. Although most applicants pass the bar exam on the first attempt, every lawyer knows at least one person who failed and was forced to retake the exam at a later date.

In most states, the only people who can take the bar examination are law students who have graduated from an accredited law school. In addition to graduating from an approved school, a person who plans to take the bar exam must also submit a lengthy application to the state bar. This application will contain a complete list of the applicant's work history, references, and background. The state bar, or some other agency, is empowered to investigate all applicants and certify that they do not have some legal or ethical problem that would bar them from becoming an attorney, such as conviction of a crime. In some states, this is called "moral certification." This certification is required before the applicant will be allowed to sit for the bar examination.

 **To become an attorney, a person must have a bachelor's degree, good grades, and a minimum score on the LSAT.**

B. ADMISSION TO THE STATE BAR

Once a person has graduated from an accredited law school and passed the state bar exam, she can be admitted into the state bar. After everything that the applicant has been through, admission into the state bar is often anti-climactic. The new attorney raises her hand, swears to uphold the standards of the profession, and then a judge administers the oath, signs a certificate indicating that the person is now a licensed lawyer, and it is over. She is now a lawyer and can represent clients, offer legal advice, and follow in the footsteps of a great and noble profession.

An attorney will remain a member of the state bar, and thus licensed to practice, as long as she meets certain conditions, such paying yearly bar dues and abiding by the state bar's rules. Most attorneys who lose their licenses (referred to as **disbarment**) do so because of some ethical violation.

Disbarment
A temporary or permanent revocation of an attorney's license to practice law

Once an attorney graduates from law school and passes the bar exam, she may practice in any legal area.

ISSUE AT
A GLANCE

1. THE IMPORTANCE OF ETHICAL RULES FOR ATTORNEYS

An attorney can be disbarred for any number of reasons, including conviction of a crime and violating ethical standards. The vast majority of attorneys who are disbarred every year — and these are only a small percentage of attorneys — lose their licenses because they steal money from their clients. Attorneys who use client funds to pay their own expenses engage in a practice known as **commingling.** This ethical violation is the equivalent of a professional death sentence: The attorney's license to practice law in the state will be permanently revoked. After all the time, energy, and money it has taken to acquire the license, losing it is one of the worst things that can happen to an attorney.

Commingling
Improperly mixing client trust funds with fee payments; a form of theft

Not all ethical violations justify this most drastic of remedies. Attorneys who engage in less serious unethical practices might face some sanction short of disbarment. These sanctions range from a private reprimand from the state bar, to a public reprimand (a reprimand notice published in legal magazines and case reporters in the state), to temporary suspension from the practice of law.

C. CIVIL ATTORNEYS

Once an attorney has become a member of the state bar, she can decide what area of law appeals to her. There are no additional certifications or licenses needed for attorneys who wish to specialize. An attorney is an attorney and is permitted to practice in almost any area of law that she wishes. However, most new attorneys already have a good idea, fostered by their experience in law school, of what area appeals to them. Many new attorneys choose either plaintiffs' firms or insurance defense firms.

1. PLAINTIFFS' ATTORNEYS

When a person wishes to sue another, she often hires a lawyer to handle the details of the suit. The person who brings the suit is called the plaintiff and the attorneys who represent such people are called plaintiffs' attorneys. Although there is no prohibition against an attorney representing plaintiffs in one case and defendants in another, most attorneys specialize in one area or the other. There are several reasons for this. For one thing, when attorneys specialize in one area of law, such as representing plaintiffs who have been injured in car wrecks or through medical malpractice, they learn this particular area of law thoroughly. The different areas of law are vast and complex and no one person can master them all. Therefore most attorneys focus on the area that appeals to them.

What makes a person choose to represent plaintiffs instead of defendants? There are many reasons. Some attorneys like the challenge of proving a case.

They believe that they are helping people who have been injured by the actions of others. The financial or other rewards might appeal to them. We explore the world of plaintiffs' firms in greater detail in Chapter 8.

2. DEFENSE ATTORNEYS

Insurance companies regularly pay the fees for firms that specialize in defense work. When a motorist is sued, her insurance policy often contains a provision that guarantees that an attorney will represent her. Many firms have standing arrangements with insurance companies that they will represent all people in a geographic area who are sued. These firms are commonly referred to as insurance defense firms.

3. THE ORGANIZATION OF THE LAW OFFICE

Although law is a noble profession, it is also a business. An attorney who routinely takes on cases for the principles involved and fails to pay attention to the bottom line will soon find herself without an office, a staff, or a paycheck. Attorneys work hard to maintain a balance between these competing interests.

Law firms are organized in almost as many different ways as there are attorneys and paralegals. A firm may consist of a single attorney working closely with a paralegal who also does double duty as a secretary. On the other end of the spectrum are huge, multinational law firms with hundreds of attorneys and thousands of support staff scattered in major cities across the globe. When you go to work for a firm, you will probably find yourself somewhere between these two extremes. Although there are many different ways to organize a law office, there are some basic elements that will be found in almost any size firm, be it two attorneys or two thousand. For one thing, most firms have partners and associates.

a. Partners and Associates

Suppose that you are hired to work at a ten-attorney firm. The firm handles primarily plaintiffs' work, representing people who have been injured in car wrecks. There are many other types of firms, but personal injury firms are common and many paralegals will have experience with these firms at some point in their legal careers.

Partners
Attorney-owners of a law firm

Associates
Attorney-employees of a firm

With ten attorneys in the firm, there will be some attorneys who are classified as **partners** and some who are classified as **associates.** An associate is usually a young lawyer, perhaps even fresh out of law school. The associate earns a set salary. Although the associate is well paid by most people's standards, the associate's salary doesn't compare to the partner's salary. Partners own the firm. They split the profits among themselves. Once all staff and other overhead charges have been paid, whatever is left over is divided among the partners. If it has been a particularly profitable year, this could be a huge amount of money. On the other hand, if the firm has suffered a string of losses, the pot may be small. However, most law firms make excellent money.

A law firm is a business and is generally organized with owners (partners) splitting the profits while associates, paralegals, secretaries, and others receive a fixed salary.

ISSUE AT A GLANCE

Associates handle many of the less glamorous aspects of the firm's business, such as drafting pleadings, interrogatories, and motions. Partners often concentrate on bringing in new clients and keeping current clients happy. Associates may work for years, making relatively little money, but with the ultimate goal of being promoted to partnership. If an associate "makes partner," it means that she is ushered into the prestige (and profits) shared by the other partners.

D. CRIMINAL ATTORNEYS

Attorneys who handle primarily criminal cases can also be divided into two distinct camps. On the one hand are prosecutors and on the other are criminal defense attorneys.

1. PROSECUTORS

A prosecutor is an attorney who works for the state or federal government. Future prosecutors attend the same law schools and have the same training as all other attorneys. They are hired fresh out of law school or after they have worked several years in other legal areas. Once they are hired, however, their role in the American legal system is unlike any other type of lawyer.

Prosecutors go by many different names. They may be called assistant district attorneys, state's attorneys, people's prosecutors, assistant attorneys general, and solicitors. By whatever name, a prosecutor is responsible for bringing the official charge against a person accused of a crime, arranging for and conducting a trial of that person, and recommending a sentence if that person is found guilty. Prosecutors, like judges, have an ethical code. Prosecutors are sworn to seek justice, not merely to get convictions.

Unlike other areas of law, prosecutors earn relatively low salaries. Given the fact that these attorneys could go to work for a law firm and earn two or three times the annual salary of a prosecutor, why do so many attorneys choose to become prosecutors?

There are several possible answers to this question. Some attorneys become prosecutors simply for the experience. They realize that they will try many more cases as prosecutors than civil attorneys will. Prosecutors often try two or three cases every month. A civil attorney might only try two or three cases a year. This trial experience is invaluable. After all, practice does make perfect and if a young attorney prosecutes a lot of cases, she will make herself more marketable to firms who wish to hire a veteran litigator. For some attorneys, working as a prosecutor brings a strong sense of satisfaction that outweighs the low pay. They wish to make a contribution to their communities and see prosecuting criminals as a way to do that.

Sidebar

Unfortunately, paralegals cannot become partners at a law firm. Their pay may increase as the firm's profits increase. In fact, in one notable case, a paralegal shared a multimillion dollar verdict. But situations such as the one in the movie Erin Brockovich are rare. In most situations, associates, paralegals, secretaries, and other support personnel earn a standard salary with occasional bonuses.

Sidebar

A prosecutor's salary varies considerably from state to state. In California, a beginning prosecutor could earn $50,268 a year in some heavily populated counties, while the same prosecutor earns $24,030 in Kentucky.

FIGURE 3-1

Annual Budget for State
Prosecutors' Offices,
1992–2005*

Highlights

Median annual budget for State prosecutors' offices, 1992-2005

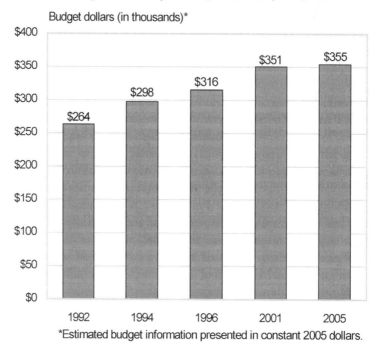

Budget dollars (in thousands)*

*Estimated budget information presented in constant 2005 dollars.

• At least two-thirds of the State court prosecutors had litigated a computer-related crime such as credit card fraud (80%), identity theft (69%), or transmission of child pornography (67%).

• Nearly all the prosecutors' offices (98%) reported their State had a domestic violence statute; 28% of the offices maintained a domestic violence prosecution unit.

• A quarter (24%) of the offices participated in a State or local task force for homeland security; one-third reported an office member attended training on homeland security issues.

• Most prosecutors (95%) relied on State operated forensic laboratories to perform DNA analysis, with about a third (34%) also using privately operated DNA labs.

• Two-thirds of prosecutors' offices had prosecuted a juvenile case in criminal court during 2005. A third of the offices had a designated attorney for these special cases.

• In 2005 nearly 40% of the prosecutors considered their office a community prosecution site actively involving law enforcement and the community to improve public safety.

* U.S. Department of Justice, Bureau of Justice Statistics. Prosecutors in State Courts, 2005.

Sidebar

Lawyer's salaries used to be a taboo subject. Not any more. Today you can actually find them reported on the web. Findlaw.com, for instance, http://careers.findlaw.com lists not only typical lawyer salaries, but also job advertisements for attorneys and paralegals.

Besides acting as the government representative in all criminal actions, prosecutors often also serve as legal advisors to the police. They draft the charging documents against defendants and present evidence and witnesses against an accused to prove her guilty of a crime.

Careers in the Law

▶ Prosecutor Keith Miles

Keith Miles has been a prosecutor for 14 years. If he had taken a job with a private firm, he could be bringing home over $200,000 a year now. But he's an assistant district attorney and he makes a fraction of that figure. Even though the job isn't what it's made out to be on television, he still wouldn't trade it for anything, even the big money at a firm. "When I was a kid, all I wanted was to be a lawyer," he says. When asked what drew him to prosecution he laughs and says, "the money, definitely the money." His first prosecution job out of law school paid a whopping $22,500. That was in 1987. In those days, top graduates from his law school could earn a starting salary of $60,000 at a downtown law firm. Today, top graduates have starting salaries of over $100,000. Miles makes less than half that amount after 14 years as a prosecutor. He has prosecuted almost every kind of crime there is, from brutal rapes and murders to hundreds of more run-of-the-mill crimes such as forgery, arson, and shoplifting. With two children approaching college age, why does he stay? The answer: satisfaction. "I like helping to put someone away who really needs it; that's what I enjoy the most. You've got a rapist or a murderer, somebody who's really hurt somebody and you put him away. It just doesn't get any better than that."

Prosecutors draft charging documents against defendants, handle trials against defendants, and act as legal advisors to the police on matters such as arrest and search warrants.

ISSUE AT A GLANCE

---

a. The Role of Prosecutors in Criminal Trials

U.S. v. DEVINE
787 F.2d 1086 (C.A.7 (Ill.) 1986)

WILLIAMS J. CAMPBELL, Senior District Judge.

Defendant John J. Devine was convicted of knowingly and willfully devising and participating in a scheme to defraud in violation of 18 U.S.C. §§1341, 1951 and 1962(c). Judge Susan Getzendanner of the Northern District of Illinois sentenced him to numerous concurrent 15-year terms of imprisonment. For the reasons set forth below, we affirm.

Defendant, a former Cook County Associate Judge, was convicted of orchestrating deals with attorneys to fix cases for monetary payments. At trial two attorneys, Martin Schachter and Arthur Cirignani, testified they paid defendant to secure favorable results and to be "court-appointed" to represent defendants in future "deals." Devine usually requested one-third of the attorneys' fees for a fixed case. The attorneys usually secured their fees from clients' bond money. In addition to the testimony of the two attorneys mentioned above there was the testimony of F.B.I. agent/informant Terrence Hake who worked "undercover" in defendant's courtroom as part of the now famous Operation Greylord investigation. He verified defendant Devine accepted money from him. A third attorney, Howard Shaffner, testified he personally had an encounter with defendant and believed defendant was trying to "shake him down." Additionally, Chicago police officer Joseph Trunzo testified he witnessed an attorney named Harry Klepper leave defendant's courtroom upset one day because defendant demanded he be paid additional dollars to secure the result Klepper desired. We believe there is little need to detail other testimony at the trial. In sum, we find no paucity of evidence from which defendant could have been found guilty as charged.

Defendant claims reversible error occurred because the district court refused to allow a linguist, Dr. Robert Shuy, to testify concerning difficult to hear sections of a "body-bug" tape produced by F.B.I. agent Hake. Hake produced such tapes while "dealing" with defendant and his courtroom personnel. Defendant claims that since the government was allowed to present transcripts of its version of the conversations to the jury, the exclusion of Dr. Shuy's testimony denied him his right to a fair trial and his Sixth Amendment right to present an adequate defense. Defendant adds Dr. Shuy's testimony was reliable and helpful and therefore should have been presented to the jury under Rule 702 of the Federal Rules of Evidence. We note that Dr. Shuy testified during defendant's offer of proof and stated, contrary to defendant's assertions, that if defense counsel were allowed to play the tapes to the jury and present its argument it would have the same effect as any transcripts given to them. The tapes were played. Shuy also rejected defendant's argument that he would be using his expertise in understanding the context and dynamics of conversations in analyzing the tape. Shuy claimed he would rely instead on auditory and phonetic indicia, i.e., listening skills. The district court concluded Shuy's testimony would "not have given the jury significant help in understanding the evidence or in determining a fact in issue, and understanding what is said in a tape recorded conversation is not outside the average person's understanding." (D. Ct. Op. of Dec. 17, 1984 at 3) We agree. "We will reverse the court's ruling on the admissibility of expert testimony only upon a clear showing of abuse of discretion." We see no clear abuse of discretion here. We also reject defendant's argument he was unable to present his version of what the tapes said. Defendant's counsel cross-examined Agent Hake for three days. The tapes were played during this cross-examination on equipment identical to that used by Dr. Shuy. Portions of the tapes contested by defendant were deleted when given to the jury in transcript form during deliberations. We see no reversible error.

Defendant claims the district court erred in refusing to allow defendant complete discovery concerning the entire scope of the "Operation Greylord" investigation of which Agent Hake's activities were a part. Defendant asserts, "It cannot be said that . . . no set of facts could be proven upon which the Defendant would have been entitled to suppression of the tape recordings." (Defendant's br. p. 57) We note the propriety of the tactics employed in the "Operation Greylord" investigation was upheld in United States v. Murphy, 768 F.2d 1518, 1528-1529 (7th Cir. 1985). Importantly, defendant was allowed discovery concerning cases which involved him. We see no error here.

Defendant asserts the trial court erred in admitting the hearsay statements of Harold Conn and Harry Klepper. We believe it rather obvious from evidence independent of Conn's statements that Conn was a part of the conspiracy at issue in this case. We therefore find no error in admitting the Conn statements under Federal Rule of Evidence 801(d)(2)(E) as a statement of a co-conspirator. The district court admitted the relevant Klepper statements through Officer Trunzo because they were not offered for the truth of the matter asserted, but instead to explain Trunzo's actions. We do not believe the admission of these statements amounts to reversible error in this case.

Defendant's final argument is that the district court erred in limiting his cross-examination of Agent Hake. Defendant particularly objects to his inability to ask Hake about the absence of confirming statements by Hake at certain times after Hake gave a co-conspirator bribe money. Hake, for obvious reasons, would try to document the giving a bribe whenever possible by making a confirming type of remark. Defendant claims, for example, he should have been able to ask Hake the question "When you left on February 3, did you say anything on that tape recorder about giving Judge Devine money?" (see defendant's br. p. 61). The district court found evidence of a lack of a confirming statement by Hake at any given time legally irrelevant, stating there may have been no opportunity for Hake to make any confirming statements in certain instances when giving bribe money for fear he would tip off the conspirators. We see no abuse of discretion on the part of the district court here. We note defendant was allowed extensive cross-examination of Agent Hake over a three-day period which covered 650 pages of trial transcript.

We close by stating we leave this case with the impression that the evidence presented against defendant Devine at trial was very strong. Testimony from several reliable, credible and independent sources indicates defendant Devine was properly convicted of conduct so despicable we will not engage in a battle of adjectives in an attempt to describe it. The evidence speaks for itself.

One final caveat is appropriate. Defendant asked for and was mercifully granted leave to file an oversized brief by this court. The brief was desultory in nature; in general a poorly written product with numerous typographical errors. It was obviously never edited by a caring professional. As a panel of judges already overburdened with cases and paper, we find it insulting to have to dutifully comb through a brief which even its author found little reason to give such attention. We condemn this type of shoddy professionalism.

For the reasons set forth above, the decision of the district court is hereby AFFIRMED.

QUESTIONS ABOUT THE CASE

1   What crimes is the Judge in this case accused of committing?
2   Was the defendant denied his rights when the trial court refused to present testimony from his expert about the content of audio tapes made between the defendant and an undercover FBI agent?
3   What is the defendant's allegation concerning discovery in his case?
4   Explain the basis of the defendant's complaints regarding hearsay testimony.
5   What comments does the appellate court make about the nature of the evidence against the defendant?

2. CRIMINAL DEFENSE ATTORNEYS

Criminal defense attorneys represent people charged with crimes. Many states have a public defender's office, staffed with attorneys who are paid by the state and who have the responsibility to represent individuals who cannot afford to hire their own attorneys. Like prosecutors, public defenders are members of the state bar.

However, not all criminal defense attorneys work for public defenders' offices. Many law firms also handle criminal defense work. In fact, some of the most famous names in our legal system belong to private attorneys who practice criminal defense. Who can forget Johnny Cochran's successful defense of O.J. Simpson or F. Lee Bailey's role in several prominent cases in the twentieth century?

Retainer
A fee paid to an attorney to secure the attorney's services

Private criminal defense attorneys charge their clients a fee to represent them in such cases. Criminal defense attorneys often charge an up-front, one-time **retainer** that can be tens of thousands of dollars. This up-front fee is designed to cover the attorney's fee and related expenses. The reason behind a retainer system is that once a criminal case is resolved, it might be difficult to get any additional payments from the client. If he or she is serving a prison sentence, the attorney probably will not receive any further payments on her fee. On the other hand, if the client is found not guilty and released, the client is often reluctant to pay any additional fees, often believing that his case was so simple and straightforward that an attorney wasn't necessary.

IV   PARALEGALS

Paralegals are an indispensable and continuously growing part of the legal system in the United States. They are found in every phase of legal practice, from arbitration to workers' compensation. Paralegals also work for criminal defense attorneys and for prosecutors. What makes paralegals so critical to legal practice is that they are the glue that holds the system together. They act as intermediaries for attorneys, handling client issues when the attorney is unavailable. They also perform many of the day-to-day activities of a legal practice, from billing clients and researching the law to trips to the courthouse or accident scenes. On any given day they may interview witnesses, photograph damage to an automobile, draft a brief to the state supreme court and answer dozens of telephone calls. In many ways, it is an exciting and rewarding career.

A. LEGAL ASSISTANT OR PARALEGAL? WHAT'S IN A NAME?

Depending on the part of the country in which you practice, the term for a professional who works closely with an attorney varies. In many areas, this professional is referred to by the term *paralegal,* while in others the term *legal assistant* is used. Some object to the term *paralegal* because they feel that it connotes a lack of professional standing. Others object to the term *legal assistant* because it lacks historical perspective and ignores the long fight these professionals faced to be recognized by attorneys for the important and crucial role that they play. There is no apparent consensus about which term to use. Therefore, we use the term *paralegal,* simply because it has existed longer than the term *legal assistant.*

FIGURE 3-2

Personnel in State Prosecutors' Offices, 2005*

Table 1. Personnel employed in State prosecutors' offices, 2005	
Personnel category	Percent of total personnel in prosecutors' offices nationwide
Total	100%
Chief prosecutor	3%
Assistant prosecutors	31
Civil attorneys	2
Managers/supervisors[a]	6
Legal services[b]	6
Victim advocates	6
Staff investigators	9
Support staff[c]	33
Other	3
Estimated total personnel	78,000

Note: Detail may not add to 100% due to rounding. Data were available on the number of chief prosecutors for all offices. Data were available on the number of assistant prosecutors, civil attorneys, managers, legal services personnel, victim advocates, staff investigators, support staff, and other personnel for 100% of prosecutors' offices.

[a]Includes any attorneys in non-litigating, managerial, or supervisory positions. If managers/supervisors litigate cases, they are included in the number of assistant prosecutors, as well as civil attorneys.

[b]Includes law clerks and paralegals.

[c]Support staff includes secretaries, clerks, and computer specialists.

* Bureau of Justice Statistics, U.S. Department of Justice. Prosecutors in State Courts, 2005.

Although the term *paralegal* has only been used for a few decades, attorneys have always had support personnel to help them in the day-to-day practice of law.

ISSUE AT A GLANCE

B. DEVELOPMENT OF THE PARALEGAL PROFESSION

In the 1970s, the conservative world of lawyers began to see a quiet revolution. The staff members who had always worked for lawyers, and without whom lawyers could not function, began to organize. They realized that they shared similar experiences and that by forming local and national organizations they could not only gain valuable insight into their day-to-day activities, but also earn additional respect. They formed two national organizations: NFPA, the National Federation of Paralegal Associations, Inc., and NALA, the National Association of Legal Assistants. Both these national organizations, and hundreds of local chapters, began to network and to demand higher pay for a job that required intensive training, discipline, and long hours and dedication.

C. ACTIVITIES CARRIED OUT BY PARALEGALS

Paralegals carry out a dizzying variety of tasks. Depending on where they work, they might interview witnesses, draft legal documents, and meet with clients. They might also find themselves in court, assisting an attorney who is trying a case. Paralegals who work in criminal defense firms are often called upon to interview clients, obtain police reports, draft motions and other criminal discovery pleadings, and attend court with the attorney. Paralegals play such a large role in the legal system and carry out so many different activities that instead of attempting to list them all here, we will address them as we discuss specific areas of law in future chapters.

Paralegals are playing an ever-increasing role not only in private firms, but also in government positions. Prosecution offices have begun hiring paralegals to help draft charging documents such as indictments and accusations, coordinate witness appearances with victim-witness programs, and work closely with the prosecutor and police when further investigation of a case is called for. Just as in private practice, many government offices are beginning to see the advantages of having someone who is trained in the law to assist attorneys with cases.

D. LICENSING PARALEGALS

In recent years, there has been a strong push toward licensing or certifying paralegals in the same way that other professionals are licensed. Various legislative initiatives have been put forward that would create paralegal licensing boards similar to the boards that govern accountants, dentists, doctors and attorneys. There appears to be a strong momentum toward licensure and it is probably simply a matter of time before a state creates such a rule. The impact on the paralegal profession will be immense. Licensure will undoubtedly include minimum educational or experience requirements and continued legal education. It may also raise the overall profile of paralegals in the same way that licensure increased the stature of nurses over one hundred years ago.

CLIENTS

No discussion of the participants in the U.S. legal system would be complete without a reference to clients. When a person hires an attorney it is often because that person has been unsuccessful in attempting to resolve the problem himself. Most people are

Profiling a Paralegal

▶ Rena Harp

 ena Harp is a graduate of an associate l level paralegal program. Although she l enjoyed her courses, she found that the l everyday practice of being a paralegal was more complicated than her paralegal courses originally suggested. "My paralegal classes gave me good general background on exactly how things work. I knew the difference between different types of pleadings. But I wasn't prepared for the many different things that you need to know in the day-to-day practice of being a paralegal. For instance, local court rules vary from jurisdiction to jurisdiction. Some judges require pleadings to be filed in duplicate or triplicate while others don't care. There is a lot variation among the jurisdictions.

"The thing that I found interesting was the role of computer software in the law office. I use QuickBooks™ for all the firm's finances. In the course of the day I'll use WordPerfect™, Westlaw, Lexis-Nexis, and other billing software. I also keep track of all the attorneys' appointments not only by using software, but also the old-fashioned way. I keep a handwritten calendar for both their professional and personal appearances and double-check it with my own.

"If I had to give a paralegal student advice, I'd say to concentrate on those practical courses, like law office management and accounting. Being able to keep track of accounts receivable is an important skill for any paralegal."

reluctant to speak with attorneys and would much prefer to avoid conflict and controversy. However, there are times when hiring an attorney is inevitable. When a client first appears at an attorney's office, she is often confused and anxious. As a legal professional, you should keep in mind that the client is not only seeking legal advice, but also some reassurance. Law is a people business. Attorneys and paralegals work to make society a better place by resolving individual conflicts. That statement might sound hopelessly naive, but many attorneys and paralegals firmly believe it. They see themselves as helpers and confidants. They hope that when the case is resolved, the client will be satisfied with the result and be able to move on with his life. It isn't always possible to resolve a case in the client's favor, but it should be possible to resolve the issues and bring the matter to a close.

 LAW ENFORCEMENT AND PROBATION

Although we have spent a good portion of this chapter discussing civil law, it is important to point out some of the important players in criminal law. We have discussed prosecutors, but they make up only a tiny fraction of law enforcement professionals. We begin our discussion with law enforcement officers.

FIGURE 3-3

Police Officer Selection
Process

Police officer selection is based on many different criteria. Candidates must succeed in all of the following areas:

- Written examinations
- Video simulation assessment
- Panel interview
- Background investigation
- Polygraph tests
- Drug screen
- Medical Examination
- Psychological Examination[3]
- Physical Agility Test

  - Applicant must complete a 550-yard run in 2 minutes and 25 seconds or less.

- Applicant must be able to remove a 150-pound object (simulated injured human being) from a vehicle and drag object 25 feet in 25 seconds or less.
- Applicant must complete an untimed 1.5 mile run without walking at any time.
- Applicant must be able to perform 15 proper sit-ups in 2 minutes.
- Applicant must be able to perform 15 proper military push-ups in 2 minutes.

[3] 2000 City of Asheville, North Carolina, Police Department Police Candidate Screening Form.

A. LAW ENFORCEMENT OFFICERS

Law enforcement officers gather evidence, interview witnesses, and interrogate people accused of crimes. They are responsible for arresting suspects. They play an absolutely essential role not only in the criminal justice system, but also for society in general.

Law enforcement officers undergo rigorous training before they are certified to make arrests. A police officer is usually certified by some state licensing board and this certification gives them the right to make arrests. There are many different types of law enforcement officers, from local police, sheriff's deputies, and county marshals to federal law enforcement officers such as agents employed by the Federal Bureau of Investigation. Whatever agency a law enforcement officer works with, all police officers are responsible for investigating crime and making arrests.

Once the arrest has been made, the case is then forwarded to a prosecutor's office for disposition. In addition to investigating the case, an officer is often called upon to testify at the trial of the accused.

ISSUE AT A GLANCE

When a person is a licensed (or certified) police officer, it means that she is qualified to make arrests whether on duty or off.

Probation
The portion of a criminal sentence that is served outside of prison; usually involves supervision and strict behavioral rules

B. PROBATION OFFICERS

When a person is found guilty of a crime and sentenced to a fine and **probation,** she often comes under the jurisdiction and authority of the probation office.

Probation refers to the portion of a person's sentence that is served outside of prison. While a person is on probation, she may not consume alcohol or commit other offenses. Such an infraction could revoke her probation and result in her serving the remainder of her sentence in prison, in addition to any jail time she also receives for the new offense. Probation and parole officers are responsible for monitoring people who have been released from prison. They schedule meetings with these individuals and ensure that they are abiding by the terms of their sentences, including making payments on their fines or restitution to their victims. The probation officer also ensures that the defendant is gainfully employed.

 **COURTHOUSE PERSONNEL**

In the final section in this chapter, we discuss various departments in the local courthouse and the critical role they play in the daily activities of attorneys and paralegals. Understanding the function of these various departments is absolutely essential to any legal professional.

A. CLERK OF COURT

Clerks are responsible for storing and maintaining all records of court proceedings. Clerk's offices are open to the public. Clerks and deputy clerks keep track of every case filed in the courthouse and store documents relating to all cases. Their role is central to the orderly administration of justice, because it is the clerks that keep track of the payment of fines, the assessment of sentences, and the organization of the mountain of paperwork generated by even the most routine cases. Deputy clerks are often found in the courtroom during calendar calls and hearings, because they are charged with the duty of keeping a record of the disposition of every case.

The clerk's office maintains records about all civil and criminal cases in the county. Most clerks' offices are computerized and simply by entering a person's last name, you can find out whether that person has been sued, divorced, or convicted of a crime. The clerk's office is a good place to start if you are investigating anyone or trying to locate information about other pending or closed cases.

The professionals who work at courthouses know a great deal about the legal system.

ISSUE AT A GLANCE

B. REGISTRAR OF DEEDS

Also called the registrar's office or the land office, the deed room is where all records of real estate transactions are stored. Here you can find out how much a person paid for her house and get a complete picture of what real estate this person owns. However, the deed room has a wealth of other information. UCC filings can tell you whether a person has financed her car, and for how much. Does a defendant claim that she has no assets and therefore cannot pay a judgment? UCC filings can show you that she recently purchased a boat or a recreational vehicle. Many deed rooms also maintain a record called vital statistics, or birth and death records. These records show the names of a person's children, if they were born in that county. They show whether a person was the beneficiary of a will. Attorneys often check these records — called asset searches — before bringing a lawsuit to make sure that they can recover something from the other side. A defendant who has no assets cannot pay a judgment and may not be worth the trouble of suing.

C. PROBATE COURT

The probate court is responsible for administering the estates of people who have died in the county. If a person has had her estate probated in that county, you can locate a record of the will here as well as the names of her beneficiaries and a list of what each received. In many states probate court also keeps records of marriages.

D. TAX OFFICE

The tax office is required to keep extensive records about real estate and all this information is open to the public. Many people never think about going to the tax office for information, but it has more raw data than any other office. Of course, the tax office keeps records about whether a person has paid her property taxes, but there is a great deal of other data here. If you want to find a person's address that isn't listed in the telephone book, it's a simple matter to enter the name in the tax office database and find out where she lives. Tax offices even keep information about the basic floor plan of a house and list how many bedrooms and bathrooms the house has. In some areas, the tax office has a digital photograph of every structure in the county and you can see this photo simply by clicking on it. The tax office also maintains information about sales, acreage, and assessed value.

 **Public records contain a wealth of information about people.**

SKILLS YOU NEED IN THE REAL WORLD

USING TECHNOLOGY

If you are unfamiliar or uncomfortable with technology, you may find that your job prospects are more limited than those people who have extensive Internet skills. Ten years ago technology had very little impact on the practice of law. Attorneys and paralegals functioned in much the same way that they had for decades. However, technology has made huge inroads in the legal field in much the same way that it has affected every other profession. Whether by using word processing programs such as Word or Wordperfect, accounting software such as Quick-books™, or contacting clients by e-mail, law firms have begun to recognize that technology can save thousands of dollars a year. Firms are requiring their existing personnel to receive additional training in software, computers, and Internet searching techniques. They will expect job seekers to possess these skills already.

If your skills aren't what they should be, consider enrolling in a local college or online course in basic computer technology. These courses are available almost everywhere and an Internet connection can open up a world of educational possibilities. However, not all these programs have the same high standards. You should look for local schools that are accredited and online programs that are offered through established colleges and universities. Acquire computer skills any way you can — they will make you more marketable to prospective employers.

CHAPTER SUMMARY

There are many different participants in the American legal system. Judges play an important role by enforcing rules and controlling the actions of the parties in a suit. Judges can be either appointed or elected depending on the jurisdiction. When a judge has a conflict of interest in a suit, she should recuse herself and allow a different judge to hear the case.

Attorneys also form an important part of the legal system. Generally speaking, attorneys fall into two broad groups: civil attorneys and criminal attorneys. Civil attorneys handle a wide variety of cases, from real estate to divorce, as well as many other areas. A prosecutor represents the state and acts to enforce criminal law. Attorneys who represent people accused of crimes are commonly referred to as criminal defense attorneys. These attorneys can practice both civil and criminal law, although many attorneys specialize in one area or the other. Paralegals also form an important part of the American legal system. There has been a strong push in recent years to license paralegals in much the same way that attorneys are licensed.

Criminal law has many different participants. For instance, police officers investigate crimes and make arrests. Probation officers supervise people who have been convicted of crimes and have been released from prison.

Other participants in the legal system are the many support people, such as clerks of court, and deed office and tax office personnel. Understanding the role and function of these professionals is essential to any paralegal's success in the legal field.

ETHICS: PRACTICING LAW WITHOUT A LICENSE

A paralegal must avoid the unauthorized practice of law (UPL). Traditionally, practicing law without a license involved carrying out any activity usually associated with an attorney. However, these days, paralegals have begun to perform many of the duties that were restricted to attorneys only a few years ago. Paralegals routinely do legal research, draft pleadings (but don't sign them), and are even authorized to represent clients in some court proceedings, such as Social Security and Medicaid hearings. All these areas were traditionally associated with lawyers, but are now more often than not handled by paralegals. The practical result is that it is often difficult for a paralegal to know exactly where the dividing line is between permissible activities and those that could be considered unauthorized practice of law. Adding to the burden is that UPL is illegal in all states. Is there a guideline that a paralegal can use to safely negotiate this legal minefield? One test used by many jurisdictions is to consider whether the paralegal is giving legal advice.

Giving legal advice is still considered to be the province of attorneys. Any action by a paralegal that crosses that line will probably be considered unauthorized practice of law. A paralegal can provide information, but cannot give a client guidance about she should do. When in doubt, the safest course is to state that you are not a lawyer and cannot give anything that even sounds like legal advice. Such a statement will often protect you from a claim of unauthorized practice of law.

CHAPTER REVIEW QUESTIONS

1 What is the judge's role in the U.S. court system?
2 Explain the various ways that judges are selected for judicial positions.
3 What is a recusal motion? What are some grounds that would justify the recusal of a judge?
4 Explain how a person qualifies to enter law school.
5 Describe the process of becoming an attorney.
6 Explain the role of ethical rules in an attorney's professional life.
7 What is the difference between a prosecutor and a civil attorney?
8 Explain the basic organization of a law office.
9 What is the role of the public defender's office?
10 Why is the paralegal's role so important to the practice of law?

11   Explain the various legislative initiatives to license paralegals.
12   Describe the concerns that a client might have when seeking out an attorney.
13   What role does a probation officer play in the criminal justice system?
14   Explain the process of becoming a police officer.
15   What is a clerk of court and what role does this person play?
16   What is the deed office and why is it significant?
17   Provide some examples of activities that occur in probate court.
18   What types of information can be found at the tax office?
19   Why is it important to have a solid grasp of technology, such as the Internet?
20   What qualifies as unauthorized practice law?

DISCUSSION QUESTIONS

1   Should judges be appointed or elected? Explain your answer.
2   Would you rather work for a criminal firm or a civil firm? Why?
3   Should paralegals be licensed? Why or why not?
4   Is too much information about private individuals available in the public records? Explain your answer.

PERSONALITY QUIZ

Is the legal field right for you? Take this personality quiz and see.

1   I operate very well under pressure.
   0-strongly disagree   5-agree   10-strongly agree

   Points: _____

2   I don't have trouble meeting deadlines.
   0-strongly disagree   5-agree   10-strongly agree

   Points: _____

3   I prefer to watch television shows about legal issues.
   0-strongly disagree   5-agree   10-strongly agree

   Points: _____

4   I like each day to be different.
   0-strongly disagree   5-agree   10-strongly agree

   Points: _____

5   I'm a big fan of Court TV.
   0-strongly disagree   5-agree   10-strongly agree

   Points: _____
   Total Points: _____

If you scored between 30-50 points, you would probably enjoy a job as a legal professional.

If you scored between 20-29 points, you might do well in the legal field, but you might also do well in some other profession.

If you scored 19 or lower, the legal field is probably not a good choice for you.

PRACTICAL APPLICATIONS

1   Go to your local courthouse and locate a motion for recusal filed in a civil or criminal case. What does this motion allege? What was the result of the motion? Was the judge recused or allowed to remain on the case?
2   Go to the land office or deed office and locate your own or someone else's title to real estate. How much can you learn about a person from the records in the deed office?
3   Review a file in the clerk's office. What types of pleadings and other materials are contained in this file? What type of case is it? Has the case been resolved? If so, what was the result?

WEB SITES

National Association of Legal Assistants
http://www.nala.org

National Federation of Paralegal Associations, Inc.
http://www.paralegals.org

You can also do a search in your own area for prosecutors and public defenders offices. Most of them are online in some form or another.

TERMS AND PHRASES

Associates	Disbarment	Recuse
Commingling	Partners	Retainer
Contempt	Probation	

Bringing a Legal Action

4

Chapter Learning Objectives

After completing this chapter, you should be able to:

■ Demonstrate your understanding of the basic steps involved in bringing a civil case

■ Explain the importance of interviewing witnesses and documenting their testimony

■ List and describe the basic steps in bringing a civil lawsuit

■ Explain the difference between direct and circumstantial evidence

■ Describe the differences between mediation and arbitration

 **INTRODUCTION TO BRINGING LEGAL ACTIONS**

There are two broad categories in which nearly any type of case falls: civil cases and criminal cases. Although we examine criminal cases in detail in Chapter 10, it is important to understand the differences between these two categories.

 COMPARING CIVIL CASES TO CRIMINAL CASES

A criminal case involves an infraction of a statute or ordinance. Criminal cases are brought by the government on behalf of the citizens. The lead attorney in a criminal case is the prosecutor. The prosecutor's burden of proof is **proof beyond a reasonable doubt.**

By contrast, civil cases are brought by individuals in their own right. They are called plaintiffs. These individuals may hire an attorney to represent their interests

Proof beyond a reasonable doubt
The proof required in a criminal case; not mere conjecture, but without a doubt that would cause a reasonable person to have some hesitation in reaching a specific conclusion

Preponderance of the evidence
The proof required in a civil case; "more likely than not to be true"

at trial or they may represent themselves. The burden that plaintiffs must meet is **preponderance of the evidence.**

Civil cases have a different burden of proof than criminal cases.

When people believe that they have been the victims of a crime they call the police and the government takes over. When people believe that they have a civil action, they must pursue the case individually.

However, none of these distinctions really helps to answer the question: What makes a civil case different from a criminal case? If we apply these differences to a real case, perhaps they will become more apparent.

Consider this scenario:

Joanne and Paula have been in business together for three years. They formed a partnership to sell women's clothing at an exclusive boutique that they own together. Paula has begun to suspect that Joanne is stealing money from the business. She claims that she has proof that Joanne has been taking money without permission and can even specify the amount taken and the dates that the money was taken. She has just arrived for her appointment at the law firm where you work. Your firm handles a wide variety of civil actions, but only prosecutors can bring criminal charges. Should the firm send Paula to the local prosecutor or should the firm consider filing a civil action against Joanne?

In a situation like this, in which another person's actions sound like a crime, the smartest thing to do would be to send the client to speak to the police or a member of the local prosecutor's office. Suppose that Paula has already met with the police and they have refused to take the case. What options are left for Paula?

Can the firm force the police or the prosecutor to bring charges against Joanne? These decisions are the prerogative of law enforcement and part of the discretion that they are granted under the law. If law enforcement refuses to pursue the matter, there is virtually no way of forcing them to change their minds. However, there is still the option of bringing a civil suit against Joanne.

Civil cases and criminal cases operate independently of one another. Regardless of what the police do, Paula may still pursue her civil action. Many people are under the mistaken impression that all criminal charges must be terminated before a person can bring a civil suit. This is not true. A civil case can be brought before, during, or after the conclusion of a criminal case. However, there is a practical reason why many firms wait until the criminal case is concluded. If the defendant is sentenced to a lengthy prison term, there is little point in bringing a civil suit against her. If the defendant ends the criminal case by pleading guilty to the crime, that evidence may be admissible in the civil case and will simplify the process enormously. There is no legal prohibition against bringing a civil case while a criminal case is still pending; however, there are other concerns that must be addressed before the civil case is brought. These include an evaluation of the facts, the likelihood of recovery, and the applicable law.

A. EVALUATING A CIVIL CASE

Simply because Paula claims to have a solid case against Joanne is not sufficient justification for bringing suit against Joanne. Before the firm can act for Paula and file suit, there are some preliminary issues that must be addressed. For instance, the case against Joanne must be evaluated and that always means a factual investigation.

1. INVESTIGATING A CIVIL CLAIM

Investigation is not only important to the ultimate outcome of the case, but it is also an ethical requirement in civil cases. Most states follow the model set by Rule 11 of the Federal Rules of Civil Procedure. The text of this rule is set out in Figure 4-1.

Rule 11 (or its counterpart in your state) requires that attorneys investigate any claim brought by a client. Attorneys are not allowed to rely on the client's representations. They must conduct a separate investigation to verify the claims brought by the client. Rule 11 was created to prevent people from using groundless lawsuits as a means to harass and intimidate others.

> **When an attorney signs a complaint, it signifies that the attorney has researched both the law and the facts and is not filing a groundless suit.**

ISSUE AT A GLANCE

a. How to Investigate a Claim

Paralegals are often called upon to carry out basic investigative work in the cases to which they are assigned.

i. Interviewing Witnesses

Any claim by one person against another involves witness testimony. Sometimes the only people who will testify at trial are the plaintiff and the defendant, but both sides will try to locate other witnesses to substantiate their client's version of the case.

We will assume that when Paula came to the firm with all her information against Joanne, she had some independent corroboration of her story. For instance, suppose that Paula mentions her conversation with one of Joanne's friends who told Paula that Joanne had come "into a lot of money" recently. The firm will definitely need to speak with this person and any others who might know something about this case.

The signature of the attorney acts as a certificate by the attorney that he has read the pleading and that there is a good faith basis for the pleading. | The signature requirement was meant to do away with actions brought simply to harass or annoy another party.[4]

FIGURE 4-1

Rule 11

---

[4] Rule 11, Federal Rules of Civil Procedure

FIGURE 4-2		

FIGURE 4-2

Factual Investigation
Questions

Who?	When?
Identify all witnesses, including those mentioned only in passing.	Identify the precise dates and times when the particular action occurred.
What?	How?
What are the allegations and what evidence proves these allegations?	What process did the defendant use to carry out the action?

Interviewing witnesses is as much of an art as it is a science. The ability to obtain information from others to help substantiate the case is an absolutely essential skill for any legal professional. See Figure 4-2 for the types of questions that should be asked of any witness.

When we speak of factual investigation we are drawn into the world of evidence law.

EVIDENCE

When we use the term *evidence* we are talking about anything that tends to prove or disprove a point in contention in the trial. Evidence can be classified into three broad categories: direct (real), circumstantial, and documentary.

A. DIRECT EVIDENCE

Direct evidence
Proof of a fact by presentation of specific evidence

Sometimes referred to as real evidence, **direct evidence** is conclusive of a particular point. For instance, if Paula actually saw Joanne take money out of the cash register and put it in her pocket, this would be direct evidence that Joanne took the money.

ISSUE AT A GLANCE

Direct evidence is conclusive of a fact; circumstantial evidence suggests a conclusion about a fact.

B. CIRCUMSTANTIAL EVIDENCE

Circumstantial evidence
Evidence that suggests a conclusion or proves a fact indirectly

On the other hand, **circumstantial evidence** suggests a conclusion. Circumstantial evidence is open to interpretation. The classic example of circumstantial evidence is finding a fish in your glass of milk. Although you didn't see anyone put the fish there, its presence suggests a conclusion: that someone put it there.

In Paula's case against Joanne, circumstantial evidence could include the fact that Joanne only took money from the register on days when Paula was not working. The conclusion: Joanne didn't want Paula to see what she was doing.

C. DOCUMENTARY EVIDENCE

Documentary evidence consists of writings, such as contracts, letters, and notes. Documents can be used in a trial, but there are special rules about when and how they can be used. Because documents can be altered and forged, there are limitations about handling and presenting these documents during the trial.

Documentary evidence
Writings, contracts, letters, and any other evidence preserved on paper or digital media

D. ADMISSIBILITY

Evidence is important because it is how the parties prove their various contentions during the trial. However, parties are not free to present any evidence that they wish. Before a jury is allowed to see any evidence, the judge must rule that it is **admissible.** When a judge rules that the evidence is admissible it means that the jury will be allowed to see it. A ruling of inadmissibility prevents the jury from seeing the evidence.

Admissible
Evidence that is relevant to the issues in the suit and helps prove or disprove a contention in the case

---

 ## DETERMINING A CAUSE OF ACTION

Although the factual investigation is absolutely essential to the case, it is only one part of the evaluation that occurs before a firm can decide to file suit on a client's behalf. Equally as important as the factual investigation is answering the legal question: Does the client have a **cause of action?**

Simply because someone suffers a loss does not mean that this person is authorized to file suit. The law does not allow a person to sue for any loss. Instead, the law limits suits to the legally recognizable losses. Consider the following scenario:

Cause of action
A claim that the law recognizes as actionable

You are at a party and a man is staring at you. Whenever you look in his direction, he sneers at you and makes other rude faces at you. At one point, he even sticks out his tongue. You leave the party and don't see the man again, but his face stays in your memory and you have nightmares about him. You decide to sue the man. Do you have a legally recognized claim against him? Put another way, is this the type of action that can result in a lawsuit?

Most of us would readily answer no. There are some things in life that we must all put up with, and allowing a suit under these facts would result in the court system being flooded with cases by people who didn't like the looks they got from a stranger. If you tried to bring this suit, the court would dismiss it by ruling that ugly looks from strangers do not give you a cause of action.

Therefore, the initial evaluation that must occur in any case involves not only a factual investigation but also a legal one. The legal team must research the law to ensure that the action complained of is the type of action that the court recognizes.

Fortunately for Paula, theft is a well-known cause of action. However, there may be other issues in this case that deserve additional research. For instance, even if the firm can prove that Joanne is at fault, can she pay a judgment?

ISSUE AT A GLANCE   Before a person can file a civil suit, the legal team must determine that the client has a cause of action.

A. DETERMINING THE LIKELIHOOD OF RECOVERY

There is one more determination that must be made before the case can be brought. No matter how good a case the client may have against another person, the firm is in business and that means that the legal team must consider the issue of being paid for its services. In cases in which the firm will be paid out of the ultimate settlement in the case (referred to as contingency fee), the firm must consider how likely it is that the defendant will have any money to pay the settlement. If the defendant has no financial resources, the firm will probably decline to take the case. After all, there is little point in incurring the costs associated with a lawsuit when there is no possibility of recovering money. A law firm that takes on several such cases would quickly find itself filing for bankruptcy.

Another issue is the amount of the client's losses or damages. If the client has incurred little or no damages, the effort involved in bringing suit will not be worth the effort.

Careers in the Law

▶ Legal Nurse Consultant

In recent years nurses have begun to work with attorneys on a wide variety of cases. The benefits are so obvious that it is a wonder this arrangement hasn't been a feature of the legal system for decades. Nurses have gone back to school to learn more about the legal system and have formed their own association: the American Association of Legal Nurse Consultants.

"I think that legal nurse consultants are getting more popular because attorneys are starting to appreciate the benefits of using someone with a medical background," says Mary Ann Shea, president of the American Association of Legal Nurse Consultants (AALNC). "In the past, they would have used doctors. Legal nurse consultants are a lot more cost effective."

One of the advantages that nurses bring to the legal field is their broad experience. "The knowledge base of a nurse really extends far beyond their area of practice. It used to be, just a few years ago, that attorneys didn't even know that nurses could help them. Actually, the AALNC has been working hard to increase our exposure, to let the general public know, to let attorneys know how they can help."

Legal nurse consultants are nurses who have legal training. Ms. Shea, for example, was a nurse for several years before going back to school to become an attorney. Legal nurse consultants work for insurance companies evaluating claims; they are in risk management; they work for law firms and federal and state government.

"They can really help the attorneys figure out if they have a case. A LNC is going to provide information about the case that is going to help the attorney to determine if the case has merit. They can help fill in the knowledge gap about medical issues. They can go through and organize and analyze the medical records. They have the medical background to figure not only what's there, but also what's missing. They can also advise the attorney along the way."

B. DAMAGES

When a civil case goes to trial, one of the decisions that the jury must make is whether the plaintiff has incurred any **damages** and, if so, how much of these monetary losses the defendant should be forced to pay. There are three categories of damages: general, special, and punitive.

Damages
Monetary payments designed to compensate the plaintiff for an injury

1. GENERAL DAMAGES

General damages are those losses that the plaintiff suffers that are often difficult to quantify. For example, if the plaintiff suffers pain or mental suffering because of the defendant's actions, how much is that worth in dollars? The jury must first decide if the plaintiff should be awarded any general damages, and then they must put a dollar amount on those damages. As you can imagine, such an award is open to interpretation and two different juries presented with the same case could come up with wildly different general damage amounts.

2. SPECIAL DAMAGES

Special damages are those plaintiff losses that can be stated with specificity. Such damages would include lost time from work, medical bills, and any other bill that could be stated with certainty. In Paula's case, special damages would include the exact amount of money that Joanne stole.

3. PUNITIVE DAMAGES

The third category of damages is reserved for special situations. Punitive damages—as the name suggests—are designed to punish the defendant. The jury would award punitive damages to the plaintiff as a way of punishing the defendant. In some cases punitive damages might easily exceed the total of the general and special damages combined, especially when the defendant's actions are unusually egregious, such as stealing from his business partner.

Damages come in three broad categories: general, special and punitive.

ISSUE AT A GLANCE

 DRAFTING A COMPLAINT

Once the legal team has determined that a valid cause of action exists, the next step is to draft a **complaint.** The complaint sets out the factual contentions of the client's injury, explains why the person to be sued is responsible for those injuries, and also makes a demand that the court award damages. In most situations, the client is requesting monetary award to compensate him for his losses.

Complaint
The pleading filed by the plaintiff and later served on the defendant; it sets out the details of the wrong suffered by the plaintiff and the reasons why the defendant is liable for those wrongs

FIGURE 4-3

A Civil Complaint

> STATE OF PLACID
> IN THE SUPERIOR COURT
> COUNTY OF BURKE
>
> Paula Plaintiff   Civil Action File No. _____
>
> v.
>
> Joanne Defendant
>   Complaint

A. TERMINOLOGY USED IN CIVIL CASES

Plaintiff
The party who files suit through a complaint, seeking damages from a person who caused personal, financial, or emotional injuries

Defendant
The party who is sued in a civil case

At this point, we must pin down the terminology used in civil cases. The person who brings a complaint is a **plaintiff.** The person against whom suit is filed is the **defendant.** Filing the complaint and serving it on the defendant officially begin the lawsuit.

B. SERVICE OF PROCESS

Once the complaint has been drafted it is then served on the defendant. This is referred to as service of process. A sheriff's deputy or a professional process server may serve the defendant. When the defendant is served, the process server files a document with the court stating the date and time that the defendant was served. The defendant has a specific number of days from the service of process to file his answer.

ISSUE AT A GLANCE A complaint must be served on the defendant before the lawsuit can begin.

C. THE DEFENDANT'S ANSWER

Answer
The defendant's response to the complaint, containing the defendant's denials and any counterclaims that the defendant may have against the plaintiff

When the defendant is served with a complaint, he must respond with a document that is known as an **answer.** An answer contains the defendant's denials of the factual allegations in the complaint, denial of responsibility for the plaintiff's injuries, and a request that the court not award damages to the plaintiff. If the defendant has any claims against the plaintiff, he will raise them in the answer.

			Plaintiffs			
Type of disposition	Number	Total	Individual	Government	Business[a]	Hospital[b]
All trial cases	11,849	100%	82.8%	0.8%	16.0%	0.3%
Jury trial cases	8,815	100	91.2	0.7	8.0	0.2
Bench trial cases	2,816	100	56.5	1.2	41.5	0.8
Other trial cases[c]	217	100	86.1	0.9	13.0	--
			Defendants			
	Number	Total	Individual	Government	Business[a]	Hospital[b]
All trial cases	11,828	100%	47.1%	4.8%	41.9%	6.2%
Jury trial cases	8,800	100	47.3	5.3	39.5	7.9
Bench trial cases	2,812	100	46.9	2.7	49.6	0.8
Other trial cases[c]	216	100	42.2	12.9	40.4	4.5

Table 3. Type of plaintiffs or defendants, by disposition of civil trials in State courts in the Nation's 75 largest counties, 2001

Note: Plaintiff or defendant type for each case is whichever type appears first on this list:
1) hospital/medical company, (2) business, (3) governmental agency, and (4) individual.
Data on plaintiff type were available for 99.5% of all trial cases and jury trials, 99.6% of bench trials, and 98.5% of other trials. Defendant data were available for 99.3% of all trial cases and jury trials, 99.4% of bench trials, and 97.5% of other trials.
Detail may not sum to total because of rounding.
--No cases recorded.
[a]Includes insurance companies, banks, and other businesses and organizations.
[b]Includes medical companies.
[c]"Other cases" include directed verdicts, judgments notwithstanding the verdict, and jury trials for defaulted defendants.

FIGURE 4-4

Type of Plaintiffs or Defendants in Civil Cases in the Nation's 75 Largest Counties*

*Bureau of Justice Statistics, U.S. Deptartment of Justice. Civil Trial Cases and Verdicts in Large Counties, 2001.

Once the answer is served on the plaintiff and filed with the court, the lawsuit has officially begun. After this point, the discovery phase begins.

DISCOVERY

Discovery refers to the process of learning information about the other side's contentions in the suit. In civil cases, there are a wide variety of methods by which parties can learn about the other side's contentions. They include depositions, interrogatories, and request for production of documents and others.

Discovery
The exchange of information between the sides involved in a lawsuit

A. DEPOSITIONS

A **deposition** is a face-to-face session between the attorneys in the case and a witness. The witness is sworn in and then asked a broad range of questions about the case. Each question and answer is taken down by a court reporter and then printed up in a transcript. If the witness becomes unavailable to testify during the trial, the transcript of the deposition can be read instead. Attorneys have wide latitude in the types of questions that they can ask during a deposition.

Deposition
Oral questions of a witness, taken under oath, by an attorney; this testimony is preserved in a transcript

B. INTERROGATORIES

Interrogatories
Written questions posed by
one side of a civil action to the
other side

Interrogatories are written questions sent to the parties in the case. The party must respond in writing and thoroughly answer the questions. Interrogatories are often used to pin down important points in the case, such as the plaintiff's explanation of why the defendant is at fault.

ISSUE AT A GLANCE

In civil cases, all aspects of the case can (and should) be known long before the trial ever begins.

C. REQUESTS FOR PRODUCTION OF DOCUMENTS

Another discovery device is to serve a request for production of documents on the opposing side. This request asks for copies of all relevant documents, photographs, videotapes, and any other evidence in the case. The party must produce the evidence so that the other side can see it.

D. COMPLETING THE DISCOVERY PROCESS

Although most jurisdictions have rules that limit the discovery process to six months, the parties may request judicial permission to the extend the limit. The process of discovery can take months or even years. At some point, the discovery phase ends and the case is scheduled for trial. Civil trials and criminal trials resemble each other very closely and for that reason we devote an entire chapter to trials later in this book (Chapter 6). We examine only a few aspects of the trial process here.

 ## THE TRIAL OF A CIVIL CASE

At the trial, the plaintiff presents his case to the jury first. The plaintiff goes first because the plaintiff is the person who raised the accusations and must therefore prove them. The plaintiff presents witnesses and evidence to prove the allegations in the complaint. When the plaintiff is finished, the defendant has the right to present his case.

Once both sides have presented their respective cases, the jury retires to consider who should win. This is referred to as jury deliberation. No one other than the jurors is allowed to be present while they reach a verdict.

A. VERDICTS IN CIVIL CASES

In a civil case, the jury's verdict is usually presented as "We, the jury, find for the plaintiff" or "We, the jury, find for the defendant." Verdicts in civil cases have nothing to do with guilt or innocence. Instead, the jury determines which side is **liable** to the other. If the jurors determine that the defendant should win, the plaintiff is not entitled to damages. However, if the jurors have found for the plaintiff, they must then determine the amount of damages that the defendant should pay to the plaintiff. When the jury announces its verdict, the judge then enters the verdict and the monetary award as a judgment. Judgments can be enforced against the losing party.

Liable
A determination that one party has some obligation to another party, usually in the form of monetary payments

 **APPEALS IN CIVIL CASES**

Whoever loses in a civil case has the right to appeal that verdict to a higher court. The appeal may be based on evidence that was submitted at trial, purported judicial error, or some other factor. We discuss appeals in both civil and criminal cases in Chapter 7.

 MEDIATION AND ARBITRATION

Most civil cases do not reach trial. Many are settled prior to trial through negotiations between the parties. Other cases may be settled through **mediation** or **arbitration.**

Mediation
The process of submitting a claim to a neutral third party who then makes a determination about the ultimate liability and award in a civil case

A. MEDIATION

When a case is mediated, a third party is appointed to act as the mediator. The mediator reviews the case and may listen to presentations from both sides as to why they should win. The mediator's decision about the issues in the case is final and binding on the parties. Mediation is a much less expensive process for the parties than taking the case to trial.

Arbitration
The process of bringing both sides in a civil suit together to negotiate a resolution

B. ARBITRATION

Arbitration is similar to mediation in many ways. When a case is arbitrated, a third party attempts to get the parties to reach a settlement of the case. In many cases arbitration is voluntary and not binding on the parties. If a party is not satisfied with the arbitration process, he may still take the case to trial.

Mediation and arbitration are alternatives to the costs and the time involved in trying a case to a jury.

ISSUE AT A GLANCE

C. SETTLEMENT

Settlement
A negotiated termination of a
case prior to a trial or jury
verdict

When a case is settled, it means that the parties have reached an agreement about terminating the case. A case that has settled will no longer be tried by the jury. **Settlement** often involves payment by the defendant to the plaintiff in exchange for the plaintiff dismissing her claim. When the case is dismissed through settlement, it cannot be brought against the defendant at a future date.

THORNTON v. GENERAL MOTORS CORP.
136 F.3d 450 (C.A.5 (La.) 1998)

PER CURIAM:

Appellant attorney, Berney L. Strauss, was sanctioned under Federal Rule of Civil Procedure 11 by the district court on its own initiative for filing a lawsuit on behalf of Donna Thornton against General Motors, Inc. for punitive damages without first having made a reasonable inquiry into the facts underlying Thornton's claim. In imposing the sanctions, the district court suspended Strauss from the practice of law before the Western District of Louisiana for two years and ordered him to reimburse General Motors, Inc. its reasonable attorney's fees incurred in defending the suit. This appeal concerns only the propriety of the imposition of sanctions upon Strauss, Thornton having failed to file a timely appeal from the district court's summary judgment dismissing her complaint. We reverse and vacate the district court's sanctions order.

Federal Rule of Civil Procedure 11(c)(1)(B) requires that, when the district court itself initiates sanctions proceedings, it shall enter an order describing the specific conduct that appears to violate Rule 11(b) and directing the attorney to show cause why he has not committed a violation with respect to that specific conduct. In the present case, the district court entered a show cause order that did not describe the specific conduct for which it subsequently sanctioned Strauss. Accordingly, the district court did not, prior to imposing sanctions, afford Strauss adequate notice to afford him an opportunity to respond to charges of specifically described conduct as prescribed by Rule 11(c)(1)(B).

Donna Thornton, was employed by General Motors Corporation ("GMC") at its headlamp manufacturing plant in Monroe, Louisiana. Thornton worked in an area called the "BAT Room" (Base Coat/Aluminize/Top Coat Room) where headlamp housings are cleaned and painted. In this process the chemical n-Butyl Acetate is used as a solvent for the paint and as a wash to clean the housings. On April 8, 1994, Thornton was hospitalized and received treatment after reporting to the GMC infirmary complaining of dizziness, nausea, vomiting, and exhibiting a skin rash. Another GMC employee, Arlene Young, who worked near Thornton, was also hospitalized after she too broke out in a rash. Subsequently, GMC discovered that in the area in which Thornton and Young worked a filter canister containing n-Butyl Acetate had developed a crack and was emitting fumes into the BAT room.

On February 17, 1995, Thornton met with an attorney, Berney Strauss, in New Orleans and sought legal representation in connection with her April 8, 1994 accident and resulting injuries. Strauss discussed with Thornton the events surrounding her hospitalization and reviewed documents provided by her relating to both GMC's reaction to the leak and the properties of n-Butyl Acetate. A GMC service report verified that two employees had been admitted to the hospital for chemical exposure on April 8, and a "Material Safety Data Sheet" ("MSDS") revealed the hazardous nature of n-Butyl Acetate. In addition, the GMC document confirmed other key components of Thornton's story-that a crack had developed in a "solvent wash" canister and that it had resulted in the release of n-Butyl Acetate. The report, signed by Bruce DeBruhl, GMC's senior manufacturing engineer, referred to the leak as a "safety problem." Thornton also told Strauss that, following the accident, DeBruhl disclosed to her that her supervisors "should have" detected the leak hours before they did.

On March 20, 1995, Strauss filed a complaint on Thornton's behalf in United States District Court for the Western District of Louisiana seeking punitive damages from GMC under Louisiana Civil Code article 2315.3 in connection with her accident. Article 2315.3 allowed for an award of exemplary (or punitive) damages in cases of wanton or reckless disregard for the public safety in the storage, handling, or transportation of hazardous or toxic substances. The complaint alleged that Thornton's injuries were the result of the defendant "failing to maintain" machinery, "failing to take proper precautions" to prevent toxic emissions, "failing to rectify a known hazard," and, lastly, requiring Thornton to work in an area known to be dangerous by GMC. These acts and omissions, Thornton claimed, constituted a "wanton or reckless disregard for the public safety."

Following discovery, GMC moved for summary judgment on March 14, 1996. GMC asserted that Thornton had not presented a genuine issue of material fact that her injury was based on the "wanton or reckless" conduct of the company as required by La. Civ.Code art. 2315.3 under its interpretation by the Louisiana state supreme court in Billiot v. B.P. Oil Co., 645 So.2d 604, 613 (La. 1994). On April 8, 1996, the district court granted GMC's motion for summary judgment and dismissed Thornton's claims with prejudice. In its memorandum ruling, the district court stated that Thornton, in response to the motion for summary judgment, had "failed to come forth with any evidence even remotely raising a genuine issue of material fact as to whether GM stored or handled n-Butyl Acetate in a wanton or reckless manner."

Previously, on April 4, 1996, the district court, on its own initiative, had ordered Berney L. Strauss to show cause why he had not violated Federal Rule of Civil Procedure 11(b). The district court's order and reasons stated:

> The court, pursuant to F.R.C.P. Rule 11(c)(1)(B), hereby ORDERS Berney L. Strauss to show cause why he has not violated subsections (b)(2) and (3) of this rule.
>
> Berney L. Strauss is ORDERED to produce evidence that supports a claim pursuant to La. Civ. code art 2315.3 and which meets the standards set forth in Billiot v. B.P. Oil Co., 645 So.2d 604 (La.1994), for seeking punitive damages under Article 2315.3. Mere argument by Mr. Strauss will not be sufficient. Rule 11(b)(2) and (3) require that Mr. Strauss have a reasonable basis in fact to support a claim under Article 2315.3. To this point, Mr. Strauss has not produced any evidence which supports making a claim for $10,000,000 in punitive damages under 2315.3. Thus, Mr. Strauss is ORDERED to produce evidence to show cause why he should not be sanctioned under Rule 11(b).

After reviewing Strauss' written response, the district court, on June 21, 1996, issued an order sanctioning Strauss by suspending him from the practice of law in the Western District of Louisiana for two years and by ordering him to reimburse GMC its reasonable attorney's fees incurred in defending this suit. The district court, however, did not quantify the amount of attorney's fees. Subsequently, and prior to a final determination as to the amount of attorney's fees owed, Strauss filed a timely appeal from the district court's order sanctioning his conduct.

The district court's sanctions ruling stated that it had initiated the sanctions proceeding "[d]ue to the complete absence of evidence produced by Thornton in response to GM's motion [for summary judgment]." Consistent with this reasoning, the district court's show cause order had directed Strauss "to produce evidence that supports" Thornton's claim, because "Rule 11(b)(2) and (3) require that Mr. Strauss have a reasonable basis in fact to support" the claim, and "[t]o this point, Mr. Strauss has not produced any evidence which supports making" the claim.

The district court's show cause order did not allege that Strauss failed to make a reasonable inquiry prior to filing suit or that this was the specific conduct that appeared to have been a violation of Rule 11(b). Instead, the district court's show cause order cited Strauss for his general conduct in failing to produce evidence in support of Thornton's claim prior to the district court's ruling on GMC's motion for summary judgment. Strauss argues, with merit, that he reasonably read the court's show cause order to call upon him to produce evidence supporting Thornton's claim as of the time he opposed GMC's motion for summary judgment, not to show that he had made a reasonable inquiry before filing the initial complaint, the lack of which the court's order ultimately found was Strauss' only omission that called for sanctions.

Given the timing of the court's ruling and the lack of precision in the show cause order, we do not believe that Strauss was adequately placed on notice as to the "specific conduct" that the court ultimately found to be sanctionable. Four days before granting GMC's motion for summary judgment, the district court issued the show cause order demanding "evidence" of GMC's liability and lamented the lack of evidence that had been produced "[t]o this point." Although the court invoked subsection (b)(2) and (3) of Rule 11 and indicated that it found Thornton's claim lacked a reasonable basis in fact, these references do not sufficiently clarify what conduct Strauss needed to explain and justify in his response to the court.

As a consequence of the court's action, Strauss was misled and hampered in presenting his defense. The district court's sanctions order evaluated his pre-filing conduct according to the factors elucidated by the en banc court in Thomas v. Capital Sec. Serv., Inc., 836 F.2d 866 (5th Cir. 1988)(en banc). These factors include: the time available for investigation; the extent to which an attorney relied on his client for factual support; the feasibility of a pre-filing investigation; whether the attorney accepted the case from another member of the bar; the complexity of the factual and legal issues; and the extent to which the development of the factual circumstances of the claim requires discovery. The district court's rule to show cause, issued more than one year after the filing of suit, did not reasonably and fairly put Strauss on notice that the district court's decision to sanction him would hinge on his showing under the pre-complaint conduct factors.

Despite the show cause order's failure to notify Strauss adequately that he might be sanctioned for a pre-complaint failure to investigate rather than a failure to produce evidence in response to a motion for summary judgment, the court found that Strauss had violated Rule 11(b) by not conducting a reasonable investigation of the evidence supporting the claim prior to initially filing suit. Thus, the show cause order did not comply with Rule 11(c)(1)(B) which provides that, when a trial court itself initiates the proceedings for sanctions, it shall "enter an order describing the specific conduct that appears to violate subdivision (b)[the substantive subdivision of the Rule] and directing an attorney, law firm, or party to show cause why it has not violated subdivision (b) with respect thereto." This requirement imposed on district courts when acting on their own initiative under Rule 11(c)(1)(B) was intended to ensure due process.

We review the imposition of Rule 11 sanctions for an abuse of discretion. In this case the notice and due process requirements for a district court's imposition of sanctions on its own initiative were not followed. Thus, the district court abused its discretion by sanctioning Strauss without giving him notice of the specific conduct for which he ultimately was suspended from practice and ordered to pay GMC's attorney's fees.

Moreover, where sanctions are imposed under Rule 11(c)(1)(B) by a district court on its own initiative, neither the award of attorney's fees nor the suspension from practice before the court constitute a valid sanction. Specifically, an award of attorney's fees is authorized only "if imposed on motion and warranted for effective deterrence." Fed. R. Civ. P. 11(c)(2). Furthermore, when a district court finds that a disciplinary sanction more severe than admonition, reprimand, or censure under Rule 11 is warranted, it should refer the matter to the appropriate disciplinary authorities. See Fed. R. Civ. P. 11 advisory committee notes to the 1993 Amendments. Thus, in this case, even if the notice and due process requirements of Rule 11(c)(1)(B) had been followed, the order suspending Strauss from practice and the award of attorney's fees imposed on Strauss would have been improper.

Therefore, it is hereby ordered that the district court's order imposing sanctions on Appellant-movant Strauss is REVERSED and VACATED.

QUESTIONS ABOUT THE CASE

1   Why was the attorney in this case sanctioned by the court?
2   What does Federal Rule 11 require before sanctions are imposed on an attorney?
3   According to the appellate court, did the attorney have adequate notice about the nature of the hearing and the sanctions to be imposed against him?
4   Did the trial court's sanctions focus on a violation of the purposes of Rule 11, i.e., to require an attorney to conduct a thorough investigation before filing suit?

Profiling a Paralegal

▶ Jane Huffman

When I organize discovery, I dig through everything that we've received. I pull out pertinent documents that help establish the case and show what the other side did. I make four copies of everything: one for attorney, one for judge, one for opposition and one for the witness. I organize our attorney's copy first. I put it in an order that makes sense. I like to have a clean set of discovery. The attorneys tend to make notes on their copies, so I always keep a clean set that hasn't been marked. It's a lot harder to get a document admitted at trial if it's got handwritten notes written across it.

Once I've gone through the discovery, I start working the file to get it ready for trial. You can't start too soon for that. I put together a list of the evidence that we'll be using at trial and put it in a notebook. That way, when the witness is on the stand, we can just hand them the notebook, or even leave it on the witness stand and just ask them to turn to a specific page.

I enjoy working in the legal field. In fact, now that I've gotten my bachelor's degree, I actually teach part time at the college where I originally got my associate's degree. You never know what doors will open to you once you enter the law.

SKILLS YOU NEED IN THE REAL WORLD

ORGANIZING DISCOVERY MATERIALS

One of the absolutely essential skills that any paralegal should have is the ability to organize a file in such a way that attorneys, paralegals, investigators, and other staff can quickly retrieve information. One way of organizing a civil file is to put the material in different subcategories. For instance, some litigation firms divide a civil case into the following categories:

- Correspondence — includes all letters sent and received in the case.
- Discovery — includes all interrogatories, deposition transcripts, and requests for production of documents.
- Pleadings — includes the complaint, answer and other motions filed in the case. Billing information — includes the contract between the firm and the client and information about how and when to bill the client.
- Client information — includes background information on the client, such as contact numbers including cell phone, address, e-mail address, and employment history.
- Legal research — includes all legal research, such as the research done to confirm that the client has a cause of action and any other legal research topics.

▓ Memoranda — includes all internal memoranda from attorney to paralegals concerning a wide variety of issues in the case.

Once these subdivisions are created, a paralegal goes through the entire file and sorts the material into these various folders. Obviously, some of the folders will be much larger than others. In a lengthy and detailed civil suit, the discovery section could easily fill several cardboard boxes. The discovery section contains not only interrogatories, but also transcripts of depositions with witnesses and the material that has been produced pursuant to the interrogatories and requests for production of documents.

Many personal injury firms create a separate sub-folder for medical issues. This folder contains all the information about the plaintiff's injuries, including all doctors' bills, medical notes, and evidence about current or preexisting injuries. Other firms create additional folders prior to trial. These trial folders might contain information about the jury panel, the judge, or any other matter that could be of significance during the trial.

CHAPTER SUMMARY

Civil cases follow a set pattern. When a person believes that he has been injured by the actions of another, he usually seeks the services of an attorney to bring suit against this person. The legal team's responsibility in a civil case is to investigate the claim, research whether a cause of action exists, determine the likelihood of recovery, and then draft a complaint. The complaint sets out the facts detailing the plaintiff 's injury, the reasons that the defendant is the person liable for those injuries, and the plaintiff's demand for damages. The defendant has the right to file an answer to the complaint that sets out his denials of the factual allegations, denial of responsibility for the plaintiff's injuries, and his request that the plaintiff receive no monetary award from the defendant. The filing of the complaint and answer officially begins the civil suit.

Once the pleadings have been filed, the discovery process begins. Discovery is the process through which both sides in a civil case learn the factual details of the allegations made by the other side. There are numerous methods used in the discovery process. For instance, a party might use depositions to question witnesses under oath to pin down their testimony. Interrogatories are written questions to a party. Rules concerning discovery requests are liberally interpreted. Parties are allowed to ask wide-ranging questions to build up as complete a picture of the case as is possible. When the discovery phase is over, the stage is set for the trial.

Trials in civil cases also follow a set pattern. The plaintiff always goes first, presenting his case to the jury through witness testimony and presentation of evidence. After the plaintiff presents his case, the defendant can present his own witnesses and evidence. At the conclusion of the trial, the jury retires to deliberate and reach a verdict. Civil juries determine liability, not guilt. The jurors also determine monetary awards or damages.

ETHICS: WHEN THE CLIENT CONCEALS INFORMATION

The civil discovery process is designed to encourage a broad range of information exchange. Clients often do not wish to be forthcoming in answering interrogatory or deposition questions in the mistaken belief that if they do not volunteer negative information the other side will not learn about it. This is common when the client has a preexisting injury that he claims was caused by a recent accident. The client may believe that by not bringing up the fact that he had a similar injury ten years ago the other side will not learn about it. In fact, in most situations the other side usually does learn about the preexisting injury and will then use this information to make the client appear to be deceitful about all aspects of the case. The best advice to give clients is to be as forthcoming as possible. Reveal all information, whether good or bad. If the firm knows about a problem, it can take steps to limit the impact during the trial. There is nothing worse than learning about your client's negative information during the trial. You should always encourage clients to answer all direct questions honestly and thoroughly.

CHAPTER REVIEW QUESTIONS

1   What is the difference in levels of proof between criminal cases and civil cases?
2   Explain how a civil case begins, focusing on the investigative process involved.
3   What are some of the methods that law firms use to investigate a claim?
4   What are some of the details that should be pinned down in an initial investigation?
5   What is the difference between direct and circumstantial evidence?
6   What is the significance of a ruling of admissibility of evidence?
7   Explain the term *cause of action.*
8   What are the different types of damages available in civil cases?
9   What are the names of the documents involved in a civil case? What is the name of the document brought by the plaintiff? What is the name of the document brought by the defendant? Explain the purpose that these documents serve in a civil suit.
10 List and explain the terms used to describe the two parties in a civil lawsuit.
11 What is service of process?
12 What is the function of an answer?
13 What is discovery? Explain.
14 List and explain various types of civil discovery.
15 Why is it important to be able to organize discovery materials?
16 What is the difference between a deposition and an interrogatory?
17 What is mediation?
18 What is settlement?

19 Explain how arbitration is different from mediation.
20 Explain how a jury in a civil case reaches a verdict.

DISCUSSION QUESTIONS

1 Explain the process of evaluating a civil claim.
2 Explain the various types of evidence that can be used in a civil case.
3 It has often been said that paralegals who work at litigation firms must be able to juggle several tasks at the same time. Why would this be true?

PERSONALITY QUIZ

Is civil litigation the right field for you? Take this personality quiz and see.

1 I am very good at multitasking.
   0-strongly disagree   5-agree   10-strongly agree

                                       Points: _____

2 I have strong organizational skills.
   0-strongly disagree   5-agree   10-strongly agree

                                       Points: _____

3 I enjoy pinning down details.
   0-strongly disagree   5-agree   10-strongly agree

                                       Points: _____

4 I have strong people skills.
   0-strongly disagree   5-agree   10-strongly agree

                                       Points: _____

                             Total points: _____

If your total points are between 25-40, you should strongly consider working in the litigation field.

If your total points are between 18-24, the litigation field may not be the best choice for you.

If your total points are less than 18, you should strongly consider working in some non-litigation field.

PRACTICAL APPLICATIONS

1   Go to your local courthouse and locate a civil case file. Make a copy of the complaint and then answer the following questions:

   ▨ Who is the plaintiff?
   ▨ Who is the defendant?
   ▨ What are the plaintiff's allegations?
   ▨ Has the defendant filed an answer? If so, what defenses does the defendant raise in his answer?
   ▨ Does it sound as though the plaintiff has a strong case? Explain your answer.

2   Using your local telephone book, locate firms that specialize in civil cases. What specialties are listed in their telephone ads?

3   Contact a local firm and speak with the firm's paralegals. Ask about the types of cases they handle and the qualities that these paralegals believe would make a person good at doing those particular types of tasks. Do the paralegals recommend any particular courses that you absolutely should take if you are considering a career as a litigation paralegal? Are there particular skills that the paralegals recommend that you should develop before going to work at a litigation firm?

WEB SITES

The Federal Judiciary Home Page
http://www.uscourts.gov

Federal Rules of Civil Procedure
http://www.law.cornell.edu/rules/frcp/overview.htm

Nation's Court Directory
http://www.courts.net

Florida State Courts
http://www.flcourts.org

California State Courts
http://www.courtinfo.ca.gov

New York State Unified Court System
http://www.courts.state.ny.us/home.htm

TERMS AND PHRASES

Admissible	Defendant	Mediation
Answer	Deposition	Plaintiff
Arbitration	Direct evidence	Preponderance of the
Cause of action	Discovery	evidence
Circumstantial evidence	Documentary evidence	Proof beyond a reasonable
Complaint	Interrogatories	doubt
Damages	Liable	Settlement

Ethics

Chapter Learning Objectives

After completing this chapter, you should be able to:

■ Explain the role of model ethics rules on the practice of law

■ Describe the types of sanctions that can be brought against attorneys who violate ethical codes

■ Explain the ethical codes that govern paralegal actions

■ Describe how a paralegal can help prevent legal malpractice

■ List and explain the most common types of ethical violations

INTRODUCTION TO ETHICS

In this chapter we explore the vitally important topic of ethics. A firm grasp of ethical rules is a must for any legal professional, whether paralegal, attorney, or legal secretary. Throughout this chapter we address not only the importance of ethical rules for both attorneys and paralegals, but also the role that the paralegal plays in helping to avoid a claim of legal malpractice.

ETHICAL CODES

All attorneys are governed by ethical codes. Before we can discuss the role that ethical codes play in the day-to-day practice of law, we must first address a more fundamental question: What is the role of a lawyer?

A. THE ATTORNEY'S ROLE

Officer of the court
A person who is either employed by a court or has an obligation to uphold ethical and moral standards. Attorneys are officers of the court

Attorneys act as representatives of clients. They have an obligation to zealously represent their clients' interests and to seek resolutions of their problems. But an attorney is also an **officer of the court.** An officer of the court has a special relationship with the court system, stemming from the attorney's admittance to practice law in the state and from the long history of ethical and moral obligations imposed on the bar.

Here is how the Florida State Bar defines the role of an attorney: "A lawyer is a representative of clients, an officer of the legal system, and a public citizen having special responsibility for the quality of justice."[5]

This obligation is part of the benefits and burdens that an attorney assumes when she becomes a member of the state bar.

B. STATE BAR MEMBERSHIP

Integrated bar
A state bar that requires attorneys to be members before they are allowed to practice

Most state bars are **integrated bars**, meaning that an attorney must be a member of the state bar before she will be allowed to practice law in the state. State bars have membership requirements that usually include the following:

- Successful completion of the state bar examination
- Moral certification
- Membership in good standing in other state bars, if applicable

ISSUE AT A GLANCE   To practice law, an attorney must be a member of the state bar.

A conviction of a misdemeanor such as driving under the influence of alcohol will not automatically revoke an attorney's license to practice, but a conviction of a more serious crime probably will.

In Chapter 3, we explored the process of becoming a lawyer. When a person graduates from law school, she is permitted to take the bar examination; upon successfully completing it, she is eligible to be admitted to the state bar. An applicant must not only pass the state bar examination, but be of moral character. This means that she cannot have a criminal record involving crimes of dishonesty or felonies.

When an attorney is a member of the state bar, it means that she is authorized to practice law. Practicing law is a generic term that takes into account a wide range of activities, including representing clients in court, giving legal advice, and generally acting as an advisor. As long as an attorney pays annual dues and does not violate ethical or criminal statutes, she is entitled to practice law in the state.

C. STATE ETHICS RULES

All states have ethical codes for attorneys. These codes are often worded identically to the Model Rules of Professional Conduct established by the American Bar

[5] Florida Bar Rules, Preamble

Association (ABA). Each state regulates its own attorneys. The ABA does not regulate, license, or sanction attorneys. The ABA acts as a lobbyist for attorneys and promulgates model rules, but has very little impact on the day-to-day practice of law.

Attorney ethical rules are usually found in the state statutes. These rules govern everything from the process of admission to the state bar, to different types of ethical violations and the resulting sanctions.

The American Bar Association

- **Does not regulate attorneys**
- **Sets policies and creates model rules that can be adopted by state bars**
- **Promulgates one of the most important sets of rules, the Model Rules of Professional Conduct**

ISSUE AT
A GLANCE

D. THE ABA'S MODEL RULES OF PROFESSIONAL CONDUCT

The ABA's Model Rules of Professional Conduct are simply guidelines that jurisdictions are free to adopt as their own. The vast majority of states have adopted the Model Rules for the simple reason that they are well organized and create a standard framework for ethical rules that do not vary from state to state.

There is no requirement that an attorney be a member of the American Bar Association to practice law. However, an attorney must be a member of a particular state's bar before she can practice there.

E. STATE BAR ASSOCIATIONS AND THE REGULATION OF ATTORNEYS

Admittance to the state bar carries several important responsibilities. One of the most important is that the attorney must act in an ethical manner in all transactions. The state bar not only establishes what the rules are, it also investigates claims brought by clients and others that a specific attorney acted in an unethical manner.

State bars usually do not sanction attorneys. They create rules and investigate claims, but the authority to sanction attorneys normally falls to the state's highest court (usually called the state supreme court).

All state bars have ethical codes to which attorneys must conform.

ISSUE AT
A GLANCE

 **SANCTIONS FOR VIOLATING ETHICAL CODES**

Attorneys can receive several different forms of sanctions for violating ethical rules. The bar sanctions run from the mildest (private reprimand) to the most severe (disbarment).

FIGURE 5-1

Sanctions for Unethical
Actions

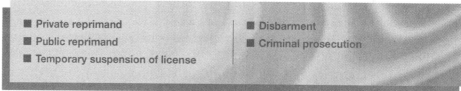

- Private reprimand
- Public reprimand
- Temporary suspension of license
- Disbarment
- Criminal prosecution

A. PRIVATE REPRIMAND

When an attorney has committed a minor ethical violation, or has engaged in questionable practices, an investigatory committee might recommend a simple, private reprimand as a sanction. A private reprimand usually takes the form of a letter from the state bar to the attorney outlining the violation and suggesting that the attorney change practices. Private reprimands are not published and usually the only parties who know about them are the attorney and the state bar.

B. PUBLIC REPRIMAND

A public reprimand, on the other hand, is a reprimand that states the attorney's unethical practice and is usually published in the state's appellate reporter. These reprimands become part of the state supreme court reporter (if the highest court goes by that name). Public reprimands are considered a midpoint between a private reprimand and the much more serious sanction of temporary suspension.

C. TEMPORARY SUSPENSION

An attorney who receives a temporary suspension is barred from the practice of law for a specified period. This period could be as short as a few days or as long as several years, depending on the seriousness of the offense.

D. DISBARMENT

Disbarment
When an attorney's right to
practice law is rescinded

An attorney who has committed a serious ethical violation, or been convicted of a major crime, can be disbarred. **Disbarment** strips the attorney of her license to practice law. An attorney who is disbarred in one jurisdiction is usually disbarred in all other jurisdictions as well. When an attorney is disbarred, she cannot practice law in any form. Disbarment can be considered a professional death sentence. A disbarred attorney can sometimes petition to have her license reinstated, but many disbarments are permanent.

ISSUE AT A GLANCE

Disbarment is the permanent suspension of an attorney's license to practice law.

E. CRIMINAL PROSECUTION

An ethical violation can also rise to the level of a crime. When an attorney embezzles client funds, for example, this is both an ethical violation and a crime. The attorney may face not only state bar sanctions, but also a fine and a prison sentence if convicted of the crime. This result is often seen in cases of commingling client funds.

 ## THE MOST COMMON TYPES OF ETHICAL VIOLATIONS

Attorneys who commit ethical violations often do so for three general reasons: (1) financial difficulty; (2) drug or alcohol problems; or (3) personal problems. Attorneys whose problems fall into the first two categories are often tempted to engage in the practice of commingling.

A. COMMINGLING FUNDS

When an attorney **commingles** funds, she uses client trust accounts as though they were her personal accounts. The attorney transfers the proceeds of a client's settlement or some other funds into her own account to cover an expense, and plans to replace the missing funds from future client payments before anyone notices. Commingling is a form of embezzlement and is a serious ethical violation. Many of the attorneys who are disbarred each year have been brought up on ethics charges relating to client funds.

Commingling
Combining funds from different sources into one. The practice is unethical when the attorney does not have the right to use the funds entrusted to her keeping.

B. LACK OF DILIGENCE

Some attorneys are cited in ethics investigations for failure to follow through on client matters. They receive a retainer, deposit it, then fail to take any action. Attorneys have a duty of diligence toward their clients. This means that they must follow through on the client's problems and take all legal actions to bring the case to a successful resolution.

C. ZEALOUS REPRESENTATION

Closely related to the issue of diligence is the ethical obligation of zealous representation. An attorney must place the client's interests foremost and seek the best possible resolution of the case. Zealous representation does not equate with illegal representation. An attorney cannot violate the law on a client's behalf, but must exercise the diligence, competence, skill, and knowledge that a client deserves.

FIGURE 5-2

Rule 1.1 Competence

A lawyer shall provide competent representation to a client. Competent representation requires the legal | knowledge, skill, thoroughness and preparation reasonably necessary for the representation.[6]

PARALEGAL CODES OF ETHICS

Paralegals and legal assistants have worked at law firms for decades, but it was only in the 1970s that they formally organized themselves under the title of paralegals. National paralegal organizations trace their origins to this period. Of the many national paralegal organizations, two stand out: the National Federation of Paralegal Associations (NFPA) and the National Association of Legal Assistants (NALA). Each group has created its own model rules of ethical conduct for paralegals. NFPA has maintained an ethics board since 1995. It posts ethical opinions on its website so that other paralegals can obtain guidance on specific issues.

National paralegal associations resemble the ABA in that they have created model ethical rules but cannot actually impose on them on a state level. Many states have codified paralegal ethical codes in the same way that they have codified attorney ethical standards. However, there are some important differences between the professional standing of paralegals and that of attorneys. One of these important differences revolves around the issue of **certification** versus **licensure**.

Certification
Completion of the minimum requirements for admission into a professional body

Licensure
Prerequisite to practicing in a particular field

Licensure is an action by the state or federal government that serves as a prerequisite to practicing a profession. Attorneys are licensed. They operate under state statutes and their licenses can be revoked by action of the state bar. Certification, on the other hand, usually refers to the standards set by a private group.

ISSUE AT A GLANCE

Licensure is a state action; certification is carried out by a private organization.

Although several states are actively considering the issue of licensing paralegals, most do not. Paralegals in unregulated states operate in a gray area: They are not attorneys, but they work closely with them. They are legal professionals, but they have no state license that clearly states their qualifications. Faced with this dilemma, many paralegals opt for certification from one of the national paralegal associations. The National Association of Legal Assistants offers a certification program that entitles paralegals to use the credentials "Certified Legal Assistant" when they successfully complete the intensive testing.

---

[6] Indiana State Bar Rule 1.1, p. 177

 THE ROLE OF THE PARALEGAL IN PREVENTING ETHICS VIOLATIONS

The paralegal plays an important role in preventing ethics violations and must master not only the paralegal code of ethics, but also the attorneys' ethical standards. Negligence or unethical practices by paralegals are imputed to the attorneys with whom they work. Paralegals should be vigilant against office practices that call the legal team's ethics into question and never engage in questionable practices themselves. If acting ethically is not rewarding in itself, there is also the added inducement of avoiding claims of legal malpractice.

 LEGAL MALPRACTICE

Legal malpractice is a claim brought by a former client against her legal team. The client alleges that but for the legal team's negligence she would have achieved a more favorable result in her case. Legal malpractice cases once were exceedingly rare, but they are becoming as common as medical malpractice claims. A paralegal who is knowledgeable in both office procedures and ethical rules can help the firm both avoid legal malpractice claims and prevail in the ones that are brought.

A. THE ELEMENTS OF A LEGAL MALPRACTICE CLAIM

To bring a claim of legal malpractice, the plaintiff must prove that:

- An attorney-client relationship existed
- The attorney breached the duties inherent in that relationship
- The breach was a proximate cause of the unfavorable ruling in the client's case
- The client suffered actual loss or injury because of this violation of duty

---

Legal malpractice is a suit by a former client claming that the attorney failed to live up to the standards of the profession.

 ISSUE AT A GLANCE

B. THE ATTORNEY-CLIENT RELATIONSHIP

The **attorney-client relationship** creates a set of duties and responsibilities on the part of the attorney. Among these duties is diligence and zealous representation, but this relationship also creates other obligations. An attorney must exercise competence, knowledge, and skill in handling the client's matters. One of the most important duties created by the attorney-client relationship is confidentiality.

Attorney-client relationship
The legally recognized and protected relationship between a client and her attorney. This relationship gives rise to the attorney-client privilege

C. CONFIDENTIALITY

Confidentiality
The ethical obligation of an attorney and her staff to protect the secret information relayed to them by a client

An attorney owes her client **confidentiality.** A client's communications with her attorney are secret. An attorney must guard these communications and refuse to reveal them to others. Some have argued that confidentiality is the very essence of the legal profession. Without a guarantee that her statements will not be repeated to others, a client would not give complete information to her attorney. This duty of confidentiality also gives rise to a special privilege.

D. THE ATTORNEY-CLIENT PRIVILEGE

Attorney-client privilege
An evidentiary privilege that can be invoked by the attorney or the client to refuse to answer questions about confidential communications between them

Communications between attorneys and clients are **privileged.** This means that attorneys cannot be compelled to reveal what clients have told them. If an attorney is subpoenaed to testify, she can refuse to answer questions about private conversations with her client. This privilege was created to protect the attorney-client relationship. There are similar evidentiary privileges, such as those between medical doctors and patients and clergy and penitents.

E. WAYS TO AVOID LEGAL MALPRACTICE CLAIMS

A paralegal can help the firm avoid claims of legal malpractice by doing the following:

- Communicating with clients
- Following office procedures
- Avoiding unauthorized practice of law

1. COMMUNICATING WITH CLIENTS

One of the biggest complaints that clients have is that their attorneys fail to communicate with them. Clients are often nervous and apprehensive about their legal troubles and do not understand that the attorney may spend a great deal of time away from the office. Clients want, and deserve, feedback about the status of their cases. One of the best ways to avoid a legal malpractice claim and keep clients happy is to simply keep them informed. Communicate with clients by telephone, fax, e-mail, and letters. Tell the client about any changes in scheduling or other developments in the case. Sometimes a thirty-second telephone call can make all the difference.

One important element to keep in mind when communicating with clients is that client information is confidential. Remember that although e-mail is a very convenient form of communication, it is not as secure or as confidential as other forms of communication.

2. FOLLOWING OFFICE PROCEDURES

Most law firms have procedures in place for initial meetings with clients, accepting a client's case, depositing retainer fees, and a whole range of other activities associated with law practice. Familiarize yourself with your firm's procedures and

---

Sidebar

The attorney-client privilege does not apply to all communications. For instance, the privilege usually does not apply to:

- *The client's identity*
- *The client's current location*
- *The fee arrangement*

FIGURE 5-3

Plaintiff Award Winners in
Nation's 75 Largest Counties,
2001*

Table 6. Plaintiff award winners in the Nation's 75 largest counties, 2001

Case type	Number of all trial cases with a plaintiff winner[b]	Final amount awarded to plaintiff winners		Percent of plaintiff winner cases with final awards —	
		Total	Median	Over $250,000	$1 million or more
All trial cases[a]	6,487*	$4,346,072,000	$33,000	18.3%	6.8%
Tort cases	4,069	$2,299,957,000	$27,000	18.8%	7.7%
Automobile	2,565	526,435,000	16,000	8.6	2.8
Premises liability	522	400,653,000	59,000	22.9	9.1
Product liability	70	199,153,000	450,000	64.6	39.1
Asbestos	19	86,275,000	1,650,000	90.7	59.7
Other	51	112,878,000	311,000	54.7	31.4
Intentional tort	214	128,428,000	37,000	25.4	16.3
Medical malpractice	311	600,746,000	422,000	66.1	29.7
Professional malpractice	51	43,108,000	93,000	30.6	13.9
Slander/libel	39	17,067,000	121,000	39.6	6.0
Animal attack	66	6,741,000	18,000	11.7	--
Conversion	13	926,000	23,000	--	--
False arrest, imprisonment	19	2,185,000	30,000	14.6	--
Other or unknown tort	199	374,514,000	106,000	39.9	15.5
Contract cases	2,369	$2,043,211,000	$45,000	17.7%	5.4%
Fraud	358	768,506,000	81,000	30.2	12.0
Seller plaintiff	925	165,336,000	34,000	10.5	2.9
Buyer plaintiff	477	130,585,000	45,000	17.7	4.8
Mortgage foreclosure	13	2,731,000	70,000	13.6	13.6
Employment discrimination	73	44,913,000	166,000	39.4	14.4
Other employment dispute	162	265,939,000	78,000	23.8	4.8
Rental/lease	176	24,112,000	20,000	11.9	2.6
Tortious interference	83	580,211,000	94,000	30.7	6.9
Partnership dispute	19	52,462,000	97,000	41.8	12.8
Subrogation	44	2,047,000	8,000	4.1	--
Other or unknown contract	41	6,369,000	22,000	13.9	7.1
Real property cases[c]	49	$2,904,000	$15,000	6.1%	--

Note: Data for case type and final awards were available for 99.3% of all plaintiff winners. Award data were rounded to the nearest thousand. Final award amount includes both compensatory (reduced for contributory negligence) and punitive damage awards. Detail may not sum to total because of rounding.
*The number of plaintiffs awarded damages may differ from the number calculated from the percentage of plaintiffs who successfully litigated the case (table 5). Missing award data, the fact that in some cases plaintiff winners receive nothing because of award reductions, and the inclusion of plaintiff winners in bifurcated damage trials (a group excluded from table 5) account for some of this difference.
--No cases recorded.
[a]The number of trials includes bench and jury trials, trials with a directed verdict, judgments notwithstanding the verdict, and jury trials for defaulted defendants.
[b]Excludes bifurcated trials where the plaintiff won on only the liability claim. Bifurcated trials involving only damage claims, however, have been included.
[c]Eminent domain cases are not calculated among final awards because there is almost always an award; the issue is how much the defendant (whose property is being condemned) will receive for the property.

*Bureau of Justice Statistics, U.S. Department of Justice. Civil Trial Cases and Verdicts in Large Counties, 2001.

follow them. This is particularly true when the firm refuses to take a case. All legal actions have a deadline, referred to as the statute of limitations. If a legal action is not brought within this time period, it cannot be brought at all. When the firm decides not to take a case, it will often issue a letter explaining its refusal and urging the client to take action on a claim before the statute of limitations runs.

3. AVOIDING UNAUTHORIZED PRACTICE OF LAW

Unauthorized practice of law (UPL)
When a person who is not an attorney gives legal advice or does any action traditionally reserved for members of the state bar

Another way to avoid a claim of legal malpractice is to avoid practicing law without a license. **Unauthorized practice of law** (UPL) occurs when a person who is not a member of the state bar engages in a practice normally reserved for attorneys. Although a paralegal who engages in UPL cannot be sued for legal malpractice, the attorney for whom the paralegal works can be. In addition to civil suits, a paralegal who practices law can also be sued or even imprisoned. Read the following sample case and then ask yourself, according to the court, when did this freelance paralegal commit UPL?

SUSSMAN v. GRADO
192 Misc. 2d 628 (N.Y. Dist. Ct. 2002)

JOEL K. ASARCH, J.

There is an unmet need for legal representation of a large portion of the state's population in civil proceedings. Despite laudable efforts by the practicing bar to provide free and reduced rate legal services to the public (pro bono publico), many people still cannot afford to obtain the assistance of counsel in civil cases. However, as the Ad Hoc Committee for Non-Lawyer Practice of the New York State Bar Association found, "[t]he employment of educated and trained legal assistants presents an opportunity to expand the public's accessibility to legal services at a reduced cost while preserving attorneys' time for attention to legal services which require the independent exercise of an attorney's judgment." To help in the delivery of "high quality, cost effective legal services to the public" (id.), paralegals work under the supervision of attorneys, who are fully responsible for such representation. The paralegal does not practice law — an "act requiring the exercise of 'independent professional legal judgment.'" In fact, a traditional paralegal may not practice law. When a paralegal declines to work under the direct supervision of an attorney, problems may occur.

This small claims case, which the undersigned tried on April 9, 2002, emphasizes the problems involved.

FINDINGS OF FACT

The plaintiff had obtained a judgment against a debtor on November 14, 2001 for $1,472. When the plaintiff attempted to enforce the judgment, he learned that there were two joint bank accounts at different banks in the names of the judgment debtor and his wife, for which the sheriff's department required a turnover order. The plaintiff went to the defendant, "an independent paralegal" and president/sole shareholder of Accutech

Consulting Group, Inc., and explained what he needed. He paid the defendant $45 for the services. Despite the defendant's claim that she did not know what a turnover order was, she accepted the case and the fee. The plaintiff alleged that the papers prepared by the defendant were deficient and, as a result, the "Sheriff's Department closed the case." He sues to recover the amount of the judgment plus the fee paid to the defendant (which she admittedly would refund). In fact, by letter dated February 21, 2002, the defendant sent the plaintiff a check for $45 (which he denied receiving), refunding the $45 for the turnover order which "was executed in good faith by this office. You indicated an error and we did not ever refuse to make the correction. This is not a usual type of court order. In fact, the three attorneys that we did speak with about it understood the relevance, but had never heard of it or done such an order." The defendant indicated that because the plaintiff had challenged the "integrity" of the defendant's office, his business "will not be welcome here."

The fact that the sheriff's department closed the case with respect to the two joint bank accounts does not mean the judgment is unenforceable. Rather, if docketed properly, the small claims judgment acts as a lien on real property. Further, the judgment is good for up to 20 years. The plaintiff has failed to prove that but for the defendant's act or omission, he would have collected on the judgment. There was no proof that the restraint was released from the bank accounts. Generally, restraining notices are good for one year. Accordingly, the plaintiff has failed to prove entitlement to recover the underlying judgment from the defendant. However, just because the plaintiff cannot recover the amount of the judgment from the defendant does not end this court's inquiry. The defendant testified that she's a graduate from a paralegal certificate program and has been a paralegal for 13 years and she "help[s] a lot of people."

In response to the court's question: "Do you work under the authority of an attorney?" the defendant answered: "I'm an independent. I assist the general public. I assist attorneys with work. And Mr. Sussman came to me of his own free will and asked me to do this work for him." To this court, there is a difference between assisting someone to fill out a form and preparing a form on a subject with which the "assistan[t]" is unfamiliar. Instead of referring this plaintiff to an attorney, the defendant allegedly asked three attorneys about what a turnover order was ("none of them had ever heard of it") and called the sheriff's office who informed her that "they needed something to direct the bank to research [its] files and find out the assets of the debtor."

"So I prepared for Mr. Sussman the turnover order that you're looking at." When asked by the court how she got the form, the defendant answered: "I patterned it based upon what I know of other orders petitioning money from the court." The petition stated, in part, "That on the 13th day of October, 2001 under the above stated index number, plaintiff was awarded a money judgment against [judgment-debtor] in the amount of one thousand four hundred forty-three and 00/100 dollars ($1,443.00) by the Hon. Alfred D. Cooper, Sr. (See copy of the judgment annexed hereto). The plaintiff caused the Nassau County Sheriff to serve a levy upon the First National Bank of Long Island, on December 3, 2001, under Sheriff's File . . . in connection with defendant's bank account number-ed. . . . That plaintiff requests said bank to research its files as to the assets of [judgment-debtor] in the aforesaid account and turn over to the sheriff of Nassau county the sum of $1,443.00 as and for satisfaction of judgment against the said [judgment-debtor]." The petition was signed and verified by the plaintiff herein. At the bottom of the page was a "turn over order," ordering "that the Bank of New York turn over to the

Nassau County Sheriff the sum of ($1,443) plus accumulated interest." There was a line for a District Court Judge's signature. The papers were filed with the court, but no action was taken on them, as the clerk's office properly rejected the papers.

WAS THE DEFENDANT PRACTICING LAW?

The American Bar Association has defined an independent paralegal as "a person who is not supervised by a lawyer, provides services to clients with regard to a process in which the law is involved, is not functioning at the time as a paralegal or a document preparer, and for whose work no lawyer is accountable." However, New York State bar associations have not recognized the "legal technician/independent paralegal" for reasons obvious from this case — the independent paralegal, working without the supervision of an attorney, may cross the line between assisting a person in need to hurting a person in need through lack of knowledge and supervision. Even the National Association of Legal Assistants, Inc. recognizes that a "legal assistant may perform any task which is properly delegated and supervised by an attorney, as long as the attorney is ultimately responsible to the client, maintains a direct relationship with the client, and assumes professional responsibility for work product" (Canon 2). "The prohibition against the practice of law by a layman is grounded in the need of the public for integrity and competence of those who undertake to render legal services. Because of the fiduciary and personal character of the lawyer-client relationship and the inherently complex nature of our legal system, the public can better be assured of the requisite responsibility and competence if the practice of law is confined to those who are subject to the requirements and regulations imposed upon members of the legal profession." A turnover proceeding is a special proceeding under article 52 of the CPLR. Preparation of legal papers (in this case a notice of petition and petition) and service of those papers must be in compliance with CPLR 5225 and/or 5227. A turnover proceeding is a common procedure in the collection of outstanding judgments.

The defendant has, in this court's opinion, crossed the line between filling out forms and engaging in the practice of law by rendering legal services. The defendant "was going to attempt to prepare an order that would hopefully affect the bank turning over the portion of the account of [the judgment-debtor]'s assets to Mr. Sussman on his judgment. That was the intention" (defendant's testimony). "The practice of law involves the rendering of legal advice and opinions directed to particular clients." "[W]hen legal documents are prepared for a layman by a person in the business of preparing such documents, that person is practicing law whether the documents be prepared in conformity with the law of New York or any other law." This court finds that the defendant used independent judgment on a subject with which she had insufficient knowledge. As indicated above, the defendant did not follow proper procedure with respect to the turnover proceeding. Failure to comply with CPLR 5225 and/or 5227 prevented the court from issuing a turnover order. Such document preparation was not "customary and innocuous practices," nor were the turnover order documents the preparation of legal forms or text simply designed to say what the law is. Rather, the defendant herein purported to "give personal advice on a specific problem" with respect to the turnover proceeding vis-á-vis the plaintiff's judgment. Regardless of her intentions to help the plaintiff, this independent paralegal operated without the supervision of an attorney. She tried to create a legal document without the required knowledge, skill or training. As a result the plaintiff may have lost the ability to execute against two bank accounts. Just as a law school graduate, not admitted to practice law, cannot undertake to collect overdue accounts on behalf of prospective clients, so is an independent paralegal barred from attempting to collect a judgment. There is no doubt that the public needs assistance in navigating the court system. This is one reason for the Chief Judge's work in creating offices for the self-represented in the courts. The hundreds of thousands of hours which the practicing bar devotes annually in voluntary pro bono services also go a long way to protecting the rights of those who cannot afford legal representation. However, the guidance of an attorney and his or her professional staff seems much preferable to an "independent paralegal" who has not gone through law school, has not passed the bar exam and who is not licensed in New York State (it should be noted that an attorney's license to practice law is subject to discipline if ethical standards are not met). Section 484 of the Judiciary Law is designed "to protect the public in this State from 'the dangers of legal representation and advice given by persons not trained, examined and licensed for such work, whether they be laymen or lawyers from other jurisdictions.' " This court finds that the actions of the defendant constituted a deceptive act "likely to mislead a reasonable consumer acting reasonably under the circumstances" and that "the acts or practices have a broader impact on consumers at large." Such action by the defendant in accepting the task to prepare a turnover proceeding when she was not qualified or legally able to prepare the necessary papers violated section 349 of the General Business Law. Here, the court finds that the accepting of the assignment was misleading in a material respect to the consumer and that the consumer was injured — he was unable to collect his judgment from the two restrained bank accounts. Accordingly, the court finds that the plaintiff is entitled to treble damages (General Business Law §349[h]) in the sum of $135. In addition, the court is sending a copy of this decision to the New York State Attorney General's Office for consideration in his discretion as to whether any action should be taken against the defendant pursuant to sections 476-a (1) and/or 485 of the Judiciary Law. In summation, the court finds for the plaintiff against the defendant in the sum of $135.

QUESTIONS ABOUT THE CASE

1   Explain who the defendant and plaintiff are in this case.
2   How long has the defendant worked as a paralegal?
3   According to the court, what is the difference between a paralegal who assists attorneys and one who helps members of the general public to fill out forms?
4   How does the court define the practice of law?

4. UPL AND THE INTERNET

The pervasiveness of the Internet has increased the likelihood of practicing law without a license. A search for "will kits" or "independent paralegals" in any popular search engine will yield thousands of hits. Many of these services originate from questionable sources and any site that claims a "one size fits all" form for child custody, divorce, or other legal problems is misleading at best and probably unauthorized practice of law at worst.

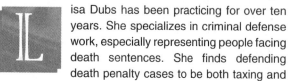

Careers in the Law

▶ Lisa Dubs, Death Penalty Attorney

isa Dubs has been practicing for over ten years. She specializes in criminal defense work, especially representing people facing death sentences. She finds defending death penalty cases to be both taxing and rewarding. "We don't have the government's resources behind us, "she says." We have to use our personalities to get information from people; we appeal to their sense of fairness. The state can always compel people to testify by offering them a reduced sentence. We don't have that option and that makes us more creative. What I usually tell people is that we need your testimony in this case out of fairness and justice. You'd be surprised how many times people will respond to that.

"The biggest difference between criminal defense and prosecution is the resources that we have. Just about everything that we do, we do ourselves. If we need to have a handgun tested, we have to find our own experts. In some ways I think this is a real advantage. It makes you more knowledgeable about your case. When you have to go out and meet with witnesses and go into neighborhoods trying to locate people it gives you a more personal

feel about the case. You know the people involved. You've been to the scene. It's not like the prosecutors who can send detectives out to do the legwork. I do it myself.

"We have our own network of professionals that we rely on in these cases. Sometimes, when we're trying a capital murder case, the entire office closes down. I take my secretary and my paralegals with me to the trial and have them help me pick the jury. I like to get everybody's impression about people who will serve on the jury. I rely on my staff a lot.

"A trial paralegal has to be able to coordinate a lot of different things at the same time. You might have witnesses coming in from out of state. The paralegal needs to know where you are in the trial and has to be able to formulate some kind of idea about when the witness will be called to testify."

Why does she represent people facing the death penalty? "My role is to make sure that United States Constitution is applied fairly. I try to see my client as a human being. No matter what he or she has done, they have mothers and brothers and children. All of those people will be devastated by what happens in the case."

Profiling a Paralegal

▶ Jean Jurasin

started in the legal field when I was fifteen. I took a secretarial program in high school and part of the curriculum called for an internship at the local courthouse. I worked for the local prosecutor, a couple of hours a day, ten hours a week. It was a great job. I learned that when you work for a team, everybody has to pull their weight. I typed up pleadings, did filing, answered the phone, and even took out the trash. I also learned the importance of ethical practices.

It's impossible to be too worried about ethics. If you aren't ethical, word gets around pretty quickly, especially in a small town. One of the biggest ethical problems that new paralegals run into is violating confidentiality. You

think that you are just talking with friends, and you even phrase everything as though you are talking about a "hypothetical" client, but people put it together pretty quickly. When you get into trouble for that, you never forget it. Sometimes you learn very quickly when you've been embarrassed.

Another ethical problem is caused by your clients. Sometimes they want to bring you things that you don't want to have anything to do with. They'll say, "I've got this recording of so and so," and my first question is, "where did you get it?" If they've broken laws to get it, we don't want to have anything to do with it. We will not touch evidence like that. You have to be very careful about what your clients bring you.

SKILLS YOU NEED IN THE REAL WORLD

RESEARCHING ATTORNEYS' STANDING

There will be times in your legal career when you need to know an attorney's standing with the state bar. The attorney might be representing the other side in a divorce action, or may be someone your firm retains to handle a case in another state. Whatever the situation, you will want to know that the person with whom you are working has not been charged with ethical violations. There are several ways to investigate an attorney. When an attorney receives a public reprimand, a suspension, or disbarment, this action is usually published in the state's appellate reporter. You can search for the attorney's name the same way that you would search for a particular case, including online. Many state bars maintain web pages on which they publish not only the names of attorneys who have been sanctioned, but also the names of attorneys who are in good standing. When a member is in good standing, it means that she is not currently under sanction by the bar and has followed all other state bar rules.

CHAPTER SUMMARY

All legal professionals should know and understand the various ethical codes that govern them. Paralegals, in particular, should not only master attorneys' ethical codes, but their own as well. Paralegals work closely with attorneys and any impropriety committed by the paralegal is imputed to the attorney. When attorneys violate ethical codes, they are subject to sanctions by the state supreme court or the state bar. The lightest form of sanction is a private reprimand, in which the state bar sends a letter to the attorney informing her of the nature of the ethical violation and warning her about the consequences of future violations. The next level of sanction is a public reprimand, in which the attorney's reprimand is published, usually in the state appellate reporter. More serious ethical violations may result in a temporary suspension of the attorney's license. During a temporary suspension, the attorney is prevented from practicing law in any way and must petition the state bar to be reinstated. The most severe form of sanction for an attorney is disbarment. When an attorney is disbarred, it means that she is prevented from ever practicing law again.

Paralegals have a separate code of ethics. Paralegals are not bound by an attorney's ethical code and will not face sanction by the state bar if they violate this code. Instead, the attorney with whom they work will be sanctioned. The most common ethical violation for attorneys and paralegals is commingling of funds. Commingling refers to using client funds for personal expenditures and is a form of embezzlement.

Another important ethical concern for paralegals is to avoid unauthorized practice of law. At its simplest, unauthorized practice of law refers to giving legal advice to clients. When paralegals commit unauthorized practice of law, it is not only an ethical violation, but also a criminal one.

ETHICS: MASTERING ETHICAL RULES

You should always have a firm handle on your ethical rules. Spend some time going through the attorneys' code of ethics and read the opinions and other material written by the state bar ethics committee. What does the state bar say about particular practices? When in doubt about a particular action, you should see if there has been a case or ethics opinion that addresses the issue. (You'll be surprised how often you'll find a case on point.) Learn the rules for attorneys and paralegals and be prepared to apply them.

Most paralegals get into ethical trouble by ignoring the rules or doing "favors." Ignoring ethical rules comes from a belief that the rules somehow do not apply to you or your firm. They do. Friends will often approach you and ask for help with a legal document or some other procedure. Always tell your friends that you can give them procedural information, such as what a hearing is, or what discovery means, but you cannot give them legal advice or guide them as to what they should do at a particular hearing. Should your friend get into trouble at the hearing, the first thing she will do is give your name to the judge to deflect some of the judge's anger. Having a standing policy that you do not give legal advice will generally help you avoid this problem.

CHAPTER REVIEW QUESTIONS

1   Explain the term *officer of the court.*
2   What is meant by the term *integrated bar?*
3   What effect does a conviction for a crime of dishonesty or a felony have on a person's ability to join the state bar?
4   How is the American Bar Association involved in the creation of ethical rules?
5   Explain the functions of the American Bar Association.
6   How are ethical complaints investigated?
7   What is the lightest sanction that can be imposed against an attorney for an ethical violation?
8   What is the most severe sanction that can be assessed against an attorney by the state bar? Explain.

9   What is the most common reason for an attorney to run into ethical trouble?

10 Explain an attorney's ethical obligation to "zealously represent the interest of the client."

11 Do paralegals have ethical codes? Explain.

12 What is the difference between certification and licensure for paralegals?

13 What is legal malpractice?

14 What are the elements of a legal malpractice action?

15 Why is confidentiality so important to legal professionals?

16 What is the attorney-client privilege?

17 What are some of the methods that a paralegal can use to avoid legal malpractice?

18 Why did the court rule against the independent paralegal in *Sussman v. Grado*, this chapter's sample case?

19 Why has the Internet provided more opportunities for unauthorized practice of law?

DISCUSSION QUESTIONS

1   Why is it important for paralegals to know and understand the ethical code that applies to attorneys?

2   Should paralegals have an ethical code that provides for sanctions similar to those applicable to attorneys? Explain.

3   Why are more clients bringing legal malpractice actions against their attorneys and paralegals?

PERSONALITY QUIZ

Take the following ethics test and see how well you do:

1   My friend asked me about a client today and I said that I'd rather talk about something else.

0-strongly disagree   5-agree   10-strongly agree

Points: _____

2   When I get a telephone call from someone asking about a particular case, I don't give out information unless the person is the client or I've been authorized to do so.

0-strongly disagree   5-agree   10-strongly agree

Points: _____

3   I like to discuss my work with friends, and I enjoy their reactions when I tell them about some of the weird stuff that I see.

    10-strongly disagree   5-agree   0-strongly agree

                                                                    Points: _____

4   I don't think that ethical rules will be much of a concern for me.

    10-strongly disagree   5-agree   0-strongly agree

                                                                    Points: _____

                                                               Total Points: _____

If you scored between 30-40 points, you have a solid understanding of the dilemmas created by ethical rules.

If you scored between 20-29 points, you should spend some time brushing up on your ethical rules.

If you scored 19 or lower, you need to become familiar with ethical rules.

PRACTICAL APPLICATIONS

1   Create a table showing the possible sanctions for ethical violations, with the lightest sanction at the bottom of the table and the most severe at the top. Give the name of each sanction with a second column that explains the sanction.
2   Locate recent publications of attorney suspensions or disbarments in your state's appellate reporters.

WEB SITES

Cornell Law School's Ethics Page
http://www.law.cornell.edu/ethics

American Bar Association
http://w3.abanet.org/home.cfm

Ohio State Bar
http://www.ohiobar.org

Illinois Paralegal Association (Code of Ethics)
http://www.ipaonline.org

TERMS AND PHRASES

Attorney-client privilege
Certification
Commingling
Confidentiality

Disbarment
Integrated bar
Licensure
Officer of the court

Unauthorized practice of
law

Trials

Chapter Learning Objectives

After completing this chapter, you should be able to:

- Explain the process of jury selection
- Describe the differences between opening statements and closing arguments
- Explain the purpose of direct and cross-examination
- Describe the function of jury charges
- Explain how the jury reaches a verdict

 **INTRODUCTION**

Hollywood is fascinated with trials. Every night you can see courtroom dramas on television and every year major motion pictures are produced that feature a trial as an important aspect of the story. Why are people so fascinated with trials? We explore this question as we describe the various phases of trials throughout this chapter. In many ways, a trial is the ultimate drama because in trials, as in good mystery novels, you don't know what will happen until the very end.

 **THE VARIOUS PHASES OF A TRIAL**

In this chapter we do not draw many distinctions between civil trials and criminal trials. The reason for this is simple: Civil jury trials and criminal jury trials resemble each other very closely. The phases of trials are identical and so are most of the rules governing testimony and evidence. Where there are important differences, we examine them in greater detail. One of the similarities between civil and criminal cases is the calendar call.

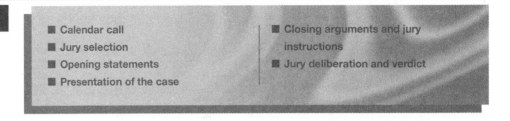

FIGURE 6-1

The Phases of a Trial

- Calendar call
- Jury selection
- Opening statements
- Presentation of the case
- Closing arguments and jury instructions
- Jury deliberation and verdict

A. CALENDAR CALL

Calendar call
A mandatory court hearing in which the judge inquires about the readiness of the parties to go to trial; also known as a docket call

On the day that trial is scheduled most judges have what is referred to as a **calendar call** or docket call. This is a hearing in which the parties in all pending cases must appear to give a status report. In civil cases, for example, the judge will have a calendar call to see which of the pending cases is ready for trial and which need additional time. If a plaintiff fails to appear for the calendar call, the judge may dismiss the suit. This makes calendar calls very important. If the attorney representing the plaintiff has to be in more than one courtroom on the same day (a common experience), the attorney will file a **conflict letter** with the court listing the various court appearances and requesting permission to report later in the day.

Conflict letter
A letter sent by an attorney to the judge explaining that the attorney has several different appearances scheduled for the same date and detailing which courts the attorney will go to first

When the parties announce that they are ready for trial, the judge often schedules them to appear later that week. Suppose that there are 30 cases on the current calendar. It is obvious that in only one week (sometimes two) it would be impossible to try all 30 cases. However, by requiring the parties to appear for the calendar call, the judge can exert some subtle (and sometimes not so subtle) pressure on the parties to settle the case. This brings us to some important differences between civil and criminal cases.

Some litigation attorneys have their paralegals answer calendar calls while they are appearing in another courtroom.

B. SETTLEMENT VERSUS PLEA BARGAINING

There are important differences between how civil cases and criminal cases terminate prior to trial. The vast majority of civil cases settle prior to trial.

1. SETTLEMENT

When we first discussed the evaluation of civil cases (Chapter 4), we mentioned that among the factors that the plaintiff's attorney considers are the legal basis of the claim and the likelihood of recovery. Plaintiffs' attorneys and paralegals must research the law before filing a complaint to address the first factor and research the defendant to address the second. Before taking a case to trial, the plaintiff must seriously reevaluate the case. There are different considerations in filing a complaint and in taking a case before a jury. All these factors weigh heavily in the parties' decision to reach a **settlement** in the case. When a settlement is reached, it means the case is terminated prior to jury trial and it usually involves a monetary payment by one party to the other in exchange for dropping the case.

Settlement
A negotiated termination of a case prior to trial or jury verdict

A settlement is a negotiated end to a civil case.

a. Evaluating Possible Verdicts in Civil Cases

Prior to trial, the legal teams for both parties must seriously consider the possibility of losing at trial. For the plaintiff, a loss means that all the time and energy put into the case will have been for nothing. For the defendant, a loss may mean a hefty monetary judgment paid to the plaintiff, in addition to paying the attorney.

There are some methods that civil attorneys can use to evaluate the likelihood of winning a jury trial. For instance, the attorneys and paralegals can review recent jury decisions from the same jurisdiction to see how other juries, faced with similar issues, have ruled. Suppose, for example, that research has shown that cases brought for intentional infliction of emotional distress have routinely failed before juries in this jurisdiction. Although this is no guarantee of what the jury in a given case will do, it is a strong indication. Conversely, if jurors in the jurisdiction have routinely awarded large damages in such cases, the plaintiff's team might feel more at ease about going to trial. The defendant, of course, will be doing the same research.

2. PLEA BARGAINING

Plea bargaining is reserved for criminal cases. A **plea bargain** is an offer made by the prosecutor to the defendant. The prosecutor offers to make a recommendation to the judge for a specific sentence and fine, in exchange for the defendant's guilty plea prior to trial. If the defendant accepts the state's offer, there will be no trial and the judge will sentence the defendant pursuant to the negotiated deal. Prosecutors make plea offers in nearly every case and the vast majority of criminal cases pending on the trial calendar end with the defendant's plea bargain. Why is this so?

Plea bargain
An offer made by the prosecution to a defendant in which the prosecution offers a reduced sentence or fine in exchange for the defendant's plea of guilty prior to trial

A plea bargain is an arrangement in a criminal trial whereby the prosecution agrees to recommend a specific sentence in exchange for the defendant's guilty plea.

There are several important reasons that prosecutors offer plea bargains in criminal cases:

- Trials are expensive and time-consuming for the state
- The caseload for most prosecutors is huge
- The case against the defendant may have evidentiary or witness problems

a. Trials Are Expensive

One consideration rarely discussed in television dramas is the expense the state incurs in both civil and criminal cases.

To bring a case to trial, the state must first have a place to hold trials. Constructing a courthouse is an expensive proposition, but necessary for the administration of justice. In addition to building and staffing a courthouse, jury trials also incur additional expenses. Most courthouses maintain a separate department whose sole duty is to arrange for jury trials. This department must send out notices to potential jurors and arrange for all potential jurors to appear on a specific day and time. In addition to this responsibility — and the fact that nearly everyone called for jury duty would rather be somewhere else — the government usually pays jurors a token amount for their time and inconvenience. This amount can be as small as $10 per day, which hardly makes up for the lost time from work, the inconvenience, and the aggravation that this public duty often entails.

b. Prosecutors Have Heavy Caseloads

The economics of jury trials are not the only consideration for prosecutors. There are other, more immediate problems to consider. For one thing, most prosecutors have heavy caseloads. Consider a simple example:

Paula Prosecutor has been assigned to Judge North's courtroom. This month, there are 30 cases still pending on the docket that were left over from last month's calendar. This month, Paula receives an additional 40 new cases to add to her current load. (After all, crime is a year-round occupation and doesn't stop simply because prosecutors have lots of pending cases.) This means that Paula now has 70 cases pending and only one week set aside this month to dispose of them. Obviously, she cannot try all 70 cases. She could concentrate on one or two cases and take those to trial this month, while ignoring the others. However, this temporary solution is no solution at all. Next month, she will probably receive an additional 30 or 40 new cases to add to her current docket. If she doesn't resolve some of these cases without trials, her docket will continue to grow until it becomes unmanageable. The solution: Make offers on most of her pending cases, have them plead guilty, and clear them from her docket.

c. The Case Against the Defendant Has Problems

Another reason that a prosecutor might offer a deal on a case is because the case has evidentiary or witness problems. This is not to say that the prosecutor cannot prove the case. If the prosecutor has reason to know that the defendant is not guilty, or that she can never prove the defendant's guilt, the only proper course is for the prosecutor to dismiss the case. However, most problems with cases do not rise to this level but are more like the following scenario:

Paula is preparing to try a burglary case. The victim in the case is reluctant to testify because he doesn't want to spend too much time away from his business. Paula cannot guarantee the exact date and time that the trial will begin until the calendar call has been completed. The burglary victim tells Paula that he would rather see the defendant enter a plea to some lesser offense than waste time and money away from his business testifying in the case. In this scenario, Paula probably will offer the defendant a reduced sentence or fine in exchange for a guilty plea to a lesser offense.

There is one other factor that weighs heavily on the minds of all attorneys, both civil and criminal: What will the jury do with the case?

SELECTING A JURY

The issues in any case, whether civil or criminal, have developed in the weeks and months prior to the trial. In a civil suit, the complaint and answer, along with pre-trial motions, have helped to frame the issues that will be brought out in trial. As we have seen in previous chapters, the complaint is the pleading in which the plaintiff sets out his claims against the defendant. The defendant responds to these claims in the answer. The allegations that the defendant denies form the issues that must be proven in the case. If the defendant admits to some of the allegations, they are no longer part of the case; the jury is instructed that the defendant has waived any objection through his admission.

In criminal cases, things are more straightforward. The defendant has been accused in an indictment or other charging instrument and it is the responsibility of the government to prove those allegations beyond a reasonable doubt. The defendant is not permitted to bring countercharges against the government in a criminal case. The issue is whether the jury members believe that the government has proven the guilt of the defendant. This often results in criminal trials taking less time than civil trials, although some criminal cases can become quite complex. People are often surprised to learn that a typical car wreck civil suit takes more time to try than a typical murder case.

Selecting a jury is actually the process of dismissing panel members until 12 jurors remain.

ISSUE AT A GLANCE

A. JURY DUTY

Whether a jury trial is a civil case or a criminal case the trial always begins with the selection of the jury. In the U.S. court system, it is not completely accurate to say that juries are selected. What actually happens is that a group of citizens are empaneled and then members of this group are eliminated until 12 jurors remain. We discuss the process of removing these panel members in the next few paragraphs.

Before we do, we should provide some definitions to keep the discussion from getting confusing. When citizens are called in for jury duty, they appear in court as part of a **panel.** Panel members are removed until 12 people remain. Those 12 people are then called **jurors.** The process of carrying out jury selection is often referred to as *voir dire.*

Panel
A group of people who have been called for jury duty; the final jury is selected from this group; also known as venire

Jurors
Those people who have been selected to sit on a jury; they will consider the evidence and reach a verdict in the case

Voir dire
(Fr) To look; to speak. The process of questioning jurors about their potential biases in the case

B. PEREMPTORY JURY STRIKES

Jury strike
The removal of a jury panel member, also known as a jury challenge

Peremptory jury strike
The removal of a jury panel member for any legally permissible reason, also known as a peremptory jury challenge

Both sides in a jury trial have a permitted number of **strikes** or challenges that they may use to remove panel members. Suppose, for example, that in a civil case both the plaintiff and the defense have 10 strikes. If the panel consists of 32 persons and if both sides use all their strikes, the result will be a 12-person jury. Such strikes are called **peremptory** strikes because each side may use them in any manner they see fit to remove panel members.

The number of strikes that the parties may use varies on the type of case. In some cases, the parties have equal numbers of strikes, but in most criminal cases, the number is uneven. It is common for defendants in criminal cases to have twice as many peremptory strikes as prosecutors.

Example: On the day of the trial, 42 panel members are brought in to go through jury selection in a criminal case. The defense has a total of 20 strikes that she may use, while the prosecutor has 10. When they both use all their strikes, 12 jurors will remain.

In the past, there were no limitations on the use of peremptory strikes. However, in recent decades, the U.S. Supreme Court has begun limiting a party's ability to use peremptory strikes, especially when the strike is based on race.

In some jurisdictions, peremptory removal of a juror is called a strike, while in other jurisdictions it is called a challenge. The terms are used interchangeably throughout this chapter.

C. LIMITATIONS ON PEREMPTORY CHALLENGES

Although we have said that parties may use their peremptory strikes for almost any reason, in the case of *Batson v. Kentucky*,[7] the Supreme Court created an important limitation on this right. In *Batson*, the Court ruled that prosecutors could not use their peremptory challenges to remove black members of a jury panel simply because the defendant was also black. The prosecutor in *Batson* freely admitted that he had used his peremptory strikes to remove all black panel members because he believed that black panel members would not convict a black defendant. The Supreme Court was not inclined to allow prosecutors to use the court system to further racist policies under the guise of peremptory strikes and announced that this use of peremptory strikes would no longer be permitted.

The *Batson* decision stands for the proposition that when a party uses peremptory strikes to remove panel members, there must be a racially neutral reason for doing so. In subsequent years, white defendants have used the *Batson* principle to challenge strikes to remove white panel members during jury selection as well. This is a so-called reverse *Batson* practice and the Supreme Court held that it is equally unfair. The principle underlying the *Batson* decision has been applied in several other contexts as well. For instance, suppose that a prosecutor uses all her peremptory strikes to remove women from the panel? Such a practice would be unconstitutional under *Batson* and later cases.

Although *Batson* was a criminal case, courts have begun looking very closely at the use of peremptory jury strikes in civil cases as well.

[7] 476 U.S. 79 (1986)

Recent court decisions have begun to seriously limit the use of peremptory jury strikes.

D. CHALLENGES FOR CAUSE

There is a second method that parties can use to remove panel members. When a party makes a **challenge for cause,** it means that the party is requesting the judge to remove the panel member. A party might make a challenge for cause for several reasons; for example, if a panel member has stated in open court that she will not obey the court's orders, or will not actively participate in the jury deliberations, or

Challenge for cause
When a panel member is removed because she cannot sit on the jury

Jury panel members may be challenged for cause and removed when they indicate that they cannot be fair or that they have religious, philosophical, or other reasons that prevent them from sitting on a jury.

FIGURE 6-2

Jury Sheet

Jury Selection Sheet

1 John Smith *bad response to Q2. Strike*	**2 Mary Doe** *very nice Keep her!*	**3 John Roe** *?*	**4 George Bush** *likes client, Smiles engineer. keep!*	**5 Patricia Burke** *Very conservative good juror!*
6 Deborah Bolstridge *nurse— good juror keep*	**7 Lisa Burnett** *another nurse no problems*	**8 Robert Bevans** *good response to Q2!*	**9 Mary Robinson** *Strike!*	**10 Chuck Soe** *doesn't want to here. Strike if other side doesn't*
11 Betsy Buster *Says she has 'moral' reasons. challenge for cause?*	**12 Jack Rocky** *nice guy! possible jury for person? Keep*	**13 Hanna Bow** *Very negative Strike*	**14 Lucy David** *Bad answers to Q2 + 3. Strike*	**15 Belle Darcy** *doesn't seem to understand ?*
16 Jane Doe *no opinions~?*	**17 Katie Burnett** *smart, but young.?*	**18 Benjamin Rod** *knows about sports Keeper*	**19 Tara Christopher** *nice lady. Keeper*	**20 Debbie Neal** *Says she 'distrusts' lawyers? Strike*
21 Katherine Bodie *Sweet old lady, but . . .?*	**22 James Carter** *Too busy, wants to be somewhere else. Strike*	**23 William Clinton** *unemployed.*	**24 Ron Reagan** *Seems conservative, nice smile. Keep?*	**25**

has religious objections to being seated on a jury. If the judge accepts the challenge, the panel member is removed and the removal is not assessed against any side's number of peremptory strikes.

Once a jury has been selected to serve on the case, the next step is the opening statements.

OPENING STATEMENTS

An opening statement is a brief speech made by the attorneys for both sides, in which they outline what will happen in the case and what evidence the jury can expect to see. The purpose of an opening statement is to provide some framework for the jurors, who have no independent knowledge of the case. The attorneys use the opening statement to explain the issues to the jurors, and as a roadmap of where the trial will go and what witnesses will testify. Although opening statements are often depicted on television as dramatic presentations in which attorneys forcefully argue major points in their cases, the reality is that opening statements are usually dry and formal. Attorneys are barred from arguing points; the best that they can do is to provide a foretaste of what will happen in the course of the trial.

In a civil case, the plaintiff's attorney presents opening statements first. The reason for this is simple: The plaintiff is the person who brought the allegations and must now prove them. Once the plaintiff has given an opening statement, the defendant is permitted to address the jury. Although a defense attorney may wait to give his opening statement until after the plaintiff's case has been presented, the common practice is for both attorneys to address the jury shortly after jury selection. Once the opening statements have been made, the next phase is the presentation of the plaintiff's case.

In a criminal case, the prosecution gives its opening statement first, for the same reasons that a plaintiff goes first in a civil case. The prosecution has leveled the accusations, and now the government must reveal what it intends to prove at trial.

BEGINNING THE TRIAL

The plaintiff has the burden of going first in a civil case. The plaintiff presents its case through two primary methods: witnesses and evidence. Attorneys are not allowed to address the jury and tell them about pertinent evidence, or to offer opinions about the legal position of their client. Instead, the attorneys must prove their case through witnesses.

A. WITNESSES

We have all seen witnesses testify in movies and television dramas. Although some of the fictional accounts may be overly dramatic, the basics are usually correct.

When a witness testifies, he is called to the stand, sworn in, and then asked questions. This is called direct examination.

B. DIRECT EXAMINATION

The witnesses who testify on **direct examination** are usually friendly to the plaintiff, or at least neutral about the outcome of the case. Let's take a typical example and explain how direct examination proceeds.

Direct examination
The questioning of a witness by the side who called the witness to the stand

   Maya was injured in a car wreck. The defendant, David Doe, ran a red light and struck Maya's car broadside. Maya brought suit against David Doe and the trial has now begun. After giving her opening statement, Maya's attorney, Lois Lawyer, calls her first witness to the stand. Wanda Witness was another driver at the intersection who saw the entire incident. The direct examination might go something like this:

LAWYER: Please state your name for the record.
WITNESS: My name is Wanda Witness.
LAWYER: Ms. Witness, were you present at the intersection of Elm Street and First Street in this city on May first of last year?
WITNESS: Yes, I was.
LAWYER: What, if anything, did you see that day?
WITNESS: I saw the defendant fail to stop at the red light and strike the car driven by that lady over there.
LAWYER: Let the record reflect that the witness has identified the plaintiff in this case. Ms. Witness, how can you be so sure that the defendant ran the red light that day?
WITNESS: Well, I was in the car right behind him and I saw the light turn red. I turned to my daughter, who was in the car with me, and I said, "That guy's crazy. He's running a red light."
LAWYER: What happened after the defendant ran the red light?
WITNESS: He slammed into that lady's car and both cars sort of rolled sideways.
LAWYER: What did you do then?
WITNESS: I parked my car and ran to the lady's car. I asked her if she was okay. That man, the defendant, had already gotten there.
LAWYER: Did the defendant say anything to you?
WITNESS: Yes, he said that he should have been paying attention and that he hoped he hadn't killed someone.

   Notice that the way the attorney phrases questions on direct examination is different from the way that a person would question the witness on the street. The lawyer uses stilted questions such as, "What, if anything, did you see that day?" The reason that attorneys phrase questions this way is that direct examination has strict limits on how attorneys question witnesses. For one thing, attorneys are not allowed to testify for the witness; the witness must tell her own story. If the attorney puts words in the witness's mouth (called *leading* a witness), the other attorney may object.

When the plaintiff's attorney has asked the witness all the questions she thinks are necessary, the plaintiff's attorney turns the questioning over to the defendant's attorney for cross-examination.

C. CROSS-EXAMINATION

Cross-examination
The questioning of a witness to show bias, prejudice, or lack of knowledge

Cross-examination occurs after direct examination and is always done by the other side's attorney. The rules about asking questions on cross-examination are much more liberal than the rules governing attorneys on direct examination. Attorneys are allowed to ask leading questions, such as, "You weren't even looking at the light, were you?" Attorneys are also allowed to be more confrontational with witnesses on cross-examination. Cross-examination is more dramatic than direct examination and this is probably why you are more likely to see it depicted on television courtroom dramas.

Attorneys are allowed to explore a witness's potential biases or lack of knowledge on cross-examination. The attorneys can also impeach a witness by showing that the witness is not someone who should be believed. Impeachment can occur through a demonstration that the witness has no knowledge of the event, such as the fact that the witness was not at the scene on the day of the accident, or that the witness has been convicted of a crime involving dishonesty, such as perjury.

D. EVIDENCE

We have said that there are only two ways that a case against the defendant can be proven. One is by witness testimony; the other is through evidence. When we explored the topic of evidence law in Chapter 4, we saw that there are several different types of evidence. A witness may testify about something she observed, or the attorneys may offer evidence to substantiate a fact, such as photographs of the damage to the plaintiff's car. The important point about evidence is that attorneys rely on it to prove their case. The plaintiff's attorney will present evidence to bolster its assertions against the defendant; the defendant will present evidence to mitigate or contradict the plaintiff's conclusions. Ultimately, the jury must decide about the weight to give any particular piece of evidence.

E. RESTING THE CASE

The plaintiff's attorney proceeds through his case, calling witnesses and presenting evidence, until he believes that he has proven all his allegations against the defendant. When he is finished, the attorney will announce, "Your Honor, the Plaintiff rests."

This announcement informs the court that the plaintiff does not plan on presenting any additional witnesses or evidence and that the plaintiff is finished with his side of the case. At this point, the focus turns to the defendant, who is free

to present evidence and witnesses. However, before the defendant begins his case, it is common for the defense attorney to raise a motion.

VI   MOTIONS

Parties can raise motions at many different points throughout a case. Motions are a common feature of the discovery phase of a civil action. During the trial, there are at least two motions that are seen in nearly every case. The first is a motion in limine and the second is a motion for directed verdict.

A. MOTION IN LIMINE

A **motion in limine** is an oral motion made during the trial that asks for the court's ruling on a particular evidentiary question. For instance, the defendant might bring a motion in limine when a witness testifies that the "defendant was at fault." The defendant's motion in limine would probably sound something like this: "Your Honor, I object. The witness is not qualified to give an opinion about who was or was not at fault in this case. I ask you to direct the witness not to give such testimony in the future."

> **Motion in limine**
> A motion made during the trial

The judge is free to sustain (agree) with the motion or overrule (disagree) with it.

B. MOTION FOR DIRECTED VERDICT

A **motion for directed verdict** almost always comes at the end of the plaintiff's or prosecution's case, shortly after that party has announced that it rests. When a defendant brings a motion for directed verdict, he is saying that the plaintiff has failed to prove all the allegations raised in the complaint. Because the plaintiff has failed to prove its case, the defendant is entitled to a verdict entered by the judge that essentially dismisses the case and ends the trial. This is a directed verdict. Motions for directed verdict are routine in both civil and criminal cases. Defendants in both cases raise these motions because there is no reason not to. If the defendant brings the motion and the judge overrules it, the defendant is in no worse position than he was before. However, if the judge sustains the motion, the trial will end and the defendant wins. Given that situation, it is little wonder that defense attorneys in both civil and criminal cases routinely bring a motion for directed verdict at the conclusion of the other side's case.

> **Motion for directed verdict**
> A motion by the defense that asks the court to enter a verdict in the defendant's favor because the plaintiff (or government) has failed to prove all material allegations against the defendant

A motion for directed verdict requests the judge to end the case and declare the defendant not guilty because the government has failed to prove its case.

ISSUE AT
A GLANCE

 **VIII** ## THE DEFENSE CASE

When the plaintiff has rested her case, the defendant is permitted to present his case. The rules for the defendant's case are identical to those that bind the plaintiff. The defendant can present witnesses and testimony to attempt to disprove the plaintiff's allegations. At this point, there is another important difference between civil and criminal cases.

A. PRESENTING THE DEFENSE (CIVIL)

In a civil case, although the defense is under no obligation to present a case, most defense attorneys do. The defense reasons that if the jurors hear only the plaintiff's version of the case, they will probably reach a verdict favorable to the plaintiff. The defendant therefore presents witness testimony and evidence that tends to disprove, or mitigate, the defendant's liability.

B. PRESENTING THE DEFENSE (CRIMINAL)

Defendants in criminal actions are also under no obligation to present a defense to the government's case. However, there are some important constitutional protections that protect criminal defendants. For one thing, not only is the defendant under no obligation to present a defense, the fact that he fails to do so cannot be used against him. It is human nature for someone to think, "If he isn't guilty, why didn't he deny it?" However, the Constitution has enacted safeguards to prevent that simple logic from injuring a criminal defendant. If the defendant does not testify (and most defendants do not), the prosecution is not permitted to comment on that failure, and the jury is instructed that they cannot draw any negative inference from that fact. (Whether they actually do is an open question.)

Why would a criminal defendant not take the stand in his own case? There are several possible answers to this question. When the defendant takes the stand in some jurisdictions, he opens himself up to questions about his criminal history. If the defendant has an extensive criminal history, he may not wish for the jury to learn about it. (In most cases, the prosecution is barred from telling the jury about the defendant's prior criminal record, unless the defendant takes the stand.) Another reason for the defendant's reluctance to testify is that the prosecutor is usually a skilled cross-examiner and might make the defendant look bad to the jury.

C. THE DEFENSE RESTS

Whether in a civil case or a criminal case, once the defendant has presented his case, he also makes the announcement, "The defense rests." This signals that the defendant has no additional testimony or witnesses. The trial will now move into its final phase. At this point, the jury is usually sent back to the jury room or given a recess while the court conducts a charge conference.

 **CHARGE CONFERENCE**

A charge conference is a meeting between the judge and the attorneys for both sides during which they discuss the type of instructions that will be given to the jury. As we will see, the judge always gives the jurors instructions about what they should consider while they deliberate in the case and how they should announce that they are finished. The charge conference is when the judge gives the attorneys for both sides the opportunity to suggest specific types of instructions for the jury.

Attorneys know that in addition to the judge's instructions about what they should do in the jury room, the judge will also instruct the jurors about what the law is on particular topics. The attorneys will research different cases, hoping that the judge will use language in his instructions to the jury that might slightly favor their side over the other. Consider the following jury instruction:

Plaintiff's Suggested Jury Charge No. 1
Ladies and gentlemen of the jury, I charge you that the defendant has been impeached by proof of a crime of dishonesty. Impeachment suggests that the witness is not capable of being believed. How much weight you give to that testimony is for you to decide.

Now, let's consider the defendant's suggested jury charge on the same topic.

Defendant's Suggested Jury Charge No. 1
Ladies and gentlemen of the jury, I charge you that whether or not a person has been impeached in this case is solely a matter for you to decide.

A jury "charge" and a jury "instruction" are the same thing.

ISSUE AT
A GLANCE

Notice that although both suggested jury charges state the same basic idea, the way that the defendant has worded the charge lessens the impact on him, while the plaintiff's suggested charge focuses attention on the defendant's testimony. The difference may be simple semantics, but attorneys do not take anything for granted. The entire case may hinge on how the jury considers this one issue.

The judge is free to accept or reject any of the parties' proposed jury charges. Once the court has considered all suggested jury instructions, the judge will call for the jury to return and announce that closing arguments may commence.

Part I   Introduction to Law

FIGURE 6-3

Civil Trials Disposed of in State
Courts, 2001*

Table 1. Number of civil trials disposed of in State courts in the Nation's 75 largest counties, 2001

Case type	Number of trials[a]	Percent
All	11,908	100.0%
Tort cases	7,948	66.7%
Automobile	4,235	35.6
Premises liability	1,268	10.6
Product liability	158	1.3
Asbestos	31	0.3
Other	126	1.1
Intentional tort	375	3.1
Medical malpractice	1,156	9.7
Professional malpractice	102	0.9
Slander/libel	95	0.8
Animal attack	99	0.8
Conversion	27	0.2
False arrest, imprisonment	45	0.4
Other or unknown tort	390	3.3
Contract cases	3,698	31.1%
Fraud	625	5.2
Seller plaintiff	1,208	10.1
Buyer plaintiff	793	6.7
Mortgage foreclosure	22	0.2
Employment discrimination	166	1.4
Other employment dispute	287	2.4
Rental/lease	276	2.3
Tortious interference	138	1.2
Partnership dispute	40	0.3
Subrogation	69	0.6
Other or unknown contract	73	0.6
Real property cases	262	2.2%
Eminent domain	52	0.4
Other real property[b]	210	1.8

Note: Data for case types were available for 100% of the 11,908 trial cases. Detail may not sum to total because of rounding.
[a]Trials include bench and jury trials, trials with a directed verdict, judgments notwithstanding the verdict, and jury trials for defaulted defendants.
[b]Includes title disputes, boundary disputes, and other real property cases.
See *Methodology* section for case type definitions.

*Bureau of Justice Statistics, U.S. Department of Justice. Civil Trial Cases and Verdicts in Large Counties, 2001.

CLOSING ARGUMENTS

In a closing argument, the attorneys summarize their cases and show the jury why they should win. Unlike opening statements, attorneys are free to engage in their full range of dramatic abilities to sway the jury to their side. Attorneys can appeal not only to logic, but also to emotion. They can argue that the verdict they want is good not only for their client, but also for society in general. Closing arguments in real cases have come to resemble their fictional counterparts on television, with attorneys pulling out all the stops to convince the jurors that they should win. Unlike fictional trials, however, most real closing arguments last a lot longer than the few seconds seen on television. In many cases, attorneys have an hour or more to sum up their case. In previous decades, attorneys might have taken several days to complete a closing argument.

Just as we saw in opening statements, the plaintiff goes first in presenting a closing argument. When the plaintiff is finished, the defense gives its closing argument. This is also the pattern in criminal cases, with the government giving its closing argument first, followed by the attorney for the criminal defendant.

 **JURY CHARGE**

When the closing arguments are complete, the judge then reads the **jury charge.** Among other things, the judge's charge instructs the jury what they must do in the jury room. For instance, a judge might read, "Once you have retired to the jury room, your first task is to select one member of the jury to act as foreperson. This person will act as the jury spokesperson for any questions the jury might have and for any communications, such as requests for breaks or meals, that the jury might need to make to the court."

Jury charge
Oral instructions given by the judge to the jury about how they should deliberate and what law they should follow

In addition to instructing the jury about the practical matters about how to deliberate, the judge also instructs the jury about the law. The judge might instruct the jury about the burden on the plaintiff to prove the case against the defendant and that if the jurors feel that the plaintiff has failed to prove the case that they should vote a verdict for the defendant.

A jury charge in a complex case could easily last for several hours. The court must go over not only procedural matters, such as where the jurors should write their verdict, but also the full range of legal issues that have arisen in the case.

 JURY DELIBERATION

When the jury charge is complete, the jurors are led from the courtroom to the jury room where they can finally discuss the case among themselves. Jury deliberations are private; no one other than jury members are permitted to be inside the jury room while they deliberate. How does a jury actually deliberate on a case? The most common approach is for the jurors to discuss the case and then vote, often by secret ballot, who they believe should win. The foreperson collects the ballots and then tabulates them. In most cases the final verdict must be unanimous, so if the majority votes for one party and two or three people vote for the other, the majority will then spend some time trying to talk the minority over to their side. This process can take minutes, hours, or even days. Although the length of the trial is an indication of how long the jury will deliberate (longer trials usually result in longer deliberations), there are no rules when it comes to juries. Any

If the jurors are unable to reach a unanimous verdict, the judge will declare a mistrial. This is referred to as a "hung" jury and the case will be tried again before a different jury.

experienced trial attorney will be quick to tell a client that there are no guarantees with jurors. This is why many trial attorneys refer to jury deliberations as "rolling the dice."

When the jurors finally reach a unanimous verdict, the jury spokesperson will knock on the jury room door and tell the court bailiff that they are ready to make their announcement. The bailiff will not ask about the verdict. Instead, he will conduct the jury back into the courtroom, where the judge will ask about the final verdict.

VERDICT

In civil cases, when the plaintiff wins, the jury's announcement will be, "We find for the plaintiff." If they have decided that the defendant should win, their verdict will be, "We find for the defendant." If the jury has decided to make a monetary award, the jury spokesperson will then announce the amount and the party to whom it is awarded.

A. VERDICTS IN CRIMINAL CASES

Jurors in death penalty cases make two determinations. In the first phase of the trial, they determine guilt or innocence. If they find the defendant guilty, the trial moves into a second phase during which the government requests the death sentence. Jurors in those cases must often recommend a sentence of death before it can be imposed.

Here is another important difference between civil and criminal trials. When the jury announces its verdict in a criminal case, there are only a few options. If the jury believes that the government has proven its case against the defendant beyond a reasonable doubt, the jury verdict will be, "We find the defendant guilty." If, on the other hand, the jurors do not believe that the government has proven its case, the verdict will be, "We find the defendant not guilty." Jurors in criminal cases usually have no input as to sentencing or other factors. Their deliberations are limited to a finding of guilty or not guilty.

B. JUDGMENT

After the jury has announced its verdict, the judge officially enters this verdict as the final outcome in the case. This is referred to as the judgment. The jurors are released from duty and are now free to discuss the case with anyone that they wish. Entering judgment has several important consequences. For one, the entry of judgment gives the winning party in a civil case the right to collect the amount awarded by the jury. It also gives the losing party the right to file an appeal.

C. SENTENCING IN CRIMINAL CASES

In criminal cases, the entry of judgment usually comes in the form of the defendant's sentence. If the defendant has been found not guilty, the defendant will be released. The guilty defendant's sentence will be recorded and, barring any appeal, the defendant will begin serving the sentence immediately.

Profiling a Paralegal

▶ Donna Cooper

I was working in industry and when the economy went into a decline, I got laid off. I went back to college and took paralegal courses. I wasn't sure what I was going to do. One day, I saw a flyer for paralegal courses. I took a crash course at a local private technical school. We really had some good instructors. I interned and then went to work for a lawyer in Houston. We did a lot of litigation, especially personal injury cases. The firm also did a lot of federal discrimination cases, age discrimination, sex discrimination.

When you work for a litigation firm, you need good accounting skills. You need to have a handle on case management. You are going to be handling a lot of paper. You also have to have a certain temperament. Everybody who comes to a lawyer's door has a problem. Their worlds have fallen apart. The paralegal needs to be able to listen, be sympathetic, and keep the client focused. Most of the client contact is between the paralegal and the client. The attorney interviews them and gets the basics, but the paralegal interacts with them all the time.

Careers in the Law

▶ Court Reporter

Laura Hamilton has been a court reporter for several years. "I went to school in Massachusetts at a time when court reporters were in high demand. In order to become a court reporter, you have to master the steno machines. The keyboard on a steno machine doesn't have the full range of the alphabet. Instead, it has letter combinations that allow you to make just about any sound people make when they speak. One of the hardest things about becoming a court reporter is getting your speed up. You need to be able to write 225 words per minute to qualify as a court reporter.

"I've done all kinds of court hearings, but the hardest thing I do is taking medical testimony at depositions. It's especially difficult when you come across a medical term that you never heard before. I've been doing orthopedics for several years now and I've really gotten those terms down.

"When paralegals work with court reporters, there are some important things to keep in mind. One is scheduling a reporter for a deposition. Paralegals should always fax or send us a copy of the notice so that we have all the information as to time, date, location, and case name on hand. Also, if they know the attorney will need the transcript before the normal turnaround time for trial or whatever, if they can tell us that when scheduling the job, it will enable us to adjust our schedules accordingly to make sure we can get a completed transcript to them by the date they would like it. Lastly, sometimes we are overlooked when jobs get canceled for whatever reason and the paralegals forget to notify us."

FIGURE 6-4

Federal Civil Trials*

Federal civil trials

Federal district courts exercise jurisdiction in civil actions that —
(1) deal with a Federal question arising out of the U.S. Constitution,
(2) are between parties that reside in different States or countries and that exceed $75,000 at issue,
(3) are initiated by the U.S. Government, or
(4) are brought against the U.S. Government. (See *Federal Tort Trials and Verdicts,* NCJ 172855, February 1999, and "The Jurisdiction of the Federal Courts," <www.uscourts.gov/understand03>, viewed 3/9/2004.)

• In fiscal year 2001 Federal district courts disposed of 1,964 tort, contract, and real property cases by jury or bench trial.

• As in State courts, a small percentage (2%) of the 87,852 terminated Federal tort, contract, and real property cases reached trial.

• A jury verdict disposed of a majority (67%) of Federal tort, contract, and real property trials.

• Federal tort cases (79%) were more likely to be decided by jury trial than contract (50%) and property (26%) cases.

• In about half of Federal tort, contract, and real property trials, the plaintiff won the decision. Plaintiffs won 51% of jury trials and 56% of bench trials.

• The median amount awarded to plaintiff winners was larger in Federal district courts than in the sampled State courts. The median award for plaintiff winners was $216,000 for all Federal tort, contract, and real property cases disposed of by trial. The median award was $228,000 for jury trials and $177,000 for bench trials.

Federal tort, contract, and real property trials terminated in U.S. district courts, 2001

	All trial cases				Jury trial cases			Bench trial cases		
Case type	Number plaintiff winners	Number of plaintiff monetary awards	Total award	Median award	Number plaintiff winners	Number of plaintiff monetary awards	Median award	Number plaintiff winners	Number of plaintiff monetary awards	Median award
Total	801	636	$976,156,000	$216,000	483	405	$228,000	318	231	$177,000
Tort	434	358	$462,943,000	$179,000	316	261	$201,000	118	97	$139,000
Contract	324	266	508,543,000	272,000	159	140	330,000	165	126	226,000
Real property	43	12	4,670,000	125,000	8	4	773,000	35	8	105,000

Note: Award data were rounded to the nearest thousand.
Source: Administrative Office of the U.S. Courts, Civil Master File, fiscal year 2001.
Published reports on Federal District Court data are also available from the U.S. Administrative Office of the Courts: <http:\\www.uscourts.gov\statisticalreport.html>.

*Bureau of Justice Statistics, U.S. Department of Justice. Civil Trial Cases and Verdicts in Large Counties, 2001.

MARTINEZ v. STATE
259 Ga. App. 402, 577 S.E.2d 82 (2003)

A Gwinnett County jury convicted Rigoberto Martinez of trafficking in cocaine, OCGA §16-13-31(a). He appeals from the denial of his motion for new trial, contending the trial court erred in limiting his cross-examination of witnesses, his voir dire of the jury pool, and his closing arguments. He claims the trial court should have excused a juror for cause, and that there was insufficient evidence to support his conviction. Finding no error, we affirm.

On appeal from a criminal conviction, this Court does not weigh the evidence or judge the credibility of witnesses. We view all evidence in the light most favorable to the jury's verdict, and the defendant no longer enjoys the presumption of innocence.

Viewed in this light, the evidence showed that, on October 4, 2000, a confidential informant ("CI") worked with a Gwinnett County Drug Task Force investigator to arrange a controlled buy of 17 ounces of cocaine for the price of $9,350 from Roberto Morales. Morales told the CI that several cars would be carrying several people to the designated location of the sale, the Checkered Parrot Restaurant in Gwinnett County. The investigator and CI arrived at the restaurant just after midnight on October 5, 2000. Morales and Martinez, the defendant, arrived shortly thereafter.

The investigator, pretending to be a drug buyer, got out of his car and talked with the men. The investigator told them that he needed to see the cocaine before he would give them the money. Morales and Martinez walked back to the car. Morales retrieved a one-ounce bag of cocaine from the car and then walked back to the investigator and gave it to him. Martinez waited by the car. The investigator testified that he was concerned about Martinez because he perceived the defendant's presence as a "show of force" by Morales in case trouble erupted. A few moments later, the investigator gave the "take down" signal and the men were arrested. The arresting officers searched the car and discovered an additional 16 ounces of cocaine on the floorboard. The cocaine weighed a total of just over 450 grams. The entire transaction was videotaped, and the State played the tape for the jury at trial.

Martinez complains that the trial court erred when it failed to excuse for cause a retired firearms investigator who had been employed by the Georgia Bureau of Investigation Crime Laboratory. We disagree. There was no evidence that he was a sworn police officer or that he had arrest powers. During voir dire, the juror stated that his former employment would not cause him to be biased in this case and that he would decide this case based on the evidence presented. Accordingly, we find no error.

Martinez asserts that the trial court erred in refusing to allow him to question a potential juror about his opinion on the country's "ongoing war against drugs." Martinez relies on OCGA §15-12-133, which provides that during voir dire, the State and the defendant each have "the right to inquire of the individual jurors examined touching any matter or thing which would illustrate any interest of the juror in the case, including . . . any fact or circumstance indicating any inclination, leaning, or bias which the juror might have respecting the subject matter of the action or the counsel or parties thereto." While we agree that this provision gives wide latitude to the parties during voir dire, we have previously held that the single purpose of voir dire is the ascertainment of the impartiality of jurors, their ability to treat the cause on the merits with objectivity and freedom from bias or prior inclination. Counsel on voir dire should confine his questions to those which may illustrate any prejudice of the juror against the accused or any interest of the juror in the cause. The trial court still "retains the discretion to limit the examination [of prospective jurors] *to questions dealing directly with the specific case and to prohibit general questions.*" We find that the trial court in this case did not abuse its discretion in refusing to allow Martinez's general question about the country's war on drugs.

In two enumerations, Martinez contends the trial court improperly limited his closing argument and commented on the evidence in violation of OCGA §17-8-57. The exchange at issue was initiated by the following statement of defense counsel during closing argument: "Ladies and gentlemen, you know, if you don't think that police officers will subtly shade their testimony in order to make it look better. . . ." The State interrupted with an objection, arguing that there had been no evidence presented to support this accusation. Without ruling on the objection, the trial court told counsel that he could argue reasonable assumptions if there was evidence to support the assumption. Defense counsel then stated that he had "the utmost respect for our officers in blue, but they enforce the rules, they should play by the rules, and when they take an oath, they should take the oath. . . ." Again the State objected, and the trial court sustained the objection. The court questioned counsel as follows: "Counsel, we're getting back in there. If there's anything in this case — you're lambasting officers in general, but what is there in this case that would authorize such a statement to be made as to any officers that appeared here today?" Counsel did not respond to the question, but abandoned this argument.

Even though parties are given great latitude during closing arguments, the allegation that *police officers in general* routinely shade their testimony at trial and violate police rules was not appropriate, as Martinez was unable to show *any evidence* to support this allegation. *See Terrell v. State,* 271 Ga. 783, 787(5), 523 S.E.2d 294 (1999) (inferences during closing argument must be supported by evidence at trial). As to counsel's insinuation that the testifying officers in this case were committing perjury or otherwise "shading" their testimony, the court gave counsel the opportunity to point to trial evidence that supported his allegations, and counsel failed to do so. "The trial court has discretion to determine the range of proper closing argument." After review of the record, we find the trial court did not abuse its discretion in sustaining the State's objection to counsel's arguments.

Although Martinez failed to move for a mistrial or object to the court's comments about the lack of evidence to support his allegations of police misconduct, we must still "consider whether the court violated OCGA §17-8-57 and, if so, whether the violation constituted an obvious error or one that seriously affected the fairness, integrity, and public reputation of this judicial proceeding." *Hunt v. State,* 247 Ga. App. 464, 468(5), 542 S.E.2d 591 (2000).

We find that the trial court's statements were clearly intended to explain his ruling that this line of argument was impermissible. "A trial judge's explanation for a ruling on an objection neither constitutes an expression of opinion nor amounts to a comment on the evidence." We find no error.

Martinez's remaining enumeration is deemed abandoned due to his failure to cite to any authority for it in his brief. *See* Court of Appeals Rule 27(c)(2).

Judgment affirmed.

QUESTIONS ABOUT THE CASE

1   What are the defendant's contentions on appeal?
2   Do appellate courts weigh the evidence or evaluate witness testimony?
3   Should the former firearms investigator have been dismissed from the jury?
4   How does the court rule on the defense allegations about police officers during closing argument?

SKILLS YOU NEED IN THE REAL WORLD

BECOMING A TRIAL PARALEGAL

If one of your career goals is to become a trial paralegal, there are many different sets of skills that you must master. They include the ability to handle:

- Stress, stress, and more stress
- Unreasonable and scared people
- Shifting deadlines
- A certain loss of control
- Unexpected developments

STRESS

Trial work is stressful for everyone involved. Witnesses are scared about testifying. Most people are afraid of speaking in public and witnesses are often afraid of looking silly or stupid on the stand. Attorneys, even those who have done trial work for years, are usually tense and nervous before a trial starts. You will also be under stress, not only because you are dealing directly with these other people, but also because you will be wondering what you may have missed in preparing for the trial and what surprises are in store for you during the trial.

You must learn how to handle stress or it will quite literally kill you. Many people deal with stress by turning to alcohol or other drugs. You must develop healthy alternatives. Exercise is great for stress reduction. With the long hours it takes to prepare a case, your exercise regimen is often the first thing to go. It shouldn't be. Even if you can take only a 20-minute break each day, go for a walk or stretch or do some exercise that you enjoy. In the long term, it will make you better at your job.

UNREASONABLE AND SCARED PEOPLE

Many people respond to anxiety with unreasonable demands and anger. You must be able to recognize that these mood swings are in direct response to the growing anxiety about the upcoming trial.

SHIFTING DEADLINES

If all of this weren't enough, trials are often rescheduled at the last moment. It is common for a trial to be continued until next week or next month. That means that all the preparation must be repeated. You will be the person who must explain this to witnesses and clients.

A CERTAIN LOSS OF CONTROL

Because they are not in control of the schedule or the individual events in the trial, trial paralegals often experience a feeling that they have no control over events. To a certain extent that is true. Rather than wondering why a certain cross-examination is taking twice as long as you thought, concentrate on what you can control: your level of preparation and the way you handle stress.

UNEXPECTED DEVELOPMENTS

Believe it or not, many of the people who are drawn to trial work like the fact that there are always unexpected developments in trials. This element makes trial work very exciting. There is a rush of adrenalin as you readjust to sudden changes in the trial, such as a witness failing to appear on time, or the judge announcing that she will allow the jury to go to the accident scene after all. Trial paralegals must be able to think on their feet. They must be able to adjust their plans, rethink their strategy, and work closely with the trial attorneys to ensure that the trial continues to flow smoothly.

CHAPTER SUMMARY

Trials follow a set pattern. Whether the trial is a civil or a criminal case, there are certain procedures that courts follow. Jury selection is the process of creating a jury that will hear the testimony and consider the evidence in the case. A jury is selected from a larger panel. Members are removed until 12 jurors remain. The attorneys for both sides in the suit can use peremptory challenges to remove panel members. Peremptory challenges can be based on almost any reason. However, U.S. Supreme Court decisions, such as *Batson v. Kentucky*, have limited the use of peremptory challenges in criminal cases, especially when the strikes are used to remove members of a particular race from the jury panel.

After jury selection, the attorneys representing each side are allowed to give an opening statement that outlines the basic facts of the case and gives the jury an overview of the witnesses and evidence that will be offered during the trial. When both sides have given their opening statements, the party who bears the burden of proof must first present witness testimony and evidence to prove the allegations. In a civil case, this means the plaintiff; in a criminal case, this means the government.

Parties prove their cases by calling witnesses to the stand who testify on direct examination and by presenting evidence. When a party is finished questioning its witness, the other side's attorney is allowed to question the witness on cross-examination. The case proceeds from witness to witness until the plaintiff believes that she has proven all the points of her case. At that point, the plaintiff rests and the defendant presents his case. At the conclusion of the trial, the attorneys give a closing argument in which they appeal to the jurors to vote for their clients. The judge then instructs the jury about the procedures to follow in the jury room and the law that applies to the case. After that, the jurors go into the jury room, where they deliberate on the case and reach a verdict. When the jurors reach a decision, it is announced in open court and the judge enters the decision as the judgment. The jurors are then released and the trial is over.

ETHICS: COACHING WITNESSES

Part of the work that goes into preparing for a trial is to meet with witnesses and go over what they will testify to while they are on the stand. Most of these witnesses are cooperative and friendly to your client and there is a natural tendency to want to guide them in their testimony. However, there are strict ethical rules about preparing witnesses. The legal team can discuss the case with witnesses, go over the facts in the case, discuss the questions that will be asked and confirm the answers that will be given, all without violating an ethical rule. The problem arises, however, when a paralegal or attorney begins suggesting answers to witnesses. Telling a witness what to say is considered coaching, is unethical, and, in some cases, illegal. Here are two examples, one that involves coaching and one that does not. Can you spot the difference?

Scenario 1

PARALEGAL: If they ask if you had anything to drink that day, what are you going to say?

WITNESS: That I had a beer in the morning, but hadn't had anything to drink at least five hours before I witnessed the wreck.

Scenario 2

PARALEGAL: If they ask if you had anything to drink that day, say that you hadn't had anything to drink all day and that you were completely sober.

WITNESS: Okay, that's what I'll do.

If you identified Scenario 2 as coaching, you are correct. Coaching is unethical because it puts the legal team's words in the witness's mouth. The witness must testify from his own recollection. If this means that there are slight variations among the witnesses about the same event, the team must deal with it. Paralegals and attorneys cannot tell witnesses what they must say.

CHAPTER REVIEW QUESTIONS

1   What are the various phases of a jury trial? List each.
2   What is the purpose of a calendar call?
3   What is settlement in a civil case?
4   What is a plea bargain?
5   What is the difference between a settlement and a plea bargain?
6   What are some of the reasons given in the chapter that support plea bargaining?
7   How are juries selected?
8   What is the difference between a juror and a panel member?
9   What is a peremptory jury strike?
10 What is the significance of *Batson v. Kentucky* on criminal jury selections?
11 What is a challenge for cause?
12 What is the purpose of an opening statement?
13 In a civil trial, which side gives their opening statement first? Why?
14 What is direct examination?
15 How does cross-examination differ from direct examination?
16 What is the significance of this announcement? "Your Honor, we rest."
17 What is a motion in limine?
18 What is a motion for directed verdict?
19 What considerations does a criminal defendant have in presenting her case that a civil defendant does not have?
20 What is witness coaching?

DISCUSSION QUESTIONS

1   Why do most criminal cases end with a plea bargain?
2   Considering that most criminal cases end with the defendant's plea of guilty, is there something wrong with our system, or something right?
3   Why is the entry of judgment in civil and criminal cases so important?
4   Should criminal juries have input as to the defendant's ultimate sentence? Why or why not?

PERSONALITY QUIZ

Is trial work right for you? Take this personality quiz and see

1   I enjoy high-stress environments.
    0-strongly disagree   5-agree   10-strongly agree

                                                              Points: _____

2   I like to work on several different projects at the same time.
    0-strongly disagree   5-agree   10-strongly agree

Points: _____

3   I find that my mind works more clearly under looming deadlines.
    0-strongly disagree   5-agree   10-strongly agree

Points: _____

4   I can deal effectively with people who are under a great deal of stress.
    0-strongly disagree   5-agree   10-strongly agree

Points: _____

5   I can think on my feet and adjust to rapidly changing situations.
    0-strongly disagree   5-agree   10-strongly agree

Points: _____

Total Points: _____

If you scored between 30-50 points, you have many of the qualities that it takes to succeed in trial work.

If you scored between 20-29 points, you might do well in trial work, but you might not enjoy it very much.

If you scored 19 or lower, trial work is not a good choice for you.

PRACTICAL APPLICATIONS

Contact your local courthouse to find out when the next trial is scheduled. Attend the trial and then answer the following questions:

- What type of trial was this?
- Was it a civil case or criminal case?
- What were the issues involved?
- Who won?
- Were there any unusual or surprising aspects to the trial?
- Did you enjoy the trial process? Why or why not?

WEB SITES

Jury Selection, Superior Courts, California
http://www.glenncourt.ca.gov/court_info/trial_jury.html

Fundamentals of a Jury Trial
http://www.da.saccounty.net/info/fundamentals.htm

Judge or Jury Trial: Which Is Better?
http://www.nolo.com

TERMS AND PHRASES

Calendar call	Jury charge	Peremptory jury
Challenge for cause	Jury strike	strikes
Conflict letter	Motion for directed	Plea bargain
Cross-examination	verdict	Settlement
Direct examination	Motion in limine	Voir dire
Jurors	Panel	

Appeals

Chapter Learning Objectives

After completing this chapter, you should be able to:

- Explain the function of a motion for new trial
- Describe the basis of appellate jurisdiction
- Explain the purpose of the record
- Define certiorari
- List and describe the contents of an appellate brief

INTRODUCTION TO APPEALS

When a party loses at trial, she is almost always entitled to appeal that loss to a higher court. There are some exceptions to this rule, however. The government is not permitted to appeal a finding of not guilty at trial. However, criminal defendants, plaintiffs, and civil defendants may all appeal an unfavorable verdict. In this chapter, we explore the issues associated with appeals.

BRINGING THE APPEAL

A party can bring an appeal from any final determination in a lawsuit. Although we often phrase appeals in terms of a loss at trial, this is not the only finding that justifies an appeal, although it is the most common. If a judge grants a defendant's motion to dismiss the case prior to trial, thus ending the case, the plaintiff may appeal from this judgment. In this chapter, we use a hypothetical case of a party that has lost at trial: Tamika Tenant versus Larry Landlord.

Tamika has lived in an upstairs apartment for several months. There is a single stairway leading to the only door to the residence. Several of the steps are loose and Tamika is afraid that they will break as she walks on them. Tamika has written letters complaining about the condition of the stairway several times. Larry

Landlord has replied to each complaint by saying that the stairway appears to be in good condition and that he has no plans to repair it.

One day, as Tamika was rushing downstairs to go to work, one of the stairs cracked and she fell through, breaking her ankle. She came to our firm to pursue an action against Larry Landlord. We took this case to trial and the judge refused to allow into evidence Tamika's prior correspondence with Larry in which she registered her complaints about the stairway. The judge also refused to allow into evidence Larry's responses that he had inspected the stairway and found it to be in good condition. The jury returned a verdict for the landlord. Tamika would like to appeal her loss.

Motion for new trial
A motion filed at the end of the trial by the losing party requesting another trial

In the last chapter, we examined trials of both civil and criminal cases. We saw that when a jury returns a verdict, the judge enters that finding as the official judgment of the court. When the judge enters the judgment, the losing party has the right to file a **motion for new trial.** A request for a new trial is a prerequisite to bringing an appeal. The losing party must ask the trial judge for a new trial, alleging any impropriety that occurred during the trial. In this case, Tamika's attorney filed a motion requesting a new trial on the basis of the evidence that the judge refused to admit. Of course, the judge who hears this motion is the same judge who just tried the case. It is unlikely that the judge will grant the motion, but this is the procedure. When the judge denies the motion for a new trial, the jurisdiction in the case shifts to the appellate courts.

ISSUE AT A GLANCE   Most appeals begin when a motion for new trial is denied.

APPELLATE JURISDICTION

Jurisdiction is an important term in any court proceeding. When we say that a court has jurisdiction, we mean that the court has the power to hear the issues involved in the case and to render binding decisions. An appellate court does not have jurisdiction in a case until the trial court's jurisdiction has been exhausted. The trial court's jurisdiction ends when a final judgment has been entered and a motion for new trial has been denied. At that point, the losing party can file a **notice of appeal** with the appellate court.

Notice of appeal
Docketing of a case on appeal

A. NOTICE OF APPEAL

We discussed the organization of appellate courts in Chapter 2, but another word about the topic of appeals is appropriate here as well. We have seen that the court system is often represented as a pyramid, with the trial courts at the bottom of the pyramid and the highest appellate court at the top. Most states, and all federal jurisdictions, have trial courts, intermediate appellate courts, and a supreme court.

On the state level, the intermediate appellate court is usually called the state court of **appeals.**

When Tamika's attorney files a notice of appeal in her case, the attorney files it in the state court of appeals. This notice contains the names of the parties, a brief statement outlining why the court has jurisdiction, and a request that the trial court be transferred to the state court of appeals. Although some features of this notice are self-explanatory, some parts need further examination. What, for instance, is the statement of appellate jurisdiction?

Appeal
A request to an appellate court that it reverse or modify a decision made in a lower court

---

A notice of appeal is the first step in bringing an appeal.

ISSUE AT A GLANCE

B. ESTABLISHING APPELLATE JURISDICTION

Tamika's notice of appeal must inform the court why it has **jurisdiction** to hear the case. If Tamika's legal team fails to set out the jurisdictional basis of the claim, the court may refuse to hear the case. Appellate jurisdiction must be established before the court will accept the case. Here is one way to allege appellate jurisdiction:

Jurisdiction
The power of a court to render a decision on issues and to impose that decision on the parties in the case

> Appellant, Tamika Tenant, shows that jurisdiction is proper in this Court because of a final judgment entered on a jury's verdict for the Appellee, dated August 10, 2003. There are no further issues pending in the trial court and jurisdiction is proper in this court according to Rule 10, Appellate Rules of Procedure.

Appellate courts must have jurisdiction before they can rule on cases.

ISSUE AT A GLANCE

You probably noticed that the terms used for the parties on appeal have changed. As we noted in Chapter 2, the party bringing the appeal is referred to as the **appellant,** while the party who won at the trial level is referred to as the **appellee.**

Appellant
The party bringing the current appeal from an adverse ruling in the court below

Appellee
The party who won in the lower court

C. THE RECORD

The notice of appeal not only informs the appellate court that an appeal will be forthcoming, it also requests that the trial court forward the **record** to the appellate court. The record consists of all the evidence and pleadings that have been admitted at trial. This record, along with the transcript of the witness testimony, will be forwarded to the appellate court and stored there while the appeal is pending.

Record
The evidence, pleadings, motions, transcript of the trial, and any other documents relevant to the case

D. DOCKET NUMBER

When a case is filed with the appellate court, it receives a docket number similar to the case file number that was given to the case when the complaint was originally filed in the trial court. This appellate docket number should appear on all documents filed in the appellate court, especially the briefs.

BRIEFS

Once a case has been docketed, the next phase of the appeal is for the parties to file written briefs explaining their positions. Although we discussed briefs in Chapter 2, the focus there was on reading appellate decisions. Here we focus on the process of creating an appellate brief.

A. APPELLANT'S BRIEF

The purpose of the appellant's brief is to explain the party's position and argue a position. This argument is based on an analysis of the facts of the case and the law that applies to those facts. Appellate court briefs have a specified format, often set out in the state's rules of appellate procedure.

 A brief presents one party's argument and reasons why that party should win on appeal.

FIGURE 7-1

Appellate Court Rules Regarding Formatting of Briefs

All briefs and responses shall be typed or printed on letter size (8½" × 11") paper with covers on the front and back, STAPLED on the left-hand side in booklet form. Covers shall be of recyclable paper, heavier than regular stationery, and shall bear the style of the case, the case number, and the name or names of the persons preparing the brief, along with their bar numbers, if attorneys.[8]

[8] Ga. Sup. Ct. Rules, Rule 18

1. CONTENTS OF AN APPELLATE BRIEF

An appellate brief has specific subsections, including:

- Title page
- Statement of facts
- Enumerations of error
- Argument
- Conclusion

a. Title Page

A brief must have a title or cover page, listing the names of the parties, the appellate docket number, and the name of the court.

b. Statement of Facts

After the cover sheet, the legal team prepares a statement of facts that describes the incident that gave rise to the lawsuit and the events of the trial that feature prominently in the appeal. Tamika's brief will contain not only a recitation of the facts surrounding her injury, but also the fact that the judge refused to allow her to present specific evidence at trial. See Figure 7-3 for a sample statement of facts.

IN THE COURT OF APPEALS
FOR THE STATE OF MADISON

TAMIKA TENANT,
Appellant

v.   Court of Appeals Docket No: 03-908

LARRY LANDLORD,
Appellee

FIGURE 7-2

Appellate Brief Title Page

STATEMENT OF FACTS

Appellant Tamika Tenant, hereafter referred to as Appellant, was a tenant of the Appellee Larry Landlord, hereafter referred to as Appellee. Appellant had resided at 1000 Maple Lane, Anytown, Madison, for seven months. (Trial transcript, p. 11.) During that time, appellant complained to appellee about the deteriorating condition of the stairway that led to the appellant's apartment. (Trial transcript, p. 22.) The stairway was the sole means of access to appellant's apartment. (Trial transcript, p. 40.) On October 20, 2002, appellant was descending said stairs when one of them gave way, severely injuring the appellant. (Trial transcript, p. 54.)

FIGURE 7-3

Statement of Facts

 A statement of facts must contain accurate information about the case.

Notice that the statement of facts not only sets out specific incidents, but also cross-references these details to the transcript of the trial. This makes it easier for the appellate justices to double-check facts and locate specific testimony.

c. Enumerations of Error

Once the party has set out the basic facts of the case, the next section of the appellate brief contains the enumerations of error. This is usually a single, bold-faced paragraph that explains why the court's ruling was wrong.

Most appeals have several enumerations of error, but we will limit our hypothetical brief to one. Notice that this enumeration of error not only sets out the basic allegations, but also seeks to phrase the complaint in the appellant's favor. This is one of the skills that brief writers acquire: the ability to set out facts while still shading them in their client's favor. If this enumeration of error were written by the appellee, it would certainly look very different. Consider the example provided in Figure 7-5.

 An enumeration of error is a party's contention that something improper happened during the trial that unfairly prejudiced the party.

FIGURE 7-4

Enumeration of Error

ENUMERATION OF ERROR

I. The trial court committed reversible error when it refused to admit relevant evidence about the appellant's communications with appellee in which appellant complained of the dangerous condition that eventually injured her.

FIGURE 7-5

Appellee's Enumeration of Error

I. The trial did not commit reversible error by failing to admit irrelevant, duplicative, and unduly repetitive information to bolster the appellant's weak factual case.

As you can see from comparing these two enumerations of error, wording has everything to do with how the statement is perceived.

d. Argument

The real meat of an appellate brief is the argument. Everything up to this point has been mere preparation. The argument is where the parties set out the facts and the law that support their contentions. As we saw in Chapter 2, this is where legal research comes to play. We know that courts are bound by the principle of *stare decisis*. This is the principle that dictates that an appellate court must reach a similar decision as a previously decided case that had similar facts and similar issues. In Tamika's case, her legal team has located a series of cases that stand for the following proposition:

> Communications between landlords and tenants are relevant to the issue of a dangerous condition on the leased premises.

Tamika's brief plays up the similarities between the cases that had this ruling and Tamika's case. (Conversely, the brief downplays any cases that go against this position.) The argument continues, often for several pages, explaining the facts and the applicable law and urging that the court adopt the appellant's version.

e. Conclusion

The conclusion is usually a brief statement at the end of the brief that reiterates the party's position and requests specific relief.

2. FILING DEADLINES

Both parties on appeal have strict time limits for preparing and submitting their briefs. Failure to meet the time limits will often result in the appeal being dismissed, or some other sanction.

3. SERVING COPY ON APPELLEE

Once the appellant's brief has been written, copies are served on the appellee and filed in the clerk of appellate court's office. The appellee then has a specific time limit in which to respond to the appellant's brief.

For all of the foregoing reasons, appellant urges the Court to reverse the decision of the trial court and order a new trial.	**FIGURE 7-6** Conclusion

4. APPELLEE'S BRIEF

The appellee's brief will be very similar in appearance to the appellant's brief. It will contain the same elements. The only differences are in the way that the statement of facts and argument are presented. The appellee's statement of facts will tend to emphasize her position in the case and her argument will obviously encourage the appellate court to leave the judgment as it stands.

B. ORAL ARGUMENT

Most appeals before the state court of appeals are conducted in writing. Although there are provisions that allow for oral argument before appellate courts, the vast majority of appellate litigants do not make this request. Oral argument is usually reserved for unusual cases in which the justices feel the need to ask additional questions of the attorneys about the consequences of a ruling.

If oral argument is scheduled for a case on appeal, the attorneys representing the parties will appear before the appellate justices and present an argument. Attorneys cannot present new evidence or new witness testimony. In fact, there are no witness boxes or juries in an appellate court. The attorneys stand at podiums and address the justices, arguing the facts of their case and the applicable law. The justices may interrupt the attorneys at any time during the argument. There are also strict rules about how long the argument can take. Given the restrictions of oral argument, most attorneys waive it in favor of their written briefs.

ISSUE AT A GLANCE **Oral argument of an appeal is rare.**

THE POWERS OF THE APPELLATE COURTS

We have said that the court system is organized as a pyramid, with the trial courts at the bottom and the appellate courts at the top, but this oversimplifies the organization and the powers of these courts. Although appellate courts are considered to be higher courts, in many ways their powers are more limited than trial courts. In fact, appellate courts have very limited options in what they can do with a case on appeal. The options for appellate courts are limited to the following:

- Affirming a decision
- Reversing a decision
- Modifying a decision
- Remanding a case for further proceedings

Appellate courts have strict limitations on the decisions they can make in cases on appeal.

ISSUE AT A GLANCE

A. AFFIRMING A DECISION

Returning to our hypothetical case of Tamika Tenant v. Larry Landlord, we saw that Tamika lost in the trial court. She has now appealed her case to the state court of appeals. If that court agrees with the decision in the lower court, it will issue an order affirming the decision. When a higher court **affirms** a lower court decision, it leaves the decision intact and does not change it. An order affirming the lower court ruling would be a loss for Tamika.

Affirm
The appellate court agrees with the verdict, or some ruling, entered in the lower court and votes to keep that decision in place

B. REVERSING A DECISION

When a higher court **reverses** a lower court ruling, it issues an order disagreeing with that court's decision and making the appellant the winner in the case.

Reverse
To reverse a decision is to set it aside; an appellate court disagrees with the verdict, or some ruling, in the lower court, and overturns that decision

C. MODIFYING A DECISION

Appellate courts are also authorized to create a hybrid decision that partly affirms and partly reverses a lower court decision. This is common when there are numerous issues in the appeal. However, with only one issue in Tamika's case, it is unlikely that the court would modify a lower court decision.

D. REMANDING A CASE

If an appellate court requires additional information, such as witness testimony or evidence, the only option for the court is to return the case to the trial court for additional hearings. Appellate courts are not equipped to hear new testimony. They are not trial courts and no one ever testifies before these courts. When an appellate court remands a case, they return it to the trial court with directions that the court have a hearing on specific issues.

A **remand** in Tamika's case is a distinct possibility. Before the appellate court can rule about Tamika's letters and communications with Larry Landlord, the court must know what they contain. Because no new evidence is ever presented in an appellate court, the only option left is to return the case to the trial court for additional hearings and then to have the case resubmitted to the appellate court.

Remand
The appellate court requires additional information or an evidentiary hearing; it cannot conduct such a hearing itself, so it sends the case back to the trial court for the hearing, and then considers the appeal based on that hearing

THE COURT OF APPEALS RULING IN THE CASE OF TAMIKA TENANT v. LARRY LANDLORD

When Tamika takes her case to the state court of appeals, it remands the case to the trial court and then considers the appeal again. This time it enters an order reversing the trial court's decision to exclude the evidence and ordering a new trial. Larry Landlord vows to appeal the case to the state supreme court.

ORGANIZATION OF THE APPELLATE COURT SYSTEM

On the state level, the court occupying the top position of the court system pyramid is usually called the state supreme court. This court has the final say on all issues involving the interpretation of state law and cases. Almost all states have three levels to the court system: the trial court at the bottom, the state court of appeals in the middle, and the state supreme court at the top. We have discussed the function and limitations of the court of appeals, and we now focus on the role played by the state supreme court.

A. THE STATE SUPREME COURT

When Larry Landlord loses his case in the state court of appeals, he tells his attorney to take the case to the state supreme court. Larry's attorney explains that although this court can overrule a decision by any court in the state, bringing an appeal to this court isn't as simple as bringing an appeal before the state court of appeals. First there is the issue of certiorari.

B. CERTIORARI

Certiorari (Cert)
(Latin) "To make sure." The court's authority to decide which cases it will hear on appeal. A denial of certiorari means that the court has refused to hear the appeal

State supreme courts have the right to decide which cases they will hear. All litigants must pass an administrative hurdle before the supreme court will consider the case. This hurdle is **certiorari,** or cert. State supreme courts, like the U.S. Supreme Court, refuse to hear the vast majority of cases that apply to them for a hearing. Supreme courts have different standards than courts of appeal. Before a supreme court will agree to consider an appeal, the parties must show that the case has statewide significance or involves an interpretation of the state constitution. Simply showing that the case is important to the individual parties is not enough. The parties make their case for statewide significance in their petition for certiorari.

Appellant Larry Landlord shows that the   code and the significance that unduly
issues involved in this appeal involve an   duplicative written communications
interpretation of the State's evidentiary   have in bolstering oral testimony at trial.

FIGURE 7-7

Excerpt from Larry Landlord's
Petition for Cert

1. PETITION FOR CERT

Bringing an appeal in the state court of appeals was a relatively straightforward affair. The parties filed a notice of appeal, received a docket number, and the trial record was forwarded to the court. However, before the parties can bring their appeal to the state supreme court, they must file a petition for cert. This petition outlines the importance of the case and the impact that a ruling will have on case law interpretation or a provision of the state constitution.

Notice that in Larry Landlord's petition for cert. in Figure 7-7 the terms for the parties have changed. Larry Landlord is now the appellant — he is the person requesting court intervention from the court of appeals ruling. That means that Tamika Tenant is the appellee in the state supreme court.

Tamika Tenant will file a motion with the supreme court requesting that the court deny the petition for cert. She would obviously be happy to leave the situation exactly as the court of appeals decided it.

Certiorari is almost universally referred to as "cert," not only because the word itself is difficult to pronounce, but also because appellate courts commonly abbreviate the term that way in reporting decisions, as in "petition for cert. denied."

2. GRANTING CERT

When the state supreme court grants cert, it means that the court has agreed to hear the case. The appeal will now proceed in an almost identical fashion as the procedure followed in the state court of appeals. The parties will submit written briefs that include a statement of facts, an argument, and all the other features that we saw in our previous discussion of appellate briefs. Simply because a party has been granted cert does not mean that she will ultimately win the appeal. Granting cert simply authorizes the continuation of the appeal. The Court is free to rule any way that it sees fit.

You will notice when reading documents that refer to the state supreme court, the "c" in court is always capitalized. This is a tradition that sets this court apart from other courts in the state.

3. DENYING CERT

When the state supreme court denies cert, it means that the Court has refused to hear the appeal. At this point, the appellate process is essentially over. The appellant can file a motion for rehearing that asks the Court to reconsider its ruling, but a court rarely overturns its own decision. At this point, the only option left to a litigant is to file a petition for cert with the U.S. Supreme Court, discussed in the next section.

What effect does the state supreme court's denial of cert have on Tamika's case? It means that the state court of appeals ruling — that the case is reversed and a new trial is ordered — now stands as the final decision in the case. Tamika will have

FIGURE 7-8

The State Supreme Court's
Ruling in Tamika Tenant v.
Larry Landlord

Appellant Larry Landlord's Petition for Cert is denied.

a new trial and her letters to the landlord will be permitted as evidence in this new trial.

4. CRIMINAL APPEALS

So far, we have not mentioned any differences between civil appeals and criminal appeals. The reason is that for almost all purposes, there are no differences in the way that a civil case and a criminal case go up on appeal. However, there is one important difference that deals with petitions for cert.

a. Cert Not Required in Death Penalty Cases

When a criminal case involves the imposition of the death penalty, the state supreme court (and the U.S. Supreme Court) cannot refuse to hear the case. There is no cert requirement in such cases. Death penalty cases can always be heard before these courts.

VII THE UNITED STATES SUPREME COURT

A. ORGANIZATION OF THE FEDERAL APPELLATE SYSTEM

In the 2000 presidential election, the U.S. Supreme Court declared George W. Bush as President of the United States after hearing an appeal about contested votes in certain states.

Our discussion of appeals has so far centered on the state appellate system. The federal appellate system is organized in almost exactly the same way. However, instead of covering a single state, the federal system covers the entire nation. Because of the size of the United States, the country has been divided up into different circuits, with one circuit encompassing several states. Appeals from federal trial courts (called Federal District Court) are brought to the Federal Circuit Court of Appeals that has jurisdiction over those states. These courts are situated in a major city in one of the states inside that federal circuit.

The federal court system is also arranged as a pyramid, with federal trial courts at the bottom, Federal Circuit Courts of Appeal in the middle, and the U.S. Supreme Court at the top.

Like a state supreme court, the U.S. Supreme Court has the final say about interpretations of the U.S. Constitution, case law, or statutes. In the United States, there is no court higher than the U.S. Supreme Court.

FIGURE 7-9

Petitioner's request for grant of certiorari to the United States Supreme Court is hereby denied.

Larry Landlord's Petition for Cert to the United States Supreme Court

B. THE U.S. SUPREME COURT IS FINAL AUTHORITY FOR STATE COURTS

Along with its role as the final arbiter of federal questions, the U.S. Supreme Court has an additional responsibility: It is the court of last resort for all state law questions as well. When a party loses in a state supreme court, such as when Larry Landlord's petition for cert was denied, the only remaining option is to file a petition for cert with the U.S. Supreme Court. State court litigants are not required to start at the bottom of the federal court system and work up. Instead, they go directly from the state supreme court to the U.S. Supreme Court. However, in cases in which a state supreme court has denied cert because a case lacks sufficient importance, it is highly unlikely that the U.S. Supreme Court would grant cert.

Careers in the Law

▶ Cyndie Callaway, Former Appellate Law Clerk

 hen I worked in the North Carolina Court of Appeals, we often saw attorneys who used what we called the "shot gun" approach to appeals. They would go through the trial transcript and write up an enumeration of error on any questionable decision by the trial judge, no matter what it was. The problem with this approach is that it makes your entire brief look like it has very little legal validity. For instance, in most routine appeals, the party would allege 25-50 errors. The majority of them would have absolutely no merit, but the appellate court would have to address each one. One of the biggest problems is that they would allege grounds for things that they hadn't objected to at trial. On appeal, the rule is simple: You object or you've waived it.

Another problem is that some parties on appeal didn't realize that the appellate courts don't consider questions of fact. As far as the court is concerned, the facts were established at trial. The appellate courts consider the law and error. They don't decide factual questions.

In order to practice good appellate law, you have to know the court's rules. You should know about filing deadlines, formatting, and even their paper requirements. You should also know the basic ground rules for writing any appellate brief. One of the best things that a paralegal can do is work from an appellate brief bank. If you don't have one, you should create one.

Profiling a Paralegal

▶ Sarah Roman

I started out working as a paralegal, making appointments for attorneys and assisting on preparing intake information for new clients. Now I'm a case manager and I handle all aspects of client contact. I do all the typing of complaints, take the forms to the courthouse, file them, make arrangements for civil summonses, and make sure that all of the files are up to date. I also keep track of all court dates and go through our files to make sure that they are ready for the attorney when he takes them to court.

Whenever you deal with any kind of case, the number one rule is to pay attention to filing deadlines. They all have different deadlines and you might lose your case if you miss one.

The thing that surprised me the most about law is how much your clients rely on you. Some of them are dealing with heart wrenching issues and they just need someone to talk to. They call you up for help and it's wonderful when you can give it to them. I never realized how busy I would be. There's so much more to the job than just typing or filing. You're talking with clients, keeping up with deadlines, staying organized. Organization is the key. I enjoy it; there's never a dull moment.

HENDERSON v. DEPARTMENT OF PUBLIC SAFETY AND CORRECTIONS
901 F.2d 1288 (C.A.5 (La.) 1990)

E. GRADY JOLLY, Circuit Judge:

Houston T. Penn is before this court for the second time, complaining that the district court's imposition of sanctions against him without notice and an opportunity to be heard violates due process rights guaranteed to him by the fourteenth amendment, and that the district court abused its discretion in finding him in violation of Rule 11 and in imposing the sanctions. For the reasons discussed below, we affirm.

I

Penn, who is an Assistant Attorney General employed by the Louisiana Department of Justice, represented the defendants, the Louisiana Department of Public Safety and Corrections, C. Paul Phelps (former Secretary of the Department), and D.R. Guillory (former Warden of Wade Correctional Center) in a lawsuit filed by Assistant Warden Robert Henderson, an employee of the Louisiana Department of Public Safety and Corrections. After a trial on the merits, the district court entered judgment for the defendants, Mr. Penn's clients, and no appeal was taken. The judgment on the merits is final and the merits are not relevant to the issue presently before this court.

What is relevant is what occurred before the trial of the case. On October 27, 1988, approximately one month prior to the scheduled trial, Penn filed a motion for change of venue and a motion in limine or, alternatively, motion for summary judgment asserting several grounds for relief. Shortly thereafter, the district court received a letter from plaintiff's counsel advising that he had had difficulty in contacting Penn to prepare the pretrial order. On October 28, 1988, the district court warned counsel that:

> This court expects all parties to work amicably toward the completion of an appropriate pretrial order which will assist the ultimate resolution of the case. The failure of any party to proceed in good faith or obey this court's standing instructions will result in sanctions under Fed. R. Civ. P. 16(f).

On November 1, 1988, Penn filed a motion for a continuance, contending that counsel for the plaintiff had failed to provide defense counsel with a copy of his witness and exhibit lists in a timely manner. The lists were ultimately received by Penn prior to the deadline for filing the pretrial order. On November 2, 1988, the magistrate denied the motion for continuance and noted several deficiencies in Penn's proposed insert to the pretrial order. In conclusion, the magistrate stated: "Counsel are warned that any dilatory tactics will result in sanctions."

On November 2, 1988, Penn filed a "Motion to Recusal [sic] of the Trial Judge." According to the memorandum in support of the motion, the defendants sought recusal pursuant to 28 U.S.C. §455. The motion asserted two reasons for recusal: (1) "opposing counsel related that the judge presiding over this case (Judge Stagg) has known the opposing counsel since he was a kid and that the judge presiding over this case was friends [sic] of opposing counsel and opposing counsel's father"; and that (2) the judge had already ruled adversely upon the credibility of one of the defendants in a prior matter.

On November 8, 1988, the district court denied the motion for recusal and the motion for change of venue. After addressing those motions, the court stated:

> The motion for recusal and for change of venue have not been well founded, either in fact or law. Apparently, counsel for defendants has used these motions, as well as the motion for a continuance, for dilatory purposes. Counsel for defendants is warned that this court will scrutinize future motions for compliance with Fed. R. Civ. P. 11.

Penn was undeterred. On November 17, 1988, Penn filed a motion for reconsideration of the district court's order denying the motion for recusal, which added nothing new to his previous motion. Attached to the motion was an affidavit by Penn attesting that the contents of the motion to recuse and the motion for reconsideration were true and accurate to the best of his knowledge and belief. The district court construed the motion for reconsideration as a new motion for disqualification under 28 U.S.C. §144. The court noted that, under §144, actual bias must be sufficiently alleged. After observing that Penn had failed to conduct a reasonable inquiry into the law, and that Penn either had not read the relevant cases or, having read them, had chosen to ignore their authority, the court ruled that the affidavit filed by Penn was legally insufficient under §144.

Following the completion of the trial, the court's memorandum ruling finding a violation of Rule 11 and imposing sanctions on Penn was unsealed. Referring specifically to the motion for change of venue, motion for summary judgment, motion for continuance, motion for recusal, and motion for reconsideration filed by Penn, and noting that its three warnings had been ignored by Penn, the court found that those filings had been made by Penn "for the dual purpose of trying to delay the proceedings and harass the opposing party. In addition, most of the recent filings have not been submitted after a reasonable inquiry into the factual basis and law."

With respect to the motion for reconsideration, the court stated:

> [T]he court is convinced that these motions, as well as the presently pending motion for reconsideration, were designed solely for dilatory purposes. The current motion asserting an argument under 28 U.S.C. §144 fails to cite a single authority in support of the relief requested. Even the most minimal inquiry into the law governing motions under §§144 and 455 would have revealed that the asserted bias or impartiality must result from an extrajudicial source. Moreover, even a reading of the clear language of §144 demonstrates that it applies to "parties" instead of counsel. . . . Mr. Penn's allegations as to the basis for the alleged impartiality were not made on personal knowledge, but rather hearsay. Mr. Penn conducted no further inquiry into the factual basis. Had such an inquiry been conducted, Mr. Penn would have discovered the lack of factual merit.

The true reason for the filing of these motions became apparent at the pretrial conference. It was at that time that Mr. Penn's state of unpreparedness for trial became evident. This court is left with no other conclusion but that the recent filings of Mr. Penn, including the current motion for reconsideration, were designed solely to delay the November 28 trial date.

The court concluded that Penn had violated all three of the affirmative duties placed upon him by Rule 11, and imposed sanctions of $250 upon Penn, individually. The court further ordered Penn to read and brief the facts and law of the cases cited in its rulings on Penn's time during nights and holidays or days off and to deliver a "letter-perfect brief" to the judge's chambers by February 3, 1989.

Penn appealed to this court, assigning two bases of error: (1) lack of notice and an opportunity to be heard before sanctions were imposed resulting in violation of the due process rights guaranteed to him by the Fourteenth Amendment to the United States Constitution; and (2) an abuse of discretion by the district court in finding him in violation of Rule 11 and in imposing the sanctions. Because Penn did not argue to the district court either of the issues presented for review, this court remanded the case to the district court so that the district court could consider the issues.

In this case, the record speaks for itself. Mr. Penn tried every avenue possible to delay resolution of this matter. The poorly-written briefs were submitted without making a reasonable investigation into the facts and law. This court had no discretion to ignore such activities. Rule 11 sanctions were required. . . . The sanctions imposed were carefully tailored to Mr. Penn's situation. . . .

In sum, this court's decision to impose sanctions was not made lightly. Rather, sanctions were imposed only after reviewing repeated filings by Mr. Penn in violation of Rule 11.

The due process clause is not mentioned in either the motion to reconsider or in the memorandum filed by Penn in the district court after remand from this court, but Penn did make the following statements in the memorandum:

> This Motion was also denied by this (District) Court without a hearing and in the same ruling this Court without prior specific notice of the charges and without giving Assistant Attorney General Penn an opportunity to respond or to defend himself found that Assistant Attorney General Penn violated Rule 11 . . . and imposed sanctions against him personally. . . .

The Rule 11 action was brought through the District Court's own initiative and Assistant Attorney General Penn was not given notice of the specific charges and was not afforded any opportunity to respond or defend himself prior to the finding of a Rule 11 violation and imposition of sanctions.

The statements quoted above are inadequate and inept attempts to raise properly a due process argument. Although it is true that this court ordinarily will not consider issues not properly before the trial court, we will do so in this case for two reasons: (1) the issue can be resolved as a matter of law; and (2) a refusal to consider the issue would not advance the interests of justice or judicial economy.

Rule 11 provides that, "[i]f a pleading, motion, or other paper is signed in violation of this rule, the court, upon motion or upon its own initiative, shall impose upon the person who signed it, a represented party, or both, an appropriate sanction. . . .". Penn contends that, "[a]s a minimal [sic], due process requirements [sic] the procedure used to find a Rule 11 violation and to impose sanctions should include at least adequate and timely notice of the specific charges and opportunity to address the charges in writing or orally before a relatively neutral arbitrator, who would thereafter render written reasons for the judgment." Penn complains that the district judge cannot be considered a "neutral arbitrator," and that he had no opportunity to present evidence on any factual issues. According to Penn, "fundamental fairness" requires that, when a trial judge invokes Rule 11 sanctions on its own initiative, the trial judge must inform the attorney "in writing of the particular conduct which the Trial Judge suspects to be in violation of Rule 11."

In addition to the imputed notice Rule 11 itself imparts, the district court and the magistrate warned Penn three times that sanctions would be imposed if his dilatory tactics continued. Furthermore, when the court denied Penn's first motion for recusal, it informed him that it considered his arguments to be without basis in fact or law. Penn was specifically given notice in the November 8, 1988 order that future motions may result in Rule 11 sanctions; yet Penn persisted in flogging the same mule. We therefore conclude that Penn had ample notice of the possible imposition of Rule 11 sanctions and of the reasons for their imposition.

The district court's memorandum ruling of November 22, 1988, which imposed the sanctions at issue, thoroughly sets forth its reasons for the sanctions. Penn has had an ample opportunity to respond and to attempt to justify his actions. Following remand from this court, he once again filed his motion for reconsideration of sanctions. Penn was advised by the court that it would decide the matter based upon the briefs. Penn did not object, did not request a hearing, and did not request leave to supplement the brief that he had already filed. "Rule 11 does not require that a hearing separate from trial or other pretrial hearings be held on Rule 11 charges before sanctions can be imposed. . . ." An evidentiary hearing was unnecessary here. There are no issues of fact, only conclusions to be drawn from undisputed facts. The district judge's participation in the proceedings and the record itself provided the judge with sufficient knowledge of the relevant facts with respect to Penn's dilatory tactics. Penn acknowledged as much, in his motion for reconsideration of sanctions filed in the district court, and in his brief filed in this court:

[A] careful review of the case record in this matter reveals that there was no actual (or attempted) delay in the adjudication [sic] of this case that can be contributed [sic] directly to defendants' counsel. The record reflects both a clear and concise factual basic [sic] for counsel's various motions and requests as well as the legal (procedural and substantive) basis which support defendants' concerns and contentions.

It is apparent from the record itself that Penn's motion for recusal and the motion for reconsideration of the denial of that motion have no basis in law and that Penn failed to conduct even the minimum amount of research that would have been necessary for him to be aware of that fact.

We therefore conclude that the procedures used by the district court for finding that Penn violated Rule 11 and for imposition of sanctions do not offend due process.

For the foregoing reasons, the district court's order denying Penn's request to vacate its order imposing Rule 11 sanctions is *Affirmed*.

QUESTIONS ABOUT THE CASE

1 Who did Houston represent in the case at the center of this appeal?
2 What is a motion for recusal?
3 For what purpose did the trial court consider the motions filed by Houston?
4 Did Houston conduct adequate legal research before filing his motions?
5 What was the court's view of Houston's allegations concerning the sanctions imposed on him?

SKILLS YOU NEED IN THE REAL WORLD

CREATING A BRIEF BANK

If your firm does not already have a brief bank, consider creating one. A brief bank is an archive of the appellate briefs filed in previous cases that can be quickly and easily retrieved. There are many issues in appeals that recur over and over again. Why reinvent the wheel each time, when you can rely on previous research and writing to speed up the process of creating a new brief? In the old days, paralegals would make hard copies of appellate briefs and then file them according to subject, or put appellate subjects on index cards to help retrieve the brief later. These days, most paralegals keep brief banks on a computer. After all, the briefs are almost always created using a word processing program such as Word or WordPerfect. Why not use this same system to create a brief bank?

Each argument section of old briefs can be pulled and indexed separately. The subjects can be saved on the computer hard drive (and backed up on a floppy disk or CD) under headings such as:

- Appeal — Waiver of issue by failure to object at trial
- Appeal — Failure to conform to appellate rules
- Cert — Petition for cert to state supreme court
- Cert — Petition for cert to U.S. Supreme Court
- Evidence — Hearsay exceptions
- Evidence — Demonstrative
- Witnesses — Unavailable for trial
- Witnesses — Expert witness in auto reconstruction
- Witnesses — Expert witness in medical standard of care

No matter how you do it, creating a brief bank can save you hours of work on future briefs. Just remember that no matter how well you researched the previous brief, you should always make sure that there are no recent cases that affect the brief you're working on.

CHAPTER SUMMARY

When a party loses at trial, she has the right to appeal the decision to an appellate court. The appeals process begins when the losing party files a motion for new trial. If that motion is denied, the party then has the right to file a notice of appeal and have the case transferred to the jurisdiction of the appellate court. In most states, and on the federal level, the first level of appellate court is called the court of appeals. Parties file appellate briefs to contest the decision in the trial court and to argue their positions on appeal. Appellate briefs have a standard format, with specific subsections appearing in all such briefs. These subsections include a statement of facts, argument, and enumerations of error.

Appellate courts are limited in the actions that they can take in an appeal. When an appellate court affirms the lower court's decision, it agrees with that court's decision and allows it to stand. However, when a court reverses a decision, it disagrees with the lower court's decision. Appellate courts can also modify lower court decisions or send the case back to the trial court for additional hearings in a remand.

Appellate courts form a hierarchy, with the most powerful court at the top and the trial courts at the bottom. On the state level, the highest court is usually called the state supreme court and it has the final say about interpretations of state law. The U.S. Supreme Court is the highest court in the United States. It is the court of last resort for all types of appeals.

ETHICS: CASES THAT GO AGAINST YOUR CLIENT

There is a natural tendency among researchers to downplay or even ignore adverse case law. This situation can arise in several contexts, but the most common is when you are given a research assignment such as the following:

Please locate some case law that supports our client's action in seizing personal property from a tenant who has not yet been evicted, but who will be shortly.

As you research the case law on this issue, you locate several cases directly on point, but that go against your client's position. However, you also locate a few cases in which the language is ambiguous enough to be interpreted to support the client's position. You write down these cases and ignore the others. Later, when the attorney is arguing before the court, the judge asks if there are adverse cases and the attorney says no. Has an ethical violation occurred?

The answer could easily be yes. Many courts have rules that specifically require attorneys to notify the court about cases that go against their position. The rule stems from a philosophy that an attorney should always advocate for the client, but not to the point of misstating the law.

When researching case law, you should always inform the attorney and the court about any adverse cases. In the long run it is not only the ethical thing to do, but also the most practical. If there are numerous cases going against your client's actions, perhaps it would be better to change tactics in the case rather than use an approach the court is sure to deny.

CHAPTER REVIEW QUESTIONS

1 What is a motion for new trial?
2 Explain the basis of appellate jurisdiction.
3 What is a notice of appeal?
4 What is an appeal?
5 What is the appellate "record?"
6 What is a brief ?
7 List the basic components of an appellate brief.
8 What is the purpose of a statement of facts in an appellate brief?
9 What is an enumeration of error?
10 What is oral argument?
11 Explain the limited powers of appellate courts.
12 What is the difference between affirming and reversing an appeal?
13 What is the purpose of a remand?
14 Explain the organization of state courts.
15 What is certiorari?
16 What is the basis for granting or denying certiorari?
17 What type of case does not have certiorari requirements?

18 What is the name of the highest court in the United States?
19 What is the purpose of federal circuits?
20 What is a brief bank?

DISCUSSION QUESTIONS

1 If you were going to organize a system for appealing cases, which aspects of the current system would you keep and which aspects would you eliminate? Explain your answer.
2 What are some reasons for and against certiorari?
3 Are there some types of cases in which appeals should not be allowed? Explain your answer.

PERSONALITY QUIZ

Is appellate law right for you? Take this personality quiz and see.

1 I enjoy researching the law.
   0-strongly disagree   5-agree   10-strongly agree

   Points: _____

2 I always take the time to get the details right.
   0-strongly disagree   5-agree   10-strongly agree

   Points: _____

3 I can meet deadlines.
   0-strongly disagree   5-agree   10-strongly agree

   Points: _____

4 I am very organized.
   0-strongly disagree   5-agree   10-strongly agree

   Points: _____

5 I have a good memory for case law.
   0-strongly disagree   5-agree   10-strongly agree

   Points: _____
   Total Points: _____

If you scored between 30-50 points, you have many of the qualities that it takes to do well in researching and helping to write appellate briefs.

If you scored between 20-29 points, you might do well in appellate law, but you might do better in some other area.

If you scored 19 or lower, appellate law is not a good choice for you.

PRACTICAL APPLICATIONS

Locate the web site for your state supreme court (if it goes by that name). What types of resources are available? Does the court publish any of its opinions on the web? Can litigants file their briefs electronically? Does the court provide a link for appellate rules?

WEB SITES

Maryland Appellate Court Opinions
http://www.courts.state.md.us/opinions.html

Opinions of the New Jersey Courts
http://lawlibrary.rutgers.edu/search.shtml

MacMillan Law Library (Emory Law School) Federal Courts Finder
http://www.law.emory.edu/FEDCTS

First Court of Appeals–Texas
http://www.1stcoa.courts.state.tx.us

Illinois Supreme Court Opinions
http://www.state.il.us/court/OPINIONS/recent_supreme.asp

Arizona Court of Appeals
http://www.cofad1.state.az.us

TERMS AND PHRASES

Affirm	Certiorari	Record
Appeal	Jurisdiction	Remand
Appellant	Motion for new trial	Reverse
Appellee	Notice of appeal	

Specific Types
of Law

Personal Injury Law (Torts)

Chapter Learning Objectives

After completing this chapter, you should be able to:

- Explain the difference between intentional torts and negligence torts
- Explain the differences between the torts of assault and battery
- List and explain the four elements of a negligence suit
- Explain the legal basis for product liability suits
- Describe the elements of both legal and medical malpractice

 INTRODUCTION TO TORT LAW

In Chapter 4, we outlined the general phases of a civil case. In this chapter, and in subsequent chapters, we address specific areas of law. Each of these chapters introduces you to a specialized area of law, but is not intended to be an exhaustive treatment of the topic. Many of the topics discussed in future chapters may form the basis of entire courses in your paralegal education. In this chapter, we focus on personal injury law, including intentional torts, negligence, and malpractice cases.

The term **tort** has been used for centuries to refer to a civil action that one person has against another for a personal injury. Because the term is not descriptive of this area of the law, many commentators have adopted the phrase *personal injury* or *civil injury* to describe it.

When we discuss the subject of tort law, we often encounter confusing terminology. For instance, in the area of intentional torts, we find references to the torts of assault and battery. These are also terms used in criminal law. There is a simple reason why many of the tort terms are also criminal law terms: They originate from the same branch of the law. Several hundred years ago, the courts did not make a

Tort
A personal injury, often resulting from a breach of duty, that gives the injured party a cause of action

distinction between a crime that injured a person and a civil wrong that injured a person. An injury was an injury. Only in the last two centuries have criminal law and tort law become two separate areas of law.

 The term *tort* refers to any case involving a physical, financial, or emotional injury. Many commentators have gradually phased out this term, replacing it with the more general term *civil injury.*

A. THE MANY DIFFERENT TYPES OF TORTS

Tort law is an area rich in subspecialties and full of interesting branches: intentional torts, negligence, medical malpractice, and many others. We examine each of these areas in this chapter.

 ## INTENTIONAL TORTS

We mentioned earlier that some torts have a great deal in common with crimes. The area that has the closest relationship to criminal law is the topic of intentional torts.

An intentional tort is a civil action brought by one person against another for an injury. As the name suggests, the defendant is being sued for an intentional action. Consider the following scenario:

Juan and Al have hated each other for a very long time. One evening, while they are both at a local bar, Juan calls Al a name. Al rushes toward Juan and swings his fist at Juan's face. Al misses. Juan punches Al and Al falls over unconscious. Juan takes another swing at Al after Al passes out, but this time Juan misses. Several people subdue Juan before he can try again.

When Al recovers, he decides to sue Juan for the injuries he sustained in the fight.

The first question we must answer in any scenario is: What type of case is this? Because both men were acting intentionally, we know that if this is a civil action at all, it must be an intentional tort. (Later, we discuss another area of tort law, negligence actions, that do not involve intentional actions.)

If you think this case sounds like it might be a crime as well as a civil action, you're right. It is fairly common for intentional tort cases to be both civil actions and criminal actions at the same time. Despite the close affinity between some torts and crimes, it is important to keep in mind the important distinctions between these two areas of law. A crime is an infraction of society's law. Prosecutors charge people with crimes in the name of the government. The possible punishment includes jail time and fines. Torts, on the other hand, are injuries to a specific individual. Plaintiffs bring suit against defendants in their own names. The possible

	Intentional Torts	Crimes
Name of legal action	Particular torts often have same name as crime	
Parties	Individual versus individual	State (government) versus individual
Procedural rules	Civil rules	Criminal rules
Burden of proof	Preponderance of evidence	Beyond a reasonable doubt
Pleadings	Complaint and answer	Indictment
Outcome	Monetary judgment	Fines, jail, restitution

FIGURE 8-1

Similarities and Differences Between Intentional Torts and Crimes

punishment is monetary loss (damages). A winning plaintiff might be awarded a monetary judgment against a defendant, but the defendant will not be put in jail and will not be fined. We discuss criminal law in greater detail in Chapter 10. See Figure 8-1 for a breakdown of the important differences between intentional torts and crimes.

When a plaintiff brings a suit against a defendant for a tort, it is critical to categorize the type of tort involved. Different torts have different rules and different bases of proof. A claim that the defendant intentionally injured the plaintiff is very different than a claim that the defendant injured the plaintiff through negligence. These claims involve different elements of proof, different types of testimony, and finally, a different consideration by the jury.

In the scenario involving Juan and Al, we have several possible intentional torts. We discuss the two most common, assault and battery, below and then see if either one applies to this factual situation.

The first question that must be answered in any civil injury is whether the defendant's actions were intentional or caused by negligence.

 ISSUE AT A GLANCE

A. THE REQUIREMENT OF INTENTIONAL ACTIONS

One aspect of intentional torts that makes them so different from every other type of tort action is the allegation that the defendant acted with intent. People often misunderstand the term *intent*. Under the law, intent does not mean the intent to do a specific harm. For instance, a child on a playground might defend his action of striking a classmate by saying, "I didn't mean to hurt you." This is not the legal standard for intent. Instead, the law asks, "Did the defendant act voluntarily?" In almost all situations involving intentional torts, the inquiry does not focus on the end product. Courts do not ask, for example, did the defendant intend to commit the tort of battery? Instead, courts simply require that the plaintiff prove that the defendant acted knowingly and voluntarily.

Under this definition of intent, if a person acts involuntarily, is that a defense to an intentional tort? Absolutely. If the defendant loses consciousness and slips from his chair, and in so doing injures the plaintiff, the defendant has the best possible defense to a lawsuit for battery: He did not act intentionally.

Let's examine some specific types of intentional torts.

B. ASSAULT

Assault
The defendant causes the plaintiff to have fear or apprehension of a harmful/offensive contact

The intentional tort of **assault** involves the following elements:

1   The defendant, acting intentionally
2   Caused the plaintiff to experience fear or apprehension of a
3   Harmful or offensive contact

When a person is assaulted, at least as that term is defined under the law, no physical contact occurs. People use the term *assault* in a wide variety of contexts, but the legal definition is simply fear or apprehension of contact, not the contact itself.

Is there an assault in the case involving Juan and Al? When Al rushed toward Juan and swung his fist (and missed), he committed an assault. Attempting to strike a person is assault. Assault requires that the victim be aware of the attempt to strike. In our scenario, when Al slumped to the floor unconscious, Juan attempted to strike Al a second time and missed. Because assault requires fear or apprehension on the part of the victim, Juan did not assault Al. However, he did batter him.

C. BATTERY

Assault and battery are often mentioned in the same context, because they involve nearly identical elements and because they often occur together. However, where as assault involves the fear or apprehension of a harmful contact (but no actual contact), **battery** involves the actual touching.

Battery
The defendant causes harmful or offensive contact to the plaintiff

The elements of battery consist of:

1   The defendant, acting intentionally
2   Caused the plaintiff to experience
3   Harmful or offensive contact

In examining the scenario, we have a clear case of battery against Juan. He did, after all, cause Al to experience harmful or offensive contact. If Juan had actually struck Al after Al had become unconscious, he would have committed a second battery. While reviewing this scenario, you may have said to yourself, "It seems that Juan was acting in self defense." Under these facts, this is probably right. A defense, such as self defense, doesn't affect the analysis of the initial action. Self defense may excuse the battery, but does not alter the fact that a battery occurred.

D. FALSE IMPRISONMENT

Another common intentional tort is false imprisonment. When a plaintiff brings a suit for false imprisonment, he is saying that he was intentionally, unlawfully restrained against his will by the use of force or the threat of force.

The elements of false imprisonment consist of:

1   The defendant, acting intentionally
2   Without lawful basis
3   Restrained the plaintiff
4   By the use of force, threat, or intimidation

When a plaintiff raises a claim of false imprisonment, the plaintiff is saying that the defendant restrained him without legal basis. Claims of false imprisonment are commonly seen in situations in which a person is wrongfully detained on suspicion of shoplifting. When store personnel hold a person in an office while waiting for the police to arrive, they have committed the tort of false imprisonment, assuming that the plaintiff did not actually commit the shoplifting. If the plaintiff did actually steal from the store, the detention would be lawful (and would therefore negate the second element of false imprisonment).

 NEGLIGENCE

A **negligence** case is considerably different than an intentional torts case. The biggest difference between these two types of cases involves the defendant's mental state. In an intentional tort, the plaintiff must prove that the defendant knowingly and voluntarily injured him. In a negligence action, the plaintiff must prove that the defendant caused the injury through indifference, carelessness, or with reckless disregard for the safety of others. In the first scenario, the defendant intentionally causes injury; in the second, the defendant causes injury through inattention.

Other differences between negligence torts and intentional torts become apparent as we examine the elements of a negligence action. Individual intentional torts have different elements. However, all negligence cases have the same four elements that must be proven in every case. If the plaintiff can prove the existence of these elements, he has gone a long way toward winning his case.

The four elements of a negligence case involve proof that:

1   The defendant owed a duty to the plaintiff
2   The defendant breached that duty

Negligence
The theory of tort law that gives the plaintiff a cause of action against a defendant who owed the plaintiff a duty not to injure him, who then breached that duty, such that there was proximate cause between the breach of duty and the plaintiff's resultant injuries

3   There is causation between the defendant's breach and the plaintiff's injuries

4   The plaintiff has the type of injuries that can be compensated at law

We can reduce these elements to four words:

1   Duty
2   Breach
3   Causation
4   Damages

Let's explore negligence concepts by examining the issues that develop in a typical automobile accident.

One morning, Larry is driving while talking with his wife on his cell phone. He fails to notice that the traffic light he is approaching has turned red. He runs the red light and strikes the driver's side of a car being driven by Keisha. The impact of the collision causes extensive damage to her body and her car. She tears a ligament in her shoulder and injures the soft tissue in her neck. The police arrive and cite Larry for failure to stop at the red light. Keisha is treated at the hospital. Later she approaches a local attorney about bringing suit against Larry for her property damages and her medical bills.

As with the previous scenario involving Juan and Al, we must decide what type of case this is. There is no allegation that Larry knowingly and voluntarily injured Keisha, so this is not an intentional tort. The remaining option is a negligence action. Keisha is alleging that Larry injured her because he failed to keep a proper lookout and failed to abide by the rules of the road. He did not set out to strike Keisha's car; the collision was a result of his inattention, or negligence. Can Keisha prove all four elements of a negligence action?

 **In any negligence claim, the plaintiff must prove four elements:**

- Duty
- Breach
- Causation
- Damages

A. DUTY

Duty
An obligation to conform one's conduct in such a way as to avoid causing injury to another

Duty is a legal obligation owed by one person to another. Duty can arise from many different situations. Parents owe duties to their minor children to care for them. Innkeepers owe duties to their guests to provide safe hotel rooms. Motorists owe a duty to others to drive in a reasonable manner and to abide by the rules of road. A person can owe a duty to someone he does not know, just as in our hypothetical, Larry owes a duty to Keisha not to run a red light.

B. BREACH

The contentious issue in many negligence cases often is whether the defendant owed a duty to the plaintiff. Once that duty has been established, proving a **breach** of duty is often a straightforward proposition. If Larry owes a duty to other drivers to abide by the rules of the road, did he breach that duty? Under the facts of this scenario, the answer is obviously yes. He failed to stop at the red light and therefore breached his duty to Keisha.

Breach
The defendant fails to act according to a legal standard, or violates a duty

C. CAUSATION

Establishing a duty and the defendant's subsequent breach of that duty are only the first two elements of a negligence case. Each of these elements builds on the previous one. Without duty, there can be no progression to the other elements. In a similar vein, if the plaintiff fails to prove **causation,** her case against the defendant will fail. What is causation?

The term used most often to describe this element is *proximate causation,* or *legal causation.* This is the element that establishes that as a direct result of the defendant's breach, the plaintiff was injured. Causation is the requirement that the plaintiff prove that his injuries are directly linked to the defendant's negligence. In the case that we have been examining, there do not appear to be any causation issues. After all, Larry ran a red light and struck Keisha's car. As a result of this

Causation
Also known as proximate cause; the requirement that the defendant's actions be the primary cause of the plaintiff's injuries

Careers in the Law

▶ **Clerk of Court**

abel Lowman has been working in the clerk of court's office since 1976. "I applied for a job with the clerk's office in April 1976. A job came open in July of that same year and I've been here ever since."

She was elected to the position of clerk of court in 1998. "Working in the clerk's office requires you to know a little bit about everything," she says. A solid understanding of the workings of the clerk's office is important for any legal professional. "We get young attorneys in here all the time who say that law school never teaches the things you'll see here everyday."

The clerk's office not only keeps track of all civil and criminal filings, it also maintains files on incompe-tency hearings, divorce actions, and foreclosures. "Foreclosures are the hardest thing that we do. It used to be that you never saw the people who were being foreclosed on, but with the recent trouble we had with the economy, we had people coming in all the time trying to find some way of avoiding foreclosure."

Advances in technology have brought about some of the biggest changes she has seen in the clerk's office. "In 1976, everything was done manually. We didn't even have an electric typewriter. Today, everything is done on PCs and word processors. We used to use old-style mimeograph machines to make copies; now we have computerized copy machines. In a few years, we will be moving to paperless offices. Police officers will write citations on palmtops and they will automatically transmit to our computers. When a person pays the fine, they'll do it at a terminal. It will save a lot of processing time."

collision, her neck and shoulder were injured. But causation could become an issue simply by changing one of the facts in this case.

Suppose that Keisha wasn't injured in the car wreck with Larry, but did have injuries from earlier that day when she was lifting a heavy box and fell. Although Larry certainly violated a duty by running the red light, there is no direct connection between Keisha's injuries and Larry's actions. There is no legal causation running from Larry's negligence to Keisha's injuries. Without that causation, Keisha's case against Larry, at least for her medical injuries, must fail.

Throughout a negligence case, all parties pay close attention to the cause and effect equation: Is the defendant responsible for all injuries? If not, what injuries is he responsible for? If the defendant is not responsible for some injuries, then who is? Should that person also be sued? These are all questions that must be resolved in the pre-trial investigation discussed in Chapter 4.

D. Damages

Damages
Monetary payments designed to compensate the plaintiff for an injury

The final element of a negligence case is the requirement of **damages.** No matter how strong a case the plaintiff has, if he cannot prove that he has been damaged by the defendant's actions, he has no case. Suppose that when Larry ran the red light, instead of striking Keisha's car, he narrowly misses it. Keisha is shaken up and suffers from nightmares for the next several nights. She loses sleep and is cranky for several days at work. She brings suit against Larry. Can she prove a negligence case? She can make out duty, breach of duty, and at least a minimal case about causation, but her case begins to fall apart when the court examines the issue of damages. Is loss of sleep a recoverable loss? By itself, no. In states that would allow Keisha to recover for a form of psychological injury, she would have to substantiate a lot more than a few sleepless nights before the court would award her damages.

In addition to referring to the plaintiff's expenses or other losses, damages also refers to the monetary amount awarded by a jury if it should find that the plaintiff is entitled to win. We explored the various types of damages in Chapter 4.

ISSUE AT A GLANCE   Damages refer to the plaintiff's monetary losses, such as lost time from work and the medical bills attributable to the defendant's negligence.

 PERSONAL INJURY CASES

When attorneys and paralegals specialize in lawsuits involving car wrecks, they are usually said to be involved in *personal injury* cases. This term is more descriptive — and more accurate — than the broader term of *tort law.* Personal injury lawyers often specialize in representing one side of a case exclusively. For instance, some lawyers build a practice concentrating on representing plaintiffs in personal injury cases, while other attorneys specialize in representing defendants in such cases.

There is no shortage of work for these attorneys and paralegals, because car wreck cases are one of the most common type of lawsuits in the United States.

As you can see in Figure 8-2, motor vehicle cases are the largest category of tort trials in federal courts.

FIGURE 8-2*

Highlights

Changes in the tort caseloads of U.S. district courts primarily related to litigation involving asbestos and other product liability claims

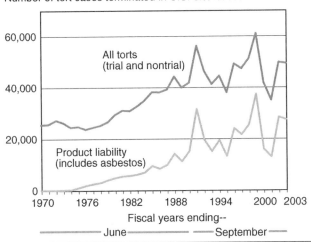

Number of tort cases terminated in U.S. district courts

- U.S. district courts terminated approximately 512,000 civil cases during fiscal years 2002-03. Nearly 20% or 98,786 of these cases were torts in which plaintiffs claimed injury, loss, or damage from a defendant's negligent or intentional acts.

- Of the 98,786 tort cases terminated in U.S. district courts in 2002-03, about 2% or 1,647 cases were decided by a bench or jury trial.

- An estimated 9 out of 10 tort trials involved personal injury issues — most frequently, product liability, motor vehicle (accident), marine, and medical malpractice cases.

- Juries decided about 71% of all tort cases brought to trial in U.S. district courts; judges adjudicated the remaining 29%.

- Plaintiffs won in 48% of tort trials terminated in U.S. district courts in 2002-03. Plaintiffs won less frequently in medical malpractice (37%) and product liability (34%) trials.

- Eighty-four percent of plaintiff winners received monetary damages with an estimated median award of $201,000.

- Plaintiffs won more often in bench (54%) than in jury (46%) tort trials. The estimated median damage awards were higher in jury ($244,000) than in bench ($150,000) tort trials.

* Bureau of Justice Statistics, U.S. Department of Justice. Federal Tort Trials and Verdicts, 2002-03.

A. PLAINTIFFS' FIRMS

When Keisha decides to sue Larry for the losses she incurred as a result of his negligence, she will seek representation from a plaintiffs' firm. Many personal injury lawyers specialize in representing plaintiffs exclusively. This specialization is a result of many different factors, including the attorney's temperament, the fee arrangements, and the complexity of tort law in general.

Attorneys who consistently represent plaintiffs in personal injury cases face different pressures than attorneys who practice other types of law. Although attorneys who represent personal injury plaintiffs are not barred from also representing defendants in other cases, most do not. After learning the ins and outs of plaintiff representation it is difficult to shift gears to defense work. There are also some practical limitations that push firms to specialize in one area or another, such as the issue of payment.

 Plaintiffs' firms represent people who have been injured by others' negligence. Defense firms represent people who have been sued.

1. CONTINGENCY FEES

Contingency fee
A legal fee calculated on the basis of the final amount awarded in a case

When a firm represents a plaintiff in a personal injury case, the custom is that the firm will be paid on a **contingency fee** basis. A contingency fee is a percentage of the total recovery in the case, most commonly 33 percent. This means that whatever amount the plaintiff is ultimately awarded in the case, the firm receives 1/3 or 33 percent of that amount. If the plaintiff receives nothing, the firm also receives nothing. If the plaintiff receives an enormous judgment, the firm earns a huge fee. That kind of speculative pay arrangement doesn't suit the temperament of all attorneys. For those who like a little more predictability in their fees, there is the option of insurance defense.

B. INSURANCE DEFENSE FIRMS

Firms that routinely handle the defense side of motor vehicle suits are referred to as insurance defense firms. This is because automobile insurance policies (required in all states) provide that if the policyholder is sued, the insurance company will pay an attorney to represent the policyholder. The attorney works for the policyholder, but is paid by the insurance company.

Insurance defense firms do not work on a contingency fee basis. Instead, they charge an hourly fee. This hourly fee is billed to the insurance company, often on a monthly basis. The nice thing about insurance defense is that these attorneys can predict, with a fair degree of accuracy, exactly what their monthly

Profiling a Paralegal

▶ Amanda Eury

manda Eury is currently a paralegal student. She will be graduating in a few months. "I decided to go back to school when I lost my job. I wanted a career with some stability. I'd always thought about going into the law. My grandfather was a prosecutor and I think that's why I always had it in the back of my mind that I would like to try it."

Amanda currently works part time at a local law office. "The biggest surprise I had was that everything you see on TV is not true. The law is more flexible than I thought. You run into the phrase 'reasonable person' a lot."

Since entering the paralegal program, Amanda has become more involved both on campus and off. "I was elected president of our campus paralegal association and joined Phi Theta Kappa honor society. I'm really enjoying my classes."

When she graduates, she'd like to go work for a personal injury firm. "I'd like to help people who've been injured. I think personal injury work would be very intense and in-depth. I'm really hoping to go to work for a big firm. I have my eye on a firm that employs 275 attorneys. It sounds like it would be a lot of glitz and glamour and I think the money would be better than at a small firm."

income will be. This also means that they do not have the possibility of 33 percent of a huge recovery. Attorneys in both types of firms face a trade-off: Plaintiffs' attorneys may get no fee, with the chance of a huge settlement; defense attorneys get a steady fee, with no possibility of a windfall from a huge settlement.

Having said this, however, most law firms in the personal injury field make excellent money. Some firms do extremely well and make their partners rich.

1. CONTRACTING WITH A LAW FIRM

When a person goes to a plaintiffs' firm seeking representation, he will sign a contract that sets out the details of the agreement (and the contingency fee arrangement) for the duration of the case. For an example of a contingency fee contract, see Figure 8-3.

 PRODUCT LIABILITY

Tort law is a diverse and fascinating field. Although we have been discussing intentional torts and motor vehicle cases up to this point, there are several other interesting topics in this field. One such topic is **product liability.**

Consumers who have been injured by defective products bring product liability suits against manufacturers. This is a relatively recent phenomenon in tort law. This area of law has seen a huge increase in litigation in the last three decades, with courts gradually expanding the types of cases that can be brought and manufacturers improving the overall safety of their products as a direct result.

Product liability
Suits brought by consumers for defective products that cause injury to them; such suits can be brought even when the manufacturer is not at fault in designing, manufacturing, or marketing the product

FIGURE 8-3

Contract of Representation

THIS AGREEMENT, made this _____ day of _____, 200___ is between _____ the foregoing named person(s) being herein called Client, and Clarence D. Arrow, herein called "Attorney(s)". It is understood that litigation can be expensive, and that the Attorneys are prohibited by law from becoming liable for its costs, expenses, disbursements and deposits. Attorneys may advance them, but they cannot become ultimately liable for them. The Client and the Attorneys have agreed as follows:

1. The Client this day retains, employs and authorized the Attorneys:

(a) To prosecute, administratively and judicially, if necessary in his judgment, each of the Client's following claims:

(b) To prosecute or defend any and all appeals that may be taken in connection with the Client's claims; and

(c) To receive and collect any final recovery that may be realized on the Client's claims and to satisfy the same upon the records of the appropriate agency or court. The words "final recovery" when used anywhere in this Agreement means the total gross amount of any and all monies, property and compensation of any and every kind whatsoever realized or received by any Client for any claim, whether realized as the result of settlement or litigation or otherwise, and shall include, but not be limited to, any and all monies, funds, awards, verdicts, judgments, determinations, damages, principal, interest of every kind and nature, penalties, allowances, costs, and any and all compensation of every kind, nature and description; and

(d) To deduct and retain their Attorneys' fees out of the proceeds of the final recovery, and to remit the balance, less their costs, expenses, disbursements and deposits, to the Client.

2. The Client agrees to pay the Attorneys, and the Attorneys agree to accept for all of the legal services rendered in accordance with this Agreement, the following fee:

(a) A contingent fee, paid within thirty (30) days of a final recovery or any portion thereof, computed as follows: thirty three percent (33%) of any final recovery obtained if the claim is settled without suit.

IN WITNESS WHEREOF, the parties have executed this Agreement the day and year first above written.

_____   _____

CLIENT   Attorney

Sworn to and subscribed before me
this ___ day of _____, 200___

_____

Notary Public

When consumers are injured by defective products, they are permitted to bring suit against the manufacturer. These suits can be brought even when the manufacturer is not at fault.

A. NEGLIGENT PRODUCTION

Although product liability cases can be brought against companies for negligence in the way that a product is manufactured or distributed, many states allow a plaintiff to sue a manufacturer even when the manufacturer is not at fault. Product liability is a "no fault" tort, meaning that it is not necessary for a plaintiff to prove that the manufacturer did anything wrong, only that the product injured the consumer.

A product liability case is not authorized when a consumer is simply dissatisfied with the performance of a product or its appearance. Product liability suits are reserved for cases in which the product injures a person.

Product liability cases can be based on negligence, strict liability, or breach of warranty.

B. WARRANTIES

One of the theories underlying product liability suits is that all products come with **warranties,** or promises, that are overtly stated or implied. An example of an overt warranty is: "This product can be used under water." When the product fails in water, the manufacturer has breached a warranty. However, other warranties are implied by the courts. These warranties are assumed to be given with a product, even if they are not overtly stated. See Figure 8-4 for a list of other implied warranties.

Warranty
An express or implied promise about the performance, manufacture, or use of a product

1. EXPRESS WARRANTIES

A manufacturer may also be sued when it violates one of its express warranties. An express warranty is a written or oral promise about how the product will perform, or about the health hazards associated with using the product.

2. LIABILITY WITHOUT FAULT

Product liability suits are unusual in that the plaintiff is not required to prove that the manufacturer was at fault in the way that it designed, manufactured, or marketed a particular product. This is a substantial departure from other types of torts. With intentional torts and negligence, the defendant's fault is a prerequisite to the action. However, the courts have carved out this exception because of the unusual

FIGURE 8-4

Examples of Implied
Warranties

■ Warranty of merchantability
The implied promise that the product
will perform normally and safely

■ Warranty for fitness for purpose
The product is fit for the purpose for
which it was purchased

nature of these actions. The plaintiff may find it difficult, if not impossible, to prove how the manufacturing process was at fault, although the plaintiff can clearly show that the product caused injury. Faced with the prospect of denying a plaintiff any recovery, the court opted to create a new kind of tort and eliminate fault as a requirement.

INTRODUCTION TO MALPRACTICE

In addition to suing people for intentional torts or negligence, plaintiffs are also permitted to sue professionals for failure to meet the standards of their profession. Although the most common type of **malpractice** action is medical malpractice, other professionals, such as lawyers, are increasingly facing suit by former clients.

Malpractice
The failure of a professional to exercise the degree of skill, expertise, and knowledge for the benefit of the client or patient, otherwise known as professional negligence

A. WHAT IS MALPRACTICE?

A plaintiff who sues for malpractice is alleging that the defendant, a professional, injured the plaintiff while performing his profession. A plaintiff in a malpractice action is essentially alleging professional negligence.

One of the elements that a plaintiff must prove in a malpractice action is that the defendant is a recognized professional. Under the law, the term *professional* is reserved for a select group of occupations. A professional is a person with specialized knowledge, training, and experience who is acknowledged by, and often receives special consideration from, the court system.

When a plaintiff alleges malpractice, the elements of a negligence action do not change, even if the way that the case is proved does. For instance, in establishing duty and breach of duty, the plaintiff must prove that the defendant is a professional and that, acting as a professional, the defendant failed to exercise the same degree of skill, knowledge, and care as other members of the profession. This is referred to as the **standard of care** and the plaintiff must prove not only what the standard of care is, but also that the defendant did not meet that standard. Inevitably, this requires the presentation of expert testimony. An expert from the same field as the defendant must testify as to what the commonly accepted standard of care is and how the defendant failed to live up to it. Without such testimony, a malpractice case will fail.

Standard of care
The standard used by the law to determine negligence; the standard that a professional must act in the same manner as a reasonable, prudent member of the profession

One of the essential elements of a claim for medical negligence is that the defendant breached the applicable standard of medical care owed to the plaintiff.

ISSUE AT A GLANCE

B. LIMITATIONS ON DAMAGES IN MEDICAL MALPRACTICE CASES

Medical malpractice cases have received much attention in the past couple of decades because of several large jury verdicts awarded to plaintiffs. Some of these awards have been enormous, as much as hundreds of millions of dollars. As a result, the field has undergone dramatic changes. State legislatures have enacted new statutes to modify the statutes of limitation or to limit the size of verdicts that plaintiffs may receive in such cases. One such limitation that has been imposed in numerous states is a strict limit on the amount of punitive damage awards.

Limitations on punitive damages were enacted out of the impression that juries were awarding plaintiffs windfalls based on spurious claims. Whether or not that impression was accurate, most states that have enacted limitations on damages in medical malpractice cases have usually done so through treble damages.

When a state has a treble damages limitation, it means that a plaintiff's ultimate award for punitive damages is limited to an amount that is exactly three times the total amount of the plaintiff's compensatory damages. If the plaintiff was awarded $1,000 by the jury for his out-of-pocket expenses and injuries, the most that the jury could award as punitive damages would be $3,000, no matter how egregiously the doctor acted.

C. INFORMED CONSENT

Another important issue in medical malpractice cases involves **informed consent.** Doctors routinely ask patients to sign forms indicating their agreement to the procedure to be performed. This consent often protects the doctor from suit at a later date. A patient is entitled to bring an action based on inadequate informed consent. The basis of this claim is that the patient was never made aware of the risks involved in the procedure or was never told about treatment alternatives so that he could make an informed decision about whether to risk the procedure in the first place. For a plaintiff to succeed on a claim of inadequate informed consent, he must prove the following:

Informed consent
An agreement by a person to allow some type of action after having been fully informed and after making a knowing and intelligent decision to allow the action

1 The defendant-doctor failed to adequately describe the procedure to the patient, especially the treatment alternatives and the foreseeable risks involved
2 That a reasonable and prudent person would not have undergone the pro cedure if he had been adequately informed
3 The lack of informed consent is a proximate cause of the plaintiff's injuries

FIGURE 8-5

Plaintiff Winners in Tort Cases,
2001*

Table 5. Plaintiff winners in State
courts in the Nation's 75 largest
counties, 2001

Case type	All trial cases	
	Number	Plaintiff winners[b]
All trial cases[a]	11,681	55.4%
Tort cases	7,798	51.6%
Automobile	4,121	61.2
Premises liability	1,260	42.0
Product liability	154	44.2
Asbestos	30	60.0
Other	124	40.3
Intentional tort	366	56.8
Medical malpractice	1,149	26.8
Professional malpractice	99	52.5
Slander/libel	94	41.5
Animal attack	99	66.7
Conversion	28	46.4
False arrest, imprisonment	45	42.2
Other or unknown tort	383	50.9
Contract cases	3,625	64.8%
Fraud	602	58.3
Seller plaintiff	1,196	76.8
Buyer plaintiff	779	61.5
Mortgage foreclosure	22	72.7
Employment discrimination	160	43.8
Other employment dispute	282	55.7
Rental/lease	276	64.9
Tortious interference	133	57.9
Partnership dispute	41	46.3
Subrogation	61	67.2
Other or unknown contract	73	56.2
Real property cases	258	37.6%
Eminent domain	49	40.8
Other real property[c]	209	36.8

Note: Data on plaintiff winners were available
for 99.9% of trials. Detail may not sum to total
because of rounding.
[a]Trial cases include bench and jury trials, trials
with a directed verdict, judgments notwithstanding the verdict, and jury trials for defaulted
defendants.
[b]Excludes bifurcated trials where the plaintiff
litigated only the damage claim. There were
216 trials where only the damage claim was
litigated.
[c]Includes title disputes, boundary disputes,
and other real property cases.

* Bureau of Justice Statistics, U.S. Department of Justice. Civil Trial Cases and Verdicts in Large Counties, 2001.

Table 7. Punitive damage awards in civil trial cases for plaintiff award winners in State courts in the Nation's 75 largest counties, 2001

Case type	Number awarded punitive damages[a]	Trial cases with plaintiff winners			
		Amount of punitive damages awarded		Number of cases with punitive damages —	
		Total	Median	Over $250,000	$1 million or more
All trial cases[a]	356	$1,221,877,000	$50,000	81	41
Tort cases	217	$367,149,000	$25,000	45	23
Automobile	54	48,578,000	5,000	9	7
Premises liability	8	646,000	33,000	--	--
Product liability	3	1,077,000	433,000	2	--
Asbestos	2	900,000	500,000	2	--
Other	1	177,000	177,000*	--	--
Intentional tort	78	32,653,000	16,000	16	9
Medical malpractice	15	115,577,000	187,000	4	2
Professional malpractice	7	117,000	1,000	--	--
Slander/libel	23	3,771,000	77,000	4	--
Animal attack	6	391,000	68,000	--	--
Conversion	3	289,000	100,000	--	--
False arrest, imprisonment	5	202,000	8,000	--	--
Other or unknown tort	16	163,849,000	470,000	11	4
Contract cases	138	$854,658,000	$83,000	36	18
Fraud	60	368,992,000	63,000	11	5
Seller plaintiff	9	484,000	4,000	--	--
Buyer plaintiff	16	16,509,000	275,000	9	3
Mortgage foreclosure	--	--	--	--	--
Employment discrimination	13	13,552,000	606,000	9	5
Other employment dispute	16	3,949,000	151,000	2	1
Rental/lease	9	2,282,000	15,000	2	2
Tortious interference	9	431,981,000	83,000	3	1
Partnership dispute	4	16,909,000	186,000	1	1
Subrogation	--	--	--	--	--
Other or unknown contract	2	1,000	1,000	--	--
Real property cases[b]	1	$70,000	$70,000*	--	--

Note: There was a total of 364 cases in which a punitive damage claim was awarded.
In 356 of these cases, the punitive award went to the plaintiff and in 8 cases the punitive award went to the defendant on a counterclaim. In this study, cases are classified by the primary case type, though many cases involve multiple claims (that is, contract and tort). Under laws in almost all States, only tort claims qualify for punitive damages. If contract or real property cases involved punitive damages, it involved a related tort claim.
Detail may not sum to total because of rounding.
Award data were rounded to the nearest thousand.
*Not median but the actual amount awarded.
--No cases recorded.
[a]The number of trial cases includes bench and jury trials, trials with a directed verdict, judgments notwithstanding the verdict, and jury trials for defaulted defendants.
[b]Excludes eminent domain cases.

FIGURE 8-5

Plaintiff Winners in Tort Cases, 2001*

* Bureau of Justice Statistics, U.S. Department of Justice. Civil Trial Cases and Verdicts in Large Counties, 2001.

ISSUE AT
A GLANCE

Informed consent must be based on adequate information and
the patient's understanding of what the procedure entails and
what the risks of the procedure are.

D. LEGAL MALPRACTICE

Legal malpractice
Professional negligence
committed by an attorney
during the course of his
representation of a client

Medical doctors are no longer the only professionals who are routinely sued by
former clients. In recent years, suits alleging **legal malpractice** have become
increasingly common.

When a plaintiff alleges legal malpractice, he is alleging that the attorney failed
to perform his professional duties to the minimum standard of care in the legal
community and that this failure resulted in an identifiable loss to the client. Legal
malpractice, like medical malpractice, is a question of fact and must be determined
by the jury.

In addition to attorneys and doctors, other professionals, such as certified
public accountants, have been the focus of malpractice actions.

GOFF v. CLARKE
302 A.D.2d 725, 755 N.Y.S.2d 493 (N.Y.A.D. 3 Dept., 2003)

Appeal from an order of the Supreme Court (O'BRIEN III, J.), entered January 22,
2002 in Madison County, which, inter alia, partially granted plaintiff's motion for partial
summary judgment.

On December 10, 1997, plaintiff, then a senior at Stockbridge Valley Central School
in Madison County, and a member of its varsity basketball team, was injured when he was
involved in a physical altercation with defendant who, at the time of the incident, was a
teacher at the school and plaintiff's coach. Both plaintiff and defendant relate markedly
different accounts of the incident. Plaintiff alleges, inter alia, that while waiting in the high
school gymnasium for practice to begin, he asked defendant to demonstrate a wrestling
move "without actually doing it." According to plaintiff, defendant grabbed his arm and,
despite twice asking defendant to release him, defendant continued, twisting plaintiff's
arm with even greater pressure until his wrist made a popping noise. The parties struggled
briefly before separating. Plaintiff claims that moments later, defendant grabbed him by
the knees attempting to throw him, but plaintiff overpowered defendant and fell on top
of him.

Conversely, defendant claims that the incident was jovial in nature, stemming from
what he characterized as plaintiff's "playful[ly] antagonistic" challenge of defendant
which progressed to wrestling. Defendant then alleges that plaintiff ended up on top
of him and gave defendant a "wedgie." Both parties agree at that point that defendant
conceded that plaintiff won, and plaintiff got up and then assisted defendant from the
floor. Thereafter, defendant "high-fived" plaintiff.

This action ensued, charging defendant with negligence and the intentional torts of assault and battery, and seeking damages for plaintiff's injuries, including a fracture of the right wrist. Following joinder of issue, defendant unsuccessfully moved to dismiss the complaint on the ground that, inter alia, it was time barred. Thereafter, plaintiff moved for summary judgment on the issue of liability. Supreme Court granted the motion with respect to the causes of action stemming from the intentional tort claims, but dismissed plaintiff's claim sounding in negligence. Defendant appeals. We agree with defendant that Supreme Court erred in granting summary judgment to plaintiff. A plaintiff, to recover damages for battery, must prove that there was bodily contact, that the contact was offensive, that is, "wrongful under all the circumstances" (*Zgraggen v. Wilsey,* 200 A.D.2d 818, 819, 606 N.Y.S.2d 444), and that defendant intended to make the contact (*see Messina v. Matarasso,* 284 A.D.2d 32, 35, 729 N.Y.S.2d 4; *Zgraggen v. Wilsey, supra*). Lack of consent is considered in determining whether the contact was offensive, but it is not conclusive.

In addition to his deposition testimony, plaintiff proffered the affidavits of two former classmates, both of whom averred that they witnessed the incident between plaintiff and defendant, they saw defendant twisting plaintiff's arm and they heard plaintiff, more than once, tell defendant to stop, but that defendant failed to comply with plaintiff's request. The fact that plaintiff may have been a willing participant at the outset of the activity is, as correctly observed by Supreme Court, irrelevant as to whether defendant's conduct is ultimately tantamount to battery. Upon this record, we thus conclude that plaintiff has tendered sufficient evidence to sustain his initial burden of proof that there was intended contact and that the intended contact was offensive. The burden then shifted to defendant to "produce evidentiary proof in admissible form sufficient to establish the existence of material issues of fact which require a trial of the action." At his deposition, defendant was asked if, at any time during the physical interaction that he had with plaintiff . . . did he recall plaintiff ask him to stop? Defendant answered "no." Defendant further testified that he did not remember plaintiff telling him that he was hurting plaintiff nor did he recall plaintiff saying, "You're twisting my arm, it hurts." Viewing the evidence "in a light most favorable to the nonmoving party, affording that party the benefit of all reasonable inferences" we find these statements, by themselves, sufficient to raise a triable issue of fact as to whether the intended contact between plaintiff and defendant was offensive. Rather than characterizing defendant's answers as ambivalent, as did Supreme Court, we find that they constitute a denial to plaintiff's allegations that the contact was offensive. The fact that both parties concede that the incident ended on friendly terms provides additional support for treating these answers as a denial that plaintiff made these statements to defendant. Moreover, the parties' conflicting testimony presents credibility issues which cannot be resolved on a motion for summary judgment.

ORDERED[:] the order is modified, on the law, with costs to defendant, by reversing so much thereof as partially granted plaintiff's motion; motion denied in its entirety; and, as so modified, affirmed.

QUESTIONS ABOUT THE CASE

1 What are the allegations in this case?
2 What intentional torts do the plaintiff allege against the defendant?
3 Is it significant that the plaintiff consented to the original contact?
4 Are there conflicting stories in this case?

SKILLS YOU NEED IN THE REAL WORLD

PHOTOGRAPHING AND VIDEOTAPING ACCIDENT SCENES

Many times in your career, you may be asked to go to the scene where an automobile accident occurred and to take photos and video of the scene. To get the most out of this process, here are some practical concerns to keep in mind when attempting to record the scene of an accident.

1. *Get there sooner rather than later.* Accident scenes can change in appearance quickly. If you wait even a few weeks before going out to record the site, the scene may have changed dramatically. For instance, road crews may have come through and put up barriers where none existed before. A change in seasons can mean that the foliage and underbrush has changed. Skid marks and other evidence of the crash fade and disappear over time. These are all excellent reasons to go to the scene as soon as possible.

2. *Begin recording as you approach the scene.* Whenever possible, record the approach to the scene from your client's perspective. That usually means taking photos or video through the windshield. You should have someone else drive the route followed by your client on the day of the incident and begin recording before you reach the scene. This can have a powerful impact on the jury when the video is used later at the trial.

3. *Avoid comments or dramatic effects.* If your video camera has a mute for the audio part of the recording, use it. Do not talk while the video is running. You should certainly avoid making comments such as, "Wow! Our guy must have really been speeding to go this far off the road!" For videos, the best course is no audio at all. A slightly different rule applies to photos. It might make the photo more dramatic to put a warning sign in the shot that wasn't actually there when the accident occurred, but you are there to record, not to improvise. In the same vein, you shouldn't rearrange the site to make it more picturesque or dramatic. Record the scene as it appears, not as you would like it to appear.

4. *Make every picture tell its own story.* When you are taking photographs, give the viewer some point of reference. Try to make the photo speak for itself, so that

no one else will be forced to come in later and explain what is being viewed in the photo. Take your shots so that they tell their own story and need little or no explanation.

5. *Special problems with video.* Everyone has seen poorly made home videos. They usually have the same problem: The camera scene whips around like the end of an unattended firehose. There is a natural tendency when you are operating a video camera to quickly record everything at the scene and then move on. However, the resulting video is choppy, bumpy, and difficult to watch. Suppress your natural tendencies and move the video camera slowly. Hold the camera steady and concentrate on a shot. If you must pan (move) the camera, do it very slowly. You might feel as though the scene is moving too slowly, but you'll learn later when you watch the video that slow taping translates into normal viewing.

6. *Different angles.* Finally, you should always strive for different angles and different views of the scene. Use a landmark as a point of reference for these other angles. If there was a large evergreen tree in the first shot, start with the same tree on the other side and then move the camera away from it to pan across the accident scene.

CHAPTER SUMMARY

Tort law, sometimes called civil injuries law, is a rich and diversified subject. Encompassing both intentional torts and negligence, tort law also includes product liability suits and professional malpractice actions. Intentional torts consist of deliberate and voluntary actions on the part of a defendant to injure another person. Examples of intentional torts include assault, battery, and false imprisonment. Negligence actions are among the most common type of lawsuit brought in the United States today. In a negligence action, the plaintiff is not alleging that the defendant acted intentionally, but instead that the defendant failed to keep a proper lookout or that he acted recklessly. Negligence actions consist of four basic elements: duty, breach of that duty, causation, and damages. A plaintiff must prove all these elements to establish a negligence action. Failure to prove any single element justifies a dismissal of the plaintiff's suit against the defendant.

Attorneys often specialize in personal injury law. The sheer volume of such cases has justified the decision by many attorneys to spend their entire careers in this one area of law.

Product liability lawsuits, although not as common as personal injury suits, make up another important branch of tort law. A party suing under the theory of product liability is alleging that he was injured by a defective product. Product liability lawsuits are unique in that the plaintiff is not required to prove that the manufacturer was at fault when it created a defective product.

Medical malpractice falls into the much larger category of professional negligence. Medical malpractice cases are also very common. When a plaintiff alleges medical malpractice, he is saying that a physician violated the standard of care and injured his patient. Legal malpractice cases, although not as common as medical malpractice cases, are becoming more prevalent. In a legal malpractice action, a client alleges that his former attorney violated the legal standard of care in representing a client and that this failure was a direct contribution to the plaintiff's failure to win the case.

ETHICS: COMMINGLING FUNDS

One of the most frequent reasons that attorneys are disbarred is for commingling funds. Simply put, commingling funds refers to an attorney using a client's funds as his own. When an attorney receives a settlement check, the typical practice is to deposit it in the attorney's trust account. The attorney will then deduct his fee and forward the remaining funds to the client. Attorneys who are in financial difficulty are often tempted to borrow against client funds, believing that if they can replace the funds before anyone notices, they will stay one step ahead of their creditors. Commingling funds is a serious ethical violation and justifies the disbarment of an attorney. Paralegals are often called upon to monitor deposits and withdrawals from the various firm accounts and to reconcile the balances on these accounts. This can put a paralegal in a difficult position if the attorney is using client funds for personal uses. Documentation is critical in this situation. Paralegals should document unusual or suspicious activity occurring in these accounts. Not only is commingling funds the basis of an ethical violation, it might also be the basis of a criminal prosecution for embezzlement.

CHAPTER REVIEW QUESTIONS

1 Is *civil injuries* a better term than *tort?* Explain your answer.
2 What are some of the different types of tort cases?
3 Why is the terminology used in intentional torts and crimes so similar?
4 Explain the historical relationship between tort law and criminal law.
5 Compare and contrast the elements of the intentional tort of assault with the intentional tort of battery.
6 What is the basic difference between intentional torts and negligence cases?
7 What are the four basic elements of a negligence action? Explain each.
8 Explain how the four elements of a negligence action are satisfied under the following scenario:

    Thomas is driving to work and fails to stop for a red light. He strikes Anna's car as she is proceeding through the intersection at the green light.
9 The text mentions that negligence cases are one of the most common type of suit in the United States. Why?
10 What is meant by the term *personal injury?*
11 Explain the role of the various attorneys in personal injury lawsuits.

12   What are the elements of a product liability suit?

13   What are warranties and how do they apply to product liability suits?

14   Explain the underlying concepts in professional malpractice cases.

15   How do courts determine the standard of care in medical malpractice cases?

16   What are the elements of a legal malpractice claim?

17   When is an attorney liable under a theory of legal malpractice?

18   What is commingling of client funds?

19   Why is it important to keep track of client funds in the law firm's account?

DISCUSSION QUESTIONS

1   You have just walked into a courtroom where a trial is in progress. As you sit down, you hear one of the attorneys ask the witness on the stand, "Is that the man who attacked you?"

   The woman on the stand answers yes. Can you tell from this brief exchange whether this is a civil case or a criminal case? Are there any conclusions you can reach from this snippet of testimony? Explain.

2   As you sit in the same courtroom, the testimony continues. The woman on the stand says, "He grabbed me and threw me to the ground. Just then, a police officer came up and arrested him."

   The attorney then asks, "Did you have any monetary losses associated with your injuries from the defendant?"

   Is this a civil case or criminal case or is it still too early to tell? Explain your answer.

3   The witness continues testifying, and then the judge calls for a brief recess. The judge says, "I would like the defense attorney and the assistant district attorney to approach the bench." Can you identify what type of case you have been watching? Explain your answer.

PERSONALITY QUIZ

Is personal injury the right legal field for you? Take this personality quiz and see.

1   I like the procedural aspects of law.
   0-strongly disagree   5-agree   10-strongly agree

   Points: _____

2   I like to root for the underdog.
   0-strongly disagree   5-agree   10-strongly agree

   Points: _____

3   I distrust large institutions.
0-strongly disagree   5-agree   10-strongly agree

Points: _____

4   I am more liberal than conservative.
0-strongly disagree   5-agree   10-strongly agree

Points: _____

5   I am aggressive when it comes to the rights of others.
0-strongly disagree   5-agree   10-strongly agree

Points: _____

Total Points: _____

If you scored between 30-50 points, you have many of the qualities that would suit you for a career in either a plaintiffs' or insurance defense firm.

If you scored between 20-29 points, you might do well in this field, but you might do even better in some other area of law.

If you scored 19 or lower, you should strongly consider some other area of law.

PRACTICAL APPLICATIONS

Visit your local courthouse and review the docket to locate a case involving a personal injury claim. Your best bet will be to locate a motor vehicle accident, because these are the most common types of lawsuits filed. Review the complaint and the answer. What are the plaintiff's allegations? How does the plaintiff set out the four elements of a negligence action: duty, breach of duty, causation, and damages? How does the defendant respond to the plaintiff's allegations? What was the result in this case? Did the parties settle or did they take the case to trial? Who won? Did you discover anything unusual or surprising in your review of the pleadings in the action?

WEB SITES

State Law on Tobacco Control (CDC)
http://www.cdc.gov/tobacco/research_data/legal_policy/mmwrss699.htm

National Safety Council Statistics on Accidents
http://www.nsc.org/lrs/statstop.htm

U.S. Consumer Product Safety Commission
http://www.cpsc.gov/library/data.html

TERMS AND PHRASES

Assault	Damages	Product liability
Battery	Duty	Standard of care
Breach	Informed consent	Tort
Causation	Legal malpractice	Warranty
Contingency fee	Malpractice	

Contracts and Business Law

Chapter Learning Objectives

After completing this chapter, you should be able to:

- Define the concepts of offer and acceptance
- Explain the basic elements of any legally binding contract
- Demonstrate your understanding of legal capacity to contract
- Explain the role of the Statute of Frauds in contract law
- Explain how the Uniform Commercial Code affects contract law and sales

 INTRODUCTION

Contracts are the lifeblood of business. Without enforceable contracts, there could be no commerce, no industry, and no wealth. Because of the importance of contract law to business, there has always been a close relationship between law and contracts. Without legal remedies, contract promises could not be enforced and business would grind to a halt. The relationship between business and law has existed for centuries and continues to be an important relationship today. In this chapter, we explore the law of contracts and reveal how this area is as specialized and as interesting as criminal, real property, or tort law.

Before we can examine the elements of a legally binding contract, we must first answer the question: What is a contract?

A **contract** is an agreement between two or more parties, who have legal capacity, to do some act. When a party breaches a contract, the law gives the other party a cause of action to enforce the agreement's provisions.

Contract
A legally recognized agreement that can be enforced under the law

Under this definition, a legally binding contract consists of basic elements: agreement, capacity, and the ability to enforce the agreement. From these general

FIGURE 9-1

The Elements of a Valid
Contract

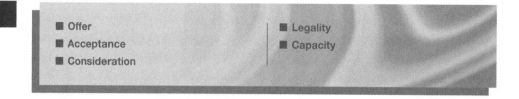

- ■ Offer
- ■ Acceptance
- ■ Consideration
- ■ Legality
- ■ Capacity

concepts, we can create a list of the basic requirements of a binding contract. These elements are set out in Figure 9-1.

A. OFFER

An offer is one party's indication of her willingness to enter into a contract. An offer is specific about the details of the proposed contract. These details include who will be bound by the contract, what the terms of the contract are, and how the contract will be performed. There is no requirement, however, that an offer contain legal expressions or that it anticipate every contingency. A valid offer can be couched in everyday language and the words used will be given their ordinary meaning. Read the following paragraph and then decide if it is a valid offer.

> Classified Ad
>
> For Sale: To the first person who appears at my house with $1,000, cash only, I will sell my 2004 Honda motorcycle. It's only been driven once, is in excellent condition, and runs great. Must sell; am leaving the country. — John Doe, 123 Maple Street, Springfield

Is this a valid offer? To be legally effective, an offer must contain enough details to answer the questions who, what, and how. Let's analyze this newspaper ad and see if it meets these requirements.

Who? Does the ad specify who is making the offer? Yes, it does. John Doe is making the offer. However, does it identify who can accept the offer? Without that level of specificity, a newspaper ad is simply an advertisement, not an offer. Can we identify the other party to this contract? Actually, we can. The other party is the first person to show up at John's house with $1,000. To be valid, the parties must be identifiable, but not necessarily named. Suppose you are the first person to show up at John's house with $1,000 in cash; under the terms of this ad, you would have accepted John's offer and you would be the other party in the transaction.

What? To be valid, an offer must be specific about what will be the focus of the contract. Again, John's ad appears to satisfy this element. He has spelled out that he is selling a 2004 Honda motorcycle. There are some potential problems here. Suppose that John has more than one 2004 Honda motorcycle? In that situation, his offer would be too vague to be enforceable. However, if John has only one motorcycle in his possession, his offer is perfectly valid.

How? The answer to how a person becomes bound in this contract is also simple and straightforward: a person shows up at John's house with $1,000 in cash. Suppose that you are interested in the motorcycle and you call John to tell him that you'll buy. Have you created a legally binding contract? Not according to the terms of the offer. In order to accept, you must abide by John's terms. How do you accept? You appear with the money. Any other action is not a valid acceptance of his offer and therefore does not create a binding contract.

An offer indicates a person's willingness to enter into a contract; it is also specific about what is being offered and how a person can accept.

ISSUE AT A GLANCE

B. ACCEPTANCE

If we have determined that John's newspaper advertisement is actually a legally binding offer, we must address the question of how a person accepts the offer. Over the centuries, courts have created specific rules about when and under what circumstances a valid acceptance is made. Courts have referred to the ability to create a binding contract through acceptance as the **power of acceptance.**

Power of acceptance
The ability of a person to create a binding, legal contract by accepting a valid offer

1. THE POWER OF ACCEPTANCE

A legally valid offer gives another person the power of acceptance. Simply put, the power of acceptance is the ability of a person to accept an offer and create a legally binding contract between the two parties.

Going back to our previous example, if you are the first person to show up at John's house with $1,000 in cash, you have accepted John's offer to purchase his motorcycle. You have the power of acceptance and by your actions you have created a legally binding contract. This is important because, if John should then refuse to sell you his motorcycle, you have a cause of action against him and can bring suit to enforce the terms of the contract. This is what the power of acceptance gives you. However, suppose we change one fact in the transaction.

When you arrive at John's house, you know that he is eager to sell because he wants to leave the country. When he answers the door, you say, "I want to buy your motorcycle, and I've got the $1,000, but I was wondering if you'd take $800 instead?"

This is a counteroffer. People make counteroffers all the time without realizing what this does to the underlying dynamic of a legally binding offer. A counteroffer rejects the original offer. It takes it off the table. Now, John has the power of acceptance. In essence, what you have done is to reject the initial offer and make an offer of your own. John can do one of three things: He can slam the door in your face, which is a fairly straightforward way of signaling his rejection of your counteroffer, he can accept your counteroffer, or he can reject your counteroffer by making a counteroffer of his own. This third scenario would go something like this:

John says, "No way, $800 is just about giving it away. I could go as low as $900, but that's it."

This is a counteroffer. It is specific about terms and gives the other person the power of acceptance. If you accept at this point, you and John are in a legally binding contract.

   **When an offer has been accepted, a contract is created.**

2. THE MAILBOX RULE

Over the years, the courts have created some specific rules that govern how an acceptance can be made. One such rule is the mailbox rule. The mailbox rule provides that an acceptance is valid at the moment that it is mailed, not when it is delivered. Under the mailbox rule, if person *A* can show that she posted an acceptance on Monday at 3 P.M. and person *B* hand delivered an acceptance on Monday at 3:30 P.M., person *A*'s acceptance would be the only legally valid one that the seller could accept. Although this rule seems to run counter to common sense, there is a practical reason for the rule. Once you post something in the mail, it is out of your hands. You cannot make any alterations to it, or even retrieve it. Although it may take two or more days for the acceptance to reach the seller, a court would rule that it is legally effective when it is posted, because to rule any other way would cause no end of confusion in business transactions. This is one of the reasons why postmarks contain not only dates, but also times.

3. UNILATERAL AND BILATERAL CONTRACTS

At this point, we should address an important distinction in the types of contracts that can be created through a valid offer and acceptance. We can divide contracts into two broad categories: unilateral contracts and bilateral contracts.

a. Unilateral Contracts

Unilateral contract
A contract that exchanges a promise for an action

A **unilateral contract** is one in which a person makes a promise in exchange for an action. The most common example of a unilateral contract is a reward poster.

> Reward! Lost Dog!
> Lost last week, our Black Lab, answering to the name of Missy. See picture below. Will pay $100 to anyone who brings her home. Call Joan, 555-1212.

In this scenario, just like in the newspaper ad for John's motorcycle, the person making the offer is requesting an action. Most contracts involve reciprocal promises: I promise to do this; you promise to do that. However, in a unilateral contract, we have a different arrangement: I promise to do this; you do that.

In the reward posted above, the only way to create a binding contract, and be entitled to receive the reward, is to produce Missy, the lost dog. If you were to call Joan and promise to produce Missy, there would be no binding contract.

An unilateral contract is a promise in exchange for an action.

ISSUE AT
A GLANCE

b. Bilateral Contracts

Bilateral contracts are the most common type of contract. In a bilateral contract, both parties make reciprocal promises to one another. Most business transactions are bilateral contracts. Consider this agreement:

Bilateral contract
A contract in which one promise is exchanged for another promise

> Asheville Scrapbooks, Inc., hereby agrees to purchase no less than 500 sheets (1 ream) of marbelized paper from Mandy Marbles Paper, Inc., per month for the sum of $100 per ream. This agreement shall remain in effect for 24 months from the date below. Mandy Marbles agrees to provide a minimum of 20 different marbelized patterns, in four different primary colors, in each of these reams. The reams will also contain no obvious flaws and will be ready for immediate resale.

If we analyze this agreement, we see that Asheville Scrapbooks, Inc., has made a bilateral contract with Mandy Marbles Paper, Inc. What are the reciprocal promises? Asheville Scrapbooks promises to pay $100 per ream and to purchase a minimum of one ream per month. Mandy Marbles Paper agrees to prepare the marbelized paper, to ship it, and to ensure that there are at least 20 different patterns in each ream and that there will be at least four different color patterns. This is a classic bilateral contract: a promise for a promise.

Classifying the type of contract created by a valid offer and acceptance is important when it comes to enforcing the contract or assessing damages for breach. Unilateral and bilateral contracts are enforced in different ways. We discuss contract damages later in this chapter.

So far, the first two elements of a legally binding contract — offer and acceptance — have been explained, but this still leaves us with the elements of consideration, legality, and capacity.

A bilateral contract is a promise in exchange for a promise.

ISSUE AT
A GLANCE

C. CONSIDERATION

The requirement of **consideration** is an ancient contract principle, rooted firmly in common sense. Before either party to a contract is bound by its terms, she must first incur some form of legal detriment. When a party incurs legal detriment, it means that she has surrendered something of value in exchange for something else

Consideration
The requirement in a contract that all parties incur some form of legal detriment in binding themselves to the contractual terms

of value. This legal detriment, or consideration, is a duty imposed by law. It shows that the parties have obligated themselves to do something that they were not otherwise obligated to do. Consideration can also work in the negative. If you have the right to do something, and you stop doing it as part of a contractual obligation, you have satisfied the element of consideration.

Consider the following example:

Rick has led a wasteful life. He hasn't held down a job for more than a month since he was 18. He is now 40. His oldest aunt, Rose, who loves him despite his bad habits, approaches him one day and says, "Rick, if you clean up your act, stop drinking and cursing, and get a job and stick to it, I'll leave you $100,000 in my will."

Rick gives up alcohol and cursing and gets a job. He remains at the job for the next 12 years until Aunt Rose dies. When her attorney reads her will, Rick discovers that he has received nothing from his aunt's estate. Rick sues. Does Rick have an enforceable contract?

If we consider Aunt Rose's offer of $100,000 as an intention to enter into a unilateral contract, Rick's actions seem to have satisfied the requirement of acceptance. However, we have also said that consideration requires a party to do something that he was not already obligated to do, or to refrain from something that he was legally capable of doing. There is no law that requires Rick to get a job, so in getting one, Rick was taking on a duty that he did not otherwise have an obligation to do. Rick also gave up drinking and cursing, both of which he was entitled to do. Rick has satisfied the element of consideration.

If we alter the details of Aunt Rose's offer only slightly, we get an entirely different result. Suppose that Aunt Rose had told Rick, "If you don't rob any banks until I die, I'll leave you $100,000 in my will." Rick doesn't rob any banks. When his aunt dies and leaves him nothing in her will, he sues her estate. Is there consideration for this contract?

Answer: No. Rick did not refrain from doing something that he was otherwise legally entitled to do. No one is entitled to rob banks; therefore there is no legally recognized consideration for his aunt's promise. Without that consideration, there is no binding contract and Rick will lose his suit.

D. LEGALITY OF CONTRACTS

One important aspect of any contract is the action that is contemplated by the parties. When the action involves an illegal activity, the contract is not enforceable. To rule otherwise would put the court system in a bizarre situation: The parties would use legal means (such as a lawsuit) to ask the court to enforce a contract that is otherwise illegal. To avoid such a predicament, courts routinely refuse to enforce contracts that are drafted for illegal purposes. Examples of such contracts would include any contract that contemplates a crime, or that involves actions deemed unenforceable by the legislature. When a contract contains a provision for interest payments in excess of the statutory maximum, for example, the courts will not enforce the contract.

E. CAPACITY

Capacity is not only a contract requirement, it is a requirement in many other types of legal documents and pleadings as well. When a person has capacity, it means that she has the legal ability, authority, and mental awareness to enter into a binding, legal agreement. A person who lacks capacity, such as someone who has been declared to be mentally incompetent, cannot enter into a contract, because the person lacks the ability to understand the consequences of that decision. When a person is intoxicated, for example, she lacks the mental capacity to enter into a contract. Similarly, a person suffering from some form of dementia would also be barred from entering into a contract.

When a person's lack of capacity is revealed, the contract is normally cancelled. However, there are provisions under the law that allow a temporarily incapacitated person, such as someone who is intoxicated, to affirm the provisions of the contract after she has regained her sobriety. In another example of lack of capacity, a contract entered into with a child is not enforceable because children (those under the age of 18 in most states) are considered to lack legal capacity.

Capacity
The requirement that all parties to a contract have the mental, physical, and legal ability to understand the nature of the obligation assumed

To be binding, both parties to a contract must have capacity, or the ability to know and understand the contract's terms.

ISSUE AT A GLANCE

 ## THE STATUTE OF FRAUDS

The Statute of Frauds was originally created in England in the 1600s and adopted later by the newly formed United States. The Statute of Frauds should actually be called the Statute to Prevent Frauds. This statute requires, as a way to avoid claims of fraud and deceit, that certain types of contracts must be in writing or they will not be enforceable. See Figure 9-2 for a complete list of the types of contracts that must typically be in writing under the Statute.

FIGURE 9-2

Categoreis of Contracts That Must Be in Writing According to the Statute of Frauds

- Wills
- Contracts to answer for the debt of another
- Contracts in anticipation of marriage (prenuptial/antenuptial agreements)
- Contracts for the sale of land
- Contracts that cannot be performed within one year of the date of their creation
- Contracts for the sale of goods exceeding $500 in value
- Contracts for the sale of securities (stocks, bonds)

FIGURE 9-3

Statute of Frauds in Texas

§ 26.01. Promise or Agreement Must Be in Writing

(a) A promise or agreement described in Subsection (b) of this section is not enforceable unless the promise or agreement, or a memorandum of it, is

(1) in writing; and

(2) signed by the person to be charged with the promise or agreement or by someone lawfully authorized to sign for him.

(b) Subsection (a) of this section applies to:

(1) a promise by an executor or administrator to answer out of his own estate for any debt or damage due from his testator or intestate;

(2) a promise by one person to answer for the debt, default, or miscarriage of another person;

(3) an agreement made on consideration of marriage or on consideration of nonmarital conjugal cohabitation;

(4) a contract for the sale of real estate;

(5) a lease of real estate for a term longer than one year;

(6) an agreement which is not to be performed within one year from the date of making the agreement;

(7) a promise or agreement to pay a commission for the sale or purchase of:

(A) an oil or gas mining lease;

(B) an oil or gas royalty;

(C) minerals; or

(D) a mineral interest; and

(8) an agreement, promise, contract, or warranty of cure relating to medical care or results thereof made by a physician or health care provider as defined in Section 1.03, Medical Liability and Insurance Improvement Act of Texas.[9]

There is no nationwide Statute of Frauds. Instead, each state has adopted its own version. Most state statutes have language similar to the statute set out in Figure 9-3.

ISSUE AT A GLANCE

The Statute of Frauds requires certain types of contracts to be in writing to help prevent fraud and deceit.

A. CONTRACTS INVOLVING TESTAMENTARY TRANSACTIONS (WILLS, ETC.)

Wills are required to be in writing under the Statute of Frauds for the very simple reason that when it comes time to interpret the provisions of the will the person who wrote it is no longer alive to explain it. By requiring wills to be in writing, the law avoids the situation in which an heir presents a purported oral promise to leave him X amount of dollars from the decedent's estate. Proving such a promise (or disproving it) would be nearly impossible. The Statute of Frauds avoids this legal minefield by requiring a written expression of the decedent's wishes.

[9] Texas Bus. & Com. §26.01

B. CONTRACT TO ANSWER FOR THE DEBT OF ANOTHER

If a person voluntarily agrees to pay another person's debt, the Statute of Frauds also requires this agreement to be in writing. The reasoning behind this requirement is similar to the rule about wills: Such an agreement would be almost impossible to prove if the only record of it was a conversation. Taking on such a burden is unusual, and requiring it to be in writing helps pinpoint the extent of the obligation being assumed.

C. PRENUPTIAL AGREEMENTS

The original Statute of Frauds addressed marriage as if it were any other type of contractual agreement. Although marriage certainly has contractual elements, most of us would agree that it involves more than simple contractual obligation. These days, the Statute of Frauds is no longer invoked to enforce one person's promise to marry another. Instead, it governs a different aspect of matrimony: prenuptial agreements.

A prenuptial agreement (also known as an antenuptial agreement) is a contract between two people who are about to be married that sets out how the marital estate will be divided if they should later divorce. Prenuptial agreements are usually seen in situations in which one party to the marriage has considerable assets, or family holdings, that she does not wish to lose through a divorce proceeding.

Prenuptial agreements must be made prior to marriage. They have no legal effect if they are created after the parties are legally married.

D. CONTRACTS FOR THE SALE OF LAND

There is a pattern emerging in our discussion about the Statute of Frauds. The contracts that it requires to be in writing appear to be the more significant and important agreements made during a person's life. This is especially true in our fourth category of transactions required to be in writing: purchase and sale of land. A home may be the biggest monetary investment most people ever make. In past centuries, land ownership was the only basis of an individual's wealth. The need for the original Statute of Frauds may have arisen from the need to prevent fraud in real estate transactions among illiterate landowners.

Almost all types of real estate transactions are required to be in writing. This includes the sale of land to another and using real estate as collateral for a mortgage. Not only are these transactions required to be in writing, they must also be recorded in the local land office or register of deeds office so that they become part of the public record. We discuss real estate transactions in greater depth in Chapter 12.

FIGURE 9-4

Contract Cases Disposed of in
2001*

Table 1. Contract cases disposed of by trial in State courts in the Nation's 75 largest counties, 2001

Case type	All contract trials		Type of trial		
	Number	Percent	Jury	Bench	Other*
All contract trials	3,698	100.0%	42.6%	55.8%	1.6%
Fraud	625	16.9%	45.6%	52.0%	2.4%
Seller plaintiff	1,208	32.7	22.7	76.3	1.0
Buyer plaintiff	793	21.4	58.1	41.0	0.9
Mortgage foreclosure	22	0.6	--	100.0	--
Employment discrimination	166	4.5	86.7	10.2	3.0
Other employment dispute	287	7.8	57.5	38.7	3.8
Rental/lease	276	7.5	22.8	76.8	0.4
Tortious interference	138	3.7	55.8	42.0	2.2
Partnership dispute	40	1.1	55.0	45.0	--
Subrogation	69	1.9	68.1	27.5	4.3
Other or unknown contract	73	2.0	48.6	48.6	2.7

Note: Data for case and disposition type were available for 100.0% of the 3,698 contract trials. Detail may not sum to total because of rounding.
-- No cases recorded.
*Other trial cases include trials with a directed verdict, judgments notwithstanding the verdict, and jury trials for defaulted defendants.
 Although these cases are typically placed in a separate category, they are a form of jury trial.

*Bureau of Justice Statistics, U.S. Department of Justice. Contract Trials and Verdicts in Large Counties, 2001.

E. CONTRACTS THAT CANNOT BE PERFORMED WITHIN ONE YEAR

When a contract cannot, by its terms, be completed within one year of the date of its creation, it must be in writing. Again, the Statute of Frauds is concerned with the duration of a legal obligation. The longer the obligation runs, the more likely that a dispute will arise about it. Putting it in writing removes many of the ambiguities that may arise.

F. CONTRACTS FOR THE SALE OF GOODS EXCEEDING $500 IN VALUE

The original Statute of Frauds required written contracts for the sale of goods when the value of the goods exceeded $500 in value. This provision, and the provision requiring written contracts for the sale of stocks and bonds, has been absorbed into the Uniform Commercial Code.

FIGURE 9-5

Types of Contract Trials, 2001*

Table 2. Types of plaintiffs or defendants, by types of contract trials, in State courts in the Nation's 75 largest counties, 2001

Case type	Number	Total	Percent of each type of plaintiff			
			Individual	Government[a]	Business[b]	Hospital[c]
All contract trials[d]	3,676	100%	53.9%	0.8%	44.3%	1.0%
Fraud	616	100%	65.1%	1.9%	32.5%	0.5%
Seller plaintiff	1,203	100	31.3	0.7	66.3	1.7
Buyer plaintiff	789	100	72.2	0.3	27.5	--
Mortgage foreclosure	22	100	--	--	100.0	--
Employment discrimination	165	100	99.4	0.6	--	--
Other employment dispute	286	100	75.9	0.3	22.0	1.7
Rental/lease	275	100	44.7	--	53.8	1.5
Tortious interference	138	100	44.2	0.7	54.3	0.7
Partnership dispute	40	100	65.0	--	25.0	10.0
Subrogation	69	100	2.9	4.3	92.8	--
Other or unknown contract	73	100	57.5	--	42.5	--

	Number	Total	Percent of each type of defendant			
			Individual	Government[a]	Business[b]	Hospital[c]
All contract trials[d]	3,675	100%	33.5%	3.2%	62.3%	1.1%
Fraud	618	100%	35.0%	1.1%	63.4%	0.5%
Seller plaintiff	1,204	100	44.1	0.7	53.8	1.3
Buyer plaintiff	790	100	16.1	0.6	83.2	0.1
Mortgage foreclosure	22	100	54.5	--	45.5	--
Employment discrimination	165	100	4.8	34.5	57.0	3.6
Other employment dispute	286	100	16.4	9.4	72.0	2.1
Rental/lease	275	100	53.5	1.5	44.7	0.4
Tortious interference	138	100	34.8	3.6	57.2	4.3
Partnership dispute	40	100	37.5	--	62.5	--
Subrogation	65	100	66.2	1.5	32.3	--
Other or unknown contract	72	100	50.0	4.2	45.8	--

Note: Plaintiff or defendant type is whichever type appears first in this list: (1) hospital/medical company, (2) business, (3) government agency, and (4) individual. For example, any case involving a hospital defendant is categorized as a hospital even if there were also business, individual, or government defendants in the case. Data on plaintiff type were available for 99.5% of contract trials and data on defendant type were available for 99.4% of contract trials. Detail may not sum to total because of rounding.
-- No cases recorded.
[a]Includes law enforcement and other governmental agencies.
[b]Includes insurance companies, banks, and other businesses and organizations.
[c]Includes medical companies.
[d]Includes bench and jury trials, trials with a directed verdict, judgments notwithstanding the verdict, and jury trials for defaulted defendants.

* Bureau of Justice Statistics, U.S. Department of Justice. Contract Trials and Verdicts in Large Counties, 2001.

 WHAT IS THE UNIFORM COMMERCIAL CODE?

During the early years of the twentieth century, many business leaders saw the need for a uniform system among the various states that would make business transactions easier and more efficient. There was recently a similar push among European nations to create the European Union. Both movements centered on creating

Profiling a Paralegal

▶ April Gardin

I was taking paralegal courses and working for a local bank. One of our clients who worked at a local law office came in and we started talking. She told me about an attorney who was looking to start a law office. I'd wanted to work in the legal field all my life and I contacted him immediately. What he needed was someone to start his office from scratch.

The first thing that I did was to sit down with him and find out what his vision for the office was. How did he want to set up files, handle clients, things like that? After that, I did a needs assessment. What kind of equipment would we need to best suit the practice that he wanted to create? I found the computer system and purchased it.

Then I had to think about other equipment: fax machines, filing cabinets, break room furniture, desks, chairs, and all of the other things that you need to run a law office.

The biggest challenge was creating a filing system that met the needs of the practice. We needed a system that would best suit his needs when he was in the courtroom. We finally settled on a combination numeric and alphabetic system. The clients all receive a specific file number, but while the files are active, we file them alphabetically by their last name. When their cases are closed, we archive them under their file number.

I really enjoy what I do and I'm planning on going on to law school and one day working with my employer as a partner.

a uniform system for business transactions that made the paperwork requirements identical no matter where the transactions took place. There would no longer be differing (and even conflicting) laws in different areas. In the United States, this movement resulted in the Uniform Commercial Code (UCC).

Just as its name suggests, the UCC is a series of proposed commercial codes governing actions as disparate as sales and security agreements. It is not federal law. Instead, it was developed by a panel of legal experts, business people, and scholars as a template that could be adopted by states. It was so effective that most states have adopted the UCC with few or no changes.

ISSUE AT A GLANCE

The Uniform Commercial Code was created as a way of making commercial transactions throughout the United States simpler, easier, and more uniform.

A. THE ORGANIZATION OF THE UNIFORM COMMERCIAL CODE

The UCC covers a wide range of transactions. To determine if the UCC covers a specific type of deal, a researcher can simply check the table of contents. All the transactions covered by the UCC are listed there. Article II, for instance, covers sales, while Article 7 covers warehouse receipts and bills of lading. Article 9 addresses secured transactions.

Careers in the Law

▶ Law Office Manager, Debra Holbrook

I graduated with a paralegal degree and worked for several years as the only paralegal for a three person law firm. The firm continued to grow and I found myself doing everything: answering the phones, making coffee, typing complaints, billing clients, and preparing HUD settlement statements. I even took care of client's children while their parents were with the attorneys. When you're going to school you have this vision of legal secretary versus paralegal and how the two roles are different. In a small town law practice, there is no difference. Your jobs overlap and everybody has to work as a team.

We started hiring more support personnel and I went back to school to get my four year degree in human services. I decided to approach the attorneys with a proposal. I said, "Why don't you let me handle the mechanics of the firm and you guys can do what you need to do? I'll become the office manger. I'll handle the mechanics, hiring and training staff, paying the bills and you could concentrate on practicing law." They thought about it and then gave me the job.

As Office Manager, I handle almost all of the financial stuff. I make sure that the trust account is administered properly and I contact clients if we get a bad check. Believe it or not, the hardest part of my job is facilitating communication between the three attorneys. They are always so busy that they hardly ever have time for them all to meet at the same time. Each of them views things differently and that makes it hard to implement any changes. But I love the challenge of it all.

When a state enacts the UCC, transactions that formerly fell under the Statute of Frauds come under the UCC's jurisdiction.

LONG v. ALLEN
906 P.2d 754 (1995)

BUSTAMANTE, Judge.

Defendant Allen (hereafter Seller) appeals from an order of summary judgment in favor of Plaintiff Long (hereafter Buyer) in an action for breach of a residential purchase agreement. Judgment was entered against Seller and his former wife, co-owners of the property at issue. Only Seller has appealed. We affirm.

DISCUSSION

Buyer made several offers to Seller and his former wife (collectively, Owners) to purchase their residence. Ultimately, Buyer made a written offer dated March 1, 1994, that was set to expire on March 3, 1994, at 6:00 p.m. unless the Owners delivered a written acceptance to Buyer before that time. The Owners signed the offer (the Agreement) on March 4, 1994, and returned it to Buyer on that date via her real estate agent. Both parties acknowledge that the Owners' execution of the Agreement on March 4 constituted a counteroffer. They dispute, however, whether uncontroverted facts establish that Buyer's performance constituted an "acceptance" that bound the Owners to the terms of the counteroffer.

The ultimate question of whether the Owners' counteroffer became a binding promise and resulted in a contract requires us to consider whether the evidentiary facts conclusively establish that Buyer accepted the counteroffer. See Orcutt v. S & L Paint Contractors, Ltd., 109 N.M. 796, 798, 791 P.2d 71, 73 (Ct. App. 1990) (offeree's acceptance must be clear, positive, and unambiguous). Acceptance of an offer is a manifestation of assent to the terms of the offer, made by the offeree, in a manner allowed, invited, or required by the offer. Id. (citing Restatement (Second) of Contracts §50 (1981)).

Seller initially contends that the specific terms of the Owners' counteroffer required a written acceptance. Seller refers us to paragraph 4.11 of the Agreement which states that "[a]ll notices and communications required or permitted under this Agreement shall be in writing." Paragraph 4.11 is a general provision which describes the mechanics for giving notice "required or permitted under this Agreement," including addresses and facsimile telephone numbers. The paragraph also defines the effective time of notices depending on the method of delivery. The paragraph does not on its face address the manner of acceptance or time within which acceptance of the counteroffer is required. We believe that the act of acceptance of the counteroffer is not a communication under the document as provided in paragraph 4.11. Rather, acceptance is an act creating an agreement. The Agreement does not otherwise address in any way Buyer's mode of response and, in our view, simply does not specify that the counteroffer can only be accepted in writing. The counteroffer thus invited acceptance by any manner reasonable under the circumstances, such as by promise or performance. See Restatement, supra, §30(2) (form of acceptance invited) and §32 (in case of doubt, offeree may accept by promise or performance).

The fact that the transaction involved the sale of land and thus was within the statute of frauds does not persuade us by itself that a written acceptance was required. The Agreement, already signed by Buyer on March 1, identified each party and the subject land and also specified the pertinent terms and conditions of the transaction. See Pitek v. McGuire, 51 N.M. 364, 371, 184 P.2d 647, 651-52 (1947). Seller suggests that Buyer's actions were not the type of partial performance which would take the transaction out of the statute of frauds. We disagree. The Agreement satisfied the requirements set forth in Pitek, and Seller, the party to be charged in this case, signed the document. Nothing more is required to satisfy the statute of frauds. See id.; Balboa Constr. Co. v. Golden, 97 N.M. 299, 303, 639 P.2d 586, 590 (Ct. App. 1981); Restatement, supra, §131.

We turn next to the facts bearing on the issue of Buyer's acceptance of the counteroffer by her performance. To the extent the pertinent facts are not in dispute and all that remains is the legal effect of those facts, summary judgment is appropriate. See Westgate Families v. County Clerk, 100 N.M. 146, 148, 667 P.2d 453, 455 (1983). The following facts are undisputed. Paragraphs 1.4(A) and 1.9 of the Agreement required Buyer to deliver a $5,000 earnest-money deposit to a named title company as soon as practical. The check was received by the title company on March 8, 1994. Buyer arranged for professional inspections of the property as urged in paragraph 2.5 of the Agreement. Pursuant to paragraph 2.1 of the Agreement, Buyer sought and obtained a financing commitment for her purchase of the property. Paragraph 1.10 specified that the closing take place within ten business days of April 8, 1994, and that the parties arrange for delivery and execution of the necessary documents and funds. Buyer appeared at the title company office on April 14, 1994, and signed all the documents necessary to close the transaction. In our view, these facts establish conclusively that Buyer accepted the Owners' counteroffer by performance of what the counteroffer requested. See Restatement, supra, §62 (where offer invites offeree to choose between acceptance by promise and acceptance by performance, beginning of invited performance is an acceptance by performance).

We recognize that Seller's affidavit states he never received any communication from Buyer specifically claiming or purporting to accept the counteroffer. However, the fact that Buyer may not have communicated her verbal or written promissory acceptance explicitly is not fatal to Buyer's position. The Restatement makes it clear that notification to the offeror of acceptance is not necessary unless the offer requests notice or the offeree has reason to know the offeror has no adequate means of learning of the performance with reasonable promptness and certainty. Restatement, supra, §54. We have already determined the offer did not require any particular form of acceptance. Further, Seller does not assert and has made no showing that he had no means of learning about Buyer's acceptance. Most tellingly, however, it cannot be disputed that Seller had actual notice of Buyer's acceptance. The following facts are undisputed. On March 9, 1994, at Seller's request, Buyer's real estate agent faxed a copy of the Agreement to Seller's attorney. The cover sheet for the fax included the statement, "We are moving very fast to get everything done." Seller directed Buyer's agent to deliver Buyer's earnest-money-deposit check to the title company and Seller knew the check was delivered. Seller was kept informed regarding property inspections and Buyer's efforts to secure financing. Seller was aware that Buyer's real estate agent arranged for a survey of the property at the Owners' expense. Seller arranged for the April 14, 1994, closing appointment at the title company. Buyer was not aware of any obstacle to closing the purchase until she appeared at the title company to sign closing documents. These facts conclusively establish that Seller was aware in the normal course of business of Buyer's acceptance by performance.

Seller argues that the statement in Buyer's affidavit that she "entered into a valid contract with Defendants" on March 4 is a conclusion of law beyond Buyer's competence. We address this contention only to note that the trial court was not required to rely on Buyer's statement as proof of the existence of a binding contract.

CONCLUSION

We hold as a matter of law that Buyer accepted the counteroffer by performance, thus making the Owners' promises binding. Accordingly, we affirm the trial court's order of summary judgment for Buyer.

IT IS SO ORDERED.

QUESTIONS ABOUT THE CASE

1   Does the court find that the buyer accept the counteroffer in this case?
2   How does the court define "acceptance?"
3   Are the sellers correct that the only proper way to accept is in writing?
4   Does the Statute of Frauds require an acceptance to be made in writing?
5   What does the court mean when it refers to the buyer's acceptance "by performance?"

SKILLS YOU NEED IN THE REAL WORLD

DECIPHERING CONTRACT CLAUSES

Contract law can be a very complicated subject. This is especially true when considering individual contract clause provisions in a large contract. Being able to decipher these contract provisions is a necessary skill for anyone contemplating a career in contract litigation. One of the best methods to decipher contract clauses is to take the clause item by item. For instance, consider the following contract clause:

> The Buyer's obligation to purchase the property is contingent upon the Buyer obtaining, from a lending institution, a commitment for a mortgage loan, secured by the property, in the principal amount of not less than $92,500, at an interest rate not to exceed seven percent (7%) per annum, repayable in equal monthly installments of principal and interest over a period of not less than thirty (30) years, and requiring the payment of points/loan origination/loan discount fees of not more than two percent (2%) of the total loan amount by the Buyer. The Buyer shall apply for such a commitment within ten (10) banking days of the date hereof.

At first, this contract clause might seem intimidating if not incomprehensible. However, if you take the clause point by point, you can easily establish what it means. When you decipher a contract clause, begin with the first phrase that precedes a comma. That would be the phrase: "The Buyer's obligation to purchase the property is contingent upon the Buyer obtaining. . . ."

What does this mean? This language states that the offer being made by the buyer has a condition. What is the condition? Continue reading the contract. The buyer's offer is "contingent upon the Buyer obtaining, from a lending institution, a commitment for a mortgage loan, secured by the property, in the principal amount of not less than $92,500. . . ." How do we interpret this language? The buyer's offer is contingent on the buyer being able to obtain a mortgage on the property for $92,500. If the buyer cannot obtain this financing, using the property as collateral for the mortgage, which is how all mortgages work, the buyer's offer is considered withdrawn.

CHAPTER SUMMARY

Contracts form the basis of nearly all types of commercial and private transactions. All legal professionals must understand the basic components of a contract. The contract is formed when a person makes an offer. An offer indicates a willingness to enter into a contract and also has definite terms. When an offer is accepted, the contract is formed. An acceptance must be unequivocal and must not change the material terms of the offer. A counteroffer rejects the original offer and substitutes a new offer. The power of acceptance is a legal concept that states that a contract can be created when one of the parties has the power and the ability to accept an offer and thereby create a binding contract. Contracts have other essential requirements. Among those requirements is consideration. Consideration is bargained-for exchange; it means that both parties have surrendered something of value in exchange for something else of value. A contract that has no consideration is not a contract. Contracts must also be supported by capacity. Capacity refers to the parties' ability to know and understand the consequences of venturing into a legally binding agreement. If an individual lacks capacity, either because of physical or mental impairment or because the individual is below the age of 18, the party cannot enter into a legally binding contract and therefore the contract is not enforceable. Finally, a contract must contemplate a legal subject in order to be valid.

The Statute of Frauds is a historical protection on particular types of contracts. Under the Statute of Frauds, before certain types of contracts can be enforced through the court system, they must first be in writing. Examples of contracts that are required to be in writing under the Statute of Frauds are contracts to answer for the debt of another, contracts to exchange ownership interests in real estate, and prenuptial agreements.

The Uniform Commercial Code has been enacted, in one form or another, in all 50 states. The UCC provides a framework for commercial transactions and has created a nationwide uniform system to improve the efficiency of business transactions.

ETHICS: AVOIDING CONFLICTS OF INTEREST

It is essential for any legal professional to know and understand the rules about conflicts of interest. A conflict of interest refers to representing two clients with interests adverse to one another. An example of a conflict of interest would be a single attorney representing both sides in a divorce action. Because clients share confidential information with their attorney, the attorney is placed in an impossible situation when she is called upon to represent both sides in a matter and to keep both sets of client confidentialities from being revealed to the other. Because of this impossible situation, all states have created ethical rules that forbid attorneys to represent clients when there is even the appearance of impropriety in doing so.

Conflicts of interest can also arise in other situations. An attorney is barred from representing a client who has an adverse claim against a former client. The problem with conflicts of interest is that the conflict is not always obvious. An attorney could have represented a person years before and not realize that the new client has a potential conflict of interest with the prior client. Attorneys frequently rely on their paralegals to review current cases and newly accepted clients to ensure that the new clients do not have interests that conflict with previous clients' interests. This is called a *conflicts check*.

Conflicts of interest can also arise when an attorney goes into business with a client. An attorney who has a client as a business partner faces a host of potential conflicts of interest. For instance, at what point is the attorney's duty to himself in conflict with his ethical duty to represent a client to the best of his ability? These potential legal pitfalls have resulted in strict rules about conflicts of interest.

CHAPTER REVIEW QUESTIONS

1   What are the elements of a legally enforceable contract?
2   What specific details must be found in a valid offer?
3   What is the power of acceptance?
4   Explain the effect of a counteroffer on the original offer.
5   Explain the mailbox rule.
6   What is the difference between a unilateral and a bilateral contract?
7   Give examples of unilateral and bilateral contracts.
8   What is consideration and why is it a requirement in a contract?
9   Explain the requirement of legality in the contract.
10   What are some types of contracts that are considered to have an illegal purpose?
11   What are some circumstances that would justify a ruling that one party to a contract lacks legal capacity?
12   When was the Statute of Frauds originally created and why?
13   List and explain the various types of contracts that are covered by the Statute of Frauds.
14   According to the Statute of Frauds, what types of contracts must be in writing to be enforceable?
15   What is the significance of the Uniform Commercial Code?
16   Why is it important for a paralegal to understand conflicts of interest?

DISCUSSION QUESTIONS

1   Why is there a strong link between business and law?
2   In drafting the Uniform Commercial Code, the framers were concerned about creating a system that would govern the entire United States. Does a uniform system improve the quality of commerce? Explain your answer.
3   The Statute of Frauds was created at a time when most people could not read. Requiring certain types of contracts to be in writing was a safeguard against fraud and deceit, primarily because someone who could read and write would

draft the contract. Is the Statute of Frauds still necessary in the twenty-first century when nearly everyone is literate? Explain.

PERSONALITY QUIZ

Is contract law right for you? Take this personality quiz and see.

1   I enjoy reading.
0-strongly disagree   5-agree   10-strongly agree

Points:_____

2   I like to pin down details in written communication.
0-strongly disagree   5-agree   10-strongly agree

Points:_____

3   I enjoy research.
0-strongly disagree   5-agree   10-strongly agree

Points:_____

4   I believe that a contract should anticipate and solve problems.
0-strongly disagree   5-agree   10-strongly agree

Points:_____

Total Points:_____

If you scored between 30-50 points, you have many of the qualities that would make you successful in contract law.

If you scored between 20-29 points, you might do well in the field of contract law, but you might do even better in some other area of law.

If you scored 19 or lower, contract law is probably not the best choice for you.

PRACTICAL APPLICATIONS

1   Examine a loan agreement, credit card agreement, or a lease and identify the various contract requirements set out in this chapter. Are there provisions for consideration, capacity, or legality?

2   Locate your state's version of the Statute of Frauds. Is it substantially similar or dissimilar to the sample provided in the text?

WEB SITES

Federal Citizen Information Center (Consumer Law)
http://www.pueblo.gsa.gov

GSA Board of Contract Appeals
http://www.gsbca.gsa.gov

U.S. Department of Commerce
http://www.commerce.gov

TERMS AND PHRASES

Bilateral contract	Consideration	Power of acceptance
Capacity	Contract	Unilateral contract

Criminal Law

Chapter Learning Objectives

After completing this chapter, you should be able to:

- Define what an arrest is and when it occurs
- Explain the role of the grand jury in criminal law
- Explain important procedural steps in a criminal case, such as an arraignment and trial
- Describe the important elements of crimes, such as murder and burglary
- Describe the basic steps in a criminal appeal

 **INTRODUCTION TO CRIMINAL LAW**

In this chapter, we explore the basic concepts of criminal law. Easily one of the most fascinating legal subjects, criminal law has been the focus of countless movies and nightly television dramas. We examine the significant phases of a criminal prosecution and highlight elements of some commonly encountered crimes. We begin where most criminal prosecutions begin: with the arrest.

 ARREST AND BEGINNING THE PROSECUTION

An **arrest** is a detention of a suspect by a police officer. To justify an arrest, the police officer must show that he had **probable cause** to believe that the person arrested had committed a crime. The requirement of probable cause stems directly from the Fourth Amendment of the United States Constitution.

Amendment IV. Search and Seizure
The right of the people to be secure in their persons, houses, papers, and effects, against unreasonable searches and seizures, shall not be violated, and no Warrants

Arrest
The detention of a person by the police

Probable cause
Objective evidence that a crime has been or is about to be committed

shall issue, but upon probable cause, supported by Oath or affirmation, and particularly describing the place to be searched, and the persons or things to be seized.

A person is usually arrested by being physically seized and handcuffed by the police, but the actual definition of arrest is more liberal than that. A person is under arrest when a hypothetical, reasonable person would believe, from the situation, that he was not free to leave. You are certainly under arrest when a police officer places you in the back of a police car and transports you to jail.

Determining the exact moment in time when a suspect is under arrest is important for several reasons. The most important is that arrest triggers several constitutional protections. After an arrest, for example, a suspect has the right to an attorney and the right to remain silent, among other rights. Police officers often read these rights, called Miranda rights, to the suspect shortly after arrest.

A. MIRANDA RIGHTS

We have all heard of Miranda rights. They begin with the famous phrase, "you have the right to remain silent. . . ." These rights were developed by the U.S. Supreme Court in the case of *Miranda v. Arizona* and thus became known as Miranda rights. These rights are read to suspects that the police intend to question after arrest, remind suspects what their rights are, and tell them how they can exercise their various rights. There are numerous misconceptions about Miranda rights. For one, there is no requirement that the police read Miranda rights to everyone who is arrested. The rights are only required when police intend to question a suspect. If they have no need to question a suspect, they have no need to read the Miranda rights. In driving under the influence of alcohol charges, police routinely do not read the rights. After all, the blood-alcohol level will determine the extent of the charge and the defendant could not be questioned anyway — he is intoxicated.

After a suspect is arrested, his official title changes from suspect to defendant. A defendant is a person charged with a crime. A suspect is a person suspected of committing a crime. Following arrest, the suspect is also officially charged with a crime. This often involves the grand jury.

 GRAND JURY

The Fifth Amendment to the U.S. Constitution requires a grand jury proceeding in certain types of cases.

> **Amendment V. Rights of Persons**
> No person shall be held to answer for a capital, or otherwise infamous crime, unless on a presentment or indictment of a Grand Jury. . . .

This Amendment has been interpreted to require grand jury proceedings whenever a person is charged with most types of felonies. A grand jury consists of 16 to 23 people selected from the community who hear testimony and evidence about pending cases and decide whether the prosecution should continue. If they decide that the case should go forward, they issue a ruling called a true bill. If they believe that there is insufficient evidence to proceed, they issue a no bill. A no bill effectively dismisses the pending case. Grand jurors do not determine guilt or innocence. They function as a buffer between the state and the defendant. If they vote a true bill in a case, the defendant will be charged with a crime in an indictment.

A. INDICTMENT

An indictment is a document that officially charges a defendant with a felony. A felony is a crime that is punishable by more than one year in custody. Felonies include crimes as varied as theft and murder. See Figure 10-1 for an example of language used in an indictment.

If the defendant is charged with a misdemeanor (a minor crime that is punishable by no more than 12 months in custody and a $1,000 fine), there is no requirement of a grand jury proceeding and the charging document is referred to as an accusation or **information.**

Information
A document filed by the prosecution that accuses the defendant of a crime; commonly used by federal prosecutors. Also known as an accusation

B. ARRAIGNMENT

Following an indictment, or the issuance of an accusation, the next step is usually an **arraignment.** An arraignment is a court proceeding in which the defendant is officially informed of the charges against him, given a copy of the indictment, and usually served with discovery. The arraignment is also the defendant's opportunity to enter a plea. Most defendants enter a plea of not guilty and then are scheduled for trial. Defendants who wish to plead guilty can be sentenced immediately after the arraignment.

Arraignment
A court appearance in which a person accused of a crime is given the opportunity to enter a plea of guilty or not guilty

C. CRIMINAL DISCOVERY

Discovery is the name for the process by which both sides of a lawsuit learn the details of other side's allegations. In civil cases, discovery is very liberal. Civil litigants are allowed to file discovery motions on the opposing side that request the names, addresses, telephone numbers, and the testimony that each witness will give. In civil cases, it is possible to learn the complete details of the case, down to what each witness will testify to, long before the trial ever begins. The discovery rules in criminal cases are not so liberal. In the past, criminal discovery was extremely limited. A defendant might learn the names of the witnesses who would testify against him, receive copies of scientific tests (such as DNA results) and any potentially helpful material, but that was all. Witness statements, police reports, and other information were not provided.

In recent years, those rules have begun to change. Many states have created new criminal discovery rules that require the state to turn over the entire prosecution file to the defendant, along with witness statements and other materials. However,

Discovery
The exchange of information between the sides involved in a suit

FIGURE 10-1

Sample Indictment

State of Placid vs. John Doe

Count I: Carrying a Concealed Weapon
Count II: Possession of an Automatic Weapon
Count III: Reckless Driving

The grand jurors of this county, to wit:

Patricia Burke, Foreperson	Clay Lambert
Bryan Gartman	Lou Szabo
Lisa Burnett	Scott Smeal
Deborah Bolstridge	David Keaton
Anne Walker	Keith Miles
Neal Pruitt	Amber Sprague
Linda Brunt	Alice Bolstridge
Andy Spradley	Shannon Wagener
Tom Walker	Donna Meyer
Rosanna Hartley	
Cheri Eddy	
Karen Blair	
Tara Bevans	
Joan Bernstein	
Mike Blackham	
Ralph Daniels	
Susan Levine	

Do hereby charge the above named defendant with:

Count I: Carrying a Concealed Weapon
And the grand jurors, in the name and behalf of the State of Placid, County of Belle, do hereby charge and allege that John Doe, on the 19th day of May, 2002, did commit the crime of carrying a concealed weapon, to wit: a 9mm handgun, in such a way that it was not open and obvious to public view, in violation of the laws of this state, the good order, peace and dignity thereof.

Count II: Possession of an Automatic Weapon
The grand jurors aforesaid further allege that said defendant, John Doe, did, on the 19th day of May, 2002, commit the crime of possession of automatic weapons, to wit: a submachine gun, in violation of state law, without proper licenses to possess or transport such weapons, in violation of the laws of this state, the good order, peace and dignity thereof.

Count III: Reckless Driving
The grand jurors aforesaid further allege that said defendant, John Doe, did, on the 19th day of May, 2002, drive recklessly and in disregard of the safety of others, in violation of the laws of this state, the good order, peace and dignity thereof.

- ■ The defendant's statement
- ■ The defendant's criminal record, if any
- ■ Transcripts of recordings
- ■ Witness statements
- ■ Scientific and Test reports
- ■ Exculpatory information (information that is helpful to the defense)

FIGURE 10-2

Discovery Normally Produced by the Government in a Criminal Case

it is doubtful that criminal discovery will ever resemble the free flow of information found in civil cases.

Civil discovery devices, such as depositions and affidavits, are seldom used in criminal cases.

ISSUE AT A GLANCE

IV   THE LAW OF PRINCIPALS AND ACCESSORIES

Just as important as the procedural steps following a defendant's arrest are the rules that apportion guilt between multiple defendants. Under the law, there are two degrees of responsibility: principals and accessories.

A **principal** is the person who actually commits the crime or is present and assists in the commission. An **accessory,** on the other hand, is someone who assists the principal either before or after the crime, but is not present when it actually occurs. Principals are punished more severely than accessories, for obvious reasons.

Many states separate accessories into two categories: accessories before the fact and accessories after the fact.

Principal
The suspect directly involved in the commission of the crime

Accessory
The person who assists a principal, but is not present when the crime occurs

A. ACCESSORY BEFORE THE FACT

An accessory before the fact helps the principal to prepare for the crime, often by helping to plan it, or by providing other resources. However, an accessory before the fact is not present when the crime occurs. Presence usually changes a suspect's classification into that of a principal.

B. ACCESSORY AFTER THE FACT

Accessories after the fact are generally punished less severely than principals or accessories before the fact. Accessories after the fact provide help or assistance to a principal after the crime has occurred. They do so in full knowledge that the principal has committed a crime. A common example of an accessory after the fact is someone who hides a suspect after the crime has occurred.

Some states have completely abolished the categories of accessories, preferring instead to lump them all together under the heading of accomplice.

CRIMES OF VIOLENCE

Human beings have been inflicting injury on one another since time began. Crimes of violence range from assault to first-degree murder. In this section, we summarize the main features of each of these crimes. The most serious of these is murder.

A. MURDER IN THE FIRST DEGREE

Murder is often classified by degree, with murder in the first degree the most serious. First-degree murder is defined by the following elements:

- The unlawful or illegal
- Killing
- Of a human being
- Done with malice
- And premeditation

Malice and **premeditation** are the elements requiring explanation. Malice is hatred or ill will toward the victim. Malice is usually easy for the prosecution to prove. However, the same cannot be said of premeditation.

Malice
The intentional desire to harm a person

Premeditation
An appreciable time period between forming the intent to kill and actually carrying out the murder

1. PREMEDITATION

Premeditation is the element that separates first-degree murder from other types of murder, such as murder in the second degree, manslaughter, and involuntary

---

FIGURE 10-3

Violent Crime, 1973-2003*

Violent crime rates
Adjusted victimization rate
per 1,000 persons age 12 and over

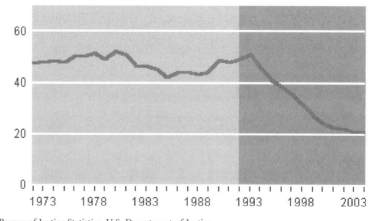

* Bureau of Justice Statistics, U.S. Department of Justice.

manslaughter. When the state alleges premeditation, it must prove that the defendant had time to consider his actions and followed through on them anyway. It is this time for reflection that defines this type of murder. When most people would have hesitated, the defendant did not.

B. MANSLAUGHTER

Unlike murder in the first degree, manslaughter is the killing of a human being with malice, but usually under the influence of some strong passion. Often referred to as a "crime of passion," manslaughter is reserved for impulse killings, in which a defendant is confronted with a certain amount of provocation and responds with deadly force. His actions are not excused, but the impact of the provocation will reduce the charge from first-degree murder to manslaughter. The practical consequence is that the defendant may face a 20-year sentence instead of life in prison for a first-degree murder conviction.

C. ASSAULT AND BATTERY

The crimes of assault and battery are so intertwined, and are the subject of so much misinformation, that separating out the details is sometimes difficult.

The elements of assault are straightforward. Assault consists of:

- Causing the victim to experience fear or apprehension of
- A harmful or offensive contact

In assault, the victim is not touched. A person is assaulted when he fears contact. Battery, on the other hand, consists of the following elements:

- Causing the victim
- Harmful or offensive contact

Battery involves an actual touching; assault does not. The reason that these two crimes are usually discussed together is that often they both appear in the fact situation of an attack. If a person tries to punch you and misses, that is an assault. If he then actually strikes you on his next punch, that is battery. He can be prosecuted for both charges, although battery is considered to be more serious, since it actually caused injury.

 **SEX CRIMES**

Forcing sex on another person is a crime, whether the person is an adult or a child. The two most common prosecutions of sex offenses are rape and child molestation.

A. RAPE

Rape is the forcible carnal knowledge of a woman by a man, without her consent. Rape is a consistently underreported crime, probably because of the continued stigma associated with being a rape victim and the embarrassing aspects of having to testify about sexual acts. Medical testimony is often used in rape prosecutions to establish bruising and trauma associated with forced sex.

1. RAPE SHIELD STATUTES

An important aspect of rape prosecutions is the protection given to rape victims under the law. All jurisdictions have some form of so-called rape shield statutes that protect a sexual assault victim's identity and also prohibit defense counsel from inquiring into the victim's past sexual encounters, unless these encounters actually involved the defendant. Rape shield statutes are specifically designed to prohibit the kind of emotionally devastating cross-examination that is commonly depicted in television shows and in movies.

B. CHILD MOLESTATION

Child molestation consists of sex with a child. In most states, a child is defined as anyone under the age of 14, although 12 is used in some states. Prohibited sexual acts with children include fondling and actual sex.

 THEFT AND PROPERTY CRIMES

Rounding out our discussion of the various types of criminal offenses are theft crimes. Theft covers a broad range of activities, from theft by shoplifting to robbery and burglary. We begin our discussion of theft crimes with larceny.

A. LARCENY

Larceny
Taking property belonging to another without permission

Larceny is a general term that is used to describe most forms of theft. The elements of larceny are:

- The wrongful taking and conversion of
- Personal property of another
- Without permission and
- With the intent to permanently deprive the owner of the property

1. WRONGFUL TAKING AND CONVERSION

A person who is entitled to take possession of property, such as repossession agent who is sent out to retrieve a car, does not commit larceny because he has the right

FIGURE 10-4

30-Year Crime Data*

Highlights

The National Crime Victimization Survey reveals long-term declines in victimization to the lowest per capita rates in nearly 30 years

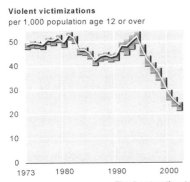

Violent victimizations
per 1,000 population age 12 or over

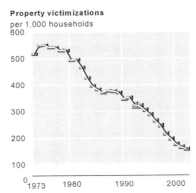

Property victimizations
per 1,000 households

The best estimate and range of estimates

Each vertical bar shows the range within which the true victimization rate was likely to fall.
For discussion of displaying estimates, see <http://www.ojp.usdoj.gov/bjs/pub/pdf/dvctue.pdf>.

• Overall violent victimization and property crime rates in 2002 are the lowest recorded since the inception of the NCVS in 1973.[1]

• In 2002 the rate for rape was 0.4 per 1,000 persons age 12 or older, 60% of the 1993 rate.

• For the decade the rate for robbery was down 63%, falling to 2 per 1,000 in 2002.

• From 1993 to 2002 victimization by aggravated assault, associated with serious injury or weapons, declined 64% to 4 per 1,000. The rate of simple assault — a crime that involves neither serious injury nor weapon — fell 47%.

[1]Based on adjustments to pre-1992 estimates to account for the 1992 redesign of the NCVS.

• The rate of violent crime dropped 21% from the period 1999-2000 to the period 2001-02.

• Reporting to the police increased from 43% of all violent crimes in 1993 to 49% in 2002; reporting of property crimes increased from 34% to 40%.

• Violent crimes against females were more likely to have been reported to the police than those against males.

• The relative increase in reporting crime to the police was greater for rape/sexual assault than it was for robbery or simple assault, 1993-2002.

• During 2002, 7% of violent crime victims faced an offender armed with a firearm.

* Bureau of Justice Statistics, U.S. Department of Justice. Criminal Victimization, 2002.

Conversion
The act of removing property from the rightful owner and reducing it to the possession of the taker

to take possession. **Conversion** of property refers to assuming control over an object and removing it from the rightful possession of its owner.

2. PERSONAL PROPERTY OF ANOTHER

Larceny always refers to personal property. Under the law, all property can be divided into two broad categories: real property and personal property. Real property refers to land and anything permanently attached to the land, such as houses. All other types of property are classified as personal property.

3. WITHOUT PERMISSION

Although this would appear to be an obvious component of theft, it is true that the government must prove, in a criminal prosecution, that the person who took the property did not have the owner's permission to do so. At some point in a theft trial, the property owner will take the stand and actually tell the jury that the defendant did not have his permission to take the property. Without this testimony, the state would be unable to prove one of the key elements in a theft case.

4. WITH THE INTENT TO PERMANENTLY DEPRIVE THE OWNER

Another key element of a theft case is proof that the defendant intended to permanently deprive the owner of the property. The facts surrounding the taking are usually sufficient to establish this element. If the defendant breaks into someone's home, steals jewelry, and leaves with it, such evidence would be enough to establish that he meant to permanently deprive the owner of the jewelry.

B. THEFT BY SHOPLIFTING

Shoplifting is a form of larceny in which a person takes property belonging to a store, without permission, with the intent to permanently deprive the store of its merchandise. Shoplifting deserves special mention because it is still one of the most common forms of theft. Stores lose billions of dollars each year in theft by shoplifting.

C. OTHER PROPERTY CRIMES

The category of other property crimes encompasses a broad range of activities from arson to burglary to insurance fraud. One of the most common types of crimes in this category is burglary.

Although burglary is discussed in the context of theft crimes, burglary is actually more of a hybrid between trespass and theft. See Figure 10-5 for the elements of the crime of burglary.

When the government charges a person with burglary, it must prove not only that the defendant entered a building without consent, but also what the

Careers in the Law

▶ K-9 Police Officer

arty McNeeley has been a K-9 patrol officer for seven years. He'd always wanted to be a police officer and he was attracted to the idea of working with a police dog. He took police dog training courses in the military.

"The first week of classes concerns dog psychology. They emphasize training, punishment, and reward trading. The kind of a world that a dog lives in is a one-minute world. That's what we were told. If a reward or punishment is not administered almost immediately, the dog won't know what it's for. After that, you take additional courses in K-9 health, conditions, medical afflictions and proper health care of your dog. They take you out and there is a kennel full of dogs, they've already been trained, and they pair you up."

Officer McNeeley has been working with Rocco for two years. Rocco has been trained to detect narcotics and he is called out whenever police suspect someone of transporting illegal drugs. He is also trained to attack and subdue suspects.

"When I pull someone over, Rocco always moves into the opening into the back seat and watches. He can come out of the patrol car if he needs to. That gives you a good feeling, knowing that he's got your back covered."

Burglary consists of the following elements: Proof that the defendant
- Entered a building or occupied structure (such as a home)
- Without consent or permission of the owner
- With the intent to commit a theft or a felony

FIGURE 10-5

The Elements of Burglary

---

defendant's intent was at the time that he entered. The government must prove either that the defendant entered with the intent to commit a theft or with the intent to commit a felony. Examples of felonies would include murder, rape, and armed robbery.

 VERDICTS IN CRIMINAL CASES

When we discussed civil cases in Chapter 4, we learned that the **verdicts** that the jurors in those cases reach are findings of liability or no liability. The verdicts in criminal cases are markedly different. Jurors in criminal cases are not only asked to determine the facts of a case, but also to apportion guilt. The verdicts in these cases reflect that responsibility.

The standard of proof in a criminal case is proof beyond a reasonable doubt. This is a much higher standard than civil cases, in which the standard is simply a preponderance of the evidence. The burden of proof in criminal cases is higher because the punishment in a criminal case is more serious. After all, in a civil case,

Verdicts
The jury's decision about the facts and responsibility in a case

the losing party may pay out a monetary award. In a criminal case, the losing party may go to prison for the rest of his life. Given this dramatic difference in result, the burden of proof in criminal cases is raised.

 **The burden of proof in criminal cases is proof beyond a reasonable doubt.**

The problem with a standard such as beyond a reasonable doubt is that legal commentators have been wrestling with a precise definition almost from the day that it was created. With the civil standard of preponderance of the evidence, the definition is simple: The plaintiff must prove that his version of the facts is more than likely to be true. However, proof beyond a reasonable doubt raises a host of questions. What, precisely, is a reasonable doubt?

We can say that reasonable doubt is something less than absolute or mathematical certainty. Beyond a reasonable doubt does not mean proof beyond all doubt, or beyond a shadow of a doubt. Most courts approach this problem by instructing the jury that a reasonable doubt means a doubt based on a specific reason. At the end of the state's case, a juror should be convinced that the state has made a case against the defendant and that the facts, as presented, are true. If not, the juror should vote not guilty, based on having a reasonable doubt.

A. GUILTY

When the jurors believe that the government has proven its case against the defendant beyond a reasonable doubt, they vote a guilty verdict. A guilty verdict is the jury's decision that the defendant is factually responsible for the crime and that the case against him has been proven to the legal standard.

B. NOT GUILTY

Criminal juries may also find a defendant not guilty. Such a finding may be based on any of a number of factors. The jurors may not believe that the defendant is the person who actually committed the offense, or they may believe that the defendant is the responsible party, but do not believe that the government has sufficiently proven its case.

When a defendant is found not guilty, the government is not allowed to appeal that verdict. The case against the defendant is over and the defendant cannot be prosecuted again for that crime. Under the Fifth Amendment's Double Jeopardy provision, once a person has been tried for a crime and found not guilty, he can never be tried for that crime again, even if new evidence surfaces or witnesses later change their stories.

C. ALTERNATE VERDICTS

Jurors are not permitted to create their own verdicts. In criminal cases, the choices are usually limited to guilty or not guilty. However, there are times when jurors have additional choices. For instance, when a defendant raises the defense of insanity, the jurors have a third option. In such a case, if the jurors believe that the defendant was legally insane when he committed the crime, they may find him not guilty by reason of insanity. In such a case, the defendant is not responsible for the crime and will not be sentenced. However, most states provide that a person who receives this verdict will be remanded into the care of the state psychiatric system. In many cases, persons may end up spending more time incarcerated in a state mental institution than they would have spent in prison had they been found guilty of the crime.

Some states have amended their insanity defense to provide a fourth verdict alternative for jurors. In these states, a jury may find the defendant guilty, but mentally ill. In such a case, the defendant is sentenced to prison, just as if he had been found guilty. According to the provisions of the statutes that create this sentencing alternative, the defendant should receive mental counseling while in custody.

In most cases, the jury's verdict options are guilty, not guilty, and not guilty by reason of insanity. Some states provide a fourth alternative: guilty, but mentally ill.

ISSUE AT A GLANCE

D. UNANIMOUS VERDICTS

Most jurisdictions provide that verdicts in criminal cases must be unanimous. All jurors must agree that the defendant is guilty before a verdict will be entered against

---

Profiling a Paralegal

▶ Cherie Eddy, Prosecution Paralegal

What does a prosecution paralegal do? Cherie Eddy has been working in a Virginia-based prosecutor's office for years. "I prepare the case files for each attorney. We get a copy of the charging document, which we call a warrant, or indictment. If it's circuit court, it's indictment; if it's district court, it's a warrant. I prepare the case file, meaning I get all of the police reports, victim-witness information, addresses, and statements. If it's a drug case, I make sure that the crime lab report is in the file."

She assists the prosecutors by preparing summaries of the case. "I prepare a synopsis of the case. I put in the key players, what they have to do with the case, so the attorney doesn't have to read through an inch of reports to find the basics. That synopsis helps the attorney get briefed on the case, get the highlights of it so that they don't go over there and not know what's going on.

"I enjoy the job very much. It's exciting and you feel as though you are making a positive impact on your community."

Hung Jury
A jury that is unable to reach a unanimous verdict

Mistrial
A judicial declaration that the trial is void and has no legal effect

him. If only one juror disagrees with the majority, and cannot. be convinced to change his vote, the judge will intercede. When jurors are unable to reach a unanimous verdict, the jury is referred to as a **hung jury.** The judge will declare a **mistrial.** A mistrial is a ruling that puts the case back on its original footing, as though the trial never occurred. The state is free to retry the defendant, and, in most situations, the state does so

Although the jurors decide factual issues in a case and apportion guilt, in almost all situations, the jury has no input as to sentencing. That decision rests with the judge.

SENTENCING

Sentence
The prison term, probation/parole, and fine imposed on a defendant who has been found guilty

Judges impose sentences. If the defendant has been found not guilty, the judge will simply release the defendant. If he has no other charges pending against him, he leaves the courtroom as a free man. When the defendant is found guilty, the judge will then consider the possible **sentence.**

There are many factors that go into a defendant's sentence. Certain crimes carry statutory minimum sentences. In such a situation, the judge's sentence must be for a term that is at least as long as the minimum sentence, although the judge is allowed to increase the sentence beyond that point. The judge will review the defendant's prior record, the facts of the current case, the violence used and injuries sustained by others, and many other factors, to determine the defendant's sentence. Sentencing factors are listed in Figure 10-6.

Many states, and the federal system, follow sentencing guidelines that dictate the defendant's ultimate sentence.

A. SENTENCING GUIDELINES

Sentencing guidelines are also known as structured sentencing.

Many jurisdictions have moved to a sentencing guideline system. Under this system, a defendant's prior convictions, current charge, and other factors are entered into a grid or numeric system that dictates the minimum and maximum sentence. Such systems remove much of a judge's discretion in drafting a sentence.

FIGURE 10-6	
Factors That Increase or Decrease a Potential Sentence	

Aggravating Factors	Mitigating Factors
■ Violence in committing the crime	■ Defendant's remorse
■ Past criminal record	■ Lack of violence in committing the crime
■ Defendant's demeanor	■ Family upbringing
■ Possibility of future dangerousness	■ Mental health

 # APPEALS IN CRIMINAL CASES

Although we discussed appeals in detail in Chapter 7 of this book, there are some issues in criminal appeals that should be brought up here.

When a defendant has been found guilty after a jury trial, he always has the right to **appeal** that conviction. We have already seen that the government does not have the same right when the defendant is found not guilty. The appellate process usually begins when the defendant files a motion for a new trial.

Appeal
A request to an appellate court that it reverse or modify a decision made in a lower court

A. MOTION FOR NEW TRIAL

When a defendant files a motion for new trial, he is literally asking the trial court to void the results of the first trial and start the case over again. As you can imagine, most motions for a new trial are denied. It is the denial of this motion that gives the defendant the right to take his case to an appellate court.

B. CRIMINAL APPEALS

Criminal cases raise unique issues on appeal. In a criminal case, the defendant can raise a wide variety of allegations about improprieties that occurred during the trial as justification for a reversal of his conviction. However, a defendant is not permitted to bring new evidence to the attention of the appellate court. Appellate courts do not consider new evidence. They only address what occurred in the trial court.

If an appellate court reverses a defendant's conviction, the government is free to retry the defendant. In many ways, an appellate reversal is similar to a mistrial. The legal effect of the first trial is voided. The government is free to try the defendant all over again and to introduce the same evidence and testimony. If the defendant is convicted a second time, he also has the right to appeal this conviction. Another appellate issue that is unique to criminal law is habeas corpus.

C. HABEAS CORPUS

A habeas corpus action is a type of appeal brought in the federal court system. When a defendant files a **habeas corpus** action, he is triggering a provision of the U.S. Constitution that requires all incarcerations to be legal and justifiable. Although it wasn't originally designed to be a second round of appeals for people convicted in criminal cases, that is how it is used. Whether the defendant is convicted in state court or in federal court, he is permitted to challenge the conviction through habeas corpus. This is one reason why appeals in criminal cases can drag on for years.

Habeas corpus
(Latin) "You have the body"; an inquiry to determine whether a person who is incarcerated has received all constitutional guarantees

MATTAROCHIA v. STATE
200 Ga. App. 681, 409 S.E.2d 546 (1991)

Alice C. Stewart, Atlanta, for appellant
Ralph T. Bowden, Jr., Solicitor, Neal R. Bevans, Asst. Solicitor, for appellee

COOPER, Judge.

Appellant was convicted in a jury trial of driving under the influence of alcohol (O.C.G.A. 40-6-391(a) and driving with a blood alcohol concentration greater than 0.12 grams (O.C.G.A. 40-6-391(a)(4)), and appeals the denial of his motion for new trial and motion for modification of sentence.

Viewing the evidence in the light most favorable to the jury's verdict, it appears that while responding to a call concerning a traffic accident shortly after 6:30 A.M., on July 13, 1989, Officer Britt of the Atlanta Police Department was flagged down by appellant en route to the reported site of the accident. Appellant said that he had been in an accident and had run off the roadway. Officer Britt testified that as appellant approached the car, he detected a strong odor of alcohol on appellant's breath and noticed that appellant was unsteady on his feet, his eyes had a glassy appearance, and his speech was slurred. Appellant got into the patrol car and directed Officer Britt to the accident site, which was approximately one-eighth of a mile away. At the site, Officer Britt discovered skid marks on the roadway and tire tracks in the dirt which led to a car which had been driven over the curb, into the grass of a city park and was resting against a tree on its right side. Officer Britt observed that the radiator was warm and the engine was steaming. Appellant, still seated in the patrol car, was then placed under arrest and was advised of his rights, including implied consent warnings pursuant to OCGA 40-5-55. No field sobriety test was given; however, appellant consented to a blood test. At trial, the parties stipulated that appellant's blood alcohol level at the time of testing was 0.12 grams.

1. At the outset we will consider appellant's various contentions that the trial court erred in its rulings on the sufficiency and adequacy of the accusation and jurisdictional questions. Appellant argues that this case was improperly bound over to the State Court of DeKalb County from the City Court of Atlanta because the citations issued by Officer Britt indicated that appellant was cited for violating local offenses and appellant did not elect to have the offenses treated as state offenses pursuant to OCGA 40-6376(b). This contention is without merit. The solicitor's decision to charge appellant with state violations was duly authorized by OCGA 40-6-376(a). Appellant's contention that the accusation and an amended accusation were improper because they were drawn more broadly than the citations is likewise without merit. Appellant's remaining arguments that the trial court was without jurisdiction to hear the case and that the traffic citations must serve as notice of the charges, due to the solicitor's failure to file the accusations with the court, will not be considered as they were not raised as error below. Moreover, it appears any objection to the amended accusation was waived by appellant's counsel's consent to the amended accusation before the trial commenced.

Appellant contends the trial court erred in denying his motions for directed verdict and new trial, asserting the general grounds. Appellant maintains that Officer Britt did not see the vehicle in motion, did not see appellant in the car, did not witness the accident and did not establish the time the accident occurred; nor did anyone else witness the accident. Moreover, despite the stipulation, appellant contends the State did not establish that his intoxication level was 0.12 grams during the time he had physical control of the vehicle, and as a result of these deficiencies, there was insufficient evidence that appellant operated the vehicle under the influence of alcohol.

Appellant is correct that to be guilty of the offense of driving under the influence one must drive or be in actual physical control of a moving vehicle while under the influence of alcohol. However, it is well settled that the driving of an automobile while intoxicated may be shown by circumstantial evidence. In order to sustain the judgment of conviction, the evidence need not exclude *every* inference or hypothesis except the guilt of the accused, but only *reasonable* inferences and hypotheses, so as to justify the inference, beyond a reasonable doubt, of guilt.

Appellant's argument with regard to the insufficiency of the circumstantial evidence totally belies his admission to Officer Britt that he drove the car off the road and his stipulation to the blood test results. These admissions together with the direct evidence provided by Officer Britt describing appellant's demeanor and the additional circumstantial evidence adduced at trial amply justified a finding by the jury that appellant was in actual physical control of the vehicle when it was driven off the road and that appellant was intoxicated while driving in accordance with the conviction of OCGA 40-6-391(a)(1) beyond a reasonable doubt.

It is also urged that because Officer Britt indicated on the traffic citation that the incident occurred in the City of Atlanta, Fulton County, that proper venue was not established at trial; however, Officer Britt's testimony at trial that the accident occurred in the City of Atlanta, DeKalb County went unchallenged. Thus, venue in DeKalb State Court was properly established beyond a reasonable doubt.

Appellant next charges that the admission of the mug shot, taken when he was booked, was without proper foundation, resulting in prejudice far outweighing any probative value. Before a photograph may be introduced in evidence, it must be authenticated by a showing that it is a fair and truthful representation of what it purports to depict. The quantum of evidence required to sufficiently identify photographs as true and accurate representations of what they purport to depict is a matter to be left within the discretion of the trial court. The mug shot was identified by Officer Britt as fairly and accurately representing appellant's appearance on the morning of his arrest. Appellant's objections to the photograph at trial asserted lack of foundation and relevance. This court has upheld the admission of mug shots to "illustrate [a] defendant's physical appearance shortly after his arrest" in cases in which an incident of driving under the influence is being re-created for the jury and the defendant's appearance is "some evidence" of his intoxication. The photograph was clearly relevant to the issue of appellant's intoxication, and the court did not err in allowing its admission. The trial transcript does not reflect that appellant's contentions — that the photograph was inflammatory, put his character in issue and deprived him of the presumption of innocence — were raised below. Hence, they were not preserved for appellate review and will not be considered by this court.

Judgment affirmed.

QUESTIONS ABOUT THE CASE

1   Who are the attorneys who argued this case on appeal?
2   What were the circumstances that Officer Britt found at 6:30 A.M. on July 13th?

3 According to the court, can a person be convicted of drunk driving by circumstantial evidence?

4 What is the standard to admit a "mug" shot of the defendant, taken at the time of the arrest?

SKILLS YOU NEED IN THE REAL WORLD

LOCATING CRIMINAL CONVICTIONS

There may be numerous times in your legal career when you will need to obtain information about a person's criminal background. The person may be a witness in an upcoming trial, or may be someone who has just applied for a job at the firm. Either way, knowing how to locate information about criminal convictions is a skill that will make you indispensable at your job.

When a person is convicted, a file of that conviction is kept in the local courthouse. This information is also added to a statewide database. In many states, you can access this database of criminal convictions through the Internet, although many courthouses still only allow access from a secure terminal in the local clerk of court's office. To search for a person's criminal record, you need to know some information about him. You will need this person's identifying information: correct legal name, date of birth, and, in many cases, Social Security number. Armed with this information you can search the local courthouse records for any indictments or other charges brought against this individual. You can also access the statewide criminal conviction database. (Most states have, or are developing, this database.)

Knowing how to quickly and efficiently locate a person's criminal record can be an absolutely essential skill for a new legal professional.

CHAPTER SUMMARY

Criminal law is a highly specialized area of law that has its own set of rules, pleadings, and concerns. A criminal case normally begins when a person is arrested and charged with a crime. An arrest is a detention of a person by law enforcement officers. Determining the point of arrest is important because once a person is arrested, he has certain constitutional rights that operate to protect him. If a person is charged with a felony, a grand jury will be convened to consider the facts of the defendant's case and to rule that there is probable cause to continue the prosecution against the defendant. A grand jury's vote of true bill gives the state authority to continue to prosecute the defendant at trial. The document that charges a defendant with a felony is referred to as an indictment. Felonies are serious crimes punishable by more than 12 months in custody. Examples of felonies include murder, rape, armed robbery, and serious theft offenses. When a person is charged with a misdemeanor, the charging document is referred to as an accusation or an information.

The arraignment is the official court hearing in which the defendant is informed of the charges against him and given an opportunity to enter a plea of guilty or not guilty. If a defendant pleads not guilty at an arraignment, he is normally served with discovery materials such as witness statements, police reports, scientific reports, and other materials. The defendant is given a court date for his trial.

Criminal trials are very similar to civil jury trials. However, at the end of a criminal trial the jury enters a verdict of guilty or not guilty. Defendants who are found not guilty are released. The government is not permitted to appeal a not guilty verdict. If the defendant is found guilty, the judge will sentence him. Defendants who are found guilty at trial are allowed to appeal their cases to appellate courts.

ETHICS: REPRESENTING GUILTY CLIENTS

Criminal defense attorneys are often asked, "How can you represent someone you know is guilty?" The answer to that question is both simple and complex. The simple part is that representing people who are charged with a crime is the attorney's job and because many of them are guilty, there is no way to avoid it. The complex answer is more interesting. Attorneys rarely discuss guilt or innocence with their clients. Instead, an attorney will tell the client about the government's case and then ask how the client intends to respond to the allegations. Most criminal defense attorneys are ethical and honest people who work hard to uphold the basic philosophy of the criminal justice system: that all people are presumed innocent until proven guilty. Criminal defense attorneys are as indispensable to our system of justice as juries, judges, and prosecutors. Everyone in the system has a role to play and ultimate justice depends on all these participants doing their duty to the best of their ability.

CHAPTER REVIEW QUESTIONS

1   What is the definition of *arrest*?
2   What are the Miranda rights and what purpose do they serve?
3   How many people normally compose a grand jury and what is the grand jury's function?
4   What is the difference between an indictment and an information?
5   Explain arraignment.
6   Compare and contrast civil discovery with criminal discovery.
7   Under the law, what is the difference between a principal and an accessory?
8   What is the difference between an accessory before the fact and an accessory after the fact? Explain.
9   What are the elements of murder in the first degree?
10 What is the difference between manslaughter and murder in the first degree?
11 Compare and contrast the elements of assault and battery.

12   Explain the elements of rape.
13   What are rape shield statutes?
14   What are the elements of larceny?
15   List and explain the elements of the crime of burglary.
16   Compare and contrast the possible verdicts in criminal cases versus the possible verdicts in civil cases.
17   Explain the role of sentencing guidelines.
18   Explain the process of appeal in criminal cases.
19   What is a motion for new trial and what purpose does it serve?
20   Explain habeas corpus.

DISCUSSION QUESTIONS

1   John has been charged with murder and his defense team is going to raise the defense of insanity. What are the possible verdicts that the jury may reach in this case? Explain the consequences of each.
2   Why are criminal discovery laws and civil discovery laws so different?
3   Sentencing guidelines were originally enacted to curtail judges' discretion in sentencing. It was felt that judges were imposing different sentences in cases that were actually quite similar. Are sentencing guidelines a good idea or a bad idea? Support your answer with material from the text.

PERSONALITY QUIZ

Is criminal law the right field for you? Take this personality quiz and see.

1   I distrust the government.

    10-strongly disagree   5-agree   0-strongly agree

                                                                        Points: _____

2   I have a strong sense of right and wrong.

    0-strongly disagree   5-agree   10-strongly agree

                                                                        Points: _____

3   I have family members in law enforcement.

    0-strongly disagree   5-agree   10-strongly agree

                                                                        Points: _____

4   I have friends who have been hassled by the police.

    10-strongly disagree   5-agree   0-strongly agree

                                                                        Points: _____

                                                                   Total Points: _____

If you scored between 0-10 points, you might be more suited for criminal defense work than prosecution.

If you scored between 20-40 points, you might prefer to work for the prosecution.

PRACTICAL APPLICATIONS

Contact your local court system and find out when the next criminal trial is scheduled. Sit in on an arraignment or a criminal trial and take note of details and events. For instance, what is the prosecutor called? The prosecutor can be referred to as a solicitor, commonwealth's attorney, assistant district attorney, state's attorney, or people's attorney, depending on the state. See if you can identify the prosecutor and the type of hearing that is being held. What procedure is followed? If the event is an arraignment, do defendants who plead guilty receive their sentences on the same day? What happens to defendants who plead not guilty? Are they given a trial date for a later time? Are they served with discovery materials at that time? If you have the opportunity, speak with a defense attorney and see if you can get answers to some of these questions.

WEB SITES

The Federal Judiciary Home Page
http://www.uscourts.gov

The United States Supreme Court Home Page
http://www.supremecourtus.gov/opinions/opinions.html

American Probation & Parole Association (APPA)
http://www.appa-net.org

Find Law.com
www.findlaw.com

National Center for Policy Analysis — Criminal Justice Issues
http://www.ncpa.org

Department of Justice Home Page (DOJ)
http://www.usdoj.gov

Court TV
http://www.courttv.com

Bureau of Justice Assistance (BJA)
http://www.ojp.usdoj.gov/BJA

Federal Bureau of Investigation (FBI)
http://www.fbi.gov

Drug Enforcement Administration (DEA)
http://www.usdoj.gov/dea

TERMS AND PHRASES

Accessory	Habeas corpus	Premeditation
Appeal	Hung jury	Principal
Arraignment	Information	Probable cause
Arrest	Larceny	Sentence
Conversion	Malice	Verdict
Discovery	Mistrial	

Administrative Law

Chapter Learning Objectives

After completing this chapter, you should be able to:

- Explain the reason for the creation of administrative agencies

- Explain the role of administrative agencies in federal and state governments

- Define "sunshine" laws

- Explain how agencies create their own rules and regulations

- Describe the role of Social Security and workers' compensation laws

 **INTRODUCTION TO ADMINISTRATIVE LAW**

There are some areas of law that you might go your entire life without ever experiencing directly. Administrative law is not one of them. Unlike specialized legal topics such as criminal law or real property law, everyone in the United States encounters administrative law, more so than any other area of law. The reason for this is simple: Administrative law is the way that governments run. Whenever you pay your taxes, apply for a loan, put gasoline in your car, or take classes through your local college, you are involved with and affected by administrative law.

 **WHAT IS ADMINISTRATIVE LAW?**

Because **administrative law** encompasses such a huge area of practice, we must begin with a foundation to the topic and then expand on that foundation to describe federal and state administrative law.

Administrative law
A broad term encompassing the power of branches of government to delegate power to governmental agencies to perform specific areas of responsibility; also refers to the power of governmental agencies to regulate themselves, such as their ability to create their own rules and regulations

Administrative law consists of the rules, procedures, and regulations that government agencies use in their day-to-day practices. We begin with a simple scenario and explain how administrative law affects the process.

Maria has recently graduated from a paralegal program. She is immediately hired by a local law firm that pays her an excellent salary. The work is challenging and interesting and she spends all her time learning as much as she possibly can. Two weeks after she starts, she gets the very first paycheck she has ever received in her life. When she looks at the check, she asks, "What are all these little debits on my check and where is this money going?"

Maria has hit the world of administrative law. Some of the debits on her paycheck go toward paying her taxes. At the end of the year, she will submit an income tax return to the Internal Revenue Service showing her income and the taxes that she paid that year. If she paid too much on her taxes, she will be entitled to a refund. If she didn't pay enough, she will have to make up the shortfall.

ISSUE AT A GLANCE   Administrative law refers to the creation, structure, and day-to-day business of government.

We all know that the Internal Revenue Service (IRS) is the governmental agency that is responsible for collecting taxes. The IRS is an administrative agency under the control of the U.S. Department of the Treasury.

Both federal and state governments are divided into three branches: executive, judicial and legislative. We know that the judicial branch is responsible for the court system and the legislative branch is responsible for drafting laws. The executive branch has the responsibility of enforcing the laws. On the federal level, the President of the United States holds the highest executive position. On the state level, the governor holds the highest executive position.

Sticking to our example of paying taxes, we know that the President has far too many responsibilities to spend his time contacting individual taxpayers to discuss their delinquent taxes. The President delegates his various powers among federal administrative **agencies.** See Figure 11-1 for a partial list of the broad range of administrative agencies that exist on the federal level.

Agency
A governmental unit or department

President of the United States

U.S. Department of the Treasury

IRS

The list in Figure 11-1 is only a small sampling of the entire federal administrative agency organization. As you can see in Figure 11-3, the IRS is only one of several agencies that fall under the jurisdiction of the Department of the Treasury,

FIGURE 11-1

A Sample of Federal Agencies Answering to the President

This list includes some of the administrative agencies that work under these various federal agencies.

- Department of Agriculture
  USDA
- Department of Commerce
  National Oceanic and Atmospheric Administration
  Patents and Trademarks
- Department of Defense
  Army
  Navy
  Air Force
  Marines
- Department of Education
  Office of Student Financial Assistance
- Department of Energy
  National energy policy
- Department of Health and Human Services
  Centers for Disease Control (CDC)
  Food and Drug Administration (FDA)
  National Institutes of Health (NIH)
- Department of Housing and Urban Development

    Office of Fair Housing and Equal Opportunity
    Government National Mortgage Association (Ginnie Mae)
- Department of the Interior
  National Park Service
  U.S. Fish and Wildlife Service
- Department of Homeland Security
  United States Secret Service
  Bureau of Citizenship and Immigration Services
- Department of Justice
  Drug Enforcement Administration (DEA)
  Federal Bureau of Investigation (FBI)
- Department of Labor
  Occupational Safety and Health Administration (OSHA)
- Department of State
  Bureau of Consular Affairs
- Department of Transportation
  Federal Aviation Administration
- Department of Treasury
  Internal Revenue Service (IRS)
- Department of Veterans Affairs (VA)
  Veterans Health Administration

and Treasury is only one of many departments. You can easily conclude from this that the President of the United States has a great deal of power.

There are hundreds of federal agencies, covering nearly every aspect of a person's life.

ISSUE AT A GLANCE

The U.S. Constitution sets the stage for administrative agencies by giving Congress the right to create agencies to carry out the business of government and to make most of them answer to the President. However, the Founding Fathers never envisioned the massive structure of governmental agencies that has come into existence in the last 200 years.

Because an administrative agency such as the IRS operates under authority delegated by the President, some interesting issues arise as an agency goes about its duties.

FIGURE 11-2

The President's Cabinet

The head of the U.S. Department of the Treasury is the Secretary of the Treasury who works directly for the President of the United States as a member of the President's Cabinet. Other members of the President's Cabinet include:

■ Secretary of Defense
■ Attorney General

■ Secretary of Labor
■ Secretary of Education
■ Secretary of State
■ Secretary of Energy
■ Secretary of Transportation
■ Secretary of Homeland Security

FIGURE 11-3

Agencies Under the U.S. Department of the Treasury

Bureau of Engraving and Printing	Designs and manufactures currency
Financial Management Services	Monitors the health and budgets of government
Internal Revenue Service	Easily the largest department under the Treasury's jurisdiction. Responsible for assessing and collecting income and other taxes
Office of Thrift Supervision (OTS)	Regulates lending institutions, such as savings and loans

For example, who creates the agency's rules and regulations? Who enforces these regulations? Where are the rules found? These were among the many questions that had to be answered by administrative agencies so that they could operate effectively.

We explore these questions throughout this chapter.

ADMINISTRATIVE AGENCIES

All complex systems develop specialization. This is as true of governments as it is of computer systems and human bodies. The U.S. federal government is one of the most complex systems ever created; its specialization is almost mind-boggling in its complexity. We first examine how an agency is created, how it creates its rules, and finally how an agency is regulated.

A. CREATING AN ADMINISTRATIVE AGENCY

The authority of an administrative agency flows directly from legislative or executive authority. In the case of the U.S. Department of the Treasury, the authority to create this agency arises from the U.S. Constitution. All administrative agencies must receive their authority to operate from some branch of the government. This authority could be the U.S. Constitution, the U.S. Congress, or Executive Order of the President. No matter how the agency is created, it operates within the strict limits of its original charter.

1. PRIMARY REASON FOR CREATING ADMINISTRATIVE AGENCIES

The primary reason for creating an administrative agency is to perform the routine activities of government. The U.S. Constitution does not provide any details about how the various governmental actions will be carried out. For instance, the word *treasury* is used only three times in the entire Constitution:

Many commentators have suggested that the federal government has become too large, with too many agencies working at cross purposes with each other. The creation of the Department of Homeland Security was a direct result of the realization that too many different governmental agencies were responsible for monitoring terrorism against the United States (and many of them were not communicating adequately with each other).

1 The Senators and Representatives shall receive a Compensation for their Services, to be ascertained by Law, and paid out of the **Treasury** of the United States. Article I, Section 6, Clause 1.
2 No Money shall be drawn from the **Treasury**, but in Consequence of Appropriations made by Law; and a regular Statement and Account of the Receipts and Expenditures of all public Money shall be published from time to time. Article I, Section 9, Clause 7.
3 . . . Net Produce of all Duties and Imposts, laid by any State on Imports or Exports, shall be for the Use of the **Treasury** of the United States; and all such Laws shall be subject to the Revision and Controul [sic] of the Congress. Article I, Section 10, Clause 2.

Notice that nowhere in any of these clauses does the Constitution explain how the U.S. Department of the Treasury actually carries out these activities. The details are left to be determined at a later date. When an administrative agency is charged with a particular duty, it must create its own rules and regulations to perform its function. In fact, agencies not only create the procedures to carry out their governmental mandate, they also must create the entire framework, infrastructure, and rules to put the principle into practice.

2. AN EXAMPLE: CREATING THE INTERNAL REVENUE SERVICE

The authority for the creation and powers of the Internal Revenue Service is found in the **Sixteenth Amendment.** (This amendment was proposed in 1909 and ratified on February 3, 1913.)

Again you will notice a lack of explanation about the details involved in collecting income taxes from individuals. In fact, neither the Internal Revenue Service nor the U.S. Department of the Treasury is even mentioned in this Amendment. However, just as we have seen with other portions of the U.S. Constitution, the lack of detail does not mean lack of authority. Implied in this Amendment is the power of the government to create an agency to carry out the work of collecting taxes. The power to collect taxes was subsequently conferred on the U.S. Department of the

Amendment XVI
The Congress shall have power to lay and collect taxes on incomes, from whatever source derived, without apportionment among the several States, and without regard to any census or enumeration

The first Form 1040 appeared in 1913, shortly after the ratification of the Sixteenth Amendment.

By the end of the 2002 tax year, the IRS had collected $2 trillion in revenue and processed 227 million tax returns.[10]

Treasury, which then created the Internal Revenue Service to carry out the duties imposed by the Sixteenth Amendment. Although we have discussed the creation of the IRS in this chapter, these same principles apply to any type of government agency, from the Internal Revenue Service to the Federal Aviation Administration.

B. ADMINISTRATIVE RULES AND REGULATIONS

One of the basic principles involved in the creation of an administrative agency is the right of that agency to create its own rules to govern the specifics of its charter. This power runs counter to our experience with the way that our government is run. For example, we know that the U.S. Congress passes a law and sends it to the President for signature. This is an example of the checks and balances scheme required in the Constitution. One branch of the government has the right to oversee at least some actions of another branch. However, an administrative agency has the right to create its own rules.

1. AGENCIES CREATE THEIR OWN RULES

Why does an agency have the right to create its own rules? One answer is that given the nature of administrative agencies, they are in the best position to set out their responsibilities. In many ways, agencies create rules and procedures as they go. Relying on some other branch of government to create routine rules and regulations would be far too cumbersome and time-consuming to allow an agency to perform its duties.

 **Agencies are empowered to create their own rules.**

Many commentators also argue that when an agency receives its mandate, it impliedly receives the right to create the rules to put its mandate into practice.

2. LIMITATIONS ON AN AGENCY'S RULEMAKING POWER

Governmental agencies have strict limits on their ability to create their own rules. For one thing, an agency can only create rules governing its own responsibilities. An agency cannot create a rule that infringes on the mandate of another agency. The IRS, for example, cannot create a rule that limits the type of baggage that travelers can carry on to airplanes. Their ability to create rules is limited to the issue of collecting taxes.

[10] *http://www.irs.gov/newsroom/article/0,,id = 108363,00.html*

An agency's power to make its own rules is strictly limited by its original charter and the statutory authority creating the agency in the first place.

ISSUE AT A GLANCE

The limitations on an agency's rulemaking power are straightforward. The agency may create rules to govern how, when, and where it can exercise its authority to do its job. However, it is not authorized to draft rules that impinge on the charter or purpose of other governmental agencies.

3. AN AGENCY CANNOT EXCEED ITS MANDATE

Other limitations on rules include the prohibition against creating a rule or regulation that gives the agency a power not originally delegated to it under statute. Similarly, the agency is not allowed to avoid its duties by creating rules and regulations that limit authority or create exemptions that effectively eliminate the agency's role. Within these restrictions, however, the agency is free to create any rule or regulation to put its policies into effect. In many ways, the agency's power to create its own rules is similar to the legislative branch's power to create laws. Some have referred to an agency's power in this regard as "quasi-legislative."

4. THE FEDERAL ADMINISTRATIVE PROCEDURE ACT

There are specific statutes that limit an agency's power to create its own rules. The most important is the Federal Administrative Procedure Act (FAPA). This statute not only limits how and when an agency can create its own rules, but also works to create a more uniform system among all agencies in the way that rules are created and maintained.

This statute also creates a level of transparency in the way that agencies create their rules. For one thing, an agency is required to publish its rules in the Code of Federal Regulations.

5. THE CODE OF FEDERAL REGULATIONS

The Code of Federal Regulations (CFR) is an annual, multi-volume publication containing rules and regulations for all federal administrative agencies. Each section is divided by the name of the administrative agency. For an excerpt from the CFR on IRS regulations, see Figure 11-4.

When you are searching for federal administrative rules and regulations, the CFR is where you find them. The CFR is available in most public libraries.

C. AGENCIES AND SUNSHINE LAWS

The federal government (and almost all states) have enacted so-called sunshine laws. These laws require that most agency meetings and rulemaking hearings be

Periodically there are movements and proposals to limit the ability of administrative agencies to create their own rules. Some see this ability as a prime example of government run amok, with an agency acting as all three branches of government rolled into one: They have executive power in the ability to carry out and enforce their rules; they have legislative power in that they create their own rules; and they have judicial power in their ability to revise their rules.

Federal legislation classifies a governmental department as an "agency" when it has considerable or substantial control over its own operations and rulemaking abilities.

FIGURE 11-4

Code of Federal Regulations:
Income Tax on Individuals

Code of Federal Regulations
Title 26, Volume 1
Revised as of April 1, 2003
TITLE 26 — INTERNAL REVENUE
CHAPTER I — INTERNAL REVENUE
SERVICE, DEPARTMENT OF THE
TREASURY
PART 1 — INCOME TAXES — Table of
Contents
Sec. 1.1-1 Income tax on individuals.
(a) General rule. (1) Section 1 of the Code
imposes an income tax on the income of every individual who is a citizen or resident of the United States and, to the extent provided by section 871(b) or 877(b), on the income of a nonresident alien individual. For optional tax in the case of taxpayers with adjusted gross income of less than $10,000 see section 3. The tax imposed is upon taxable income (determined by subtracting the allowable deductions from gross income). The tax is determined in accordance with the table contained in section 1.

FIGURE 11-5

Federal Administrative
Procedure Act

5 U.S.C. §553. Rule making

(b) General notice of proposed rule making shall be published in the Federal Register, unless persons subject thereto are named and either personally served or otherwise have actual notice thereof in accordance with law. The notice shall include —

(1) a statement of the time, place, and nature of public rule making proceedings;

(2) reference to the legal authority under which the rule is proposed; and

(3) either the terms or substance of the proposed rule or a description of the subjects and issues involved.

(c) After notice required by this section, the agency shall give interested persons an opportunity to participate in the rule making through submission of written data, views, or arguments with or without opportunity for oral presentation. After consideration of the relevant matter presented, the agency shall incorporate in the rules adopted a concise general statement of their basis and purpose. When rules are required by statute to be made on the record after opportunity for an agency hearing, sections 556 and 557 of this title apply instead of this subsection.

Sunshine laws often require agencies to post announcements about when and where their meetings will be held. It is a violation of these laws to hold a meeting at an inconvenient time, or in a room too small to admit anyone other than agency members.

held in public. Instead of meeting in secret, agencies must hold their meetings in the open, or in the "sunshine." These statutes not only require public meetings for agency hearings, but also allow members of the public to comment on proposed rules and regulations.

Sunshine laws obviously do not apply to all agencies at all times. There are many governmental agencies, such as the Department of Homeland Defense, that are permitted to hold some of their more sensitive hearings in private. However, sunshine laws do apply to a wide range of both federal and state agencies. See Figure 11-6 for an example of the federal Sunshine Act.

FIGURE 11-6

Government in the Sunshine Act

5 U.S.C. §552b

(a) For purposes of this section —

(1) the term "agency" means any agency, as defined in section 552(e) of this title, headed by a collegial body composed of two or more individual members, a majority of whom are appointed to such position by the President with the advice and consent of the Senate, and any subdivision thereof authorized to act on behalf of the agency;

(2) the term "meeting" means the deliberations of at least the number of individual agency members required to take action on behalf of the agency where such deliberations determine or result in the joint conduct or disposition of official agency business, but does not include deliberations required or permitted by subsection (d) or (e); and

(b) Members shall not jointly conduct or dispose of agency business other than in accordance with this section. Except as provided in subsection (c), every portion of every meeting of an agency shall be open to public observation.

D. ENFORCEMENT OF AGENCY RULES AND REGULATIONS

Once an agency has created a rule, it may enforce this rule. Agencies have many different methods of enforcing their rules, including citations, sanctions, injunctions, court proceedings, and criminal prosecution.

We have said that agencies have limitations on their rules. One limitation concerns the enforcement of their rules and regulations. When there is a dispute about the scope of an agency's power, the court system determines the limits, not the agency. The court system often intervenes as a consequence of an administrative hearing.

 # ADMINISTRATIVE HEARINGS

When a person wishes to contest an agency ruling, such as the denial of Social Security benefits, the person may request a hearing. Administrative hearings are often very similar to trials. Witnesses may testify, the person may have an attorney or other representative to look after the person's interests, and a judge will make rulings.

Although the procedures followed in agency matters may resemble those in a courtroom, there are important distinctions. For one thing, the rules of evidence and procedure in agency hearings are often very different than courtroom trials. In the past, agencies have attempted to use these differences to minimize or completely eliminate some of the constitutional protections that persons enjoy. There are no jury trials in agency hearings. The rules of evidence are more relaxed.

FIGURE 11-7

U.S. Department of Treasury,
National Money Laundering
Strategy Excerpt

THE 2001 NATIONAL MONEY LAUNDERING STRATEGY

Prepared by

The Office of Enforcement, U.S. Department of the Treasury,
in consultation with the U.S. Department of Justice

Priority 2:   **Provide asset forfeiture training that emphasizes major case development to federal, state, and local law enforcement officials.**

> **Lead**:   Director, Federal Law Enforcement Training Center (FLETC); Chief, Asset Forfeiture and Money Laundering Section, Criminal Division, Department of Justice.
>
> **Goals**:   Develop advanced asset forfeiture training programs. By September 2001, the Chief, Asset Forfeiture and Money Laundering Section, Criminal Division, and Director, Executive Office of Asset Forfeiture, Department of the Treasury, will assess current forfeiture training programs. FLETC, in concert with the Chief, Asset Forfeiture and Money Laundering Section, Criminal Division, and Director, Executive Office of Asset Forfeiture, will develop a new advanced asset forfeiture training program by January 2002.

This year's *Strategy* requires continued education of federal, state, and local investigators, analysts, and prosecutors concerning asset forfeiture statutory modifications and case law developments. In 2000, Congress enacted extensive changes to civil asset forfeiture law in the Civil Asset Forfeiture Reform Act of 2000 (CAFRA). The CAFRA altered the burden of proof in civil asset forfeiture cases, authorized appointment of counsel in certain circumstances, allowed for pre-trial release of property in certain circumstances, changed the requirements of the innocent owner defense, and codified *Bajakajian's* "grossly disproportional" test of excessive forfeitures under the Eighth Amendment's Excessive Fines Clause. Sweeping legislative modifications often have chilling effects on law enforcement efforts because investigators and prosecutors are uncertain of the application of the legislative changes and prefer to take the approach of "wait and see." Advanced asset forfeiture training programs, therefore, must inform law enforcement of significant statutory changes such as CAFRA, and instruct them how to investigate and prosecute successfully under the new provisions.

In previous years, many agencies did not allow individuals to be represented by attorneys, but in most (but not all) situations, this rule has been changed.

Agencies have some tremendous advantages over their judicial counterparts. For one, agency hearings and rulings happen much more quickly than they do in the court system. They also help to relieve some of the court system's burden.

Workers' Compensation cases, for example, form an enormous class of litigation that would easily swamp an already overloaded civil court system if they were heard there. Instead, workers' compensation cases are heard before an administrative agency.

Agency hearings have several advantages over courtroom proceedings, such as:

- Hearings before administrative agencies take less time and cost less money than the same hearing before a court
- Innovation spreads more quickly because administrative agencies share their information more readily than other branches of government
- Hearings are more relaxed and tend to move more quickly

Administrative hearings have different rules and are often more informal than court proceedings.

ISSUE AT
A GLANCE

A. ADMINISTRATIVE HEARINGS INVOLVE LESS TIME AND RESOURCES

When a case goes before an administrative agency, it is almost always less costly both in terms of time and resources for the parties to present their cases. There are several reasons why this is so. For one, administrative hearings can be scheduled at places other than courthouses. Workers' compensation hearings, for instance, often take place in office buildings and do not require precious space in the courthouse. For another, hearings are designed to move quickly. An administrative law judge (ALJ) makes rulings on the issues in the case. There are no juries in administrative hearings.

B. INNOVATION

In many courtrooms in the United States, upon completion of a case, the judge reads the jury instructions to the jurors. This process originated hundreds of years ago when most jurors could not read. It is considered to be remarkably innovative for a judge to simply make copies of the jury charge and give them to the jurors. Judges and courthouse personnel are not famous for embracing new technology and innovation.

Agencies are not as bound by tradition and conservative attitudes. When a new technology appears that can dramatically improve the efficiency of the process, agencies are swift to adopt it. For example, ALJs have used telephone conferences between parties for years, instead of requiring all parties to appear in court to give a status report. They have also been quick to use fax machines and e-mail to facilitate hearings and dispositions in cases.

FIGURE 11-8

Governmental Entities That Do
Not Qualify as Agencies

- President of the United States
- U.S. Congress
- U.S. Supreme Court and all courts
  falling under its jurisdiction
- Territory owned and controlled by the
  federal government
- The Judge Advocate General (military
  criminal and civil wing)

C. RELAXED EVIDENTIARY RULES

The evidentiary rules in administrative hearings are more streamlined, and more relaxed, than those found in trials. Hearsay evidence is frequently relied on in administrative hearings. Interestingly enough, the U.S. Supreme Court has consistently held that court systems are better at safeguarding the rights of individuals than are administrative hearings.[11]

D. ISSUING SUBPOENAS

When an agency has a hearing or issues a subpoena, it must use the court system to enforce the subpoena and request the court to find a person in contempt who refuses to respond.

E. APPEALING AGENCY FINDINGS

We have said that the court system may become involved in determining the limits of agency power. One way that the court system can do this is through the appellate process. A person may appeal an agency ruling through various appellate courts until it reaches the U.S. Supreme Court. Just as we have seen in other contexts, the Supreme Court has the final say about agency power.

SPECIFIC EXAMPLES OF ADMINISTRATIVE AGENCIES

Although we have used the IRS as our example in this chapter, there are numerous administrative agencies on the federal and state level that people come into contact with frequently. So far, we have only mentioned federal agencies, but there are important state agencies that figure prominently in people's lives. See Figure 11-9 for a partial list of state agencies.

We consider two such agencies, one on the federal level and one on the state level. The example from the federal level is the Social Security Administration.

---

[11] Agosto v. Immigration and Naturalization Service, 98 S. Ct. 2081, 436 U.S. 748, 56 L. Ed. 2d 677 (1978)

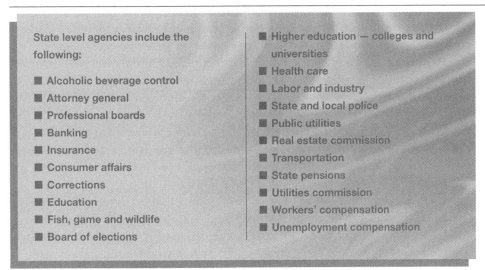

FIGURE 11-9

State Agencies

State level agencies include the following:

- Alcoholic beverage control
- Attorney general
- Professional boards
- Banking
- Insurance
- Consumer affairs
- Corrections
- Education
- Fish, game and wildlife
- Board of elections
- Higher education — colleges and universities
- Health care
- Labor and industry
- State and local police
- Public utilities
- Real estate commission
- Transportation
- State pensions
- Utilities commission
- Workers' compensation
- Unemployment compensation

A. SOCIAL SECURITY HEARINGS

When a person has been denied Social Security or Supplemental Security Income benefits, she can file a request for a hearing to dispute this finding. Administrative law judges preside at these hearings and make rulings on the evidence presented. The person contesting the ruling is allowed to have representation during the hearing. Unlike court proceedings, however, there is no requirement that the representative be an attorney. Paralegals often represent clients in these hearings and are referred to as representatives. (See this chapter's Skills You Need in the Real World.) Representatives are allowed to get information from a client's Social Security file, assist with collection of medical records, appear with the client, and question witnesses during the hearing. The representative is allowed to charge a fee for this service. Fees charged by SSI representatives may be a flat fee or a percentage of the total award, up to 25 percent.

B. WORKERS' COMPENSATION

Workers' compensation, sometimes referred to as workmen's compensation, is a state-based system that provides an alternative to lawsuits for employees injured on the job. Deductions from every paycheck paid by Qualifying employers go into the workers' compensation fund. If a covered employee is injured or killed on the job, she or her representative can file a claim with the workers' compensation board. If the board determines that the provisions of the state workers' compensation statute cover the injury, the board can make a monetary award to the employee.

   If the board denies a claim, the employee has the right to contest this decision by requesting a hearing. The employee and employer then present their cases to an administrative law judge who makes rulings on the case. When we use the term

In 2002, the New York Workers' Compensation Board received 164,402 new claims. Of those claims, 56 percent were resolved at hearings, while 44 percent were settled before a hearing. Approximately 7.9 million workers fell under the jurisdiction of the New York Workers' Compensation Board.[12]

judge in this context, we are not referring to someone who works for the judicial branch of government. The administrative law judge is employed by the workers' compensation board and makes decisions based on state and agency law.

Most workers' compensation boards were founded in the early twentieth century as a result of organizing efforts for better working conditions and benefits by workers who frequently worked six days a week, fourteen hours a day, with no minimum salary, insurance, or benefits for injury or death.

Workers' compensation is a trade-off. In exchange for coverage under workers' compensation, an employee surrenders her right to use the court system to bring suit against an employer. Any litigation that would ordinarily involve a civil suit must now be brought through the state workers' compensation board. The employer must contribute to the workers' compensation system, but receives the assurance that it will not be involved in civil suits.

Under modern workers' compensation schemes, an injured employee has the right to payments for medical bills as well as regular cash payments for living expenses.

IRVING v. AMETEK, INC.
756 So. 2d 1045 (2000)

Van Nortwick, J.

In this workers' compensation appeal, Shiwana J. Irving seeks reversal of an order of the Judge of Compensation Claims (JCC) which, primarily on the authority of *Martin Co. v. Carpenter,* 132 So. 2d 400 (Fla. 1961), denied Irving's claim for indemnity and medical treatment on the ground that she had not been truthful regarding her medical history at the time she was hired. Irving argues that *Martin* has been overruled by the adoption of section 440.15(5)(a), Florida Statutes (1993); and, alternatively, that, even if *Martin* has not been overruled, *Martin* should not serve as a bar to her claim, since there is no "causal relationship" shown between the prior medical condition that she failed to disclose in a preemployment questionnaire and the workplace injury which is the subject of the instant proceeding. Because we agree with the JCC that the *Martin* rule remains viable and we find competent substantial evidence to support the JCC's finding that such a causal relationship did exist, we affirm.

Prior to employing Irving to work as an assembler, appellee Ametek, Inc., the employer, required Irving to answer a questionnaire regarding her medical history and to submit to a physical. Among other things, the questionnaire asked: "Do you now have or have you ever had any of the following: . . . arm, hand or shoulder trouble?" If an applicant answered yes, the applicant was to provide additional information, such as the date of injury, name of the treating physician and hospital. Irving answered "no" to this question. The questionnaire further asked: "Have you ever had an injury on the job (worker's compensation) that required treatment/medical care by a doctor?" Claimant again answered in the negative.

On November 18, 1995, on her third day of work, Irving reported to Ametek's occupational nurse that she was experiencing pain in her right shoulder. A notice of

[12] New York Workers' Compensation Board web page; *http://www.wcb.state.ny.us/content/main/TheBoard/factsht.htm*

injury was filed, and Irving was referred to her personal physician. She never returned to work. On February 19, 1997, she filed a petition for temporary total disability (TTD) benefits and temporary partial disability (TPD) benefits, impairment benefits as of the date of maximum medical improvement, and medical treatment. By that time, Irving had been examined by Paul Dell, M.D., who diagnosed impingement syndrome, and Robert Martinez, M.D., who diagnosed an inflamed tendon in the right shoulder.

As a defense, Ametek and National Union Fire (jointly the employer/carrier) alleged that Irving misrepresented her medical history and that the employer detrimentally relied on that misrepresentation. In support of such defense, Marc Newquist, M.D., testified that, in September 1994, before Irving's employment at Ametek, Irving presented to a hospital emergency room for which he was on call and complained of right shoulder pain which occurred as she was packing and moving boxes at work. Dr. Newquist diagnosed muscle strain due to overuse.

At the hearing on her claim for workers' compensation benefits, Irving testified that she was confused by certain questions on the employer's questionnaire and that she circled those questions, including the questions related to her prior medical history quoted above. The original questionnaire completed by Irving was introduced into evidence, and it contained no circled questions. Further, the occupational nurse who was present while Irving completed the questionnaire testified that Irving did not ask any questions about the questionnaire.

The JCC denied the claim in its entirety on the authority of section 440.15(5)(a), Florida Statutes (1993), and *Martin, supra.* In denying the claim, the JCC found that Irving had knowingly misrepresented herself, that the employer relied on that misrepresentation to its detriment, and that the prior undisclosed shoulder injury was causally related to the 1995 workplace injury.

In *Martin,* the claimant had experienced back pain for approximately 20 years prior to her employment by the Martin Company, and sought medical treatment for her back condition on several occasions during those years. As a condition of her employment by the Martin Company, claimant was required to complete a questionnaire which asked if she had ever been subject to various diseases, including back injury or backache. To this question, claimant answered "no." Approximately seven months after beginning work for the Martin Company, following a change from seated work to employment requiring standing and bending over a table, claimant complained of increased back pain. She received treatment at the company's first aid station and, later, by a physician. Claimant was then placed on a 90-day leave of absence because of her back condition and approximately 23 months after her initial employment by the Martin Company, she filed a claim for workers' compensation and medical benefits.

In *Martin,* in considering whether the claimant was precluded from receiving benefits because she had misrepresented her physical condition to her employer, the Supreme Court noted that the applicable Workers' Compensation Act "was silent on the effect of false representations on the status of the employee in cases like this. . . ." Nevertheless, the court reasoned that the provisions of section 440.151(b), which precluded payment of benefits to employees who falsely represent in writing that the employee had not previously been disabled or compensated due to an occupational disease, demonstrate a legislative determination that an employee who misrepresents in writing a fact material to a subsequent claim for compensation shall be precluded from the benefits of the Act. As a result, in furtherance of this legislative intent, the *Martin* court held as follows:

> We therefore adopt the rule that a false representation as to a physical condition or health made by an employee in procuring employment will preclude the benefits of the Workmen's Compensation Act for an otherwise compensable injury if there is shown to be a causal relationship between the injury and the false representation and if it is shown that (1) the employee knew the representation to be false, (2) the employer relied upon the false representation and (3) such reliance resulted in consequent injury to the employer.

As this court explained in *Colonial Care Nursing Home v. Norton*, 566 So. 2d 44, 45-6 (Fla. 1st DCA 1990), an employee who has misrepresented a condition which is causally related to a subsequent claim for benefits has denied the employer the opportunity of making a choice as to whether or not to hire that particular employee notwithstanding the attendant risks. *Martin* does not, however, require a potential employee "to make a full, not specifically solicited, disclosure of all of his particular shortcomings," or create a defense when the employer asks only "nonspecific broad questions as to physical condition on employment applications." It is undisputed in the instant case that the employer's questionnaire included questions directed to specific physical conditions.

Section 440.15(5)(a), Florida Statutes (1993) provides:

> The fact that an employee has suffered previous disability, impairment, anomaly, or disease, or received compensation therefor, shall not preclude him from benefits for a subsequent aggravation or acceleration of the preexisting condition nor preclude benefits for death resulting there from, except that no benefits shall be payable if the employee, at the time of entering into the employment of the employer by whom the benefits would otherwise be payable, falsely represents himself in writing as not having previously been disabled or compensated because of such previous disability, impairment, anomaly, or disease and the employer detrimentally relies on the misrepresentation.

Irving argues that this statute has superceded the rule in *Martin* and that a party can be denied benefits pursuant to section 440.15(5)(a) only if she was previously "disabled or compensated" and falsely represents that fact in writing. Since Irving was neither previously disabled nor compensated by her shoulder condition, she argues her claim was wrongly denied under the statute. Irving reasons that the legislature's decision to allow a misrepresentation defense only in cases where the claimant has experienced a disability or has received compensation is a logical one, because only prior medical conditions which have been significant enough to have warranted compensation or have caused a disability would have an effect on future performance in the workplace. She submits that an employee who seeks worker's compensation benefits should not be punished because that employee failed to report insignificant aspects of their medical history.

We agree that section 440.15(5)(a) would not bar Irving's claim, because the record contains no evidence that she was disabled or received compensation as a result of her shoulder injury in 1994. Nevertheless, we find Irving's argument to be without merit. Section 440.15(5)(a) was enacted by chapter 90-201, Laws of Florida. Neither the preamble to the chapter law or the final staff analysis and economic impact statement prepared for the Florida House of Representatives, Committee on Commerce, refers to *Martin*. In addition, the *Martin* rule has been recently cited without any suggestion that its validity was impacted by the adoption of chapter 90-201. Further, and more significantly, the workers' compensation law in effect when *Martin* was decided included in section 440.151(b) a statutory provision substantially similar to section 440.15(5)(a), from which statute the *Martin* court gleaned the legislative intent on which to base its holding. Thus, we find no basis to conclude that the adoption of section 440.15(5)(a) was intended to overrule *Martin.*

To preclude a workers' compensation claim under the *Martin* defense, a "causal relationship" must exist between the misrepresentation and the injury which is the subject of a present claim. Irving argues, in the alternative, that, assuming the *Martin* defense remains viable, there is no causal connection between her prior shoulder condition and the instant workplace injury.

A causal relationship for purposes of *Martin* is shown by evidence of a "medical relationship" between the workplace injury at issue and the undisclosed prior injury or condition, or by evidence that the prior injury or condition contributed to or was aggravated by the subsequent injury. Here, the JCC expressly found such a causal relationship did exist. We find competent substantial evidence in the medical evidence in the record to support a finding that Irving's prior shoulder problems, which she failed to disclose, were substantially the same as her 1995 workplace injury. The similarity of the shoulder problems is clearly shown by a comparison of the testimony of the emergency room physician who examined her right shoulder in 1994 with the testimony of the physician who performed an IME in 1997. Both in 1994, when she was treated for shoulder pain, and at the time of her 1997 IME following her 1995 workplace injury, she complained of pain starting in her right shoulder and radiating down her arm. The emergency room physician who treated Irving in 1994 testified that Irving experienced generalized pain over her right shoulder and down into her arm. Similarly, Dr. Dell testified that in the 1997 IME Irving complained of tenderness over the anterior aspect of the right shoulder radiating into the anterior of the deltoid and biceps muscles of her arm. Dr. Dell also explained that it was "unusual" to show "symptoms of a repetitive motion injury after two days of working on the job." Further, when he was asked to assume that Irving had presented to an emergency room in 1994 with pain and muscle strain to her right shoulder, Dr. Dell testified that the workplace injury could be a "reexacerbation" of her previous shoulder condition. We therefore find a sufficient basis in the record for affirming the JCC's finding of a causal connection between the undisclosed prior condition and the workplace injury which is the subject of this proceeding.

We have considered the remaining issues raised on appeal and find them to be without merit. Accordingly, the order under review is AFFIRMED.

QUESTIONS ABOUT THE CASE

1   What is the basis for the finding against the worker in the original hearing?
2   What questions were asked on Ametek's questionnaire about prior medical problems?
3   What type of injury did Irving report?
4   What is the theory used by the employer to deny Irving's coverage?
5   What is the underlying theory in the court's opinion concerning why an employee who misrepresents prior medical history should be precluded from benefits?

Profiling a Paralegal

▶ Janice Johnson

I was working in a job that was making me miserable and I knew that I had to get out or I would lose my mind. I looked at different programs at the community college and I saw a listing for paralegals. I'd always been curious about the law and I knew that instead of just getting another job, I wanted to get training for a career. I've never regretted the decision to go back to school and get a paralegal degree.

I concentrate exclusively on Social Security and Medicaid cases these days. I do everything from the beginning of the case through to development and closure. I even have an assistant now. She spends most of her time ordering medical records. That's a full time job in itself.

Social Security cases begin when a client is referred to us. I'm proud to say that we even get some referrals from Social Security personnel. We also get referrals from attorneys, doctors, and other clients. I set up a client screening and we do an in-depth interview. If the interview goes less than two hours, I call that a short one. I go over everything:

work history, medical problems, education, all of the doctors you've seen throughout your life, all of the major medical events in your life. I warn people that by the time it's done, I'm going to know everything except their underwear size, and sometimes I'll know that. This exhaustive background check brings the case together. It also helps you realize the importance of asking questions. I've actually come up with diagnoses that doctors have missed. In one case, just by digging into a client's background, I found out that he had polio when he was a child. His doctors didn't even know that because they'd never asked enough questions.

Most of the clients I deal with are depressed. If you live in pain, if you can't do what you want to do, you're going to be depressed. A lot of our intake also involves making sure that these people get treatment for depression.

I also represent clients in Social Security hearings. It really helps you in your preparation to understand what you'll need during the hearing. I think it's made me better at preparing cases for the attorneys.

Careers in the Law

▶ Paralegal Educator, Leslie McKesson

Leslie McKesson is the coordinator of the Paralegal Program at Western Piedmont Community College in North Carolina.

"I graduated from paralegal school and received a certification in litigation. I went to work for Legal Services, helping senior citizens with issues like Social Security and Medicare. I enjoyed the work because it gave me a chance to represent clients in administrative hearings. I also became the community education specialist, presenting programs throughout the area on a wide variety of legal issues.

"Before becoming a paralegal instructor, I also worked for the department of social services as a child enforcement agent. I spent at least two days a week in the courtroom. We handled all aspects of establishing and enforcing child support payments.

"When I heard about an opening as a paralegal instructor at the local community college, I jumped at the chance to teach. As a paralegal educator, I get to help others begin their careers. When you are an academic, you have the chance to be a bit more innovative than you can be in the daily practice of law."

One of the innovations she has overseen in her career is the development of online paralegal courses. "When we started creating Internet-based paralegal courses, a lot of people said to us, 'there are some classes you just can't teach online.' They were concerned about quality of instruction. Quality is a major concern; that's why we have the same requirements for online courses as we do for campus classes." In recent years, enrollment in these courses has skyrocketed.

SKILLS YOU NEED IN THE REAL WORLD

REPRESENTING CLIENTS IN ADMINISTRATIVE HEARINGS

Many administrative agencies allow non-lawyers to represent clients in disputes before them. In many ways, an administrative hearing is similar to courtroom trial. We have outlined the important differences between them in this chapter, but now we focus on how you, as a paralegal, can represent clients in administrative hearings.

Here are some practical tips:

- When you represent a client before an administrative agency, make sure to notify the board as soon as possible. If they require a specific form for notification, make sure that you use it.
- If you wish to be treated like a professional, act like one. Start with your appearance. First impressions are as important in administrative hearings as they are in every other aspect of life.
- When appropriate, be cordial to the opposing side. Win or lose, you should display good judgment and maturity. You may be facing all of these people again at some future date.
- Don't forget to explain the process to your client. You may have done this a hundred times before, but this is your client's first time. Always give your client the time and attention that she deserves.

At the hearing:

- When you represent a client at a hearing, you are allowed to cross-examine witnesses. As is true in any other context, good cross-examination has more to do with preparation than performance. The secret to effective use of cross-examination is to know the case better than anyone else in the room.
- As the representative, you may also submit evidence on behalf of the client. Make sure that you have a solid understanding of the evidentiary rules used in the court. Talk to someone who has appeared before this ALJ and confirm the types of questions that this judge likes to hear before evidence is submitted. Is there a special form used to keep track of evidence? Is there a specific place where all physical evidence must be placed? Remember that although the hearing is not held in a courtroom and that everything appears very informal, the hearing is being recorded and this recording may be the basis of an appeal at a later date. Do not say anything that you would regret hearing again later. Most boards

require medical evidence to be submitted in advance. Find out how and when this evidence should be submitted and if you have submitted the appropriate number of copies.

When the hearing is over:

- Make sure that you receive a copy of the ALJ's ruling and confirm that the written ruling conforms to any verbal ruling that the judge made at the time.

CHAPTER SUMMARY

Administrative law is usually defined as the area of law that deals with the delegation of power by the executive branch to specific governmental agencies to handle the day-to-day business of government through rules and regulations created by these agencies. An agency is a government department created through authority of the Constitution, by statute, or by other enactment. Agencies are permitted to create their own rules and regulations to put their responsibilities into practice; however, they are limited to creating rules that apply directly to their duties. When a person has a dispute with an agency, she typically requests a hearing before that body.

Administrative hearings superficially resemble trials. However, hearings are more informal than trials, have more liberal rules of evidence, and are usually both faster and more cost effective than trials. Unlike in court proceedings, paralegals are allowed to represent clients at some administrative hearings.

ETHICS: CLIENT "MILLS"

One of the problems with specializing in any area of law is the temptation to create a client "mill." A mill is law firm that puts more emphasis on the quantity of cases than the quality of work. In mills, client cases are pushed through the office with a minimum of attention to the details and an emphasis on resolution, as though one approach fit all cases. Clients receive very little personal attention and their potential legal claims are ignored in favor of quick settlement so that the firm can receive its fee and move on to the next case. At best, client mills are a questionable proposition and may actually be unethical. When a client retains a law firm's services she is entitled to personal attention and thorough legal analysis. Unfortunately, the area of administrative law has a fair proportion of client mills. Attorneys and paralegals can specialize in a specific area, such as Social Security hearings or workers' compensation hearings and begin to focus on fees over client service. The client always deserves individual attention. Each case is unique and presents different factual and legal questions. When the legal team begins to see the clients as products instead of people, the firm is in danger of committing ethical violations, such as failure to adequately investigate claims or, even worse, pursuing claims that have no merit.

CHAPTER REVIEW QUESTIONS

1 Why is it so difficult to define the term *administrative law*?
2 Explain the relationship of administrative agencies with the executive branch of government.
3 Why are administrative agencies needed?
4 What areas of practice fall under administrative law?
5 Where do administrative agencies get their authority?
6 How are administrative agencies created?
7 What is the role of the U.S. Constitution in creating administrative agencies?
8 Why are there more administrative agencies in today's federal government than at any time in our nation's history?
9 What is the authority for the creation of the Internal Revenue Service?
10 Can administrative agencies create their own rules and regulations? Explain.
11 What limits are placed on an agency when it creates its rules and regulations?
12 What are sunshine laws?
13 Compare and contrast administrative hearings with court hearings.
14 What are at least three advantages that administrative hearings have over courtroom proceedings?
15 Why is an innovative technique more likely to be used in an administrative hearing than in a courtroom?
16 When would a person request a hearing over the award of Social Security benefits?
17 What is workers' compensation?
18 In the sample case, *Irving v. Ametek, Inc.*, why was Shiwana Irving's workers' compensation claim denied?
19 Explain how a paralegal can represent a person at an administrative hearing.
20 What are some of the important differences between administrative law and other types of law that you have studied in previous chapters?

DISCUSSION QUESTIONS

1 Is an agency's power to create its own rules and regulations a violation of the checks and balances system created in the U.S. Constitution?

2   Do administrative agencies give the President too much power?
3   Is there an alternative to creating a vast system of administrative agencies on both the federal and state level?
4   Why would the U.S. Supreme Court declare that a courtroom is still a better place to safeguard a person's individual liberties than an administrative hearing?

PERSONALITY QUIZ

Do you think that you would like to represent others in administrative hearings? Take this personality quiz and see.

1   I enjoy speaking in public.
    0-strongly disagree   5-agree   10-strongly agree

                                                                    Points:_____

2   I enjoy preparation for court.
    0-strongly disagree   5-agree   10-strongly agree

                                                                    Points:_____

3   When I speak in public, I make coherent points.
    0-strongly disagree   5-agree   10-strongly agree

                                                                    Points:_____

4   I have no trouble maintaining my objectivity.
    0-strongly disagree   5-agree   10-strongly agree

                                                                    Points:_____

5   I like to help people who are in trouble.
    0-strongly disagree   5-agree   10-strongly agree

                                                                    Points:_____

                                                            Total Points:_____

If you scored between 30-50 points, you would probably do very well representing others in administrative hearings.

If you scored between 20-29 points, you might be able to put together a good presentation for a client.

If you scored 19 or lower, you would probably not be very comfortable representing clients in administrative hearings.

PRACTICAL APPLICATIONS

Locate a paralegal who regularly represents clients at administrative hearings. Ask this person the following questions:

- How did you begin representing clients in these hearings?
- Are there any common misconceptions about administrative hearings?
- What do you like best about what you do?
- What do you like least?
- Are administrative hearings fair?

WEB SITES

Federal Agencies and Commissions
http://www.whitehouse.gov/government/independent-agencies.html

IRS Web Site
http://www.irs.gov/irs/index.html

New York Workers' Compensation Board
http://www.wcb.state.ny.us

California Division of Workers' Compensation
http://www.dir.ca.gov/dwc/dwc_home_page.htm

Social Security Online — Hearings and Appeals
http://www.ssa.gov/appeals/index.html

TERMS AND PHRASES

Administrative law   Agency

Real Property Law

Chapter Learning Objectives

After completing this chapter, you should be able to:

■ Explain the difference between personal property and real property

■ Define the types of interest that a real estate owner acquires in real estate

■ Explain the difference between fee simple title and leasehold interests in real estate

■ Describe the basic financing arrangements for the purchase of residential real estate

■ List and explain the various classifications of real property

INTRODUCTION TO REAL ESTATE LAW

Legal professionals can spend their entire careers specializing in real estate law exclusively. This is an area rich in complexity and variety. However, before we can discuss the various types of professions associated with real estate, we must first create a working definition of real property and what makes it so unique.

REAL PROPERTY VERSUS PERSONAL PROPERTY

All property can be divided into two different categories: real property or personal property. Although the original meanings of these terms had more to do with the types of damages associated with the civil actions, in modern times **real property** refers to land and anything permanently attached to land, while personal property refers to all other types of property. Put another way, personal property refers to non-real estate items, from apples to automobiles.

Real property
Land and anything permanently attached to land, also commonly referred to as real estate

255

ISSUE AT
A GLANCE

Real property refers to land and anything permanently attached
to land; personal property refers to all other types of property.

The reason that the law makes a distinction between these two types of property is that the classification affects many of the rights and legal remedies available to the owners. For one thing, the way that ownership is transferred in real estate is different than the way it is transferred in personal property. There are other important differences between real property and personal property. Taxes, for instance, are often assessed differently between personal property and real property.

Another important difference between personal and real property is that personal property is mobile, while land is fixed.

A. PERSONAL PROPERTY IS MOBILE; LAND IS FIXED

An item qualified as personal property is mobile. In this case, mobility does not mean that the property is easily portable; there are many items classified as personal property that are difficult to move. When we use the term *mobility* we are talking about the quality of the property in comparison to real estate. Land occupies a fixed location on the planet. It does not move; it is not mobile. Real estate maintains a static location on the globe. It cannot move. Because of this, the documents that prove real estate ownership have peculiar characteristics that we discuss later in this chapter.

B. REAL ESTATE LEGAL PRACTICE

The practice of real estate law is as specialized and unique as any other subspecialty of law. Legal professionals who work in real estate have a rich field of opportunities from which to pick. For instance, some legal professionals concentrate on residential home sales, while others work in the area of business or commercial property.

FIGURE 12-1	Real Property	Personal Property
Differences Between Real and Personal Property	Fixed	Mobile
	Generally appreciates in value over time	Generally depreciates in value over time
	Each parcel is unique	Units can be identical
	Title transferred by deed	Title transferred by physical possession

Still others work in the area of real estate investments. In fact, real property law is so diverse that entire books are written on single aspects of it, such as landlord-tenant law or the law of commercial sales. Because this chapter is designed to introduce the broad concepts of real estate, we do not devote much attention to these specialties. Instead, we focus on one of the most common types of real estate transactions where most legal professionals concentrate their talents: the sale of a residence.

Purchasing Their First Home

John and Mary have decided to purchase a home. They've never owned a home before, and currently live in an apartment. Their first step toward becoming home-owners is to meet with a local bank and to prequalify for a mortgage. Prequalification is always a good idea because it lets the buyers know exactly how much house they can afford to buy.

After meeting with a local banker, John and Mary know that they can purchase a house up to $150,000 in value and comfortably meet the mortgage payments. Their next step is to meet with a real estate agent.

C. REAL ESTATE AGENTS AND CONTRACTS

Under the law, an **agent** is a person who works on behalf of another person, called the **principal.** Agency relationships have existed in one form or another for thousands of years. Usually, the principal hires the agent to act on his behalf in securing the best deal possible. In the case of John and Mary, they have chosen a real estate agent named Rhonda. She drives them around town, showing them several houses that are in their price range. On the second day, they locate a house that they both like. It is priced at $149,000, so it is just inside their maximum limit. They tell Rhonda that they want to buy the house.

At this point, it is important to point out where the agency relationship lies. Although Rhonda has been driving around with John and Mary for two days, she is not their agent. An agent, after all, works for the benefit of a principal. The agent is paid by the principal for this service. In this case, Rhonda will be paid by the proceeds from the sale of the house they located. Rhonda is an agent for the home seller, even if she has never met him.

Agent
One who acts on behalf of another, usually in a business context

Principal
One who has an agency relationship with another who acts on his behalf

---

In a typical real estate purchase, there is a seller who is represented by a real estate agent and a buyer who usually has no real estate agent.

 ISSUE AT A GLANCE

To have a better understanding of this relationship, we should go back to the homeowner's decision to sell his home. When he contacted a local real estate company, he told them that he wanted to sell his home and what price he had in mind. The real estate agency placed a "For Sale" sign in the seller's yard and then advertised the house for sale in local brochures and in the Multiple Listing Service.

Careers in the Law

▶ Real Estate Agent, Barry Stock

arry Stock has been a real estate agent in North Carolina for 26 years. His specialty is commercial and industrial properties, but he has handled all types of real estate in the past two decades. For Barry, real estate is a family vocation. His mother was also a real estate agent. "I got my real estate license two weeks before I graduated from high school." He's never looked back.

"Real estate is a people business. There's nothing like the feeling you get when you help a young couple buy their first home." Sales of commercial properties differ from residential sales. For one thing, the people involved are different. "The people who invest in commercial property are more sophisticated." But there are other differences. "Residential property sales involve a lot more

paperwork than commercial sales. When you first meet with a residential client, there are agency disclosure forms that you have to go over. Later, you'll have to go through the offer of purchase contract and other legal documents. If you're working with a seller, you'll sign a listing agreement that gives you permission to try to sell his property."

Conflicts of interest are a big concern for real estate agents. "If I'm a seller's agent and a buyer asks me what he should offer on the house. . . . I can't go against my client, the seller, by telling the buyer confidential information. On the other hand, I don't want to waste everyone's time. I'm obligated to say that they should offer the listing price. However, when I'm working as a buyer's agent, I'm free to make suggestions about price. It depends on my role."

1. MULTIPLE LISTING SERVICE

Multiple Listing Service
The advertisement of real property among real estate brokers offering to share in a commission if a broker produces a buyer who is ready, willing, and able to purchase the real estate

When a home is listed on the **Multiple Listing Service** (MLS), it is essentially an offer that is made to local real estate agents. We discussed offers, acceptances, and contracts in Chapter 9. In that chapter, we saw that a contract is created when someone accepts an offer. In this case, the MLS makes the following type of offer: If you produce a buyer for this listing, you can get one-half of the commission. This is a powerful inducement and one of the reasons for the success of the Multiple Listing Service. Rhonda saw the house listed in the MLS and when John and Mary decided to purchase the home, she knew that she would receive one-half of the total commission on the sale of the home. Because she is paid by the seller through the MLS, she is technically the seller's agent.

Rhonda takes John and Mary back to her office, where they begin filling out a form entitled "Offer of Purchase Contract."

2. REAL ESTATE CONTRACTS

When a person lists his house for sale, he is requesting offers. John and Mary have decided to make an offer on this house. Although the sale price is listed as $149,000, John and Mary make an offer of $140,000. They think that the owner will probably counteroffer with $145,000, which is the amount that they'd like to spend. They draft an offer of purchase contract for $140,000 and also include other contingencies.

As we saw in the chapter on contracts, offers can have contingencies. In the case of offers of purchase for real estate, there are some common contingencies seen in almost every offer. Among these contingencies are:

- Inspection for damage
- Financing
- Termite inspection

a. Inspection for Damage

John and Mary's offer on the house is conditional on an inspection of the property by a licensed housing inspector. This is a commonsense provision that makes the offer conditional on the house passing an inspection. John and Mary will hire a qualified inspector to examine the property and to draft a report about any potential problems with the structure.

b. Financing

Another condition in John and Mary's offer concerns financing. Most people do not have the spare cash to buy a house outright. They must obtain bank financing. John and Mary's offer is contingent on receiving a mortgage on this property from a bank. They were smart enough to obtain prequalification for a mortgage, but they will need to finalize this arrangement. In fact, the seller will want some assurance from the bank that John and Mary actually will be able to purchase the home. We discuss the function of mortgages later in this chapter.

c. Termite Inspection

The requirement that the home be inspected for termites is something that can occur independently of the house inspection. Because termites have traditionally been the bane of a homeowner's existence, many state and federal agencies require a certification that the house is free of termite infestation before the house can be sold.

3. ACCEPTING THE OFFER

After several rounds of negotiation, the seller agrees to sell his home to John and Mary for $145,000. There is now a binding contract between them setting out the details of their agreement, including sale price, terms and closing date. Among the provisions of this agreement is the seller's requirement that John and Mary produce proof, within ten days of the contract date, that they have obtained a mortgage for the property.

 **MORTGAGES**

When John and Mary obtain a **mortgage** on the property, they are using the real estate as collateral for the loan. In essence, their arrangement with the bank is: "In

Mortgage
A pledge of real estate as collateral or security for a loan

exchange for you lending us the money to purchase the house, we will pledge the house as collateral for the loan. If we fail to make payments, you may seize the house to satisfy the loan."

A mortgage resembles other types of financing in only superficial ways. People finance the purchase of cars, boats, or other personal property items every day. Although mortgages resemble these transactions, there are important differences between traditional financing and financing the purchase of real estate. For one thing, there is the issue of foreclosure.

A. FORECLOSURE

Foreclosure
The right of another to take legal action to auction off real estate to satisfy an outstanding indebtedness, such as a mortgage

If John and Mary ever fail to make payments on their mortgage, the bank has the right to foreclose on the property. **Foreclosure** is unique to real property. When a bank acquires the right to foreclose on real estate, it does not mean that the bank holds title to the land. Unlike transactions involving personal property in which the bank retains title to the property until the final payment is made, in a mortgage situation, the new owners actually possess full title to the property. The property is listed under their names and they have a deed to prove that they have full title. When the buyers acquired a mortgage, they did not transfer title; they transferred a right. The mortgage gives the bank the right to foreclose on the property. This right becomes actionable only on specific conditions, such as the owners' failure to pay the mortgage. When that event occurs, the bank is entitled to bring a legal action to seize the property and auction it off for the remaining loan balance. The important difference between mortgages and the financing seen in personal property is that the right of foreclosure is not automatic. The bank must institute legal proceedings to seize the house. When the owner of personal property defaults on the loan, the bank will simply seize the property through repossession. After all, the bank actually has title to the personal property. Foreclosures are not repossessions. The bank must enforce its right of foreclosure through a judicial proceeding and close off the owners' rights to the property before auction.

 When a person fails to make monthly mortgage payments, the bank is authorized to foreclose and sell the property at auction.

B. MORTGAGE TERMS

Among the important terms of a mortgage are the length, monthly payment, and interest rate. Given the substantial amount of money involved in most residential transactions, the loan term for a mortgage is usually 30 years. The monthly payment is determined by the length of the mortgage, the amount financed, and the interest rate. The interest rate is set by the bank and may fluctuate, such as in adjustable rate mortgages, or may be fixed from the outset, such as in fixed rate mortgages.

Once John and Mary have obtained a mortgage on the property, their next concern will probably be to ensure that the type of property interest they will obtain in the property is fee simple absolute ownership.

 **OWNERSHIP INTERESTS IN REAL PROPERTY**

There are various types of ownership interests in real estate, such as:

- Fee simple absolute
- Life estates
- Concurrent estates
- Leasehold estates

All these interests, or estates, in property, reflect the rights of the possessor. When a person has fee simple absolute interest in property, he or she has dramatically different rights than a person who possesses a life estate or a leasehold estate.

A. FEE SIMPLE ABSOLUTE

Fee simple absolute interest gives the owner the most rights of any estate. An owner in fee simple has all the rights that we normally associate with ownership, including:

> **Fee simple absolute**
> Absolute ownership interests in the property; all rights to the property are vested in a single owner or owners

- The right to mortgage the property
- The right to sell or give away the property
- The right to leave the property to heirs
- The right to rent the property to others
- The right to use the property in any manner that does not violate the law, and many others

We have already seen that a property owner can mortgage property. An owner in fee simple has the most extensive and protected rights of any type of owner. When a person possesses fee simple title to real estate, he can leave the property to his heirs in his will, or even give the property away (assuming that there are no outstanding claims on the property). The rights of a fee simple owner are so absolute that the only limitations that can be placed on the right to use the property involve threats to public health or morals. An owner can be cited for violating local ordinances in the way that he uses property, but as long as his use is not illegal, he is free to do anything with his property that he chooses.

Many commentators have listed the various rights associated with home ownership as a bundle of rights. This bundle includes the right to use, possess, rent, mortgage, etc. The interesting aspect of fee simple absolute ownership is that an owner can transfer some of these ownership rights to others. This is what occurs when an owner creates a life estate.

Fee simple absolute is the category of real estate ownership that has the most rights and protections under the law.

B. LIFE ESTATES

Life estate
Creation of a temporary estate in which a person is given possession, use, and other rights to property, but only as long as he lives. On the possessor's death, the property reverts to another

A **life estate** is a real estate concept in which a person is given many of the rights of a fee simple owner, but the rights have an expiration date. In most cases, the rights expire when the possessor dies. The most common method for creating a life estate is to leave property to a family member in a will. Consider the following example:

Jamillah writes a will that contains the following provision: "On my death, I wish to leave my home and the land on which it sits to my niece, Vanna, for her life and then to my children."

If we construe the language of this will, on Jamillah's death, her home will transfer to Vanna. Vanna can use this home, but only as long as she lives. On her death, she cannot leave the property to her heirs. Instead, on her death, her life estate expires and title to the property vests according to the terms of Jamillah's will.

C. CONCURRENT ESTATES

A "concurrent estate" refers to the rights of multiple property owners. We have mentioned John and Mary several times throughout this chapter. When they purchased their home, they became concurrent owners. In this capacity, concurrent ownership refers to the fact that there is more than one owner. The various concurrent estates set out the limitations placed on these multiple owners in their possession, use, and ultimate transfer of the property. For instance, if John and Mary are married, they would own their property in the concurrent estate of tenants by entirety.

1. TENANTS BY ENTIRETY

Tenancy by entirety
The joint tenancy created by marriage; each spouse has the right of survivorship to the estate on the death of the other spouse

A **tenancy by entirety** is the name for a concurrent estate created when a husband and wife own property together. This estate grants specific rights and guarantees to married couples. For instance, they cannot sell the property without the signatures of both (preventing one spouse from selling the property without the other spouse's knowledge). Among the other rights guaranteed under this estate is the right of survivorship.

a. The Right of Survivorship

Right of survivorship
The right of a surviving concurrent owner to take full title to the property on the death of the other concurrent owner

The **right of survivorship** is the right of the surviving concurrent owner to take full title to the property. For instance, in a tenancy by entirety, when one spouse dies, the other spouse immediately receives full title to the property without the necessity of a court order granting such rights. This right is a powerful one. Instead of a person's property rights divesting to his heirs on death, complete ownership bypasses the heirs and vests in the surviving concurrent owner. Although the right of survivorship is a feature of tenancy by entirety, there are other concurrent estates that also possess this right. One is joint tenancy.

> **When two or more tenants own property with the right of survivorship, it means that when one dies the other gets complete title to the property.**

2. JOINT TENANCY

Joint tenancy is another form of concurrent ownership in which two or more people hold title to property jointly. In this case, the co-owners are not married (if they were, the estate would be a tenancy by entirety). Joint tenants have an undivided mutual interest in the property. Unlike tenants by entirety, joint tenants can transfer or sell their interests to others and thereby extinguish the concurrent estate. (Tenants by entirety extinguish their estate by ending the marriage.) Because the right of survivorship exists in joint tenancy, and therefore bypasses the normal probate proceedings, when two or more people wish to create a joint tenancy they must specifically state this intention in the deed that transfers ownership.

Joint tenancy
The right to real estate that exists in two or more owners who have the right of survivorship

3. TENANTS IN COMMON

A **tenancy in common** is another type of concurrent ownership in property, but it does not have the right of survivorship. When a tenant in common dies, his property interest is transferred through probate proceedings.

Tenants in common
Concurrent owners who own unequal shares to real estate and have no right of survivorship

Let's assume that John and Mary are married and that they will possess the property together as tenants by entirety. As they prepare to take possession of the property, they must consider some additional important details. One of them is the quality of the title being conveyed. In many states, purchasers hire legal professionals to investigate the title. This is called a title examination.

TRANSFERRING TITLE TO REAL ESTATE

The method used to transfer title or ownership is one of the primary distinguishing characteristics between personal property and real property. There is a great deal of symbolism in real estate transactions that arises directly from the fact that, unlike personal property in which physical transfer of the item is the best way to prove ownership, land cannot be picked up and given to a new owner. Transferring ownership interests in real estate is different, not the least because the nature of real property is different.

In a typical residential real estate transaction, there is a buyer and a seller. The seller has placed the real estate for sale, and the real estate agent has produced a buyer who is ready, willing, and able to purchase the property. At this point, the issues unique to real property surface, especially in regard to transfer of title. In the next sections, we examine many of the features of a real estate closing, including a paralegal's role in examining the title to the real estate and the role of deeds to transfer ownership to real estate.

TITLE EXAMINATIONS

Title examination
The process of examining the public records connected with a parcel of real estate to locate any encumbrances or other legal impediments

In states in which attorneys offer a legal opinion about the status of the real estate title, the common practice is to perform a title search, also known as a **title examination,** on the property's history. A title examination is a review of the public record to search for any outstanding legal interests or claims on the property that might affect the quality of the title. Not all states use the title examination system. In many states, the quality of title is determined by outstanding claims recorded against the property. In states in which the title examination system is used, attorneys are often called upon to give a legal opinion about the status of the title and the effect of any outstanding claims on the property. The purchasers obviously wish to obtain property that is free and clear of any claims and the attorney's certificate of title is one way that they can be assured that this is actually the case. We explore the issue of title examinations in detail in this chapter's "Skills You Need in the Real World."

The purchasers normally hire an attorney to conduct the title examination. However, the sellers will also retain an attorney to handle other aspects of the transaction, such as drafting the deed and conducting the closing.

 **Title examinations are required in many states and consist of a review of the public records for any ruling, judgment, or lien that could affect the new owner's rights in the property.**

 **DEEDS**

Real property interests are transferred through deeds. Unlike transactions involving personal property, almost all transactions involving real estate must be in writing. This requirement is a direct result of the adoption of the Statute of Frauds, discussed in Chapter 9. Under the Statute of Frauds, certain types of contracts must be in writing or the courts will not enforce them. Transfer of real estate interests is one of the categories covered by the Statute of Frauds.

A deed is not only a form of contract, but also a kind of symbolic transfer. Because the land itself cannot be moved, the parties cannot manifest physical possession of the land as a means of proving ownership. The land remains fixed and immobile and therefore the only way to prove ownership of land is through other evidence. When a deed is signed by the seller and delivered to the buyer, this physical act is the symbolic transfer of ownership of the property. If at the moment that the deed is delivered and accepted by the buyer, the house should catch on fire and burn to the ground, it will be the buyer's insurance company that will be forced to pay even though the buyer has not yet taken physical possession of the property.

> **Ownership in real estate transfers on the delivery and acceptance of the deed, not when the buyers actually move into the home.**

ISSUE AT
A GLANCE

A. TYPES OF DEEDS

We have already said that John and Mary wish to acquire fee simple absolute ownership in the property. There are several different types of deeds and John and Mary will want the deed that transfers the correct title to them. Among the various types of deeds are general warranty deeds, quitclaim deeds, and deeds of trust.

1. GENERAL WARRANTY DEED

It is important for any legal professional to recognize that real estate practice varies considerably from state to state. Our discussion of deeds, including general warranty deeds, will provide only an overview because of the peculiarities of real estate practice in each jurisdiction. You should refer to your own state statutes for the specifics related to deeds.

General warranty deeds contain promises (or warranties) from the seller to the buyer including a promise that the new buyers have fee simple absolute ownership in the property.

a. Seizin

The covenant or warranty of seizin is the seller's assurance that he is in legitimate possession of the property and is able to transfer that interest to others.

b. Quiet Enjoyment

The warranty of quiet enjoyment is the seller's promise that there are no outstanding claims or unresolved interests in the property that would affect the buyer's ability to use and enjoy it.

c. Against Encumbrances

The warranty against encumbrances is the seller's assurance that there are no outstanding liens, judgments, or other legal actions that will affect the buyer's ownership of the property.

FIGURE 12-2

NORTH CAROLINA,

<u>WARRANTY DEED</u>

STANLY COUNTY.

THIS DEED, made the 10th day of June, 1991, by and between DOROTHY LEE GADDY and husband, WILLIAM M. GADDY, of Anson County, North Carolina, MARILYN LEE MITCHUM and husband, ROBERT P. MITCHUM, JR., of Mecklenburg County, North Carolina, JULIAN W. LEE and wife, JOYCE G. LEE, and BILLY FRANKLIN LEE and wife, SARAH U. LEE, all of Stanly County, North Carolina, and BILLY FRANKLIN LEE and DOROTHY LEE GADDY, Executors of the Estate of Isabell Parker Lee, Deceased; hereinafter called "Grantors"; and TOWN OF NORWOOD, a North Carolina Municipal Corporation of Stanly County, North Carolina, hereinafter called "Grantee";

WITNESSETH:

That Grantors, for and in consideration of $10.00 and other good and valuable considerations to them in hand paid by Grantee, the receipt whereof is hereby acknowledged, have given, granted, bargained, sold and conveyed, and by these presents do give, grant, bargain, sell, convey and confirm unto Grantee, its successors and assigns, premises in Center Township, Stanly County, North Carolina, described as follows:

Lying and being in the Town of Norwood, Stanly County, North Carolina and beginning at a new iron rod [P.C.] in the northeasterly line of the 1.639 acre parcel of land conveyed to Herbert H. Eaton and wife by deed recorded in Deed Book 392, at page 396, Stanly County Registry, said beginning point being located S. 35-59-00 E. 7.99 feet from an existing concrete monument at the northerly corner of said 1.639 acre parcel [said beginning point also being the easterly corner of the 0.07 acre parcel of land conveyed by Herbert H. Eaton and wife to the Town of Norwood by deed dated June 10, 1991]; thence from said beginning point N. 35-59-00 W. 7.99 feet to an existing concrete monument; thence with the northeasterly terminus of an unopened street N. 34-41-21 W. 23.01 feet to an existing iron pipe; thence with a southeasterly line of the 0.09 acre parcel of land conveyed to the Town of Norwood by the Trustees of First Presbyterian Church of Norwood, North Carolina by deed dated June 10, 1991, N. 54-29-37 E. 74.55 feet to a new iron rod; thence in an easterly direction with the arc of circular curve to the right [said curve having a Delta of 25 degrees, 43 minutes, 44 seconds; a Radius of 315.40; a Tangent of 72.03; and a Chord of N. 81-04-42 E. 140.45 feet] for an arc distance of 141.63 feet to a new iron rod [P.T.]; thence S. 86-03-26 E. 119.67 feet to a new iron rod [P.C.]; thence in a southeasterly direction with the arc of circular curve to the right [said curve having a Delta of 59 degrees, 36 minutes, 45 seconds; a Radius of 265.65; a Tangent of 152.18; and a Chord of S. 56-15-04 E. 264.09 feet] for an arc distance of 276.39 feet to a new iron rod [P.T.]; thence S. 26-26-41 E. 197.26 feet to a new iron rod on the northwesterly margin of Ray Lee Street [30 feet right-of-way]; thence with the northwesterly margin of Ray Lee Street S. 60-18-24 W. 40.06 feet to a new iron rod; thence with the northeasterly margin of Lisk Street [unopened, 30 feet right-of-way] N. 26-26-41 W. 199.53 feet

FIGURE 12-2

(continued)

to an existing iron pipe; thence in a northwesterly direction with the arc of a circular curve to the left [said curve having a Delta of 59 degrees, 36 minutes, 45 seconds; a Radius of 225.65; a Tangent of 129.26; and a Chord of N. 56-15-04 W. 224.33 feet] for an arc distance of 234.77 feet to a new iron rod [P.C.]; thence N. 86-03-26 W. 119.67 feet to a new iron rod [P.T.]; thence in a westerly direction with the arc of a circular curve to the left [said curve having a Delta of 39 degrees, 26 minutes, 57 seconds; a Radius of 275.40; a Tangent of 98.74; and a Chord of S. 74-13-05 W. 185.90 feet] for an arc distance of 189.62 feet to the place of beginning and containing 0.70 acre, more or less, by survey of Rogell E. Hunsucker & Associates, Inc., dated May 14, 1991.

For reference see deed of Dr. W. L. McLeod to Ray T. Lee and wife, Isabell Parker Lee, dated May 20, 1965, recorded in Deed Book 224, at page 23, Stanly County Registry. Also see Will of Isabell Parker Lee recorded in the Office of the Clerk of Court of Stanly County [File 91-E-169]. Ray T. Lee predeceased Isabell Parker Lee. The Executors of the Estate of Isabell Parker Lee join in this conveyance pursuant to G.S. 28A-17-12[a] [2].

TO HAVE AND TO HOLD the above described premises, with all the appurtenances thereunto belonging, or in any wise appertaining, unto the Grantee, its successors and assigns forever.

And the Grantors covenant that they are seized of said premises in fee, and have the right to convey the same in fee simple; that said premises are free from encumbrances [with the exceptions above stated, if any]; and that they will warrant and defend the said title to the same against the lawful claims of all persons whomsoever.

When reference is made to the Grantor or grantee, the singular shall include the plural and the masculine shall include the feminine or the neuter.

IN WITNESS WHEREOF, Grantors have hereunto set their hands and seals, the day and year first above written.

_____ [SEAL]
DOROTHY LEE GADDY

_____ [SEAL]
WILLIAM M. GADDY

_____ [SEAL]
MARILYN LEE MITCHUM

_____ [SEAL]
ROBERT P. MITCHUM, JR.

_____ [SEAL]
JULIAN W. LEE

_____ [SEAL]
JOYCE G. LEE

_____ [SEAL]
BILLY FRANKLIN LEE

_____ [SEAL]
SARAH U. LEE

_____ [SEAL]
BILLY FRANKLIN LEE,
Executor of the Estate of
Isabell Parker Lee, Deceased

_____ [SEAL]
DOROTHY LEE GADDY,
Executor of the Estate of
Isabell Parker Lee, Deceased

d. Further Assurance

This warranty is the seller's promise that if some other party should claim an interest in the property, the seller will give further evidence or testimony to prove that the transaction was legitimate and that the buyer has full title to the property.

e. Warranty Forever

In addition to the previous promises made by the seller, this provision is the seller's promise that he will take no action to undermine the buyer's title in the property after the conveyance is made.

2. QUITCLAIM DEEDS

A quitclaim deed contains no promises or warranties and does exactly what its title suggests: it surrenders any claim that the person may have to the property. Although a quitclaim deed can convey fee simple absolute title, John and Mary would no doubt prefer a general warranty deed. A quitclaim deed contains no promises or covenants about the nature of the title or the seller's right to convey. As a result, quitclaim deeds are usually seen in probate situations in which a distant family member might have a potential claim on the decedent's estate. This relative might execute a quitclaim deed in order to clear up any potential clouds on the title. However, a buyer would be foolhardy not to insist on a general warranty deed in a typical residential real estate transaction.

3. DEED OF TRUST (MORTGAGES)

Some of the important questions that the participants in the closing always ask have to do with money. Buyers always want to know how much money they should bring in certified funds to the closing and sellers always want to know how much money they will make in the transaction. The settlement statement provides answers to all these questions.

When John and Mary seek a loan from a local bank to buy their home, the bank will undoubtedly secure its loan through a mortgage or deed of trust. A mortgage is a deed that creates the bank's right to foreclose on the property in the event of the borrower's default on the loan. The most common reason for a loan default is failure to make regular monthly payments on the mortgage. Some states use a deed of trust instead of a mortgage. Although we use these terms interchangeably here, there are important differences between them. Whether the transaction is secured by a mortgage or a deed of trust, the buyer will sign the instrument at the next important event in the real estate transaction: the closing.

 **THE CLOSING**

The closing is the end result of all of the contractual negotiations, inspections, title searches, and other activities that have occurred throughout the real estate transaction. A closing is a meeting at which the deed is delivered by the seller and accepted by the buyer. It is also when many other documents critical to the transaction are signed. At the closing, an attorney will coordinate the signing of the deed by the seller, the transfer of the deed to the buyer, the signing of mortgage paperwork by the buyer; and disburse funds to the several people involved in the transaction. The seller, for

A. **Settlement Statement** U.S. Department of Housing and Urban Development OMB Approval No. 2502-0265

FIGURE 12-3

B. Type of Loan

			6. File Number:	7. Loan Number:	8. Mortgage Insurance Case Number:
1. ☐ FHA	2. ☐ FmHA	3. ☐ Conv. Unins.			
4. ☐ VA	5. ☐ Conv. Ins.				

C. Note: This form is furnished to give you a statement of actual settlement costs. Amounts paid to and by the settlement agent are shown. Items marked "(p.o.c.)" were paid outside the closing; they are shown here for informational purposes and are not included in the totals.

D. Name & Address of Borrower:	E. Name & Address of Seller:	F. Name & Address of Lender:

| G. Property Location: | H. Settlement Agent: | |
| | Place of Settlement: | I. Settlement Date: |

J. Summary of Borrower's Transaction		K. Summary of Seller's Transaction	
100. Gross Amount Due From Borrower		**400. Gross Amount Due To Seller**	
101. Contract sales price		401. Contract sales price	
102. Personal property		402. Personal property	
103. Settlement charges to borrower (line 1400)		403.	
104.		404.	
105.		405.	
Adjustments for items paid by seller in advance		**Adjustments for items paid by seller in advance**	
106. City/town taxes to		406. City/town taxes to	
107. County taxes to		407. County taxes to	
108. Assessments to		408. Assessments to	
109.		409.	
110.		410.	
111.		411.	
112.		412.	
120. Gross Amount Due From Borrower		**420. Gross Amount Due To Seller**	
200. Amounts Paid By Or In Behalf Of Borrower		**500. Reductions In Amount Due To Seller**	
201. Deposit or earnest money		501. Excess deposit (see instructions)	
202. Principal amount of new loan(s)		502. Settlement charges to seller (line 1400)	
203. Existing loan(s) taken subject to		503. Existing loan(s) taken subject to	
204.		504. Payoff of first mortgage loan	
205.		505. Payoff of second mortgage loan	
206.		506.	
207.		507.	
208.		508.	
209.		509.	
Adjustments for items unpaid by seller		**Adjustments for items unpaid by seller**	
210. City/town taxes to		510. City/town taxes to	
211. County taxes to		511. County taxes to	
212. Assessments to		512. Assessments to	
213.		513.	
214.		514.	
215.		515.	
216.		516.	
217.		517.	
218.		518.	
219.		519.	
220. Total Paid By/For Borrower		**520. Total Reduction Amount Due Seller**	
300. Cash At Settlement From/To Borrower		**600. Cash At Settlement To/From Seller**	
301. Gross Amount due from borrower (line 120)		601. Gross amount due to seller (line 420)	
302. Less amounts paid by/for borrower (line 220)	( )	602. Less reductions in amt. due seller (line 520)	( )
303. Cash ☐ From ☐ To Borrower		**603. Cash ☐ To ☐ From Seller**	

Section 5 of the Real Estate Settlement Procedures Act (RESPA) requires the following: • HUD must develop a Special Information Booklet to help persons borrowing money to finance the purchase of residential real estate to better understand the nature and costs of real estate settlement services; • Each lender must provide the booklet to all applicants from whom it receives or for whom it prepares a written application to borrow money to finance the purchase of residential real estate; • Lenders must prepare and distribute with the Booklet a Good Faith Estimate of the settlement costs that the borrower is likely to incur in connection with the settlement. These disclosures are manadatory.

Section 4(a) of RESPA mandates that HUD develop and prescribe this standard form to be used at the time of loan settlement to provide full disclosure of all charges imposed upon the borrower and seller. These are third party disclosures that are designed to provide the borrower with pertinent information during the settlement process in order to be a better shopper.

The Public Reporting Burden for this collection of information is estimated to average one hour per response, including the time for reviewing instructions, searching existing data sources, gathering and maintaining the data needed, and completing and reviewing the collection of information.

This agency may not collect this information, and you are not required to complete this form, unless it displays a currently valid OMB control number.

The information requested does not lend itself to confidentiality.

FIGURE 12-3

(continued)

L. Settlement Charges

		Paid From Borrowers Funds at Settlement	Paid From Seller's Funds at Settlement
700. Total Sales/Broker's Commission based on price $ @ % =			
Division of Commission (line 700) as follows:			
701. $ to			
702. $ to			
703. Commission paid at Settlement			
704.			
800. Items Payable In Connection With Loan			
801. Loan Origination Fee %			
802. Loan Discount %			
803. Appraisal Fee to			
804. Credit Report to			
805. Lender's Inspection Fee			
806. Mortgage Insurance Application Fee to			
807. Assumption Fee			
808.			
809.			
810.			
811.			
900. Items Required By Lender To Be Paid In Advance			
901. Interest from to @$ /day			
902. Mortgage Insurance Premium for months to			
903. Hazard Insurance Premium for years to			
904. years to			
905.			
1000. Reserves Deposited With Lender			
1001. Hazard insurance months @ $ per month			
1002. Mortgage insurance months @ $ per month			
1003. City property taxes months @ $ per month			
1004. County property taxes months @ $ per month			
1005. Annual assessments months @ $ per month			
1006. months @ $ per month			
1007. months @ $ per month			
1008. months @ $ per month			
1100. Title Charges			
1101. Settlement or closing fee to			
1102. Abstract or title search to			
1103. Title examination to			
1104. Title insurance binder to			
1105. Document preparation to			
1106. Notary fees to			
1107. Attorney's fees to			
(includes above items numbers:)			
1108. Title insurance to			
(includes above items numbers:)			
1109. Lender's coverage $			
1110. Owner's coverage $			
1111.			
1112.			
1113.			
1200. Government Recording and Transfer Charges			
1201. Recording fees: Deed $; Mortgage $; Releases $			
1202. City/county tax/stamps: Deed $; Mortgage $			
1203. State tax/stamps: Deed $; Mortgage $			
1204.			
1205.			
1300. Additional Settlement Charges			
1301. Survey to			
1302. Pest inspection to			
1303.			
1304.			
1305.			
1400. Total Settlement Charges (enter on lines 103, Section J and 502, Section K)			

instance, will receive the net proceeds of the sale (less the amount of the sale applied to his outstanding mortgage). The real estate agent will also receive his commission.

When the closing is complete, the buyers have a deed to the property, the seller has a check for the net proceeds of the sale, the attorneys and real estate agents have checks for their services, and all these disbursements are set out in a settlement statement. A settlement statement is a written accounting of all the funds that have been received and disbursed in the closing. An example of a settlement statement is provided in Figure 12-3.

Profiling a Paralegal

▶ Deputy Tax Collector, Delinquent Taxes, Darlene Burgess

arlene began her legal career at age 16 when she worked part-time for a local attorney. She started out answering telephones and then slowly began taking on more and more paralegal duties. She continued working in the law office after graduating from high school and after a few years decided to go back to college and obtain her paralegal degree. After graduating with an associate's degree in paralegal studies, Darlene then completed the Certified Legal Assistant™ exam, a national certification. "The exam takes two days and it is very detailed. I passed it the first time." After completing her CLA certification, Darlene went on to complete her bachelor's degree at a local university. She has worked full time while completing her education. "I worked for a local firm, primarily doing their foreclosure actions. I was

at the local courthouse one day, working on a foreclosure, when I got a job offer to work in the tax department."

For the past several years, Darlene has been in charge of collecting delinquent real estate taxes. She has streamlined the tax foreclosure process and generated thousands of dollars per year in delinquent tax collection.

"I learned as a paralegal that you have to be creative in how you approach a legal problem. I'm constantly tracking down businesses that are delinquent on their taxes or trying to locate people to pay their outstanding taxes before their homes go into foreclosure. I find myself doing typical title examination work almost every day. Real Property Law was one of the most important courses I took in college. I use it every day."

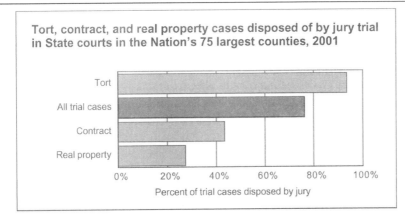

FIGURE 12-4*

Tort, contract, and real property cases disposed of by jury trial in State courts in the Nation's 75 largest counties, 2001

* Bureau of Justice Statistics, U.S. Department of Justice. Civil Trial Cases and Verdicts in Large Counties, 2001.

TAXES

Now that John and Mary have completed the closing process and own the property, they have the responsibilities shared by all property owners. Among those responsibilities is the obligation to pay real estate taxes. Taxes are assessed by the local tax assessor's office based on the local government's budgetary needs and the size of the property itself. Real estate taxes are assessed yearly and homeowners are obligated to pay these taxes or face legal action. In most states, governments have the right to foreclose on property based on unpaid real estate taxes. This foreclosure proceeding is very similar to the foreclosure proceedings seen when a person fails to pay on his mortgage.

MUSSELMAN v. WILLOUGHBY CORP.
230 Va. 337, 337 S.E.2d 724 (1985)

COMPTON, Justice.

This is an attorney malpractice case arising from a real estate transaction. The lawyer represented a corporate client and employed an untrained paralegal who played a significant role in the closing of the transaction.

The relevant facts mainly are undisputed. Appellee Willoughby Corporation, the plaintiff below, was formed in September 1974 by a large number of holders of O'Neill Enterprises, Inc., real estate bonds which had been secured by undeveloped land known as the "Willoughby Tract," lying in the City of Charlottesville and Albemarle County. When O'Neill Enterprises defaulted and went into bankruptcy, the bondholders formed Willoughby Corporation (hereinafter, the Corporation) in order to sell or develop the property to recoup their investments.

Appellant Robert M. Musselman, a defendant below, represented the bondholders in formation of the Corporation. He became attorney for the Corporation and also served as its Secretary. He was not a member of the Board of Directors. The daily operations of the Corporation were handled from defendant's law office by defendant's employees. One director testified that Musselman took "a very dominant role in the affairs of the corporation" and that the Board looked to defendant for "guidance and leadership."

In 1976, aware that the Board of Directors wished to sell a portion of the Willoughby Tract, defendant contacted Thomas J. Chandler, Jr., a local real estate broker, who obtained an offer to purchase Parcel 9. The offer was made by Charles W. Hurt, a medical doctor who had been a real estate developer in the Charlottesville and Albemarle County area for a number of years.

Initially, Hurt offered to pay $200,000 for the land. The realtor completed a standard form purchase contract dated March 26, 1976 reciting that amount and, as instructed by Hurt, showed the purchaser to be "Charles Wm. Hurt or Assign." The proposal was delivered to defendant who later asked the realtor to attend a special meeting of the Board of Directors, held at Musselman's law office on April 9, 1976.

The Board minutes of the meeting show that Chandler "presented" Hurt's offer to the Board at the meeting and that the Board fully considered "the advantages and disadvantages" of the proposed sale. The Board decided to accept the offer subject to several modifications, to which Hurt later agreed.

Subsequently, another standard form purchase contract for $215,000 was completed dated May 6, 1976. The purchaser was shown to be "Charles Wm. Hurt or Assigns."

The closing did not occur on March 1, 1977. The delay was attributed, in part, to a disagreement between Hurt's attorney and Musselman about the matter of interest on the debt as it related to the availability of sewer service to the property. The delay in closing was a subject of discussion during a meeting of the Board of Directors on September 1, 1977. Also present were Musselman and one Stanley K. Joynes, III.

Joynes had been employed by Musselman in June 1977. Joynes had just graduated from college but had no formal training either as a lawyer or a paralegal. His main responsibility, under Musselman's direction, was to "shepherd the Willoughby Project along." In the course of the September 1977 Board meeting, defendant was directed to close the Hurt transaction "as soon as possible." Three weeks later, Stuart F. Carwile, Hurt's attorney, notified Musselman by letter dated September 22, 1977 that his client desired to take title to Parcel 9 as follows:

"Stuart F. Carwile and David W. Kudravetz, as trustees for the Fifth Street Land Trust, pursuant to the terms of a certain land trust agreement dated 22 September 1977."

The paralegal then prepared the deed, with "some assistance" from other employees of defendant, in accordance with Carwile's request showing the Land Trust as grantee. Joynes arranged for Frankel to execute the deed, dated October 5, 1977, and on that day participated with Carwile in the closing of the transaction. Musselman was out of town on business on both October 4th and 5th. In the course of the closing on October 5th, the paralegal accepted the deed of trust, and other closing documents prepared by Carwile, which specifically exculpated Hurt from personal liability in the transaction as beneficiary under the land trust.

Musselman testified that Joynes, the paralegal, represented the Corporation at the closing, acting within his authority as an employee of defendant. Also, none of the Board members, prior to closing, ever examined either the proposed contract of March 26 or the final contract dated May 6. Moreover, no member of the Board knew before closing that the contract showed the purchaser to be "Hurt or Assigns." In addition, Musselman always was of opinion that the foregoing language in the contract authorized Hurt to escape personal liability under the contract by assigning his rights in the contract to whomever he chose. Also, Musselman never called the language to the Board's attention or explained its meaning to the Board. Finally, the fact that the closing documents exculpated Hurt from personal liability as beneficiary under the land trust was never revealed or explained to the Board of Directors prior to closing.

The Board of Directors met on October 6, the day after closing. Directors present were Frankel, Fox, and Lloyd T. Smith, Jr. Joynes and Musselman were also present, among others. The paralegal reported that the sale of Parcel 9 was complete. When a question arose about the date from which interest was to run, Smith asked to see Musselman's file and discovered that the property had been conveyed to a land trust and not to Hurt. He examined the note, saw that Hurt had not endorsed it, and thought the situation was "just frightening." Smith also examined the other closing documents and saw they specifically provided that Hurt would have no personal liability. As a result of the discussion at that meeting, "Musselman stated that he would speak with Dr. Hurt and his attorney . . . in an attempt to clear up these problems." The contract of sale was not exhibited to the Board until the following meeting and no discussion had taken place during the October meeting about the "or Assigns" language. At the next Board meeting held on November 3, 1977, Lloyd Smith and Musselman engaged in a discussion about the effect of the "or Assigns" language. Smith was of opinion, contrary to defendant's view, that use of the term should not permit Hurt to avoid personal liability to the Corporation. According to the minutes, "Mr. Musselman promised to have further research conducted on the question." At this time, the evidence showed, the Board was not overly concerned about the situation. The property had not been released, even though the down payment had been received, and the Board felt it had some bargaining leverage with Hurt.

Two days after the November meeting, Musselman wrote Hurt's attorney in an attempt to resolve the problems that had arisen about the transaction. In the course of the letter, Musselman discussed the "or Assigns" dispute between Board member Smith and Musselman. Defendant asked Hurt's lawyer for reference to "any Virginia authority" bearing on the question, which would support Musselman's view that Hurt could not be held personally liable.

At the Board meeting held on January 26, 1978, Musselman reported that he had negotiated a favorable change in the interest terms on the note. But the Board learned for the first time that Musselman had recorded the deed releasing three front parcels from the tract in question. The deed of partial release was executed by Frankel on the day of closing and by Musselman as a trustee on January 18, 1978, and recorded that day. Musselman was of the belief that as a trustee under the deed of trust, once the release provisions had been complied with by the purchaser, Musselman had no right to refuse to record the deed of partial release. Upon learning of this development, Smith testified that he was "astonished."

The Land Trust defaulted under the terms of the $170,000 note in respect to an interest payment due on April 1, 1978. Subsequently, this action to recover the principal sum, plus interest, due under the real estate transaction was filed in September 1978 in numerous counts against Hurt and Musselman. The proceeding against Hurt was severed and he was eventually dismissed by the trial court as a party defendant.

The Corporation's action against Musselman was based on alternative theories. The plaintiff charged that defendant breached certain fiduciary duties in his capacity as an officer of the Corporation. In addition, the Corporation alleged that Musselman, in his capacity as attorney for the Corporation was negligent and breached his fiduciary duty as counsel to the Corporation. At the March 1982 trial, the jury was permitted, under the instructions, to find against defendant in his capacity either as attorney, or as an officer of the Corporation, or as both attorney and officer. The jury found against defendant in his capacity as attorney only and fixed the damages, which were not in dispute, at $243,722.99. This sum represented the principal amount due on the obligation, plus interest through the last day of trial. The trial court entered judgment on the verdict in June 1982, and we awarded defendant this appeal in July 1983.

In the present case, the evidence showed that defendant failed to advise the Board before closing that the crucial "or Assigns" language was in the contract, and failed to explain the legal effect of the language when, in defendant's opinion, use of the language enabled Hurt to escape personal liability, a consideration of prime importance to the Board in view of the manner in which the deal was structured. In addition, the evidence demonstrated that Musselman permitted an untrained paralegal to accept formulation of final documents that further exculpated Hurt, without bringing such documents to the Board for approval. In sum, the evidence was sufficient to support the jury's finding that defendant breached his duty as an attorney to adequately inform his client and that such breach was a proximate cause of plaintiff's loss.

Inexplicably, defendant's main contentions on appeal are based on the faulty premise that he lacked corporate authority to act in executing the contract containing the "or Assigns" language and in completing the conveyance to a land trust, while, in the process, exculpating Hurt from personal liability. This argument is totally inconsistent with defendant's trial testimony that he did, in fact, have authority to execute the contract. It is also at odds with the uncontroverted evidence about defendant's "dominant role" in acting for the Corporation. This idea relies on the following circular reasoning: Even though specifically empowered to execute the contract, defendant had no authority to permit conveyance to a land trust, because the Board of Directors was unaware of the crucial contract provisions, which Musselman had the duty to disclose to the Board in his capacity as attorney. Building on this infirm basis, defendant contends that the Board should immediately have rescinded the transaction upon discovery of the "problem" at the meeting the day after closing and, in failing to rescind, the Corporation should be deemed to have ratified Musselman's unauthorized acts. As a part of this argument, defendant complains that the trial court misdirected the jury because it granted instructions which failed to recognize this theory and refused to grant tendered instructions which would have permitted the jury to consider the issue of ratification.

There is no merit to this argument. Musselman, being authorized to execute the contract and to close the transaction, had the responsibility as counsel to advise his client, immediately upon discovery of the "problem," that it should attempt to rescind the transaction, if we assume an attempt at rescission would have been successful. Instead, defendant at no time advised the Board of Directors that it should pursue rescission. At the meeting on October 6, the day after closing, Musselman merely stated that he would "attempt to clear up these problems" by speaking with Hurt and his attorney. At the next Board meeting, Musselman only promised to perform further research on the "or Assigns" question. All the while, the Board justifiably expected that the transaction would be satisfactorily completed and that Hurt would consent to become personally bound in the event of default. Finally, in January of 1978, the Board's position was made even worse when three parcels in the tract were released as the result of the recording of the deed of partial release. If Musselman did not realize the Corporation may have had the right to rescind, he will not be heard to complain that the Board should have realized it on its own. And if he knew the Board may have had the right to rescind, he will not be permitted to have withheld such advice from the Board members and then contend they have ratified his conduct by not rescinding on their own. Therefore, the trial court properly ruled the theory of ratification was not applicable and that defendant was not entitled, under the circumstances, to have that issue submitted to the jury.

For these reasons, the judgment of the trial court will be *Affirmed*.

QUESTIONS ABOUT THE CASE

1   What are the basic details of the sale arrangement?
2   What activities did the paralegal perform during the closing?
3   Why is it significant that the closing documents contained a provision absolving Hurt from all personal liability?
4   Why is it significant that the attorney raised a defense of lack of corporate authority on appeal?

SKILLS YOU NEED IN THE REAL WORLD

TITLE EXAMINATIONS

The ability to carry out a title examination is a skill that will make you very marketable to law firms. The purpose of a title exam is to review the legal status of the property by a search of the public records. Public records can reveal a wealth of information about the property, including:

- Federal or state tax liens
- Civil or criminal judgments that affect some ownership rights
- Special assessments
- Easements or liens
- Probate proceedings that divested ownership of the property to other family members
- Other individuals who have some type of ownership interest in the property

Although attorneys bear the ultimate responsibility of offering a legal opinion about the status of the property, they often rely on paralegals to gather the information to reach that conclusion.

Title examinations involve trips to the local, and sometimes a federal, courthouse. You conduct a title search in the deed office (sometimes called the registrar's office or land office). This is where deeds are filed and made part of the public record. Any person may view a deed and the office is open to the public on a daily basis. Deeds may be recorded in many different media, including paper copies, microfilm, microfiche, and digital formats. Many deed offices are beginning to computerize their records and make them available on the Internet, although we are still a long way from the time when a title search can be conducted completely online.

In addition to the deed office, you may also find yourself visiting the clerk of court's office, the tax assessor's office, and many other governmental agencies. All these agencies store public records about a wide range of activities that could adversely affect title to property. Any potential legal problem should be noted and presented to the attorney.

CHAPTER SUMMARY

Real estate law has several unique features. First of all, real property interests are a separate classification from personal property. Real property consists of land and anything permanently attached to land, while personal property consists of all other types of property. Real property has specific physical characteristics, such as enjoying a fixed point on the globe and the fact that no two pieces of real estate are identical. Real property also has several unique economic characteristics. For example, real property generally appreciates in value over time. This gradual appreciation in value allows homeowners and others to borrow against the increased value of their property, known as equity.

When people purchase real estate, they usually arrange financing through the use of a mortgage. A mortgage pledges the property as collateral for the loan. If a person fails to make the mortgage payments, the bank may foreclose on the real estate and auction it off to satisfy the outstanding debt.

Real property law also has a heavy reliance on contract law. Real estate contracts are involved at several points throughout a real estate transaction. Examples of real estate contracts include a real estate agent's listing agreement and an offer of purchase contract. The Statute of Frauds applies to many types of real estate contracts. This statute requires that transfers of real property interests must be in writing to be effective. A deed is the written expression of the transfer of ownership rights in real estate.

When real property is to be transferred, the buyers normally hire an attorney to conduct a title examination on the property. A title examination searches for any claims or interests that are recorded in the public record that might affect the buyer's interest in the property.

Title is officially transferred from the seller to the buyer at the closing. The closing is also when many of the documents, such as the mortgage, are signed. The attorney who handles the closing will also disburse funds to the various people involved in the transaction, including the real estate agent and the seller.

ETHICS: PARALEGALS HANDLING CLOSINGS

Paralegals who specialize in real estate laws can become extremely knowledgeable about closings. In fact, some attorneys turn the entire closing process over to a seasoned paralegal rather than handling the details themselves. This is a dangerous practice. Clients pay a fee to the firm for the attorney's services, which include not only legal research and advice, but also being personally involved in the closing process. There are several states that have been wrestling with the ethical consequences when an attorney turns the closing process over to a paralegal. On one hand, a seasoned paralegal can often do a better job at the closing than a novice attorney. Veteran paralegals have seen every possible complication that can occur at a closing and can often anticipate problems. Paralegals also work closely with lending institutions and clients to prepare for the closing and may have a personal relationship with the parties that an attorney has never established. On the other hand, a paralegal must avoid unauthorized practice of law and a closing is fraught with potential problems. The moment that a paralegal offers a legal opinion about a title issue, he is practicing law and is subject to criminal prosecution. The attorney who delegates complete authority to the paralegal is also playing a dangerous game. Many states have enacted ethical guidelines that require an attorney to at least be available, if not present, when the closing occurs.

CHAPTER REVIEW QUESTIONS

1   Explain the difference between personal property and real property.
2   What are some of the economic characteristics of real estate?
3   What is an agency relationship?
4   What is a realtor and what purpose does a realtor serve?
5   What is a Multiple Listing Service?
6   What are some of the basic requirements of a real estate contract?
7   What is a mortgage?
8   What is foreclosure?
9   What is meant by a "fee simple absolute" title to real estate?
10 What are some of the rights that the fee simple owner has to real estate?
11 What is a life estate?
12 What are the features of a tenancy by entirety?
13 What is the right of survivorship?
14 Explain the difference between a joint tenancy and a tenancy in common.
15 What are some of the methods used to transfer title to real estate?
16 What is a title examination?
17 What is a real estate closing and what occurs there?
18 What is a settlement statement?

DISCUSSION QUESTIONS

1   Why would any concurrent ownership in real property involve the right of survivorship?
2   Should tenancy by entirety be extended to non-married couples? Why or why not?
3   Why is it important for a paralegal to know the ethical rules about real estate closings?

PERSONALITY QUIZ

Is real estate law right for you? Take this personality quiz and see.

1   I enjoy puzzles.
    0-strongly disagree   5-agree   10-strongly agree

                                                          Points: _____

2 I like tracking down information.
   0-strongly disagree   5-agree   10-strongly agree

   Points: _____

3 I prefer the concept of tangible property versus intangible property.
   0-strongly disagree   5-agree   10-strongly agree

   Points: _____

4 I am intrigued by the idea of making money investing in real estate.
   0-strongly disagree   5-agree   10-strongly agree

   Points: _____

   Total Points: _____

If you scored between 25-40 points, you would probably enjoy the real estate field.

If you scored between 10-24 points, you might enjoy real estate, but you might also enjoy some other field.

If you scored 9 or lower, real estate law is probably not the best choice for you.

PRACTICAL APPLICATIONS

1 Go to your local deed office and examine a deed. What type of information is provided on the deed? If the deed is for a residential property, does the property description include a description of the house? If not, why not?
2 Visit your local real estate tax office and then answer the following questions:

   - How is the value of local property assessed?
   - What type of information can be learned from tax records?
   - How does the assessed value compare to the real value of property?
   - How often is property in your area reassessed for value?

WEB SITES

Findlaw.com Real Property Law Section
http://www.findlaw.com/01topics/33property/sites.html

Virginia State Bar Real Property Section
http://www.vsb.org/sections/rp/disclaimer.htm

Real Property Law
http://www.real-property-law.com

MegaLaw — Real Property Law
http://www.megalaw.com/top/property.php

Real Property Law — Wikipedia
http://en.wikipedia.org/wiki/Real_property

CataLaw — Real Property Law
http://www.catalaw.com/topics/Property.shtml

Georgetown Law Library — Real Property Links
http://www.ll.georgetown.edu/find/
resource_display_subject.cfm?topic_id=173

TERMS AND PHRASES

Agent	Mortgage	Tenancy by entirety
Fee simple absolute	Multiple Listing Service	Tenants in common
Foreclosure	Principal	Title examination
Joint tenancy	Real property	
Life estate	Right of survivorship	

Wills and Trusts

Chapter Learning Objectives

After completing this chapter, you should be able to:

- Explain the difference between testate and intestate probate proceedings
- List and describe the elements of a legally enforceable will
- Explain testamentary capacity
- Describe the administration of an estate when there is no will
- Explain the basic organization of a trust

 **INTRODUCTION**

In this chapter, we explore the law surrounding the disposition of a person's property after she dies, commonly referred to as probate. There are two methods of transferring property through probate proceedings, testate proceedings and intestate administration. We also discuss the role of trusts in probating a person's estate.

 **WILLS**

A **will** is a document created by a person who is legally competent that directs how property should be disposed of after her death. The legal history of wills stretches back for thousands of years and has a rich common law foundation. However, in modern times, wills are controlled by state statute.

Will
A written document, created by a person in anticipation of her death, that directs how her property will be devised and appoints a personal representative to act on her behalf

FIGURE 13-1

When Does a Will Take Effect?
(Georgia Statute)

> A will shall take effect instantly upon the death of the testator however long probate
> may be postponed.[13]

A. WHAT IS A WILL?

Testator
The person who distributes her
property through a will

A will is created by a person in anticipation of her death. The person who creates a will is referred to as the **testator.** The testator creates a will that specifically designates who should receive her property after she dies. Wills fall into a special category. They are not contracts or deeds or any other type of conveyance. A will is unusual because it does not come into legal effect until the person who drafted it has died. A will is a unilateral action. In a will, the testator does not promise to leave another person property in exchange for the person performing some service.

1. REQUIREMENTS FOR A WILL

Parol evidence
Oral testimony used to prove
or interpret a written provision

Wills have formal, statutory requirements. For a document to qualify as a will, the provisions of the document must meet the requirements set out in state statutes. The statutory elements must be present in the will, or be ascertainable by reference to another document. The will must stand on its own. If the document requires additional testimony (referred to as **parol evidence**) to explain the features or to establish the basic elements of the will, the document is ruled legally insufficient.

ISSUE AT
A GLANCE

**Oral testimony cannot supply a missing, statutory element for a
will, but a written document can.**

2. THE INCORPORATION BY REFERENCE DOCTRINE

Although oral testimony is not sufficient to resurrect a will that is legally insufficient, a will can refer to other, written documents to complete its terms. This is referred to as the incorporation by reference doctrine. Under this doctrine, if some other document, letter, book, or record is referred to in the will, it will be incorporated into the will as though it had actually been written in the will.

Example: Juan writes a will leaving his entire estate to the individual members of the Flat Earth Society, as those members are designated under the current year's corporate minutes. Because Juan's will refers to a written document, that document is considered to be incorporated into Juan's will. Under these provisions, the will is valid.

[13] O.C.G.A. §53-4-2

FIGURE 13-2

Incorporation by Reference (Ohio Statute)

An existing document, book, record, or memorandum may be incorporated in a will by reference, if referred to as being in existence at the time the will is executed. Such document, book, record, or memorandum shall be deposited in the probate court when the will is probated or within thirty days thereafter, unless the court grants an extension of time for good cause shown. A copy may be substituted for the original document, book, record, or memorandum if such copy is certified to be correct by a person authorized to take acknowledgments on deeds.[14]

FIGURE 13-3

Execution of Wills (Florida Statute)

Every will must be in writing and executed as follows:

(1)(a) *Testator's signature.* —
   1. The testator must sign the will at the end; or
   2. The testator's name must be subscribed at the end of the will by some other person in the testator's presence and by the testator's direction.

(b) *Witnesses.* — The testator's:
   1. Signing, or
   2. Acknowledgment:
      a. That he or she has previously signed the will, or
      b. That another person has subscribed the testator's name to it, must be in the presence of at least two attesting witnesses.

(c) *Witnesses' signatures.* — The attesting witnesses must sign the will in the presence of the testator and in the presence of each other.

(2) Any will, other than a holographic or nuncupative will, executed by a nonresident of Florida, either before or after this law takes effect, is valid as a will in this state if valid under the laws of the state or country where the will was executed. A will in the testator's handwriting that has been executed in accordance with subsection (1) shall not be considered a holographic will. . . .

(4) No particular form of words is necessary to the validity of a will if it is executed with the formalities required by law.[15]

B. HOW IS A WILL CREATED?

Because state law governs wills, we must look to statutes to determine how a will is created. Almost all state statutes provide the following minimum requirements for the creation of a will.

A will must:

- Be written
- Be signed by the testator
- Be witnessed
- Have a clearly identifiable beneficiary

[14] R.C. §2107.05
[15] F.S.A. §732.502

1. WILLS MUST BE IN WRITING

Wills must be in writing to be effective. Although there are provisions for oral wills (discussed below), these fall into a specialized category.

The will is usually set out in a formal, written document that is captioned "Last Will and Testament." However, the statutes are more liberal in their approach as to what constitutes a "writing."

Courts have held that wills are in writing when they are fixed in almost any type of permanent medium. As a result, wills have been considered to be written when they are in ink or pencil, on paper, cards, letters, envelopes, and even napkins. If the will meets the other requirements, it can be probated. However, the informal nature of a writing may have some relevance to the question of whether the document was the final draft. If it can be shown that notes on the back of an envelope were simply the testator's method of organizing her thoughts and not intended to be the final version of the testator's wishes, the envelope will not be classified as a will.

Although the legal requirements for creating a will must be met, there is no particular form in which these requirements are met. The law does not specify, for instance, that the testator write a will on stationery embossed with "Last Will and Testament." A will written on lined notebook paper is just as valid as a will prepared on expensive parchment. The important aspects of a will are not the paper used, but what the document actually says.

a. Form of Words to Create a Will

There is no particular form of words that must be used to create a will. Most of us have seen or heard of wills that begin with the famous phrase, "I, John Doe, being of sound mind . . . ." This language is not a legal requirement. The statutory rules about wills are more fluid and were designed to interpret the wide range of language that people use to communicate with one another. What is required is that the testator express **testamentary intent.** This is the legal principle that requires a will to be prepared by the testator in anticipation of her death.

> *Example:* Is this language sufficient to indicate testamentary intent?
>
> In the event that I am called to my ultimate reward, I leave my estate to my children.
>
> *Answer:* Yes. A person can use common euphemisms to indicate testamentary intent.

A testator can only convey by will such property as she owns and cannot, through her will, control the estate of another. For example, a person cannot attempt to control the estates of her children when she does not have ownership rights in their property.[16]

Testamentary intent
The demonstrated intent of a person to create a disposition of her property after her death

---

[16] *Estate of Wells v. Sanford,* 281 Ark. 242, 663 S.W.2d 174 (1984)

FIGURE 13-4	
Unusual Ways to Record Wills	

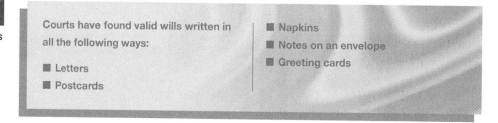

Courts have found valid wills written in all the following ways:

- Letters
- Postcards
- Napkins
- Notes on an envelope
- Greeting cards

b. Holographic Wills

Some of the statutory requirements for wills are waived in situations in which the testator has prepared a **holographic will.** A holographic will is a handwritten will. If it can be proven that the testator wrote the entire will in her own hand, some of the provisions about witnessing a will are waived.

Holographic will
A will that is in the testator's handwriting and bears the testator's signature

The principle behind waiving some of the legal requirements in a holographic will is that when the will is handwritten it shows the testator's intent and state of mind in the writing. Later, we will see that the will must establish the testator's rational mind and ability to organize the disposition of her property. When a person lacks sound judgment, it is often revealed in an inability to express coherent thoughts in print.

Some typed wills can be classified as holographic wills when they lack the proper legal requirements, but only under specific circumstances. (See Figure 13-5.)

Example: Tony writes a letter to his nephew, Ben. At the end of the letter, he writes, "By the way, in case of my death, I want you to have my entire estate. You should save this letter and present it to the proper people. Signed, Anthony Doe, Your Loving Uncle."

The courts later determined that this is a valid will.[17]

Example: Tina Roe writes the following on a greeting card:

In the event of my death, I want all of my property to go to John Doe, my next door neighbor.
—T.R. November 2, 2003

Is this a valid will?
Answer: Yes.[18]

A will which does not comply with [New Jersey's statute on wills] is valid as a holographic will, whether or not	witnessed, if the signature and material provisions are in the handwriting of the testator.[19]

FIGURE 13-5

Holographic Wills
(New Jersey)

▪ Must be completely written in the testator's handwriting ▪ Many jurisdictions also require that the will be dated by the testator	▪ The will must be found among the testator's effects after her death

FIGURE 13-6

Elements of Holographic Wills

---

[17] *Blake's Estate v. Benza,* 120 Ariz. 552, 587 P.2d 271 (1978)
[18] *Trim v. Daniels,* 862 S.W.2d 8 (1994)
[19] N.J.S.A. 3B:3-3

2. SIGNED BY TESTATOR

The law requires not only that the will be in writing, but also that it bear the testator's signature. The signature is an indication of the testator's sound mind and agreement to the terms of the will, although both of those assumptions can be attacked through a will contest, as we will see later in this chapter. We have already said that the testator must have a sound mind at the time that she executes a will. What does that term mean?

a. Testamentary Capacity

A person who has testamentary capacity has the ability to know, understand, and make decisions about her estate. She can decide which of her heirs should receive property and other issues concerning the disposition of her property after her death. Testamentary capacity is assumed to exist unless evidence is presented during a will contest that shows that the testator did not have a sound mind. There are some individuals, however, who are automatically considered to lack testamentary capacity. They include:

- Infants
- Mentally incompetent individuals

i. Infants
Under the law, an infant is any person under the age of 18. Such a person is classified as a child and, as is true in many other legal contexts, unable to engage in legally binding arrangements. Children cannot enter into contracts, vote, or prepare legally binding wills.

ii. Mentally Incompetent Individuals
When a court has ruled that a specific person is mentally incompetent, this person is barred from entering into any legal arrangements. Courts normally appoint a guardian to look after this person's affairs. When such a declaration has been made, the person cannot create a legally binding will because she lacks a sound mind.

> *Example:* David goes to a local attorney and has a will prepared. He signs the will, has it witnessed, and then goes home and commits suicide.
> Is David's suicide proof that he lacked a sound mind at the time that he signed his will?
> *Answer:* No. Suicide, by itself, does not create a presumption that the testator did not have a sound mind.[20]

3. WITNESS PROVISIONS IN WILLS

Another legal requirement of a will is that it be witnessed, usually by two people. The purpose of the witness signatures is to prove that the testator had a sound

---

[20] *Wilkinson v. Service*, 249 Ill. 146, 94 N.E. 50 (1911)

mind at the time that the will was created. Their signature is proof of the witnesses' belief that the testator was competent to handle her affairs. Like many of the assumptions that are made in estate law, this also can be challenged. For one thing, the witnesses must be aware of the testator's mental condition at the time that they sign the will. If they have no knowledge of the testator or her condition, their signatures cannot attest to the testator's mental condition at the time.

4. CLEARLY IDENTIFIABLE BENEFICIARY

When a will leaves property to a person, that person is referred to as a beneficiary under the will. (The term *devisee* is also commonly used.) Although it is helpful to have the will specifically name a person as a beneficiary under the will, it is not a requirement. What is required is that courts can identify the person. What is the difference? Consider these two examples:

> *Example 1.* I leave my entire estate to my wife, Deb, and my two children, Ben and Katy.
> *Example 2.* I leave my entire estate to my wife and children.

In the first example we have specific, named beneficiaries. The only problem with naming the beneficiaries is the possibility that the testator has another child before he dies. This would certainly complicate the execution of the will.

In the second example, we have clearly identifiable, but unnamed beneficiaries. In that example, the testator's entire estate would go to his wife, whoever she is, and his children, whoever and wherever they might be.

Now, let's consider some beneficiary clauses that do not meet the legal standard:

> I leave my estate to the one who always had my best interests at heart.

Although this sentence may have particular significance to the testator, it does not clearly identify a beneficiary. Who is this person? Can a court determine this question with any degree of certainty? Without more, this clause is invalid.

A beneficiary clause may be sufficient if the language can be interpreted by reference to some other document. Consider the next example:

> I leave my estate to the woman named in Marriage Certificate 82-675, Gannett County, Placid State, dated May 15, 1982.

Because the testator has referred to a specific person who can be identified, the clause is considered valid.

What about this clause?

> I leave my estate to my friends.

This bequest will probably held invalid because of the difficulty in identifying a person's friends. The classification of friends is not as obvious as a person's children, or even a person's family.

C. THE PROBATE PROCESS

When we use the term *probate*, such as to probate a will, we are referring to the entire process of locating, interpreting, and disposing of a person's property after her death. The probate process includes not only a determination of where the will should be probated, but also the appointment of an executor, an interpretation of what the will actually says and, finally, disposition of the testator's property according to her wishes.

1. DETERMINING WHERE TO PROBATE THE WILL

Domicile
A person's legal residence

In most situations, the will is probated where the testator was domiciled. A domicile is something more than mere presence. **Domicile** refers to a person's permanent home. Although this determination is usually straightforward, interesting questions arise when a person has several homes. In that situation, the domicile is often the location that the testator considered to be her home and where she spent the majority of her time. Consider Figure 13-7 for other tests to determine where a will should be probated.

2. APPOINTING AN EXECUTOR

Executor
The person appointed in the will to represent the testator's interests and to make dispositions according to the will's provisions

The testator normally names a personal representative, or executor, in the will. This person is responsible for handling the practical details set out in the will. For instance, if the testator has left a sum of money to a devisee, the executor is the person responsible for making sure that the money actually reaches that person. Executors must make a final accounting of all property dispositions in the estate and must answer to the probate judge or other representative for probate transactions.

FIGURE 13-7

Determining Where a Will
Should Be Probated
(Ohio Statute)

A will shall be admitted to probate:

(A) In the county in which the testator was domiciled if, at the time of his death, he was domiciled in this state;

(B) In any county of this state where any real or personal property of such testator is located if, at the time of his death, he was not domiciled in this state, and provided that such will has not previously been admitted to probate in this state or in the state of such testator's domicile;

(C) In the county of this state in which a probate court rendered a judgment declaring that the will was valid and where the will was filed with the probate court.

For the purpose of this section, intangible personal property is located in the place where the instrument evidencing a debt, obligation, stock, or chose in action is located or if there is no such instrument where the debtor resides.[21]

---

[21] R.C. §2107.11 (Ohio)

FIGURE 13-8

Who Is Qualified to Serve as Personal Representative (Virginia)

If there be no executor appointed by the will or if all the executors therein named refuse the executorship or fail to give bond when required, which shall amount to such refusal, or having qualified die, resign or are removed from office, the court or clerk may grant administration with the will annexed to a person who is a residual or a substantial legatee under the will, or his designee, and upon the failure of any such person so to apply within thirty days, to a person who would have been entitled to administration if there had been no will, upon his taking such oath and giving such bond; provided that administration shall not be granted to any person unless the court or clerk is satisfied that he is suitable and competent to perform the duties of his office. If any beneficiary of the estate objects, no husband, wife or parent who has been barred from all interest in the estate because of desertion or abandonment as provided under §64.1-16.3 shall be suitable to serve as an administrator of the estate of the deceased spouse or child, as the case may be.[22]

FIGURE 13-9

Executor Provision in a Will

I hereby nominate my son, John Doe, to act as Executor and waive any provision for the posting of surety or bond.

In many cases, the executor is required to post a bond with the probate court to insure his actions in managing the estate. However, the testator can waive this requirement by stating it in the will. Consider Figure 13-9.

3. CONSTRUING THE PROVISIONS OF A WILL

Courts follow certain guidelines in construing the language used in a will. The first, and perhaps most important, of these guidelines is that, when in doubt, the court will find that a valid will was created. Under this principle, wills that have questionable wording or come close to meeting the legal requirements will be probated. The reason behind this principle is that society wishes to follow the wishes of a testator, even when that wish is not expressed as concisely or with strict attention to the legal prerequisites. The right to pass property by will is a valuable right and is one that is vitally important to most individuals.

a. What Property Is Conveyed by a Will?

All the property owned by the testator at the time of her death will be transferred according to the will, or if there are no provisions in the will, by the court's interpretation of the testator's wishes. However, the estate is subject to any outstanding debts.

[22] Va. Code Ann. §64.1-116

FIGURE 13-10

Property Conveyed by a Will
(New Jersey)

| A will is construed to pass all property which the testator owns at his death | including property acquired after the execution of the will.[23] |

FIGURE 13-11

Paying Estate Debts Out of the
Proceeds of the Estate

| When part of the real estate of a testator descends to his heirs because it was not disposed of by his will, and his personal estate is insufficient to pay his debts, the undevised real estate shall be chargeable first with the debts, as far as it will go, in exoneration of the real | estate that is devised, unless it appears from the will that a different arrangement of assets was made for the payment of such testator's debts, in which case such assets shall be applied for that purpose in conformity with the will.[24] |

i. Estate Debts Get First Priority

The first step in probating an estate is to determine the debts owed by the testator. The executor will pay these debts out of the estate proceeds.

b. Distributing Property According to the Will's Provisions

The executor also has the responsibility for distributing the testator's property according to her wishes. Property distribution often raises interesting questions. For instance, does the state follow a per capita or per stirpes distribution system?

i. Per Capita Distribution

Per capita
(Latin) By the head; each heir
gets an equal share

Under a **per capita** property distribution system, the property is divided among all of the existing heirs equally.

Example: Tia's will states: I direct that the proceeds of my savings, checking, and investment accounts left over after the payment of my estate debts should be divided among my heirs on a per capita basis.

Tia has three children: Able, Barney, and Carlos. Barney died several years ago, leaving three children: Della, Evelyn, and Franco. Tia's estate will be divided so that Able, Carlos, Della, Evelyn, and Franco each receive an equal share.

[23] N.J.S.A. 3B:3-34
[24] R.C. §2107.53 (Ohio)

When a devise of real estate within this State to any devisee omits the words "heirs and assigns" and the will contains no expressions indicating an intent to devise only an estate for life, or the real estate is not further devised after the death of the devisee, the devise shall be deemed to pass an estate in fee simple to the devisee as if the real estate had been devised to the devisee and to his heirs and assigns forever.[25]

FIGURE 13-12

Defining Heirs

ii. Per Stirpes

Under a **per stirpes** distribution system, the property is divided up by rankings. The immediate heirs enjoy the first ranking and more distant relatives enjoy lower rankings. Consider this example:

Per stirpes (Latin)
By the root; distributing property by classification or ranking of heirs

Mary dies, and in her will she leaves her property to her "heirs, per stirpes." Mary had four children: Andy, Bruce, Candy, and David. David died several years ago, leaving two children: Eddy and Fran. Under a per stirpes distribution the estate would be divided up with all four children receiving one-fourth of Mary's estate. That means that Andy, Bruce, Candy, and David receive one-fourth of the total estate. However, because David is deceased, his share passes to his children. They must divide one-fourth between them, leaving them a one-eighth share of the estate.

The math can get become complicated when there are numerous heirs and they occupy different rankings in a per stirpes distribution system.

D. OTHER CONSIDERATIONS IN WILLS: CODICILS

A codicil is a written modification of an existing will. They are often executed several years after the original will was created, usually as a result of a change in the family's circumstances. New children, divorces, and other matters can radically change the composition of the family unit and a codicil is a way to change some of the will's provisions, without the necessity of creating an entirely new will. Codicils usually state that they are incorporating the provisions of the previous will and making specific changes. Codicils must be executed with the same formalities as the will itself.

Sidebar

"Will" means an instrument, including a codicil, executed by a person in the manner prescribed by this code, which disposes of the person's property on or after his or her death and includes an instrument which merely appoints a personal representative or revokes or revises another will.[26]

A codicil modifies the terms of a will.

ISSUE AT A GLANCE

---

[25] N.J.S.A. 3B:3-39
[26] F.S.A. §731.201

FIGURE 13-13

Oral Wills

An oral will, made in the last sickness, shall be valid in respect to personal estate if reduced to writing and subscribed by two competent disinterested witnesses within ten days after the speaking of the testamentary words. Such witnesses must prove that the testator was of sound mind and memory, not under restraint, and that he called upon some person present at the time the testamentary words were spoken to bear testimony to such disposition as his will.

No oral will shall be admitted to record unless it is offered for probate within six months after the death of the testator.[27]

E. NUNCUPATIVE WILLS (ORAL WILLS)

We have said that wills must be in writing, but many jurisdictions have a long-held exception to this rule. A nuncupative will is an oral will, made by a person who is dying and has not had the opportunity of creating a will beforehand. The terms of the will are stated before witnesses who later put the oral provisions into writing so that the will can be probated.

Some states allow an oral will to be probated if it is stated by the testator shortly before death and is rendered into written form immediately after the testator's death.

F. CHALLENGING A WILL

A will can be challenged by heirs or beneficiaries after the testator dies and the will is presented for probate. Challenging a will is not a straightforward affair. The only way to invalidate a will is to show that the legal requirements were not met, or that the testator was not of sound mind at the time that she created the will. Some of the methods used to show unsound mind are allegations of fraud or undue influence.

When an heir challenges a will on the basis of fraud or undue influence, the heir is saying that someone, presumably the person receiving the lion's share of the estate, used a position of trust to force the testator to create a will in his favor. However, proving this allegation often is difficult. We have said that courts have a stated preference for finding a will valid and will give wide latitude to a testator to make unusual or even bizarre dispositions.

A successful will challenge is rare because courts give wide latitude to testators to make dispositions of their property.

---

[27] R.C. §2107.60

G. LEGAL PROVISIONS FOR SPOUSES

All states have statutes that protect spouses of a deceased person. If a will was drafted by the testator prior to her marriage and makes no provisions for a spouse, most states have provisions that allow the surviving spouse to receive a share equal in size to what he would have received if the testator had died without a will.

There are exceptions to this rule. If the surviving spouse signed a prenuptial agreement, it is perfectly legal to make no provision for the spouse in the will. However, as we will see in the next chapter, there are strict rules for prenuptial agreements, not the least of which is that they must be signed before marriage to be effective.

Many states also allow the surviving spouse to elect the method to take property through probate. The spouse can either take the share allotted in the will, or the share she would have received through intestate laws. Most spouses in this situation opt for the choice that provides the largest share.

 ## INTESTACY PROCEEDINGS—WHEN THERE IS NO WILL

When a person dies, there is an immediate inquiry made to determine if she died with a will or without a will. If a person dies without a will, it is referred to as dying **intestate.** When a person dies with a will, it is referred to as dying **testate.**

When the deceased has no will, the court must determine how to divide the property and who should receive it. One of the first steps in making this determination is to appoint an administrator.

Intestate
The term for a person who has died without preparing a will

Testate
The term for a person who has died after preparing a will

A. APPOINTMENT OF AN ADMINISTRATOR

An administrator has duties that are similar to those of an executor. However, whereas the executor had written directions from the testator about disposing of her property, an administrator works under court direction and is bound by state statutes that control how, and to whom, property should be awarded. The problem often becomes how to locate those heirs and what percentage of the property they should receive.

B. INTESTATE SUCCESSION

All states have some type of intestate succession statute that determines who should receive the decedent's property. Most of these statutes create ranks or hierarchies of relatives who should be given preference when it comes to distributing a person's estate. One such statute is set out in Figure 13-14.

FIGURE 13-14

Statute Providing for Intestate Distribution of Property Determining Heirs of Decedent Who Died Without Will (Georgia)

(a) For purposes of this Code section:

(1) Children of the decedent who are born after the decedent's death are considered children in being at the decedent's death, provided they were conceived prior to the decedent's death, were born within ten months of the decedent's death, and survived 120 hours or more after birth; and

(2) The half-blood, whether on the maternal or paternal side, are considered equally with the whole-blood, so that the children of any common parent are treated as brothers and sisters to each other.

(b) When a decedent died without a will, the following rules shall determine such decedent's heirs:

(1) Upon the death of an individual who is survived by a spouse but not by any child or other descendant, the spouse is the sole heir. If the decedent is also survived by any child or other descendant, the spouse shall share equally with the children, with the descendants of any deceased child taking that child's share, per stirpes; provided, however, that the spouse's portion shall not be less than a one-third share;

(2) If the decedent is not survived by a spouse, the heirs shall be those relatives, as provided in this Code section, who are in the nearest degree to the decedent in which there is any survivor;

(3) Children of the decedent are in the first degree, and those who survive the decedent shall share the estate equally, with the descendants of any deceased child taking, per stirpes, the share that child would have taken if in life;

(4) Parents of the decedent are in the second degree, and those who survive the decedent shall share the estate equally;

(5) Siblings of the decedent are in the third degree, and those who survive the decedent shall share the estate equally, with the descendants of any deceased sibling taking, per stirpes, the share that sibling would have taken if in life; provided, however, that, subject to the provisions of paragraph (1) of subsection (f) of Code Section 53-1-20, if no sibling survives the decedent, the nieces and nephews who survive the decedent shall take the estate in equal shares, with the descendants of any deceased niece or nephew taking, per stirpes, the share that niece or nephew would have taken if in life;

(6) Grandparents of the decedent are in the fourth degree, and those who survive the decedent shall share the estate equally;

(7) Uncles and aunts of the decedent are in the fifth degree, and those who survive the decedent shall share the estate equally, with the children of any deceased uncle or aunt taking, per stirpes, the share that uncle or aunt would have taken if in life; provided, however, that, subject to the provisions of paragraph (1) of subsection (f) of Code Section 53-1-20, if no uncle or aunt of the decedent survives the decedent, the first cousins who survive the decedent shall share the estate equally; and

(8) The more remote degrees of kinship shall be determined by counting the number of steps in the

FIGURE 13-14

(continued)

chain from the relative to the closest common ancestor of the relative and decedent and the number of steps in the chain from the common ancestor to the decedent. The sum of the | steps in the two chains shall be the degree of kinship, and the surviving relatives with the lowest sum shall be in the nearest degree and shall share the estate equally.[28]

C. DETERMINING HEIRS

Determining an intestate's heirs is an important part of the administration of her estate. Under the law, the property is divided among a person's relatives. As far as the law is concerned, relatives are those who are related by blood. This refers to parents, children, brothers and sisters, but not relatives who are related by marriage. If a person has no heirs, the property may qualify for escheat.

Escheat
The seizure of a person's estate when she has left no heirs

D. ESCHEAT

When no heirs can be located and there is no will, the final option is **escheat.** This is the process of transferring title to the property to the local government. Although you might think that the government would welcome cash or property, in most cases it creates an administrative nightmare for the government officials involved. They must make provision to keep the property safe and maintained. That means paying someone to do regular upkeep and maintenance, as well as paying taxes.

Trustees manage the property according to the terms of the trust, usually by providing a set disbursement to the beneficiary for a period of years, and then a final transfer of the balance on a stated condition, such as the beneficiary reaching the age of 21.

 **TRUSTS**

A trust is an arrangement whereby a person transfers title to property to another for the benefit of a third party. Common trust arrangements involve setting aside money to be doled out to a child or other party for a period of years with a provision that the balance will one day be transferred in total to the child.

A. CREATING A TRUST

A trust is created when a person, the **settlor,** creates an arrangement for property to be used for a **beneficiary.** The trust is administered by a person referred to as a **trustee** who manages the property and makes regular dispersals to the beneficiary. Trust property can be real property or personal property, although in most situations it is money. The title to the property is conveyed from the original owner to two people: the trustee and the beneficiary. The trustee has the right to manage and administer the property, while the beneficiary has the right to the benefit from the property.

Settlor
The person who originally has full title to property, who creates a trust

Beneficiary
The person who receives the benefits of the trust

Trustee
The person responsible for managing and administering a trust

[28] O.C.G.A. §53-2-1

B. COMPARING TRUSTS AND WILLS

Sidebar

A testamentary trust is one that is created by the language in a will.

Wills and trusts are different instruments. A will creates a future interest that only becomes legally actionable when the testator dies. A trust, on the other hand, immediately conveys an interest to a person. The benefits of the trust may not be realized for some time, but a trust beneficiary has a recognizable claim on the trust assets.

Careers in the Law

▶ Will and Estates Attorney, Nina Neal

I always wanted to be a lawyer. I visited University of North Carolina at Chapel Hill when I was 12 years old and I knew right then that I would go there one day. I majored in criminal justice and political science. I worked for several years as a teacher before entering law school. I used to tell my students that law professors don't have any teaching skills.

When I graduated from law school, I decided to go into wills and trust work. I had a friend who did litigation, but he didn't write wills. I worked with him for a couple of years and began working with other attorneys who would contract out all of their probate work to me.

Students have a misconception about wills and trusts: They think it's boring. When we surveyed our students recently, our students listed the wills class as the most interesting (and useful) course they had taken. Real property and legal research came in at two and three.

Probate law is a very interesting topic. Before you take a wills course, however, you should have legal research and real property courses under your belt. Those courses will help you with the concepts involved in wills and estates classes. Look at all of the subjects that fall under wills and estates: You've got wills, powers of attorney, and health care agents. It's one of the most practical courses you'll ever take.

Profiling a Paralegal

▶ Tammy Atkins

Although I went to school to become a paralegal, I now work in investments. A lot of our clients are older people. They originally purchased life insurance and other policies with companies that may have been bought out by other companies years ago. I spend a lot of time using my legal skills to help me track company information. I'll track companies through the Internet, find out when they were acquired by other companies, and then submit the paperwork to the new company.

What I do is really neat. We do investments, estate planning, and offer advice on investments. I keep track of client accounts. We do a lot of stuff online. We help them research their investments.

My job involves a lot of one-on-one with clients. If they have questions about life insurance or brokerage companies, I'm the contact person. We have a problem, I try to make my boss's job easier for him. I just completed the process of scanning 30 years of old client files and storing them on computer to make them easier to access.

Everything is very fast paced in the investment world. You have to stay on top of everything. There are some things that are routine, but there's always a challenge. I've met so many different people. Every day is exciting and challenging.

ARTHUR v. MILSTEIN
949 So.2d 1163 (Fla. App. 4 Dist. 2007)

PER CURIAM.

Virgie Arthur, as natural mother and next of kin of the decedent, Vickie Lynn Marshall a/k/a Anna Nicole Smith, has filed an emergency petition for writ of certiorari. Through the petition, she asks this court to quash the trial court's February 22, 2007 order that granted Dannielynn Hope Marshall Stern's motion to recognize her sole right to determine the disposition of Smith's remains and the related ruling directing that the Guardian Ad Litem direct all aspects with respect to the handling of those remains consistent with the best interest of that child. We re-designate the case as an appeal from a final order and have expedited relief accordingly. §9.110(a)(2). Fla. R. App. P. We affirm the trial court's decision and address the second of the three points raised.

The trial court found that Arthur and the Guardian Ad Litem, on behalf of the child, both qualified as a "legally authorized person" as that term is defined in Florida Statute section 497.005(37). In finding that both were legally authorized, Florida Statute section 406.50(4) directs that priority to the remains pass in accordance with section 732.103 of the probate code. Under section 732.103, the lineal descendants of the decedent have priority.

Arthur argues that she, alone, is the "legally authorized person" to take possession of the remains, and the trial court erred in finding that the Guardian Ad Litem is an additional "legally authorized person." The phrase "legally authorized person" is found in Florida Statute section 497.005(37) (2006), which provides:

> (37) "Legally authorized person" means, in the priority listed, the decedent, when written inter vivos authorizations and directions are provided by the decedent; the surviving spouse, unless the spouse has been arrested for committing against the deceased an act of domestic violence as defined in s. 741.28 that resulted in or contributed to the death of the deceased; a son or daughter who is 18 years of age or older; a parent; a brother or sister who is 18 years of age or older; a grandchild who is 18 years of age or older; a grandparent; or any person in the next degree of kinship. In addition, the term may include, if no family member exists or is available, the guardian of the dead person at the time of death; the personal representative of the deceased; the attorney in fact of the dead person at the time of death; . . . . Where there is a person in any priority class listed in this subsection, the funeral establishment shall rely upon the authorization of any one legally authorized person of that class if that person represents that she or he is not aware of any objection to the cremation of the deceased's human remains by others in the same class of the person making the representation or of any person in a higher priority class.

In the event more than one legally authorized person claims a body in the custody of the medical examiner for interment, section 406.50(4) provides that the requests shall be prioritized in accordance with section 732.103. Florida Statute section 732.103 of the Florida Probate Code provides that the part of the intestate estate not passing to the surviving spouse under section 732.102, or the entire intestate estate if there is no surviving spouse, descends first to the lineal descendants of the decedent, and if there is no lineal descendant, to the decedent's father and mother equally, or to the survivor of them.

The trial court relied upon section 406.50(4) to determine that Dannielynn had priority over Arthur. Arthur's position is that dependence on section 406.50(4) was error in this case as she is the sole "legally authorized person" as contemplated by section 497.005(37), and as such, she is entitled to make decisions regarding the disposition of the decedent's remains.

We find that neither section 497.005(37), nor section 406.50, control the outcome of this case, which in essence involves private parties engaged in a pre-burial dispute as to the decedent's remains. Otherwise stated, the trial court was not being asked to consider whether a funeral home or medical examiner was liable for its decision with respect to the disposition of a decedent's remains.

In this case, common law is dispositive. Generally, in the absence of a testamentary disposition, the spouse of the deceased or the next of kin has the right to the possession of the body for burial or other lawful disposition. *Kirksey*. In *Cohen*, we held that a written testamentary disposition is not conclusive of the decedent's intent if it can be shown by clear and convincing evidence that he intended another disposition for his body. *Cohen* looked to decisions of other states which determined that whether to enforce the will provisions regarding disposition of the testator's body depends upon the circumstances of the case.

Having recognized certain property rights in dead bodies, many courts have announced the rule that a person has the right to dispose of his own body by will. However, courts, while paying lip service to the doctrine of testamentary disposal, have in certain instances permitted the wishes of the decedent's spouse or next of kin to prevail over those of the testator. In other instances, courts have accepted and acted upon evidence that indicated that the decedent's wishes concerning the disposition of his body had changed since the execution of his will.

Cohen noted that there were "no cases in Florida or across the country in which a testamentary disposition has been upheld even though credible evidence has been introduced to show that the testator changed his or her mind as to the disposition of his/her body." There, we found no abuse of discretion associated with the trial court's finding of the decedent's intent. We note that even under section 497.005(37), the first priority is to the wishes of the decedent "when written inter vivos authorizations and directions are provided" and that the remaining list of legally authorized persons are those who are most likely to know and follow those wishes. To the extent sections 497.005(37) and 406.05(4) provide guidance, the priorities therein could set forth a presumption, rebuttable by clear and convincing evidence of the decedent's intent, as was the will in *Cohen*, and as found here.

The "tipsy coachman" doctrine, allows an appellate court to affirm a trial court that "reaches the right result, but for the wrong reasons" so long as "there is any basis which would support the judgment in the record."

Herein, the trial court found that "Anna Nicole Smith's last ascertainable wish with respect to the disposition of her remains was that she be buried in the Bahamas next to her son Daniel Wayne Smith." This finding is not essentially disputed. In light of the trial court's extensive findings and comments associated with Smith's intent, coupled with the Guardian Ad Litem's representation and commitment to a burial in the Bahamas, we conclude that there is no need to remand the case for further proceedings.

Affirmed.

STONE, POLEN and SHAHOOD, JJ., concur.

QUESTIONS ABOUT THE CASE

1   What is Virgie Arthur requesting that she be allowed to do with Anna Nicole Smith's remains?
2   According to the court, who qualifies as a "legally authorized person" who can make decisions about the disposition of Smith's body?
3   Who has the authority, under Florida common law, to the possession of a body for burial purposes?
4   Why wouldn't a decedent's own wishes be granted about the disposition of his or her own body?
5   What is the "tipsy coachman" doctrine?

SKILLS YOU NEED IN THE REAL WORLD

DRAFTING WILLS

There will be times when your clients will approach you about drafting a will for them. The safest course to follow with such a recommendation is to consult the local bar. Does your state allow paralegals to assist people with drafting their wills or is this practice strictly limited to attorneys? Some states allow paralegals to help clients to create wills, or at least assist with the formalities, while other strictly forbid anyone but attorneys to carry out these functions. Friends, family, and others may contact you to have you help with a "simple will." There is no one-size-fits-all probate arrangement. Testamentary dispositions can become complicated even when there are relatively few assets involved. When there are children to consider, the best bet is to inform the person with a "simple will" problem that it would be wise to pay an attorney to make sure that all possible complications are considered and anticipated in the will.

CHAPTER SUMMARY

When a person dies, her estate is divided among her heirs. A person who dies with a will is said to have died testate. Her estate is probated and the provisions of her will are given effect. A will must meet specific statutory requirements, such as being in writing, signed by the testator and attested by witnesses. In addition, the testator must be of sound mind when she executed the will. A will's provisions are put into effect by an executor who is named in the will. If a person dies without a will, she is said to have died intestate. In that situation, the court must determine who should receive the decedent's property. The court will appoint an administrator who acts under the direction of statutes that determine who are the decedent's heirs and what percentage of the estate they should receive. Trusts are arrangements that transfer ownership of property to two people: a trustee and a beneficiary. A trustee manages the property so that it provides income for the beneficiary.

ETHICS: HIDING ASSETS

Some people believe that they can avoid taxes or other legal concerns by attempting to either hide assets or to transfer them prior to litigation. Clients sometimes ask for advice on how to hide assets from the government or others. You should never participate in any such transactions. Hiding assets is not only unethical, it is usually illegal. Helping a client to hide assets almost always comes the same end: the government or heirs discover the trickery and seek to void the transaction and to place the property back into the estate for distribution. The people who helped to defraud others are often prosecuted.

CHAPTER REVIEW QUESTIONS

1   What is the definition of a will?
2   What is the difference between dying testate and dying intestate?
3   What are the rules that courts use to construe the written portions of a will?
4   What are the formal requirements for creating a will?
5   What is the "four corners" test for wills?
6   Are there special words that must be used to create a will?
7   What is meant by testamentary capacity?
8   What is a holographic will?
9   Why is a signature required on a will?
10 Which classifications of people lack competence to draft a will?
11 What is the significance of the witness' signature on a will?
12 What is the difference between per capita and per stirpes distribution?
13 Which grounds can be used to challenge a will?
14 When a spouse dies, what provisions protect the surviving spouse in probate?
15 What is the term used for the person who is responsible for handling the estate of a person who dies intestate? What duties does this person have?
16 What are the rules about intestate distribution of property?
17 What is escheat?
18 What are some considerations to keep in mind when drafting a will?
19 Why is it important not to participate in schemes to help clients hide assets?
20 What is the principle set out in this chapter's sample case?

DISCUSSION QUESTIONS

1 Should every person over the age of 18 have a will? Why or why not?

2 The chapter mentions the requirement that wills should be in writing. In this age of advanced technology and the prevalence of video and digital recorders, should the laws be changed to allow videotaped wills? Why or why not? Are there any potential pitfalls in creating a videotaped or digital will?

3 Are there will provisions that would clearly indicate that the testator was of unsound mind? Suppose that the testator makes a bizarre request, such as to reduce the balance of his estate into cash and throw it out of an airplane?

4 Should the intestate succession laws be changed to reflect a person's sexual orientation and therefore include his/her significant other as an heir? Why or why not?

PERSONALITY QUIZ

Is probate law right for you? Take this personality quiz and see.

1 I enjoy assisting other people in arranging their affairs.
   0-strongly disagree   5-agree   10-strongly
                                                    agree

                                                            Points: _____

2 I can anticipate problems well.
   0-strongly disagree   5-agree   10-strongly
                                                    agree

                                                            Points: _____

3 I have a keen eye for detail.
   0-strongly disagree   5-agree   10-strongly
                                                    agree

                                                            Points: _____

4 I work well with people who are under stress, even those who are grief stricken.
   0-strongly disagree   5-agree   10-strongly
                                                    agree

                                                            Points: _____

                                                    Total Points: _____

If you scored between 25-40 points, you have many of the qualities that it takes to do well in the field of wills and trusts.

If you scored between 10-24 points, you might do well in this legal field, but you might do even better in some other area of law.

If you scored 9 or lower, this legal field is not a good choice for you.

PRACTICAL APPLICATIONS

1   Does your state probate wills in a separate Probate Court or through some other agency? Is there a local probate judge? How are wills probated in your area? Does the Probate Court maintain a web page and, if so, what types of information can you locate on the site?

2   Search the web for famous wills. You will find many sites listing the entire contents of celebrity wills, such as Princess Diana or Elvis Presley. Examine these wills for the property dispositions and other features discussed in this text.

WEB SITES

Findlaw.com (Wills)
http://www.findlaw.com/01topics/31probate

Wills & Estates Planning (Nolo.com)
http://www.nolo.com/lawcenter/ency/index.cfm/catID/
FD1795A9-8049-422C-9087838F86A2BC2B

Catalaw (Wills)
http://www.catalaw.com/topics/Estates.shtml

MegaLaw — Wills & Estates
http://www.megalaw.com/top/probate.php

TERMS AND PHRASES

Beneficiary	Intestate	Testamentary intent
Domicile	Parol evidence	Testate
Escheat	Per capita	Testator
Executor	Per stirpes	Trustee
Holographic will	Settlor	Will

Family Law

Chapter Learning Objectives

After completing this chapter, you should be able to:

■ Describe the function of prenuptial agreements

■ Explain what constitutes a common law marriage

■ Define the legal requirements to marry

■ List and describe the grounds for divorce

■ Explain how issues such as child custody and support are determined by the courts

 **INTRODUCTION**

In this chapter we explore the many aspects of family law. Covering everything from prenuptial agreements to divorce and child custody, family law is an enormous area filled with complex legal issues. During the course of your paralegal education, you will undoubtedly have an entire course devoted to the topic. Here we touch on the basics of the topic and introduce you to the many different avenues open to a legal professional considering a career in family law.

We explore family law issues in a more or less chronological method, beginning with agreements and issues that arise before marriage, continuing on through the creation of a legally binding marriage, and then the dissolution of the marriage through divorce and the issues that it generates, such as property division, separation agreements, and child custody.

 **PRENUPTIAL AGREEMENTS**

Brad Pith and Jennifer Anisette are both well-known celebrities. Brad is a successful movie star and Jennifer's sitcom "Acquaintances" has been a staple of television

entertainment for almost ten years. They have fallen in love and decide to get married. Because they both have substantial incomes and property, their managers and attorneys encourage them to enter into a prenuptial agreement.

A. WHAT IS A PRENUPTIAL AGREEMENT?

Prenuptial agreement
An agreement between future spouses about division of property and other issues in the event that the marriage ends due to death or divorce

Prenuptial agreements, also known as antenuptial agreements, are contracts between two people who plan to marry. They are contracts in which the parties agree to waive any rights to the other spouse's property or income in the event of death or divorce. Prenuptial agreements are usually entered into when one or both of the partners has substantial assets and does not wish to lose them through a divorce action. Any or all of the following situations might justify a prenuptial agreement:

- Family property
- Businesses
- Children from a previous marriage

A prenuptial agreement seeks to iron out any dispositions of property before the marriage, rather than risking litigation after death or divorce.

B. PRENUPTIAL AGREEMENTS ARE CONTRACTS

Because prenuptial agreements are contracts, they have the same basic requirements as any contract. This includes mutual assent, consideration, and capacity. Some states go further and impose additional requirements on prenuptial agreements, such as full disclosure of assets and fairness. Full disclosure provisions are imposed so that the spouse waiving rights to the assets knows exactly what they are beforehand. Other limitations in prenuptial agreements are public policy concerns.

C. PRENUPTIAL AGREEMENTS CANNOT VIOLATE PUBLIC POLICY

A prenuptial agreement will not be enforced when it contains any provision that violates law or public policy. For instance, a prenuptial agreement that made a prospective spouse waive any child support or custody of unborn children will not be enforced. Children's rights cannot be waived in a prenuptial agreement. Similarly, a provision that requires one spouse to surrender all legal rights to the other spouse would also be unenforceable.

ISSUE AT A GLANCE

Prenuptial agreements are often found in situations in which one party to the marriage has substantial assets and the other has few.

FIGURE 14-1

Excerpt from a Prenuptial
Agreement

Here is an excerpt from the prenuptial agreement between Brad Pith and Jennifer Anisette,

"This agreement also provides that Jennifer Anisette, hereinafter referred to as wife, will neither during the lifetime of Brad Pith, hereinafter referred to as husband, nor after his death take, claim, demand, or receive, and does hereby waive and release all rights, claims, titles, and interests, actual, inchoate, or contingent, in law and equity which she might by reason of her marriage to husband acquire in his property or estate, including but not limited to: dower rights, alimony and spousal support.

"Both parties covenant that they shall willingly, at the request of either party, or his or her successors or assigns, execute, deliver, and properly acknowledge whatever additional instruments may be required to carry out the intention of this Agreement. . . ."[29]

D. COHABITATION AGREEMENTS

Today it is common for men and women to live together without the benefit of marriage. Some of these relationships last for years and resemble a marriage in everything except name. Many of these couples realize that without the legal protection of marriage, their accumulated property and assets could slip away in the event of an unexpected death of the partner. To safeguard their assets, couples often create cohabitation agreements as a way of ensuring property division in the event that the relationship ends.

Cohabitation agreements are used by people who live together in a romantic relationship but do not plan to marry.

ISSUE AT
A GLANCE

 MARRIAGE

Marriage is the legally recognized union of two people. The status of marriage has been afforded special consideration under the law for centuries. Married couples cannot be compelled to testify against one another, a protection that is not afforded to any other family relationship. Married couples may own property jointly, and receive special tax considerations and many other benefits that are not accorded to unmarried couples. In the past, marriage essentially amounted to a complete surrender of a wife's rights to the husband, but we live in an age when the law and society take a more enlightened view of the rights of human beings, whether they are male or female.

---

[29] *Sieg v. Sieg*, 265 Ga. 384, 455 S.E.2d 830 (1995)

A. WHO CAN MARRY?

States are allowed to limit who can marry on the basis of blood relationships. For instance, none of the following relatives are permitted to marry:

- Parent and child (including adopted child)
- Brothers and sisters (including half-siblings)
- Uncles and nieces; aunts and nephews
- Grandparent and grandchild

First cousins have traditionally been able to enter into marriage with one another, although there are states that prohibit this union as well. When the relationship is more distant than first cousins, the marriage is usually lawful.

B. PREREQUISITES FOR MARRIAGE

Like any legally binding relationship, parties to a marriage must meet certain requirements. Traditionally, marriage has always been considered to be a form of contract, with the husband and wife exchanging promises to one another in a bilateral contract (see Chapter 9). The marriage vows, in fact, reflect the contract relationship between the parties. Both parties make reciprocal promises. When one party breaks a promise, such as by committing adultery, he has broken a promise and given the other party the right to sue for breach of contract. In this case, the action is termed a divorce, but the basic idea remains the same.

1. CONTRACTUAL ABILITY

Because marriage has many of the same elements as a contract, the couple must meet many of the same requirements as any other contracting party. This means that each must have capacity and other contractual abilities. A person who is insane, for example, can neither enter into a contract nor marry. Capacity is also a feature of marital relationships when we consider another issue: the minimum age of the husband and wife.

2. AGE

States are permitted to limit marriage to individuals above a certain age, although this age varies considerably from state to state. In most jurisdictions that allow underage persons to marry, parental consent is required. If either party in a marriage is underage, the courts may declare the marriage unlawful and annul it.

FIGURE 14-2

Common Marriage Vows

I promise to love and honor you, forsaking all others, until death parts us.

Even in states that allow underage marriage, most have cut-off ages, such as 16. Courts will intercede in any marriage in which the parties are younger and declare the marriage void. No state allows a child to marry, under any circumstances.[30]

3. INCARCERATION

States may impose other restrictions on marriage, such as the necessity that both parties be free. When a person has been sentenced to life in prison, states are free to restrict that person from marrying. A person serving a life sentence is considered "civilly dead."

4. MENTAL STATUS

The prospective husband and wife must be able to understand the consequences of entering into a marriage. As with contractual capacity, a party who is acting under duress, fraud, or insanity lacks capacity and any marriage performed under these circumstances is void.

5. CONSENT

Similarly, a marriage vow must be given with consent. A person cannot be tricked into a valid marriage. Consent must be given freely and with knowledge of the legal consequences of the arrangement. This does not mean that a person must understand all possible ramifications of a marriage vow, but it does mean that he must understand that a marriage is taking place and that when the ceremony is over, he will be bound to the other person as a legally recognized spouse.

> *Example:* Yesterday on the soap opera "Our Lives in Chaos," Mindy asked Ralph to sign what she referred to as a "legal form" for her business. After he signed, Mindy informed Ralph that they were now married and revealed that the document he had signed was in fact a marriage license. Ralph turned to the camera and wondered aloud if there was any way out of this clever trap?
>
> *Answer:* Ralph is not married. A person cannot be tricked into marriage.

> *Example:* In today's episode, Mindy has turned her attention to Ralph's father, Stone Masterton, who runs a multimillion dollar industry, and asks him to stand in for Ralph during the marriage rehearsal ceremony. They go through the vows and the minister, who is in Mindy's employ, pronounces them husband and wife. They all laugh, but when Stone turns to leave, Mindy announces that they are, in fact, husband and wife. Stone rushes to his attorney's office and asks the question, "Is this legal?"
>
> *Answer:* No. Consent to a marriage must be freely given. A party can no more use trickery or deceit to obtain a marriage vow than he can to obtain consent to any other contract.

---

[30] *State v. Wade,* 244 Kan. 136, 766 P.2d 811 (1989)

C. THE MARRIAGE CEREMONY

1. INCLUDES BOTH RELIGIOUS AND CIVIL ELEMENTS

Marriage ceremonies often combine religious and civil elements. Many people are married in religious ceremonies that are sanctioned by their religions. But a marriage is also a government affair. For a marriage to be recognized, a marriage license must be completed and the ceremony must be performed by someone licensed to do so under state law. The license is filed in the same jurisdiction where the marriage was actually performed and becomes a part of the public record.

2. MARRIAGE LICENSES

Legal professionals look up marriage licenses for a wide variety of legal reasons. Title searchers may review a marriage license to determine if a particular person was married when he conveyed property to another. Private investigators often review marriage records for clues about a person's past or current whereabouts. A license is the official recognition of a person's marriage. A marriage can be perfectly legal even when it is not performed in a religious institution, but a marriage performed in a church or synagogue will not be legally binding unless it is registered with the state. There are certain exceptions to this general rule, such as common law marriage, discussed later in this chapter. Before we leave the topic of the marriage ceremony, we discuss gay marriage, a recent controversial issue that has caused many legal scholars to rethink the issues involved in marriage.

D. FEDERAL DEFENSE OF MARRIAGE ACT

In 1996, the U.S. Congress passed a bill that was later signed into law by President Clinton. This act, known as the Defense of Marriage Act, defined marriage as referring to heterosexual couples only. See Figure 14-3.

This legislation was passed partly in response to a case pending before the Hawaii Court of Appeals that might sanction gay marriage. Under the Full Faith and Credit Clause of the U.S. Constitution, a valid, legal ruling in one state must be observed by other states, unless preempted by federal legislation.

The question about the definition of marriage was considered settled by the Federal Defense of Marriage Act until a Massachusetts decision in 2003 put the

---

FIGURE 14-3

Defining Marriage Under the Defense of Marriage Act (1996)

In determining the meaning of any Act of Congress, or of any ruling, regulation, or interpretation of the various administrative bureaus and agencies of the United States, the word "marriage" means only a legal union between one man and one woman as husband and wife, and the word "spouse" refers only to a person of the opposite sex who is a husband or a wife.[31]

[31] 1 U.S.C.A. §7

Full Faith and Credit Clause under Article IV of U.S. Constitution
"Full Faith and Credit shall be given in each State to the public Acts, Records, and judicial Proceedings of every other State. And the Congress may by general Laws prescribe the Manner in which such Acts, Records and Proceedings shall be proved, and the Effect thereof."

ISSUE AT A GLANCE

entire matter back on the national stage. In *Goodridge v. Department of Public Health*, 440 Mass. 309, 798 N.E.2d 941 (2003), the Massachusetts Supreme Court ruled that banning homosexual couples from the benefits of marriage was unconstitutional and gave the state legislature a deadline to amend the current laws to reflect this finding. This was an extremely controversial ruling, prompting national figures to both praise and condemn the finding.

In reaching its ruling, the court found that marriage ceremonies, and the issuance of marriage licenses, was a function of the state's constitutional powers to promote public welfare and there was no rational basis to deny the right to marry to homosexual couples. See Figure 14-4 for an excerpt of the *Goodridge* case.

Prior the decision in *Goodridge*, the best that homosexual couples could hope for was a civil union ceremony.

E. CIVIL UNION

Vermont is the only state that allows homosexual couples the right to some form of marriage. Vermont refers to this ceremony as a civil union and it carries some, but not all, of the privileges accorded to married couples.

FIGURE 14-4

Excerpts from *Goodridge v. Department of Public Health*

In a real sense, there are three partners to every civil marriage: two willing spouses and an approving State. Marriage is not a mere contract between two parties but a legal status from which certain rights and obligations arise. . . .

Because it fulfils yearnings for security, safe haven, and connection that express our common humanity, civil marriage is an esteemed institution, and the decision whether and whom to marry is among life's momentous acts of self-definition. . . .

In this case, we are confronted with an entire, sizeable class of parents raising children who have absolutely no access to civil marriage and its protections because they are forbidden from procuring a marriage license. It cannot be rational under our laws, and indeed it is not permitted, to penalize children by depriving them of State benefits because the State disapproves of their parents' sexual orientation.

F. COMMON LAW MARRIAGE

Common law marriage was a feature of family law for centuries. Under common law marriage, when a man and a woman held themselves out as married, or as considering themselves to be married, then as far as the law was concerned, they were.

Most states that formerly recognized common law marriage have repealed it. Common law marriage raises a host of potential legal problems, especially when a person comes forward who claims that he was married to a person who has since died. In states that still recognize common law marriage, the spouse's claim must be recognized. However, proof would be required that the man and woman had lived together as husband and wife and told others that they were married.

ISSUE AT A GLANCE

Common law marriage was originally permissible in situations in which marriage ceremonies were difficult to perform.

 **IV   ANNULMENT**

To annul a marriage is to state that a valid marriage never occurred and that any ceremony claiming to be a marriage ceremony was invalid. Annulled marriages are not marriages at all and do not create the type of legal commitment that divorce actions often do, such as property division and alimony.

A. GROUNDS FOR ANNULMENT

An annulment is a judicial decree dissolving the marriage and putting the parties back in the position that they were in before the marriage. The effect of an annulment is a decree that a marriage never occurred. Annulments can be granted for any reason that would have made the marriage invalid, such as lack of consent or the fact that one party is under the minimum age. If we consider marriage to be a contractual relationship between the parties, would intoxication provide grounds for an annulment? Consider the following hypothetical:

Most states do allow an annulment when a woman marries a man who has given a fake name or is living under an assumed name.

> Ross and Rachel were in a group of friends who took a trip to Las Vegas. One night, after they had had too much to drink, they decided to get married. They went to a nearby all-night chapel and were married on the spot. The person who performed the ceremony was licensed to do so by the State of Nevada and issued a proper marriage certificate at the end of the ceremony. Ross and Rachel promptly parted company. The next morning, Rachel woke up alone and realized that she had made a huge mistake. Does she have grounds for an annulment?

> *Answer:* Yes. Their mutual inebriation at the time of the ceremony affects their mutual assent to the marriage and it also appears that the marriage was not consummated.

A marriage can be annulled when any of the basic requirements, such as consent, are missing when the ceremony is carried out.

ISSUE AT A GLANCE

DIVORCE

As long as there have been men and women who wanted to marry there have been others who wished to divorce. Historically, men had virtually all legal rights in the marriage and a woman had no right to sue for divorce, except in circumstances of desertion or adultery. In the mid-twentieth century sweeping reforms changed the entire complexion of divorce law, allowing partners to voluntarily end their marriage.

A. A BRIEF HISTORY OF DIVORCE

Prior to the mid-twentieth-century reforms in divorce laws, divorces were difficult to obtain and often involved perpetrating fraud on the court. For instance, when a man and woman wished to end their marriage, the husband would enlist the services of a private investigator or other person and arrange a scene in which it would appear that he had committed adultery. Before the advent of "no fault" divorces, one of the few ways to obtain a judicial divorce was by proof of adultery.

We have already seen that the act of marriage places two people in a unique relationship that enjoys special protection under the law. Traditionally, marriage gave the husband nearly absolute power over his wife's property, their children, and even her body. (In many states, it was not against the law for a man to rape his wife.) Reforms and changes in societal attitudes have ended many of the heavy-handed aspects of marriage, but the union continues to enjoy special significance under the law. A divorce changes all that.

Some states have enacted statutes that require a minimum waiting period before a party can remarry after a divorce. Some of these waiting periods are for as long as six months.[32]

In recent times, most states have gradually liberalized their rules about how and when parties may divorce.

ISSUE AT A GLANCE

B. WHAT IS A DIVORCE?

A divorce is a judicial decree terminating the marital state. Called by different names in different states, such as "divorce from bed and board," or "absolute divorce," the effect of the judicial action is to dissolve the rights, duties, and obligations between the marital parties. It also divides the marital property between the parties.

---

[32] *Copeland v. Stone*, 1992 Okla. 154, 842 P.2d 754 (Okla. 1992)

Once a divorce has been declared, the parties are free to go on with their lives as single persons. They may remarry and engage in all the activities we normally associate with being single. The terms of the divorce are normally set out in a separation agreement.

C. SEPARATION AGREEMENTS

Separation agreement
An agreement between a husband and wife who are considering divorce that sets out the details of their separation and makes provisions for temporary custody of children, allocations of assets, and other issues

A **separation agreement** is the document that sets out the details of the divorce. The parties spell out who receives personal and real property, retirement benefits, and alimony. A separation agreement may also determine thorny issues such as child custody and visitation, and child support payments. Because a separation agreement is negotiated between two people who are usually hostile toward one another, legal professionals who specialize in family practice often find themselves in the difficult position of working out an agreement and avoiding a full scale war between two people who have learned to hate one another.

Separation agreements must be detailed and thorough, because they will be the basis of any continued relationship between the divorced couple. The agreement

---

FIGURE 14-5

Some Factors to Consider in Drafting a Separation Agreement

Property

■ Personal property — who will receive specific items of personal property, from family furniture, clothing, linens, and china to the family dog?

■ Real property — who will receive title to the family home and what adjustments in property or cash will offset this investiture?

Alimony

■ Who will pay and how much will this party pay?

■ Will alimony payments terminate in the future? If so, what events will trigger termination? (Remarriage, for instance?)

Insurance

■ Who will keep the children under a health insurance policy?

■ Will the other spouse continue to be covered on the divorced spouse's insurance? If not, how will the spouse be compensated for seeking his own coverage?

■ Whose insurance will continue to cover cars, boats, houses?

Child Support

■ Who will pay?

■ How much will he pay?

■ When will he pay?

■ When is a child support payment considered to be late?

■ What consequences are there for late child support payments?

Child Custody

■ Who gets custody of the children?

■ What type of custody vests in the custodial parent?

■ What type of visitation will the other parent have?

■ How often will the parent be allowed to have child visitation?

should be comprehensive about all dealings between the former husband and wife, while also anticipating problems that could arise in the future. Separation agreements should cover all assets, property, and holdings of both the husband and wife, as well as any debts incurred by the couple. Close attention to detail is a must in a separation agreement; because of the resources held by modern couples, a separation agreement can stretch to dozens, if not hundreds, of pages in length.

A separation agreement sets out all the details of the divorce, including property division and child custody and visitation, among others.

ISSUE AT A GLANCE

The court may order a divorce when the parties have lived apart for more than a stated period of time, such as six months. Some states also require, in addition to the voluntary separation, that there be no viable chance of a reconciliation between the parties. Courts may grant a divorce on other grounds as well.

D. GROUNDS FOR DIVORCE

A court may grant a divorce when there are "irreconcilable differences" between the parties. Although this term is defined in different ways in different states, most jurisdictions agree that irreconcilable differences means that there is no possibility of reconciliation between the husband and wife. Usually when one spouse makes an unequivocal statement that he no longer wishes to be married, the courts will find irreconcilable differences.

Divorce actions can also be based on other factors, such as:

- Cruelty
- Physical violence
- Mental cruelty
- Adultery
- Desertion

Any of these grounds, if proven, would be sufficient justification for a court to order a divorce. However, most couples base their divorce action not on allegations of cruelty, but on so-called no fault grounds.

1. "NO FAULT" DIVORCE

Almost all states have enacted some form of "no fault" divorce provision. These statutes permit a divorce to be granted without a finding of fault on the part of either spouse. A bare finding that the marriage is irretrievably broken is sufficient ground to justify a no fault divorce.

Many jurisdictions that have adopted no fault divorce provisions have kept the other fault-based grounds as well.

E. JUDICIAL DECLARATION OF DIVORCE

A divorce is a civil action similar to any personal injury or contract litigation. The issues involved are far more intimate than those typically found in other types of suits, but it is important to remember that they are still lawsuits. They must follow the same rules of civil procedure and they involve the same type of pleadings found in any civil suit. A plaintiff files a complaint and the defendant files an answer. The parties go through normal discovery procedures in the suit, filing interrogatories on parties and deposing witnesses. In the end, a judge enters an order in the case officially dissolving the marriage.

The court's jurisdiction in a divorce case is usually based on the fact that one or both of the marital partners reside in the same county as the court. So long as one of the parties is domiciled within the court's jurisdiction, the judge is entitled to enter orders in the case. The domicile requirement is also a way of preventing parties from shopping around for jurisdictions where they might receive more favorable treatment.

F. PROPERTY DIVISION (EQUITABLE DISTRIBUTION)

Property acquired by the parties before they were married is usually not distributed in the divorce decree. Instead, that property remains in the possession of the spouse who had it originally.

One of the issues that must be decided during a divorce is how to divide the property that the couple has acquired. In a lengthy relationship the real and personal property can be substantial. In addition to the residence, there may be vacation homes and time-share condominiums. Personal property includes all the items that the couple owns, from linens to lawn furniture. All this property must be divided between the parties. States have different approaches to the method of dividing this property, with some states requiring an exact 50-50 split, while others allow a more fluid arrangement.

G. ALIMONY

Alimony
The monetary payment made by a former spouse to the other spouse to maintain that spouse in the standard of living to which that person has become accustomed

Alimony refers to the monetary support paid by one spouse to the other following the divorce. Historically, alimony was paid by a husband to his former wife, although there have been many situations in which alimony was paid by wives to husbands. Today alimony is usually not such a consideration because of the prevalence of households in which both husbands and wives have full-time employment outside the home. When the spouses earn approximately the same amount, there is no need for alimony payments after divorce.

H. CHILD CUSTODY

Custody
The right to physical possession of the child; the parent with custody is entitled to make daily decisions about the child's clothing, education, and discipline. The child lives with this parent most of the time

When the couple has children, the divorce must also take into account who will receive **custody** of the children. This is often one of the most hotly contested issues in any divorce. When the parents cannot decide who should receive physical custody of the children, the court must make the decision. The court's decision is supposed to take into account the best interests of the child. The court might award joint custody, in which parents share custody of the children and the children live for a period with one parent and then for a period with the other parent. However, the most common arrangement is for one parent to receive custody while the other parent is given visitation rights. The reason for awarding custody to one parent is to ensure that the children have as little disruption in their lives as possible. This allows them to attend the same school and maintain their other relationships.

Sidebar

In the past, courts had a stated preference for awarding custody to mothers. These days, however, courts are just as likely to award custody to the father.

1. VISITATION

When a parent has visitation, it means that the parent can take temporary custody of the child for stated periods of times, such as weekends or vacations. When drafting a separation agreement, the issues surrounding child visitation should be reviewed carefully. The agreement should take into account all the following questions concerning child custody and visitation:

- What is the visitation period?
- Who pays for the child's expenses when the child is visiting with the other parent?
- When can the parent pick up the child?
- When should the child be returned?
- When is the child "overdue"?

I. CHILD SUPPORT

Once the court has decided the issue of child custody and the division of marital property, the next question is which parent will provide child monetary support and in what amount. The noncustodial parent is generally the one responsible for paying child support. The court sets the amount of the monthly payments and will enforce those payments by imposing sanctions against a parent who fails to make them.

 ADOPTION

Adoption is the process of bringing a child into a family and creating a new, legally recognized family relationship. When a child is adopted, he is the legal child and heir of the parents adopting him. Adopted children have the same rights as children born to the parents. Children who are available for adoption may have been abandoned by their birth parents, or their birth parents may have had their parental rights removed by action of the court. A birth parent can lose parental rights for abusing or neglecting a child. In some cases, birth parents voluntarily surrender their rights so that the child can be adopted by another family.

Adoption
A legal decree creating a parent-child relationship when one did not exist before

FIGURE 14-6

Reasons Courts May Rule That
Birth Parents Are Unfit

A birth parent can be found to be unfit
for any of the following reasons:

■ Abandonment of the child

■ Lack of interest in the well-being and
development of the child

■ Failure to take responsibility for the
child's welfare

A. WHO CAN BE ADOPTED?

*Adoptions can occur
among children who are
already related to the adult
(such as nieces or cousins)
and unrelated children.*

The common practice is for adults to adopt children. However, most states have provisions that allow adults to adopt other adults in order to make them legally recognized heirs. In most situations, the adult to be adopted must either be a relative or have lived with the adoptive parent for a minimum period of time, often two years or more.

Both couples and single individuals can adopt a child. When a couple wishes to adopt, both must join in an adoption petition. When the child is over the age of 14, the child must also consent to the adoption.

B. THE RESULT OF AN ADOPTION DECREE

When an adoption has been completed, a new birth certificate is issued for the child. The adoptive mother and father will be listed as the child's parents at the time of the child's birth. The original birth certificate is sealed and is not available in the public records. The adopted person can bring legal action later to see the original birth certificate, but without court order, the birth certificate remains sealed and unavailable to everyone. After adoption, the child takes the last name of his parents.

C. ADOPTION AGENCIES

*An adopted child no longer
has any legal claims on his
birth parents.*

There are many state-level agencies that are licensed to place children in homes. Agencies investigate the prospective parents and inspect the child's future home before granting an adoption. The investigation into adoptive parents includes a criminal history check. Adoptive parents with extensive criminal records or felonies will usually not be given the opportunity to adopt children. The child must usually be in the new home for at least six month before the agency will grant final adoptive status.

ISSUE AT
A GLANCE

An adopted child has the same rights, privileges, and duties as a child who is born of the marriage; the law does not make any distinctions between adopted children and children born of the marriage.

FIGURE 14-7

Legal Effect of Decree of Adoption (North Carolina General Statutes §48-1-106)

(a) A decree of adoption effects a complete substitution of families for all legal purposes after the entry of the decree.

(b) A decree of adoption establishes the relationship of parent and child between each petitioner and the individual being adopted. From the date of the signing of the decree, the adoptee is entitled to inherit real and personal property by, through, and from the adoptive parents in accordance with the statutes on intestate succession and has the same legal status, including all legal rights and obligations of any kind whatsoever, as a child born the legitimate child of the adoptive parents.

(c) A decree of adoption severs the relationship of parent and child between the individual adopted and that individual's biological or previous adoptive parents. After the entry of a decree of adoption, the former parents are relieved of all legal duties and obligations due from them to the adoptee, except that a former parent's duty to make past-due payments for child support is not terminated, and the former parents are divested of all rights with respect to the adoptee. N.C.G.S § 48-1-106

NEW FAMILY LAW ISSUES

Advances in technology and a gradual relaxation of societal attitudes toward traditional family issues have created a wealth of new challenges for legal professionals specializing in family law. We have already seen how separation, divorce, and adoption can become complicated legal issues. However, those are just the tip of the iceberg. Consider the possible complications that can arise when surrogate mothers are used.

A. SURROGACY

In a **surrogate mother** arrangement, a woman enters into an agreement to become pregnant and then surrender the child to another couple. As you can imagine, there are a wealth of potential legal problems with such agreements. Suppose that the birth mother changes her mind after the birth and decides that she wishes to keep the child? What if the child she carried is not a product of her body? It is now possible to implant a fertilized human egg from a husband and wife into another woman's womb for development. Who does the resulting child belong to? Suits over surrogacy agreements have become more common, raising all of these issues.

Adding to the potential problems is the fact that technology continues to develop new methods for procreation, including artificial insemination, "test tube babies," and implantation of fertilized eggs, to name just a few. What is the legal impact of a wife's use of another man's sperm to impregnate her? Is her husband the father of her child, or does the sperm donor have parental rights?

Surrogate mother
A woman who agrees to bear a child and then surrender all parental rights to that child to another, usually in exchange for money

FIGURE 14-8

Natural Father of Child Conceived by Artificial Insemination; Conditions

(a) If, under the supervision of a licensed physician and surgeon and with the consent of her husband, a wife is inseminated artificially with semen donated by a man not her husband, the husband is treated in law as if he were the natural father of a child thereby conceived. The husband's consent must be in writing and signed by him and his wife. The physician and surgeon shall certify their signatures and the date of the insemination, and retain the husband's consent as part of the medical record, where it shall be kept confidential and in a sealed file. However, the physician and surgeon's failure to do so does not affect the father and child relationship. All papers and records pertaining to the insemination, whether part of the permanent record of a court or of a file held by the supervising physician and surgeon or elsewhere, are subject to inspection only upon an order of the court for good cause shown.

(b) The donor of semen provided to a licensed physician and surgeon for use in artificial insemination of a woman other than the donor's wife is treated in law as if he were not the natural father of a child thereby conceived.[33]

Many states have addressed this issue by creating a statute to spell out the exact legal position of all parties. See Figure 14-8 for California's approach to the issue.

B. CLONING

Cloning
The creation of a genetically identical person from the tissue of the donor

The next few decades promise to raise a host of legal and ethical issues that have never been addressed before. Although there have been claims that human **clones** have been created, to date none have been proven. However, with the cloning of sheep and other higher-order mammals, it would seem to be merely a matter of time before an actual human clone is created. How will the law deal with a child who is genetically identical to one of his parents? Will the law follow the standard approach and grant the same rights to this child as it would to any other? Will the child's status as an exact genetic replica of another person change the rights and duties involved in the parent-child relationship?

The U.S. Congress has addressed this issue by passing the Human Cloning Prohibition Act, H.R. 2505, 107th Cong. (2001), which seeks to ban human cloning. Whether this Act becomes the law of the land remains to be seen. It seems clear that cloning will eventually become an important legal issue.

To date there has never been a proven case of human cloning.

[33] Cal. Fam. Code §7613

Careers in the Law

▶ Renee Collette, Sexual Assault Nurse Examiner

enee Collette is a Registered Nurse and has been working with rape and domestic violence victims since the 1970s. She graduated from nursing school in 1986 and when she began practicing, she came to a startling realization. "I found out that most RNs were not comfortable and preferred not to become involved with the rape patients. With my previous experience, the hospital asked me to set up training programs for nurses and doctors in handling rape cases, especially collecting evidence." She heard about a new movement in medicine, SANE nurses (Sexual Assault Nurse Examiners). After receiving training, Renee applied for federal grant money to begin training other nurses throughout Ohio.

"People ask me all the time why I decided to become a SANE nurse," Renee said. "I've seen the devastating effects that rape and domestic violence can have on a person. I've also seen how Emergency Room doctors are reluctant to get involved in these cases. Having nurses certified as Sexual Assault Nurse Examiners makes a lot of sense to me. It's something that we can do that makes a difference."

Renee has testified in court many times and her testimony has helped convict both rapists and abusive partners. She continues to teach other nurses to become SANEs and is a vocal advocate against domestic violence and sexual assault.

Profiling a Paralegal

▶ Lisa Mazzonetto

he thing I like about family law is that I get to go to court a lot. I'm planning on going to law school one day and the courtroom is where I'd like to be. The thing I like least about family law is that things don't always go your client's way. The hardest part is dealing with kids and placement with parents. It's awful what people can do to each other. In family law, you're dealing with very sensitive issues in these people's lives.

There is a lot of client contact in being a paralegal at a family law practice. You manage a lot of cases and you get a lot of phone calls from upset clients. There is also a lot of paperwork. The pleadings are extensive and then you have equitable distribution of the marital estate. That involves a lot of affidavits. Then you've got discovery. I do my best to stay on top of it all.

I spend a lot of time with the clients. I help prepare them for trial. Based on the initial meeting, I'll set up an outline of questions that we may ask. I like to go through the questions before they testify. It helps them get a little more comfortable with testifying. People get very nervous about taking the stand. I'll take them to an empty courtroom a few days before the trial so that they can see what it's like. The hardest part for clients when they testify is staying focused on the issues in the hearing. Some of them want to go off on tangents. I find that it helps them focus to have them work on the files with us. I'll have them go through their inventory lists and organize their files with me. I want them to be involved and not obsess about issues.

Unfortunately, we're always dealing with domestic violence issues. A lot of our clients take out domestic violence orders to keep their husbands from hurting them.

C. CHILD TRAIT SELECTION

In addition to the potential legal impacts of cloning, there are also other developments that bear close attention. Suppose that parents can choose the sex of their
unborn children? What if, in addition to simply choosing the child's sex, the
parents could also rule out some inherited diseases, and also ensure that the
child is born with specific traits? Parents might choose factors for higher intelligence, greater disease resistance, and less need for sleep. What are the legal impli-
cations of "made to order" children? When a fetus who has been genetically
manipulated becomes a viable child, can parents sue the geneticist when the child's
abilities do not match the projections? These are only some of the questions that
will make family law a fascinating area for decades to come.

IN RE GUARDIANSHIP OF SCHIAVO
932 So.2d 264 (Fla. App. 2 Dist. 2005)

ALTENBERND, Judge.

The Department of Children and Family Services (DCF) appeals an emergency order
enforcing mandate, which was entered by the probate court on March 23, 2005. This order
was entered after Theresa Marie Schiavo's feeding tube was removed on March 18, 2005,
and before her death on March 31, 2005. On March 30, 2005, this court issued a per curiam
opinion affirming the order on appeal and indicating that an additional written opinion
explaining the court's ruling would follow. This is that additional written opinion.

On March 23, 2005, the DCF filed a motion to intervene in the Guardianship of
Theresa Marie Schiavo. The motion gave notice to the court pursuant to section
415.1055(9), Florida Statutes (2004), that the DCF had received a report alleging that
the court-appointed guardian had abused the ward. The motion explained that chapter
415 gives the DCF the power to investigate claims of abuse, neglect, or exploitation of
vulnerable adults. The motion further explained that the DCF may arrange for protective
services for an abused, vulnerable adult on a nonemergency basis without the consent of
the adult by filing a petition with the circuit court. §415.1051(1). In an emergency, the
DCF may enter premises and remove a vulnerable adult to a medical facility for treatment
to prevent serious physical injury or death. §415.1051(2).

The motion alleged that the DCF had received a medical opinion that challenged the
diagnosis relied upon by the probate court when it entered its final judgment authorizing
the removal of the feeding tube. The DCF also alleged that it had received many reports of
abuse on its hotline concerning Theresa Marie Schiavo and that it had an obligation to
investigate those claims. The DCF took the position that it could not conduct its investigation if the terms of the final judgment were carried out and Theresa Marie Schiavo
died. Essentially, the DCF wished to intervene in the proceeding so that it could take
custody of Theresa Marie Schiavo and reinsert the feeding tube without violating the
court's final judgment.

At the time the DCF filed its motion, the removal of Theresa Marie Schiavo's feeding
tube was being challenged by many parties in virtually every available court. In order to
accommodate these challenges, the courts dispensed with normal time restrictions and
attempted to streamline legal procedures. The probate court was no exception.

The guardian immediately responded to the DCF's motion by making an emergency oral motion to enforce mandate. A hearing was held on March 23, 2005, with oral notice given to the DCF. All relevant parties participated in that hearing. Following the hearing, the probate court entered an order restraining the DCF "from taking possession of Theresa Marie Schiavo or removing her from the Hospice Woodside facility, administering nutrition or hydration artificially, or otherwise interfering with this Court's final judgment." This is the order that the DCF appealed.

At the broadest level, this appeal concerns the competing powers given to the judiciary in chapter 744, Florida Statutes (2004), and to the DCF in chapter 415. Chapter 744 gives extensive authority to the judiciary to establish guardianships, including guardianships for persons who fall within the definition of "vulnerable adults" under section 415.102(26). Chapter 415 gives authority to the DCF to protect vulnerable adults both before a guardianship has been established and thereafter.

When a vulnerable adult does not consent to protective services by the DCF in a nonemergency situation, the DCF typically files a petition in circuit court to obtain authority to provide those services. If the court authorizes protective services, the DCF must petition the court within sixty days to determine how to best proceed. One of the options available at that time is the creation of a guardianship under chapter 744. The rules are essentially the same in an emergency, except that the DCF can perform the removal of the vulnerable adult and begin providing protective services prior to filing a petition and holding a hearing. The petition must be filed and heard by the circuit court within four business days of the emergency removal.

Because the statutes contemplate that an extended term of vulnerability can be addressed by the creation of a guardianship under chapter 744, it might be logical to structure the respective powers of the circuit court and the DCF so that the DCF had no authority to interfere once a chapter 744 guardianship had been established. Certainly, it is probable that the DCF will rarely need to use its powers under chapter 415 concerning a person who is already the ward of a judicially created guardianship under chapter 744.

On the other hand, it is possible for a guardian to abuse or neglect a ward, and chapter 415 is written to give the DCF some power over abusive guardians. "Guardian" is defined in chapter 415 to include a guardian under chapter 744. Section 415.1051(4) contains special provisions for protective services when the vulnerable adult has a guardian. This statute expressly gives the DCF power to perform an emergency removal of a ward from the care of a guardian prior to a judicial hearing.

In this case, however, the narrower issue is whether the DCF can use these powers to remove a ward from the control of the guardian in order to restore a feeding tube that had been removed at the express order of the circuit court in a postjudgment order, after the final judgment authorizing removal of the feeding tube has been reviewed and affirmed in all available appellate venues. The primary "abuse" alleged by the DCF was the guardian's decision to obey the specific directives of the probate court's order.

We conclude that chapter 415 does not give the DCF power to declare the acts of a guardian that are in strict compliance with an explicit, lawful order of a guardianship court to be actions constituting neglect, abuse, or exploitation. Once the guardian asked the court to authorize removal of the feeding tube in 1998, the State undoubtedly had an interest in the issues that were litigated in this case. The State has participated in such cases in the past. The executive branch of state government, either through the Attorney General or through the DCF, undoubtedly had standing to intervene in this case years before the probate court entered the order on March 18, 2005, requiring the guardian to remove the feeding tube. It did not, however, have the power to wait on the sidelines until those proceedings were final and the order had been implemented and then challenge the judicial decision as "abuse" under chapter 415. This is particularly true of an order discontinuing a form of medical treatment because section 415.113 expressly provides that nothing in chapter 415 shall be construed to "require any medical care or treatment in contravention of the stated or implied objection of such person." The entire purpose of the litigation in the probate court had been to determine the treatment that the ward herself would have selected under these circumstances. See Schindler v. Schiavo (In re Guardianship of Schiavo), 780 So.2d 176 (Fla. 2d DCA 2001).

To the extent that the DCF suggested that it needed to take possession of Theresa Marie Schiavo in order to conduct its investigation of the various claims of abuse it had received on its hotline, the DCF never explained why that investigation would necessitate a further delay of the court's final judgment. The ward, of course, could not communicate or assist the DCF in any investigation, and the DCF did not provide any reasoned explanation of why its investigation required this extraordinary action. The probate court clearly had discretion to conclude that this request was not a sufficient basis for it to rescind its order.

The probate court correctly ruled that the powers given to the DCF in chapter 415 did not permit the DCF to challenge the final order of the probate court in this manner. We trust that the DCF would have obeyed the probate court without a formal restraining order, but in light of all of the circumstances in March 2005, the trial court was well within its power to issue a restraining order to assure continued compliance with its order.

Affirmed.

QUESTIONS ABOUT THE CASE

1   What is the basis of the Department of Children and Family Services' appeal in this case?
2   What allegations concerning the guardian, Shiavo's husband, had DCF received?
3   How does this case concern the power of the judiciary to protect the rights of "vulnerable" adults?
4   What does the court consider to be the central issue in this case concerning the powers of DCF?

SKILLS YOU NEED IN THE REAL WORLD

INTERNET INVESTIGATIONS

One skill that any modern paralegal should possess is the ability to use the Internet as an investigative tool. There is a wealth of information available on the Internet if you know where to look. You can use your Internet skills to locate absent witnesses, track down defendants, and search for assets, but you need to develop a basic skill set before you can call yourself a master of Internet investigations. Here are some basic steps to building your investigative skills.

1. *Learn to decipher Internet addresses.* Not all Internet sites are created equal. Some offer extremely accurate and valuable information, while others are completely unreliable. One way of separating the wheat from the chaff is to examine the pedigree of the Internet address. Commonly referred to as a "URL" (Uniform Resource Locator), an Internet address can give you many clues about its reliability. Consider the following fictitious web addresses:

www.federalbureauofinvestigation.gov

www.ihatethegovernment.org

What can you tell about these web sites just from working through the URL? The first web site is a government web site and is probably reliable. Most ".gov" sites are very reliable and are updated regularly. They are also checked and approved to make sure that they don't post inaccurate information. This doesn't mean that they are always right, but the first web site is a much safer bet than the second. The second web site has some suspicious indicators. For one thing, "I hate the government" sounds like someone with a political agenda, not someone whose primary concern is accurate information. Another indication is the .org extension. Although many quality sites are organizations, there are also more than a few crazy sites with this extension.

Learning to decode web addresses is one important skill to master in becoming an Internet investigator, but it isn't the only one.

2. *Finding people.* It is a straightforward proposition to locate someone's address on the Internet. Most general search engines, such as Yahoo.com or Altavista.com, offer people locator services for free. There are also plenty of pay sites that will provide this information.

3. *Finding criminal histories.* There are some pay sites that offer access to online criminal records checks, including *http://www.nc123.com/*, which has a broad database and competitive pricing. However, much of this information is also available for free at your local courthouse. Many have terminals tied in to state and federal criminal records. All you need to do is type in a person's name.

These are just some of the Internet investigative techniques you should learn to improve your overall effectiveness at your job—and make yourself that much more indispensable to your employer.

CHAPTER SUMMARY

When two people decide to marry, there are a host of legal issues to consider. For instance, if one of the parties has substantial assets, the couple might wish to enter into a prenuptial agreement that limits the amount of property the other spouse would receive in the event of death or divorce. Marriage itself raises several important issues. A marriage is a legally recognized union between two people. In many ways, marriage is a contract, but it is also something more. People who are married enjoy special protections under the law. Their real and personal property is held jointly and they cannot be compelled to testify against one another in criminal proceedings.

States have enacted statutes that prevent certain individuals from marrying one another. For example, certain family members are prohibited from marrying one another. Because marriage is at least partly a contract, the parties to the marriage must have many of the capacities found in any other contracting party. A marriage obtained under false pretenses or through force is no marriage at all. The legal definition of marriage has come under close scrutiny in recent years with nontraditional couples seeking the benefits and protections of legally recognized marriage.

Marriages can end in annulments or through divorce. A divorce is a court declaration officially ending the marriage. Many states have "no fault" divorce statutes that allow the couple to end the marriage without proof that either had broken the marital vows, such as by committing adultery and engaging in cruel treatment of the other. When a couple divorces, there are many issues to consider. Real and personal property must be divided and children must be supported. One parent usually obtains custody of any children while the other parent often receives visitation rights.

Family law will continue to be a relevant and fascinating field for years to come. Advances in technology, such as surrogacy, artificial insemination, and the prospect of human cloning, will provide challenges in this field on many fronts.

ETHICS: "BENDING" THE RULES

It is difficult not to become personally involved in the lives of clients when you work in a family law practice. The abstract principles of equitable distribution and custody melt away when you have actually met the children and seen the effects that the divorce has wrought on what was once a loving and viable family. Faced with these intense emotions, it is no wonder that some family law practitioners feel a strong motivation to "bend" the rules.

Bending the rules refers to taking questionable actions for the best of reasons. It can come up in a myriad of different ways. Clients may wish you to hide assets for them so that they can be used for the benefit of the children, and not for "his new girlfriend." Issues regarding child custody and rearing are fraught with potential difficulties and clients often ask their legal team to ignore, shield, or actively disguise issues as diverse as child discipline, live-in lovers, and dating rules for the children.

The important issue here is to remember that no matter how strong your motivation to help the client, you must never step outside the legal framework to do so. You might say to yourself, "I'll just do this once," but you will find that no action exists in a vacuum. The moment you break, or even bend, a rule, you must break others to conceal that fact. The safest course, and the one that keeps the firm doing valuable work for clients in other cases, is to follow the rules even when it causes hardship in a particular case.

CHAPTER REVIEW QUESTIONS

1   What is a prenuptial agreement? Why would a person wish a future spouse to sign such an agreement?
2   What are some of the legal benefits of marriage?
3   What are some examples of people who are not legally able to marry?
4   What limitations are placed on blood relatives who wish to marry one another?
5   Why would the state limit a prisoner's right to marry?
6   Explain the difference between a civil union and a marriage.
7   What is a common law marriage? What formalities are required to create one?
8   Explain when a person would be entitled to an annulment.
9   Before the advent of "no fault" divorce, what options were available to a couple who wished to end their marriage?
10   What is a divorce?
11   What are the practical effects of a judicial decree granting a divorce?
12   What is a separation agreement?
13   What is the meaning of the term *irreconcilable differences*?
14   What is a "no fault" divorce?
15   When is a court permitted to exercise jurisdiction in a divorce action?
16   Explain the process of equitable distribution.
17   What is alimony?
18   When and under what circumstances is a parent ordered to pay child support?
19   What are the guidelines that courts use when determining child custody?

DISCUSSION QUESTIONS

1   Is marriage really a contractual agreement? Why or why not?
2   Should divorce be easier to obtain than it currently is? Why or why not?
3   Should the minimum age to marry be raised to 21 or even higher? Why or why not?
4   One hundred years ago, common law marriage was common and legal in many states. Why have many of these states made common law marriage illegal?
5   Do issues such as child trait selection raise unpleasant or even dangerous possibilities? Should we as a society welcome these technological advances, or attempt to stop them?

PERSONALITY QUIZ

Is family law right for you? Take this personality quiz and see.

1 I enjoy working with people.
0-strongly disagree   5-agree   10-strongly agree

Points: _____

2 I like the challenge of finding solutions for people in trouble.
0-strongly disagree   5-agree   10-strongly agree

Points: _____

3 I work well under stress.
0-strongly disagree   5-agree   10-strongly agree

Points: _____

4 I like a balance of legal research and practical application in my daily work.
0-strongly disagree   5-agree   10-strongly agree

Points: _____

5 I have strong feelings about the treatment of children by their parents.
0-strongly disagree   5-agree   10-strongly agree

Points: _____

Total Points: _____

If you scored between 30-50 points, you have many of the qualities that would make family law a good choice for you.

If you scored between 20-29 points, you might find family law interesting, but you might also be attracted to some other field.

If you scored 19 or lower, family law is probably not a good choice for you.

PRACTICAL APPLICATIONS

1 Locate a divorce case at the local courthouse and review the file. What allegations were made in the complaint? How did the parties resolve their differences? Did the case go to trial? What was the judge's final order on property division, child support, and visitation?
2 Does your state recognize no fault divorce? Locate the statute that provides the answer.

3 What limitations are placed on adoption in your state? For instance, can adults adopt other adults? Are persons with felony convictions barred from adopting children? Locate the statute that provides the answer.

WEB SITES

Findlaw.com
http://www.findlaw.com

Washburn School of Law – Family Law
http://www.washlaw.edu/subject/family.html

Family Law Information
http://patriot.net/ crouch/fln.html

HG. Org – Family and Elder Law
http://www.hg.org/family.html

The 'Lectric Law Library — Divorce
http://www.lectlaw.com/tfam.html

Indiana School of Law WWW Virtual Law Library
http://www.law.indiana.edu/v-lib

TERMS AND PHRASES

Adoption	Custody	Surrogate mother
Alimony	Prenuptial agreement	
Cloning	Separation agreement	

Intellectual Property

Chapter Learning Objectives

After completing this chapter, you should be able to:

- Explain the federal government's role in copyright law
- Explain the nature of copyright and trademark laws
- Describe the process of registering a copyright

- Explain the basic components of patent law
- List and describe the importance of patents and trademarks to commerce

 **INTRODUCTION TO INTELLECTUAL PROPERTY**

In this chapter we explore the concepts of intellectual property, including copyright and trademarks. Copyright law has a rich history and remains an important legal specialty. Whether a case involves allegations of "pirated" music, such as the famous *Napster* case, or more mundane issues such as fair use, infringement actions, or the unlicensed use of a trademark, intellectual property is a diverse field offering many challenges to a legal professional.

COPYRIGHT

Copyright is a protection given by law to persons who create literary or artistic works. At its simplest, copyright is literally the right to make copies of a work. When an author creates a story and possesses copyright to that work, the author has the right to distribute copies to others. Distribution usually takes the form of selling copies of the work. An author may sell a copy of her book; a musician may sell a CD containing copies of her musical performances. Distribution and sale of

Copyright
The right granted to an author by the Federal Copyright Statute to reproduce, prepare derivative work, and distribute copies of the work created by the author

literary works is how authors make money. The importance of copyright was recognized as early as the drafting of the U.S. Constitution and continues to be vitally important for authors today.

However, the term *copyright* is also used in different contexts. For instance, the process of registering an original work with the U.S. Copyright Office is often referred to as copyright. When an author's work has been copyrighted, it means that she can prevent others from using it or earning money from the unauthorized sale of the work.

Copyright law seeks to balance two conflicting ideas: that the creativity and inventiveness of an author should be rewarded by legal protections while the public should be permitted access to new and interesting ideas.

 **Copyright vests in the author the moment that the work is created.**

Consider the following scenario:

Scenario 1: The Screenplay

Sal Screenwriter has just written a screenplay that he believes will make him a millionaire. The premise of the screenplay is that all human beings are actually prisoners in an enormous underground storage area, hooked to machines that drain their energies for the machines' purposes. Human beings are not even aware that they are prisoners. They live their entire lives in a computer-generated reality called the *Mailtrix.* In the screenplay, the lead character, a young man named Froto, leads a band of rebels against the machines while being pursued by a cyborg from the future called the Eliminator.

When production begins on this new movie, several motion picture studios bring copyright infringement suits against Sal. Who will win this suit?

A. THE FEDERAL GOVERNMENT CONTROLS COPYRIGHTS

1. CONSTITUTIONAL AUTHORITY

Copyright derives exclusively from federal statutes. The right of the government to regulate copyright originates in Article I of the U.S. Constitution.

> To promote the Progress of Science and useful Arts, by securing for limited Times to Authors and Inventors the exclusive Right to their respective Writings and Discoveries

U.S. Constitution, Art. I, §8, Cl. 8

There are no state statutes that control the process or creation of copyright. This puts copyright law in a rare category. Like bankruptcy, copyright issues fall

FIGURE 15-1

Determining Jurisdiction in
Copyright Issues

Patents, plant variety protection, copyrights, mask works, designs, trademarks, and unfair competition

(a) The district courts shall have original jurisdiction of any civil action arising under any Act of Congress relating to patents, plant variety protection, copyrights and trademarks. Such jurisdiction shall be exclusive of the courts of the states in patent, plant variety protection and copyright cases.[34]

FIGURE 15-2

Subject Matter of Copyright:
In general

(a) Copyright protection subsists, in accordance with this title, in original works of authorship fixed in any tangible medium of expression, now known or later developed, from which they can be perceived, reproduced, or otherwise communicated, either directly or with the aid of a machine or device. Works of authorship include the following categories:

(1) literary works;

(2) musical works, including any accompanying words;

(3) dramatic works, including any accompanying music;

(4) pantomimes and choreographic works;

(5) pictorial, graphic, and sculptural works;

(6) motion pictures and other audiovisual works;

(7) sound recordings; and

(8) architectural works.

(b) In no case does copyright protection for an original work of authorship extend to any idea, procedure, process, system, method of operation, concept, principle, or discovery, regardless of the form in which it is described, explained, illustrated, or embodied in such work.[35]

under the exclusive jurisdiction of the federal courts. When authors and others sue over copyright issues, they bring their suits in federal, not state, courts.

2. FEDERAL STATUTES ON COPYRIGHT

Copyright law is found in the United States Code, Title 17. See Figure 15-2. This title establishes not only what copyright is, but also how it is created and sold and when it expires.

Copyright protects works, not ideas.

ISSUE AT
A GLANCE

[34] 28 U.S.C.A. §1338
[35] 17 U.S.C.A §102

FIGURE 15-3

Who Is Protected by
Copyright?

(b) Published Works. — The works specified by sections 102 and 103, when published, are subject to protection under
this title if —
    (1) on the date of first publication,
    one or more of the authors is a
national or domiciliary of the United
States, or is a national, domiciliary, or
sovereign authority of a treaty party,
or is a stateless person, wherever
that person may be domiciled[36]

Notice that 17 U.S.C.A §102 specifically excludes ideas from protection. It is
one of the basic foundations of copyright law that ideas cannot be copyrighted.

B. WHO IS PROTECTED BY COPYRIGHT?

Title 17 also spells out who is protected by copyright. The exclusive right to
copyright extends to the author who created the work. The only other requirement
is that the author be either a citizen of the United States or domiciled here. (There
is also a provision for copyright protection for citizens of other countries who have
copyright treaties with the United States.)

C. THE RIGHTS CONFERRED BY COPYRIGHT

When you purchase a book at a local bookstore, you are not also purchasing the
right to use that book in any way that you see fit. Purchasing a book does not confer
copyright. Suppose that you purchase computer software (which is protected
under copyright law) and you make free copies for your friends. Have you violated
the copyright statute? The answer is yes. Your purchase of the software did not give
you the right to distribute it to others. Under the copyright statute, authors receive
exclusive rights. These rights include the following:

- To reproduce the copyrighted work in copies;
- To prepare derivative works based upon the copyrighted work;
- To distribute copies . . . of the copyrighted work to the public by sale or
  other transfer of ownership, or by rental, lease, or lending;
- In the case of literary, musical, dramatic, and choreographic works, pantomimes, and motion pictures and other audiovisual works, to perform the
  copyrighted work publicly;
- In the case of literary, musical, dramatic, and choreographic works, pantomimes, and pictorial, graphic, or sculptural works, including the
  individual images of a motion picture or other audiovisual work, to display
  the copyrighted work publicly; and

[36] 17 U.S.C.A. §104

■ In the case of sound recordings, to perform the copyrighted work publicly by means of a digital audio transmission.[37]

The rights granted to copyright holders also include the right to sell or transfer copyright to someone else. It can also be transferred by will to designated heirs. In many ways, copyright is an intangible right. It exists because a federal statute says that it exists. Because copyright ownership does not depend on possession of the physical object, such as a book, it is sometimes difficult to pin down. One way of dealing with the intangible nature of copyright is to register a work with the U.S. Copyright Office.

D. REGISTERING A COPYRIGHT

According to federal law, a copyright is created in a work the moment that it is created. There is no requirement that the work must first be registered with the U.S. Copyright Office before a person possesses authorship rights to a work.

If copyright is created the moment that a work comes into existence, why is there a need for the U.S. Copyright Office? By registering a work with the Copyright Office, an author can make her ownership of a copyright a matter of public record and can use registration as proof of ownership against others who attempt to use the work without permission.

Let's return to our example of Sal Screenwriter and his winning screenplay. A quick glance at the plot line of Sal's work reveals that Sal has apparently borrowed ideas and plot lines from three different highly successful movies: *The Matrix*®, *Lord of the Rings*®, and *The Terminator*® *Series*. The creators of each of these movies have undoubtedly registered copyrights for their screenplays and motion pictures. Because they are registered with the U.S. Copyright Office, the creators can prove that they created these works before Sal Screenwriter did and will probably be successful in a copyright infringement suit against Sal.

Registering a work with the U.S. Copyright Office involves the following steps:

1 The work must be something that can be legally copyrighted
2 The work must be submitted to the U.S. Copyright Office using the correct form and must also include the correct fee for registration
3 When the work has been registered, the author receives notification of copyright from the U.S. Copyright Office

The U.S. Copyright Office works under the auspices of the Library of Congress. It is located in Washington, D.C. In addition to registering copyrighted material, the Office also advises Congress on copyright and other issues.

Although an author has a copyright at the moment that a work is created, the best practice is to register the work with the U.S. Copyright Office to ensure protection of the work.

ISSUE AT A GLANCE

---

[37] 17 U.S.C.A. §106

E. LIMITATIONS ON COPYRIGHT

Although we have detailed the rights granted to an author under the Copyright Statute, there are limitations on these rights. One of the most important is fair use.

1. FAIR USE

Fair use
The right to use a copyrighted work without the author's permission; fair use must fall into the categories of criticism, comment, news reporting, teaching, or research

Fair use refers to the right of non-copyright holders to make use of the work for limited purposes. For instance, a person may reproduce a work for:

- Criticism
- Comment
- News reporting
- Teaching
- Research

When the use falls into any of these categories, the copyright holder is not permitted to bring suit for unauthorized use of the work.

 When use of the work falls under fair use, there is no copyright infringement.

2. COPYING COMPUTER PROGRAMS

Federal copyright statutes have recognized that computer programs present a particularly difficult issue when it comes to copyright. For example, it is not a violation of copyright to make a copy of a computer program that you have

FIGURE 15-4

Limitations on Exclusive Rights: Fair Use

In determining Fair Use, the Courts may consider:

(1) the purpose and character of the use, including whether such use is of a commercial nature or is for non-profit educational purposes;

(2) the nature of the copyrighted work;

(3) the amount and substantiality of the portion used in relation to the copyrighted work as a whole; and

(4) the effect of the use upon the potential market for or value of the copyrighted work.

The fact that a work is unpublished shall not itself bar a finding of fair use if such finding is made upon consideration of all the above factors.[38]

---

[38] 17 U.S.C.A. §107

FIGURE 15-5

Limitations on Exclusive
Rights: Computer Programs

(a) Making of additional copy or adaptation by owner of copy. — Notwithstanding the provisions of section 106, it is not an infringement for the owner of a copy of a computer program to make or authorize the making of another copy or adaptation of that computer program provided:

(1) that such a new copy or adaptation is created as an essential step in the utilization of the computer program in conjunction with a machine and that it is used in no other manner, or

(2) that such new copy or adaptation is for archival purposes only and that all archival copies are destroyed in the event that continued possession of the computer program should cease to be rightful.[39]

purchased, as long as the copy is made as part of the installation process or is created as an archive copy by the person who purchased it. These copies must be destroyed when the computer program is permanently removed from the computer's hard drive. It is a violation, however, to copy a computer program that you have purchased in order to give it to a friend.

F.   HOW LONG DOES COPYRIGHT LAST?

Once copyright is recognized in a work, how long does the protection last? Again, the answer is found in federal statutes. Copyright comes with a built-in expiration date. Giving a work copyright protection that lasts forever might benefit the author, but it would prevent others from using the work in new and creative ways. Copyright statutes provide the following provision for the duration of copyright:

> In General. — Copyright in a work created on or after January 1, 1978, subsists from its creation and, except as provided by the following subsections, endures for a term consisting of the life of the author and 70 years after the author's death.[40]

G.   DISPLAYING COPYRIGHT NOTICE

To establish copyright protections, and to proclaim copyright ownership to the world, a copyright notice should appear in a prominent position on the work. The notice can be expressed in any of the following ways:

- The symbol © (the letter C in a circle), or
  - The word "Copyright" or
  - The abbreviation "Copr."
- The year of publication[41]

[39] 17 U.S.C.A. §117
[40] 17 U.S.C.A. §302
[41] 17 U.S.C.A. §401

H. WHAT TYPES OF WORKS CAN BE COPYRIGHTED?

Copyright protects only specific types of works. The copyright statute provides that literary or artistic works can be copyrighted, but it has also been applied to a wide variety of other types of works, including motion pictures, sound recordings, and computer programs. Despite the wide variety in these categories, all these works share some of these common features: A person created the work. Someone invested time and energy and creativity in creating this work. Most of the works protected by copyright law are artistic in nature. Many of them were created by a single individual, or a small group of individuals working together. They are the product of ingenuity, creativity, and perseverance. Copyright law seeks to protect the economic and mental investment made by these individuals.

Here is a partial list of the types of works that can be copyrighted:

- Writings
- Motion pictures
- Sound recordings
- Digital recordings
- Live television "feeds"
- Computer programs
- Fictional characters

In 1912 Edgar Rice Burroughs created a character called Tarzan. This character was labeled copyrightable in two different appellate decisions.[42]

I. WORKS THAT ARE NOT COPYRIGHTABLE

Although the copyright statute has been interpreted to protect a wide range of creations, many types of creations cannot be copyrighted. When a writer prepares a nonfiction account of an event, or a person's life, those facts cannot be copyrighted. They are available to everyone and will not be protected by copyright simply because a writer has written about them.

One of the underlying themes in copyright law is that copyright protects expression, not ideas. Concepts, themes, and ideas are not copyrightable. A person cannot write down the plot for a novel, copyright it, and then prevent others from using it. Consider the following scenario:

Scenario 2: The Plot
B is a private detective who has been hired by a client to find the man's daughter. As B looks for the daughter, he comes into contact with a wide range of colorful and dangerous characters.

---

[42] *Burroughs v. Metro-Goldwyn-Mayer, Inc.,* 683 F.2d 610 (1982)

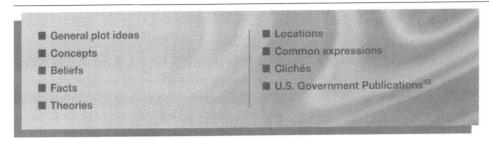

FIGURE 15-6

Items That Cannot Be Copyrighted

- General plot ideas
- Concepts
- Beliefs
- Facts
- Theories
- Locations
- Common expressions
- Clichés
- U.S. Government Publications[43]

This plot is not copyrightable because it is so general that allowing a person to copyright it would mean that any time a person writes a short story, novel, or screenplay about a private detective who is searching for a missing person, the owner of this copyright could bring suit. This would effectively stop anyone from writing in the private detective genre again.

Facts are not copyrightable

ISSUE AT A GLANCE

Other works that are not copyrightable include common expressions. Copyrighting widely used expressions would have a chilling effect on speech (and would be almost impossible to enforce).

Suppose that Al Author writes a book in which one of his characters says, "gee whiz" every time something unexpected happens. Al reads a new book in which one of the characters uses this common expression and he sues for copyright infringement. The court will dismiss his case because common expressions are not copyrightable.

J. PUBLIC DOMAIN

Works in the **public domain** are not protected by copyright. These works can be used by anyone, without permission, in any manner that the author sees fit. A work enters the public domain when the copyright has expired on the work or when the author never copyrighted the work in the first place.

Public domain
A work that was never copyrighted, or whose copyright has expired

When a work is in the public domain, it can be used by anyone for any purpose; there is no need to seek permission.

ISSUE AT A GLANCE

[43] 17 U.S.C.A. §105

K. COPYRIGHT INFRINGEMENT ACTIONS

Copyright infringement
When the holder of a copyright alleges that another has used the work without permission

When a person has a valid copyright on a work and someone uses this work without permission, the author is entitled to bring a **copyright infringement** action. This is a civil suit that seeks monetary damages from the user. Copyright infringement suits have been a staple of U.S. civil law for centuries.

> When an author's work has been used without permission, the author can sue the user through a copyright infringement action.

1. PROVING A COPYRIGHT INFRINGEMENT SUIT

When courts consider copyright infringement cases, they review the works and compare them for similarities. The court may consider any of the following factors in determining whether a work is an infringement:

- Plot lines
- Character names and traits
- Setting
- Dialogue

When the court finds a strong similarity between the works, the judge can rule that a copyrighted work has been infringed upon. This ruling justifies a monetary award for the party whose work has been copied.

Consider the following scenario:

Johnny recently wrote a book called *Lord of Rings*, the story of Randy Roe, the world's finest jeweler. He brings an infringement suit against the producers of the *Lord of the Rings* movie series. He claims that their use of the title "Lord of the Rings" is an obvious attempt by the movie producers to take advantage of the popularity of his work to bring in a larger audience for their movie.

When the court reviews Johnny's book and the *Lord of the Rings* movies, she finds that there are no substantial similarities between the two works and therefore no copyright infringement. Two works having similar titles is not enough to warrant an infringement suit.

The plaintiff in a copyright infringement case must prove the following elements:

a She is the owner of a copyrighted work
b The defendant has access to this work
c There are substantial similarities between the plaintiff's work and the defendant's creation.

a. Proving Ownership

The first element of a copyright action is relatively straightforward. The plaintiff must prove that a work is copyrighted and that the plaintiff is the owner of that copyright. This is usually as simple as producing the appropriate registration from the U.S. Copyright Office.

b. Defendant's Access to the Work

The second element usually poses no problem in an infringement action. For books or other works, the plaintiff must simply establish some evidence that the defendant had access to the work. For works in general circulation, that is a simple matter. The third element of an infringement action presents the real challenge.

c. Substantial Similarity Between the Works

The core of an infringement action is proof that the two works are substantially similar. This is not as straightforward or as simple as it might appear. If you consider the number of novels and movies that have similar plot lines, you will quickly see that substantial similarity must mean something more than a passing resemblance between the two works.

Courts approach this issue by breaking the question of substantial similarity into two tests. The first test, called the *extrinsic test*, examines the superficial similarities between the works. Here, the court examines the subject matter, the general plot, the overall construction of the work, and the themes explored. The second test, the *intrinsic test*, focuses more on the impact of the work. If an average reader would find the works to be closely associated with one another in terms of the mood, setting, and approach of the author, it is likely that the court will find the intrinsic test to be satisfied.[44] As one court has said, "to prevail on a copyright claim, a plaintiff must show substantial similarity of *both* ideas and expression."[45]

2. THE COURT'S POWER IN INFRINGEMENT ACTIONS

When an author proves a case of infringement, the court is authorized to enter an injunction preventing the unauthorized user from continuing to use the work. The court may also award monetary damages based on the unauthorized work.

 **TRADEMARKS**

Copyright applies to creative works, such as novels, motion pictures, and computer programs. A trademark, on the other hand, is reserved for goods. A trademark shows that a company has ownership and other rights in its merchandise.

A. WHAT IS A TRADEMARK?

A **trademark** is a symbol of the company, a kind of shorthand representation of the manufacturer.

Trademark
A symbol used by a company on its products; when registered under the Trademark Act, it gives the holder the exclusive rights to the symbol

[44] *Litchfield v. Spielberg*, 736 F.2d 1352 (9th Cir. 1984)
[45] *Berkic v. Crichton*, 761 F.2d 1289 (9th Cir. 1985)

Example: Darin Williams wants to open a fast-food restaurant. He has come to our firm to get some guidance about opening his business. He is going to call the business McDonald's and is going to use large golden arches to form the letter "M" in the name. He is also going to serve hamburgers, fries, and shakes. Is he facing a potential trademark action?

Answer: Yes. The McDonald's corporation will probably sue Darin for his use of both the name and the trademark arches for his restaurant. The court will almost certainly rule against Darin.

Businesses spend millions of dollars in creating and maintaining their trademarks. We can all think of symbols closely associated with a particular product, from soft drinks to real estate agencies. These trademarks are extremely valuable to companies.

Just as we saw with copyrights, federal law also controls trademarks. The Trademark Act, 15 U.S.C. §1051, governs the creation, protection, and regulation of trademarks. When a trademark is registered with the Patent and Trademark Office, it becomes the exclusive property of the company that registered it. That company may use it on all its promotional and merchandising materials and can sue to prevent others from using it without permission. In many ways trademark is similar to a copyright. A copyright holder has the exclusive right to use its work in the same way that a trademark owner has the right to use its symbol.

However, there are important differences between trademarks and copyrights. A trademark is a symbol that denotes a company and is used on its products. A copyright, on the other hand, is an author's right to make copies of a work and to sell it to others. Trademarks do not apply to creative works; they apply to products.

<table>
<tr><td>

Sidebar

The Trademark Act is also known as the Lanham Act. Both refer to 15 U.S.C. §1051 and following sections.

</td></tr>
</table>

B. ACQUIRING A TRADEMARK

A company acquires a trademark by registering it with the U.S. Office of Patents and Trademarks. A trademark must be distinctive enough from other trademarks to justify registration. Once registered, the trademark holder must renew its application every ten years.

FIGURE 15-7

Federal Trademark Legislation

U.S.C. §1051. Application for registration; verification

Application for use of trademark

(1) The owner of a trademark used in commerce may request registration of its trademark on the principal register hereby established by paying the prescribed fee and filing in the Patent and Trademark Office an application and a verified statement, in such form as may be prescribed by the Director, and such number of specimens or facsimiles of the mark as used as may be required by the Director.

(2) The application shall include specification of the applicant's domicile and citizenship, the date of the applicant's first use of the mark, the date of the applicant's first use of the mark in commerce, the goods in connection with which the mark is used, and a drawing of the mark.

Each registration shall remain in force for 10 years.[46]

---

[46] 15 U.S.C.A. §1058

Careers in the Law

▶ David Cheek, White Collar Crime Investigator

You'd be amazed how sophisticated criminals are getting. Identity theft started out in the 1990s as a minor problem, but it has really come into its own in the 2000s. People are always talking about pirating music, but the real problem is stealing someone's credit history, opening up new accounts and away they go. They'll charge up thousands of dollars and then disappear, leaving the original cardholder stuck.

We had a case a while back where a guy had manufactured 14 new identities. He's out there charging things, borrowing money on all on those names.

In the old days, criminals would literally go through your trash to get your credit card numbers. But now they've gotten more sophisticated there, too. It's a lot more common for us to find an insider at a bank or a credit card company who's selling the numbers to people on the outside.

A&M RECORDS, INC. v. NAPSTER, INC.
284 F.3d 1091 (9th Cir. 2002)

BEEZER, Circuit Judge.

This appeal involves challenges to a modified preliminary injunction entered by the district court on remand from a prior appeal, *A&M Records, Inc. v. Napster, Inc.*, 239 F.3d 1004 (9th Cir. 2001). At issue is the district court's order forcing Napster to disable its file transferring service until certain conditions are met to achieve full compliance with the modified preliminary injunction. We entered a temporary stay of the shut down order pending resolution of this appeal. We have jurisdiction pursuant to 28 U.S.C. §1292(a)(1). We affirm both the district court's modified preliminary injunction and shut down order.

Plaintiffs' action against Napster claims contributory and vicarious copyright infringement stemming from Napster's peer-to-peer music file sharing service. In the prior interlocutory appeal, we affirmed the district court's decision to issue a preliminary injunction and reversed and remanded with instructions to modify the injunction's scope to reflect the limits of Napster's potential liability for vicarious and contributory infringement. *Napster*, 239 F.3d at 1027.

We now consider the district court's modified preliminary injunction, which obligates Napster to remove any user file from the system's music index if Napster has reasonable knowledge that the file contains plaintiffs' copyrighted works. Plaintiffs, in turn, must give Napster notice of specific infringing files. For each work sought to be protected, plaintiffs must provide the name of the performing artist, the title of the work, a certification of ownership, and the name(s) of one or more files that have been available on the Napster file index containing the protected copyrighted work. Napster then must continually search the index and block all files which contain that particular noticed work. Both parties are required to adopt reasonable measures to identify variations of the file name, or of the spelling of the titles or artists' names, of plaintiffs' identified protected works.

The district court carefully monitored Napster's compliance with the modified preliminary injunction. It required periodic reports from the parties and held several compliance hearings. The district court also appointed a technical advisor to assist in evaluating Napster's compliance.

Napster was able to prevent sharing of much of plaintiffs' noticed copyrighted works. Plaintiffs nonetheless were able to present evidence that infringement of noticed works still occurred in violation of the modified preliminary injunction. After three months of monitoring, the district court determined that Napster was not in satisfactory compliance with the modified preliminary injunction. The district court ordered Napster to disable its file transferring service until certain conditions were met and steps were taken to ensure maximum compliance.

The record company plaintiffs and the music producer plaintiffs appeal the modified preliminary injunction, and Napster cross-appeals. Napster also appeals the district court's shut down order.

We review de novo the legal premises underlying a preliminary injunction. *Does 1-5 v. Chandler*, 83 F.3d 1150, 1152 (9th Cir. 1996). Otherwise, we review for abuse of discretion the terms of a preliminary injunction. *Gorbach v. Reno*, 219 F.3d 1087, 1091 (9th Cir. 2000) (en banc). "As long as the district court got the law right, it will not be reversed simply because [we] would have arrived at a different result if [we] had applied the law to the facts of the case."

Plaintiffs challenge the requirement that they provide file names found on the Napster index that correspond to their copyrighted works before those works are entitled to protection. Plaintiffs argue that Napster should be required to search for and to block all files containing any protected copyrighted works, not just those works with which plaintiffs have been able to provide a corresponding file name. Napster, on the other hand, argues that the modified preliminary injunction's articulation of its duty to police is vague and fails to conform to the fair notice requirement of Federal Rule of Civil Procedure 65(d).

We are unpersuaded that the district court committed any error of law or abused its discretion. The notice requirement abides by our holding that plaintiffs bear the burden "to provide notice to Napster of copyrighted works and files containing such works available on the Napster system before Napster has the duty to disable access to the offending content." *Napster*, 239 F.3d at 1027. Napster's duty to search under the modified preliminary injunction is consistent with our holding that Napster must "affirmatively use its ability to patrol its system and preclude access to potentially infringing files listed on its search index." *Id.* The modified preliminary injunction correctly reflects the legal principles of contributory and vicarious copyright infringement that we previously articulated.

Napster's challenge on grounds of vagueness is without merit. A preliminary injunction must "be specific in terms" and "describe in reasonable detail . . . the act or acts sought to be restrained." Fed. R. Civ. P. 65(d). We do not set aside injunctions under this rule "unless they are so vague that they have no reasonably specific meaning." *E. & J. Gallo Winery v. Gallo Cattle Co.*, 967 F.2d 1280, 1297 (9th Cir. 1992). Napster has a duty to police its system in order to avoid vicarious infringement. Napster can police the system by searching its index for files containing a noticed copyrighted work. The modified preliminary injunction directs Napster, in no vague terms, to do exactly that.

Napster challenges the district court's use of a technical advisor. Napster does not contest the appointment of the advisor but rather challenges the manner in which the district court relied on the advisor. Napster argues that the district court improperly delegated its judicial authority. We disagree.

At no time did the technical advisor displace the district court's judicial role. The technical advisor never unilaterally issued findings of fact or conclusions of law regarding Napster's compliance. The district court's use of the technical advisor was proper.

Napster challenges the district court's shut down order. The district court was dissatisfied with Napster's compliance despite installation of a new filtering mechanism. The new filter analyzed the contents of a file using audio fingerprinting technology and was not vulnerable to textual variations in file names. Napster had voluntarily disabled its file transferring service to facilitate installation and debugging of the new filtering mechanism. Users were still able to upload files and search the Napster index during this period. The district court ordered Napster to keep the file transferring service disabled until Napster satisfied the court "that when the [new] system goes back up it will be able to block out or screen out copyrighted works that have been noticed . . . and do it with [a] sufficient degree of reliability and sufficient percentage [of success]. . . . It's not good enough until every effort has been made to, in fact, get zero tolerance. . . . [T]he standard is, to get it down to zero." The shut down order was issued after the parties had filed notices to appeal the modified preliminary injunction.

Napster contends that the shut down order improperly amends the modified preliminary injunction by requiring a non-text-based filtering mechanism and ordering a shut down of the system pursuant to a new "zero tolerance" standard for compliance. Napster additionally argues that the district court lacked authority to further modify the modified preliminary injunction while the injunction was pending on appeal.

Napster argues that the new filtering mechanism is unwarranted as it lies beyond the scope of Napster's duty to police the system. By requiring implementation of the new filtering mechanism, the argument goes, the shut down order fails to recognize that Napster's duty to police is "cabined by the system's current architecture." *Napster,* 239 F.3d at 1024. We are not persuaded by this argument.

"Napster has the ability to locate infringing material listed on its search indices, and the right to terminate users' access to the system." *Id.* at 1024. To avoid liability for vicarious infringement, Napster must exercise this reserved right to police the system to its fullest extent. *Id.* at 1023. The new filtering mechanism does not involve a departure from Napster's reserved ability to police its system. It still requires Napster to search files located on the index to locate infringing material.

A district court has inherent authority to modify a preliminary injunction in consideration of new facts. Napster's original filtering mechanism was unsuccessful in blocking all of plaintiffs' noticed copyrighted works. The text-based filter proved to be vulnerable to user-defined variations in file names. The new filtering mechanism, on the other hand, does not depend on file names and thus is not similarly susceptible to bypass. It was a proper exercise of the district court's supervisory authority to require use of the new filtering mechanism, which may counter Napster's inability to fully comply with the modified preliminary injunction.

Napster argues that the shut down order improperly imposes a new "zero tolerance" standard of compliance. The district court did not, as Napster argues, premise the shut down order on a requirement that Napster must prevent infringement of all of plaintiffs' copyrighted works, without regard to plaintiffs' duty to provide notice. The tolerance standard announced applies only to copyrighted works which plaintiffs have properly noticed as required by the modified preliminary injunction. That is, Napster must do everything feasible to block files from its system which contain noticed copyrighted works.

The district court did not abuse its discretion in ordering a continued shut down of the file transferring service after it determined that the new filtering mechanism failed to prevent infringement of all of plaintiffs' noticed copyrighted works. Even with the new filtering mechanism, Napster was still not in full compliance with the modified preliminary injunction. The district court determined that more could be done to maximize the effectiveness of the new filtering mechanism. Ordering Napster to keep its file transferring service disabled in these circumstances was not an abuse of discretion.

Napster argues that the district court lacked authority to modify the injunction pending appeal. The civil procedure rules permit modifications. While a preliminary injunction is pending on appeal, a district court lacks jurisdiction to modify the injunction in such manner as to "finally adjudicate substantial rights directly involved in the appeal." Federal Rule of Civil Procedure 62(c), however, authorizes a district court to continue supervising compliance with the injunction. *See* Fed. R. Civ. P. 62(c) ("When an appeal is taken from an interlocutory or final judgment granting, dissolving, or denying an injunction, the [district] court in its discretion may suspend, modify, restore, or grant an injunction during the pendency of the appeal . . . as it considers proper for the security of the rights of the adverse party.").

The district court properly exercised its power under Rule 62(c) to continue supervision of Napster's compliance with the injunction.

We affirm both the modified preliminary injunction and the shut down order. The terms of the modified preliminary injunction are not vague and properly reflect the relevant law on vicarious and copyright infringement. The shut down order was a proper exercise of the district court's power to enforce compliance with the modified preliminary injunction.

AFFIRMED.

QUESTIONS ABOUT THE CASE

1 What is the main issue in this case?
2 What information must the music information provide to Napster as a preliminary to having Napster remove copyrighted information from its service?
3 Napster claimed that it has prevented sharing of much of A&M's works, but A&M continued to press for a complete shut down of Napster's service. What was the justification?
4 What standard did the district court establish for sharing of copyrighted material on Napster's service?

 **IV**

PATENTS

Patent
A U.S. government license recognizing that the inventor has created a new, useful, and nonobvious plant, product, or process

A **patent** is granted when a person or company has created a new invention. If the U.S. government agrees that the invention meets its standards, it will grant a 17-year monopoly to the inventor.

A. WHAT IS A PATENT?

A patent is the government's recognition that a person or company has created a unique invention. A patent gives the patent holder the exclusive right to manufacture the product. It also gives the patent holder the right to bring infringement actions against others who use the invention without permission. Patents encourage invention and creativity by giving the patent holder the exclusive rights to profits from the sale or use of the product. When a person brings a patent infringement action, this claim, similar to a trademark infringement action, allows the patent holder to sue others who use the product without permission.

1. WHO MAY OBTAIN A PATENT?

Anyone may obtain a patent, regardless of age or citizenship. The only criterion for obtaining a patent is the payment of the patent application fee and a determination by the U.S. Patent Office that the invention meets its qualifications.

Anyone may apply for a patent; age or citizenship will not disqualify an inventor.

ISSUE AT
A GLANCE

B. THREE TYPES OF PATENTS

Sidebar

Benjamin Franklin never applied for a patent for his wood-burning stove; he wanted to encourage others to copy it and use it in their homes.

There are three types of patents issued by the U.S. Patent and Trademark Office. They include:

- *Utility* patents cover mechanical, electrical, or other manufacturing processes
- *Design* patents govern the outer appearance of the invention
- *Plant* patents cover development of new types of plants or flowers

Although chemical, manufacturing, and other processes can be patented, the U.S. Patent Office will not grant patents for natural forces. For instance, a person cannot obtain a patent for lightning or sound waves. Similarly, ideas and thoughts cannot be patented. The U.S. Patent Office will also refuse to issue a patent for a simple improvement or repair of a preexisting device. The invention must meet three separate criteria to be recognized as a new invention.

C. THE CRITERIA FOR ISSUING A PATENT

To qualify for a patent, the invention must be new, useful, and nonobvious.

1. NEW

To qualify as new, the item must be unique and novel. If the item is substantially similar to a preexisting item, the U.S. Patent and Trade Office will not confer a patent.

■ Manufacturing or chemical processes	■ Designs	
■ Some improvements on a preexisting system or process		

FIGURE 15-8

What Can Be Patented?

2. USEFUL

The new invention must be useful. The invention must do something or achieve some result. If it does not, it is not patentable.

3. NONOBVIOUS

The third and final requirement for a patent is that the use is nonobvious. This is the most subjective of the three criteria used in evaluating a patent application. This element calls for interpretation and evaluation by the government employees who oversee the patent application. The standard that they use is to review the invention and to ask whether a hypothetical, reasonable person would have clearly anticipated this development. If the answer is no, the inventor can be granted a patent.

The U.S. Patent and Trademark Office employs experts in a wide variety of technical fields to examine patent applications to evaluate the invention under the three elements set out above.

D. PATENT INFRINGEMENT ACTIONS

When an inventor holds a patent, she can bring an infringement action against some-one who uses the invention without permission. A patent holder may license use to others, usually in exchange for a fee. This type of use is by permission. But when someone uses the invention without permission, the patent holder may bring a civil action. The patent holder's action may seek damages from the illegal user. These actions are similar to copyright or trademark infringement actions. Because of their complexity, there are many U.S. law firms that specialize exclusively in these types of suits.

E. PATENTS ARE PUBLIC RECORDS

Once a patent has been granted, it becomes part of the public record. Patent records are stored in the Library of Patents in Washington, D.C. This library is essential to anyone considering filing a patent application for a new invention. If the invention already exists, the U.S. Patent Office will not grant a patent. This is the primary reason for patent searches.

1. CONDUCTING A PATENT SEARCH

Because applying for a patent is expensive, it is usually worthwhile to conduct a patent search before filing. A patent search involves a search of the patent records

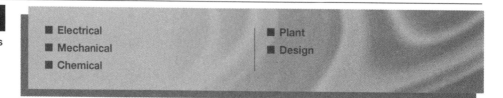

FIGURE 15-9

Five Classifications of Patents

■ Electrical   ■ Plant
■ Mechanical   ■ Design
■ Chemical

to ensure that the device has not already been invented. When a patent search is successful, the researcher comes up empty-handed. Many inventors hire a patent law firm to conduct the patent searches for them. These firms have the background, experience, and training to efficiently search the records. Most of these firms are based in Washington, D.C. and have immediate access to the Library of Patents.

While the patent application is pending in the U.S. Patent Office, the inventor can place "patent pending" on the product. Information about patents can be obtained by visiting the U.S. Patent and Trademark web site, listed at the end of this chapter.

Patent application fees range from $3 to $6000.

SKILLS YOU NEED IN THE REAL WORLD

RESEARCHING TRADEMARKS

A trademark could be something as simple as a name or as complicated as a drawing. The U.S. Patent and Trademark Office has awarded trademark status to phrases, symbols, and designs. If you have a client who wishes to create and register a trademark, you must learn how to search the database of current trademarks to ensure that your client will not use a trademark that has already been registered to another company.

Although an in-depth review of trademark searching techniques is beyond the scope of this book, you should be aware of a few provisions for such searches. For one thing, the Office of Patents and Trademarks maintains an online database of registered trademarks. You can access this database at *http://www.uspto.gov/*. It allows extensive search capabilities. However, your search for preexisting trademarks hasn't ended with a quick perusal of the U.S. Patent and Trademark Office. There are many other sources to consider before going ahead with a trademark registration.

You shouldn't neglect the obvious when searching for trademarks. See if you can locate your client's intended trademark on the web. Most companies put their trademarks on their web pages. If you can locate the symbol on a web page, there is very good chance that the company has registered it.

For more in-depth searches, there are pay sites such as Trademark.com (*http://www.trademarks.com*) or Shepard's online that will provide you with extensive information, but at a price that does not justify idle curiosity.

CHAPTER SUMMARY

Intellectual property is a broad term encompassing copyrights and trademarks. A copyright is an author's right to reproduce, sell, distribute, and otherwise modify the work. An author acquires a copyright at the moment that a work is created. An author who wishes to make her ownership a matter of public record registers the copyright with the U.S. Copyright Office. Copyright expires after a specific period of time. For works created after January 1, 1978, the time period is the author's life plus 70 years.

Some works are not copyrightable. For example, the U.S. Copyright Office will not register ideas, themes, processes, and plots because these items are too general to merit copyright protection. Works in which the copyright has expired enter the public domain. Public domain works may be used by anyone without permission. When an author believes that her work has been used without permission, she may bring a copyright infringement action in federal court. Courts may order injunctions against further use of the work and monetary damages for the unauthorized use.

Trademarks are similar to copyrights, but only superficially. Whereas copyright protects artistic works, trademarks protect symbols associated with goods. A manufacturer or seller may register a particular symbol that is used to advertise the product. When the symbol is used without permission, a trademark holder can bring an action similar to an infringement suit to stop the unauthorized use.

Patents are similar to trademarks in that the government gives an inventor the exclusive right to use a product or to sell that right to others. Patents last for 17 years and if anyone uses the product without permission during that time, the inventor is allowed to bring a patent infringement action. Patents are granted when an invention is new, useful, and nonobvious.

ETHICS: COPYRIGHT AND THE LAW

Because we discuss copyright in this chapter, we should address an issue that often rears its head in the day-to-day practice of law. When you research an issue, you may find yourself relying on the work prepared by others. Are there copyright issues involved in using language from one of the firm's old appellate briefs? In situations in which you borrow language from a previous firm writing, permission is assumed. You can usually use prior works created in your own firm without attributing them to the original author. Because the firm is the ultimate author of the work, one could argue that the copyright isn't held by individual members of the firm, but by the firm as a whole.

We have already seen that copyright does not apply to government works. Federal and state appellate reporters fall into that category. Legal professionals do not cite to cases and statutes because they have copyright concerns. Instead, they provide cites to show valid authority for the claims made in their writings.

In the vast majority of communications in the law, copyright is usually not a major concern. Of course, when you begin to use nongovernmental copyrighted material, you face the same concerns about copyright infringement as anyone else.

Copyright is a real concern in the legal community when it comes to software. Like every other profession, the legal field is undergoing a rapid change, most of it facilitated by new software that makes almost every aspect of a legal practice simpler and more efficient. The temptation to copy software and share it with others is powerful. Do not forget that this copying is a copyright infringement and could land you and the firm in big trouble.

CHAPTER REVIEW QUESTIONS

1   What is copyright?
2   What is the purpose of the U.S. Copyright Office?
3   What is the source of authority for granting copyright under U.S. law?
4   Where would you locate copyright statutes? What is the cite to the copyright statute?
5   What types of works can be copyrighted?
6   What rights are conferred on the holder of a copyright?
7   How does an author register a copyright?
8   What is fair use?
9   What are some exceptions to the exclusive rights of a copyright holder?
10 Under the copyright statutes, can you make a copy of computer software that you have purchased? Are there any limitations on making these copies?
11 How long does a copyright last?
12 How does an author symbolize copyright of a particular work?
13 List and explain some of the works that be copyrighted.
14 List and explain some of the works that cannot be copyrighted.
15 What is public domain?
16 What is a copyright infringement action?
17 What are the elements of a copyright infringement action?
18 What is a trademark?
19 When can an inventor receive a patent for an invention?
20 How is a trademark different from a patent?

DISCUSSION QUESTIONS

1   Why doesn't the law allow ideas to be copyrighted?
2   Why would copyright law have an exception for fair use?
3   Should there be a provision that never allows a perpetual copyright? Explain your answer.
4   Should computer software be excluded from coverage under copyright law? Shouldn't everyone have the right to make as many copies of computer programs as she wishes? Explain.

PERSONALITY QUIZ

Is intellectual property law right for you? Take this personality quiz and see.

1   I enjoy searching databases.
    0-strongly disagree   5-agree   10-strongly agree

                                                                    Points: _____

2   I pay very close attention to details.
    0-strongly disagree   5-agree   10-strongly agree

                                                                    Points: _____

3   I have very good computer skills.
    0-strongly disagree   5-agree   10-strongly agree

                                                                    Points: _____

4   I like to research.
    0-strongly disagree   5-agree   10-strongly agree

                                                                    Points: _____

                                                          Total Points: _____

If you scored between 30-40 points, you would probably enjoy the field of intellectual property.

If you scored between 20-29 points, you might do well in intellectual property, but you might also enjoy a different field.

If you scored 19 or lower, intellectual property is probably not the right career choice for you.

PRACTICAL APPLICATIONS

1   If you have written a story or a poem, contact the U.S. Copyright Office and order the appropriate form to register your copyright in this work. Which form is required? How much does it cost? What proof do you get that you have the copyright in the work?
2   Design a trademark for a freelance paralegal firm. Research your symbol to see if anyone else has already registered it.

WEB SITES

U.S. Copyright Office
http://www.copyright.gov

U.S. Code Collection Title 15
http://www.law.cornell.edu/uscode/15/usc_sup_01_15_10_1.html

Copyright and Fair Use (Stanford University)
http://fairuse.stanford.edu

U.S. Patent and Trademark Office
http://www.uspto.gov

TERMS AND PHRASES

Copyright
Copyright infringement

Fair use
Patent

Public domain
Trademark

The United States Constitution

We the People of the United States, in Order to form a more perfect Union, establish Justice, insure domestic Tranquility, provide for the common defence, promote the general Welfare, and secure the Blessings of Liberty to ourselves and our Posterity, do ordain and establish this Constitution for the United States of America.

Article I.

Section 1.
All legislative Powers herein granted shall be vested in a Congress of the United States, which shall consist of a Senate and House of Representatives.

Section 2.
Clause 1: The House of Representatives shall be composed of Members chosen every second Year by the People of the several States, and the Electors in each State shall have the Qualifications requisite for Electors of the most numerous Branch of the State Legislature.

Clause 2: No Person shall be a Representative who shall not have attained to the Age of twenty five Years, and been seven Years a Citizen of the United States, and who shall not, when elected, be an Inhabitant of that State in which he shall be chosen.

Clause 3: Representatives and direct Taxes shall be apportioned among the several States which may be included within this Union, according to their respective Numbers, which shall be determined by adding to the whole Number of free Persons, including those bound to Service for a Term of Years, and excluding Indians not taxed, three fifths of all other Persons. The actual Enumeration shall be made within three Years after the first Meeting of the Congress of the United States, and within every subsequent Term often Years, in such Manner as they shall by Law direct. The Number of Representatives shall not exceed one for every thirty Thousand, but each State shall have at Least one Representative; and until such enumeration shall be made, the State of New Hampshire shall be entitled to chuse three, Massachusetts eight, Rhode-Island and Providence Plantations one, Connecticut five, New-York six, New Jersey four, Pennsylvania eight, Delaware one, Maryland six, Virginia ten, North Carolina five, South Carolina five, and Georgia three.

Clause 4: When vacancies happen in the Representation from any State, the Executive Authority thereof shall issue Writs of Election to fill such Vacancies.

Clause 5: The House of Representatives shall chuse their Speaker and other Officers; and shall have the sole Power of Impeachment.

Section 3.

Clause 1: The Senate of the United States shall be composed of two Senators from each State, chosen by the Legislature thereof, for six Years; and each Senator shall have one Vote.

Clause 2: Immediately after they shall be assembled in Consequence of the first Election, they shall be divided as equally as may be into three Classes. The Seats of the Senators of the first Class shall be vacated at the Expiration of the second Year, of the second Class at the Expiration of the fourth Year, and of the third Class at the Expiration of the sixth Year, so that one third may be chosen every second Year; and if Vacancies happen by Resignation, or otherwise, during the Recess of the Legislature of any State, the Executive thereof may make temporary Appointments until the next Meeting of the Legislature, which shall then fill such Vacancies.

Clause 3: No Person shall be a Senator who shall not have attained to the Age of thirty Years, and been nine Years a Citizen of the United States, and who shall not, when elected, be an Inhabitant of that State for which he shall be chosen.

Clause 4: The Vice President of the United States shall be President of the Senate, but shall have no Vote, unless they be equally divided.

Clause 5: The Senate shall chuse their other Officers, and also a President pro tempore, in the Absence of the Vice President, or when he shall exercise the Office of President of the United States.

Clause 6: The Senate shall have the sole Power to try all Impeachments. When sitting for that Purpose, they shall be on Oath or Affirmation. When the President of the United States is tried, the Chief Justice shall preside: And no Person shall be convicted without the Concurrence of two thirds of the Members present.

Clause 7: Judgment in Cases of Impeachment shall not extend further than to removal from Office, and disqualification to hold and enjoy any Office of honor, Trust or Profit under the United States: but the Party convicted shall nevertheless be liable and subject to Indictment, Trial, Judgment and Punishment, according to Law.

Section 4.

Clause 1: The Times, Places and Manner of holding Elections for Senators and Representatives, shall be prescribed in each State by the Legislature thereof; but the Congress may at any time by Law make or alter such Regulations, except as to the Places of chusing Senators.

Clause 2: The Congress shall assemble at least once in every Year, and such Meeting shall be on the first Monday in December, unless they shall by Law appoint a different Day.

Section 5.
Clause 1: Each House shall be the Judge of the Elections, Returns and Qualifications of its own Members, and a Majority of each shall constitute a Quorum to do Business; but a smaller Number may adjourn from day to day, and may be authorized to compel the Attendance of absent Members, in such Manner, and under such Penalties as each House may provide.

Clause 2: Each House may determine the Rules of its Proceedings, punish its Members for disorderly Behaviour, and, with the Concurrence of two thirds, expel a Member.

Clause 3: Each House shall keep a Journal of its Proceedings, and from time to time publish the same, excepting such Parts as may in their Judgment require Secrecy; and the Yeas and Nays of the Members of either House on any question shall, at the Desire of one fifth of those Present, be entered on the Journal.

Clause 4: Neither House, during the Session of Congress, shall, without the Consent of the other, adjourn for more than three days, nor to any other Place than that in which the two Houses shall be sitting.

Section 6.
Clause 1: The Senators and Representatives shall receive a Compensation for their Services, to be ascertained by Law, and paid out of the Treasury of the United States. They shall in all Cases, except Treason, Felony and Breach of the Peace, be privileged from Arrest during their Attendance at the Session of their respective Houses, and in going to and returning from the same; and for any Speech or Debate in either House, they shall not be questioned in any other Place.

Clause 2: No Senator or Representative shall, during the Time for which he was elected, be appointed to any civil Office under the Authority of the United States, which shall have been created, or the Emoluments whereof shall have been encreased during such time; and no Person holding any Office under the United States, shall be a Member of either House during his Continuance in Office.

Section 7.
Clause 1: All Bills for raising Revenue shall originate in the House of Representatives; but the Senate may propose or concur with Amendments as on other Bills.

Clause 2: Every Bill which shall have passed the House of Representatives and the Senate, shall, before it become a Law, be presented to the President of the United States; If he approve he shall sign it, but if not he shall return it, with his Objections to that House in which it shall have originated, who shall enter the Objections at large on their Journal, and proceed to reconsider it. If after such Reconsideration two thirds of that House shall agree to pass the Bill, it shall be sent, together with the Objections, to the other House, by which it shall likewise be reconsidered, and if approved by two thirds of that House, it shall become a Law. But in all such Cases the Votes of both Houses shall be determined by yeas and Nays, and the Names of the Persons voting for and against the Bill shall be entered on the Journal of each House respectively. If any Bill shall not be returned by the President within ten Days (Sundays excepted) after it shall have been presented to him, the Same shall be a Law, in like Manner as if he had signed it, unless the Congress by their Adjournment prevent its Return, in which Case it shall not be a Law.

Clause 3: Every Order, Resolution, or Vote to which the Concurrence of the Senate and House of Representatives may be necessary (except on a question of Adjournment) shall be presented to the President of the United States; and before the Same shall take Effect, shall be approved by him, or being disapproved by him, shall be repassed by two thirds of the Senate and House of Representatives, according to the Rules and Limitations prescribed in the Case of a Bill.

Section 8.
Clause 1: The Congress shall have Power To lay and collect Taxes, Duties, Imposts and Excises, to pay the Debts and provide for the common Defence and general Welfare of the United States; but all Duties, Imposts and Excises shall be uniform throughout the United States;

Clause 2: To borrow Money on the credit of the United States;

Clause 3: To regulate Commerce with foreign Nations, and among the several States, and with the Indian Tribes;

Clause 4: To establish an uniform Rule of Naturalization, and uniform Laws on the subject of Bankruptcies throughout the United States;

Clause 5: To coin Money, regulate the Value thereof, and of foreign Coin, and fix the Standard of Weights and Measures;

Clause 6: To provide for the Punishment of counterfeiting the Securities and current Coin of the United States;

Clause 7: To establish Post Offices and post Roads;

Clause 8: To promote the Progress of Science and useful Arts, by securing for limited Times to Authors and Inventors the exclusive Right to their respective Writings and Discoveries;

Clause 9: To constitute Tribunals inferior to the supreme Court;

Clause 10: To define and punish Piracies and Felonies committed on the high Seas, and Offences against the Law of Nations;

Clause 11: To declare War, grant Letters of Marque and Reprisal, and make Rules concerning Captures on Land and Water;

Clause 12: To raise and support Armies, but no Appropriation of Money to that Use shall be for a longer Term than two Years;

Clause 13: To provide and maintain a Navy;

Clause 14: To make Rules for the Government and Regulation of the land and naval Forces;

Clause 15: To provide for calling forth the Militia to execute the Laws of the Union, suppress Insurrections and repel Invasions;

Clause 16: To provide for organizing, arming, and disciplining, the Militia, and for governing such Part of them as may be employed in the Service of the United States, reserving to the States respectively, the Appointment of the Officers, and the Authority of training the Militia according to the discipline prescribed by Congress;

Clause 17: To exercise exclusive Legislation in all Cases whatsoever, over such District (not exceeding ten Miles square) as may, by Cession of particular States, and the Acceptance of Congress, become the Seat of the Government of the United States, and to exercise like Authority over all Places purchased by the Consent of the Legislature of the State in which the Same shall be, for the Erection of Forts, Magazines, Arsenals, dock-Yards, and other needful Buildings; — And

Clause 18: To make all Laws which shall be necessary and proper for carrying into Execution the foregoing Powers, and all other Powers vested by this Constitution in the Government of the United States, or in any Department or Officer thereof.

Section 9.
Clause 1: The Migration or Importation of such Persons as any of the States now existing shall think proper to admit, shall not be prohibited by the Congress prior to the Year one thousand eight hundred and eight, but a Tax or duty may be imposed on such Importation, not exceeding ten dollars for each Person.

Clause 2: The Privilege of the Writ of Habeas Corpus shall not be suspended, unless when in Cases of Rebellion or Invasion the public Safety may require it.

Clause 3: No Bill of Attainder or ex post facto Law shall be passed.

Clause 4: No Capitation, or other direct, Tax shall be laid, unless in Proportion to the Census or Enumeration herein before directed to be taken.

Clause 5: No Tax or Duty shall be laid on Articles exported from any State.

Clause 6: No Preference shall be given by any Regulation of Commerce or Revenue to the Ports of one State over those of another: nor shall Vessels bound to, or from, one State, be obliged to enter, clear, or pay Duties in another.

Clause 7: No Money shall be drawn from the Treasury, but in Consequence of Appropriations made by Law; and a regular Statement and Account of the Receipts and Expenditures of all public Money shall be published from time to time.

Clause 8: No Title of Nobility shall be granted by the United States: And no Person holding any Office of Profit or Trust under them, shall, without the Consent of the Congress, accept of any present, Emolument, Office, or Title, of any kind whatever, from any King, Prince, or foreign State.

Section 10.
Clause 1: No State shall enter into any Treaty, Alliance, or Confederation; grant Letters of Marque and Reprisal; coin Money; emit Bills of Credit; make any Thing but gold and silver Coin a Tender in Payment of Debts; pass any Bill of Attainder, ex post facto Law, or Law impairing the Obligation of Contracts, or grant any Title of Nobility.

Clause 2: No State shall, without the Consent of the Congress, lay any Imposts or Duties on Imports or Exports, except what may be absolutely necessary for executing it's inspection Laws: and the net Produce of all Duties and Imposts, laid by any State on Imports or Exports, shall be for the Use of the Treasury of the United States; and all such Laws shall be subject to the Revision and Controul of the Congress.

Clause 3: No State shall, without the Consent of Congress, lay any Duty of Tonnage, keep Troops, or Ships of War in time of Peace, enter into any Agreement or Compact with another State, or with a foreign Power, or engage in War, unless actually invaded, or in such imminent Danger as will not admit of delay.

Article II.

Section 1.
Clause 1: The executive Power shall be vested in a President of the United States of America. He shall hold his Office during the Term of four Years, and, together with the Vice President, chosen for the same Term, be elected, as follows

Clause 2: Each State shall appoint, in such Manner as the Legislature thereof may direct, a Number of Electors, equal to the whole Number of Senators and Representatives to which the State may be entitled in the Congress: but no Senator or Representative, or Person holding an Office of Trust or Profit under the United States, shall be appointed an Elector.

Clause 3: The Electors shall meet in their respective States, and vote by Ballot for two Persons, of whom one at least shall not be an Inhabitant of the same State with themselves. And they shall make a List of all the Persons voted for, and of the Number of Votes for each; which List they shall sign and certify, and transmit sealed to the Seat of the Government of the United States, directed to the President of the Senate. The President of the Senate shall, in the Presence of the Senate and House of Representatives, open all the Certificates, and the Votes shall then be counted. The Person having the greatest Number of Votes shall be the President, if such Number be a Majority of the whole Number of Electors appointed; and if there be more than one who have such Majority, and have an equal Number of Votes, then the House of Representatives shall immediately chuse by Ballot one of them for President; and if no Person have a Majority, then from the five highest on the List the said House shall in like Manner chuse the President. But in chusing the President, the Votes shall be taken by States, the Representation from each State having one Vote; A quorum for this Purpose shall consist of a Member or Members from two thirds of the States, and a Majority of all the States shall be necessary to a Choice. In every Case, after the Choice of the President, the Person having the greatest Number of Votes of the Electors shall be the Vice President. But if there should remain two or more who have equal Votes, the Senate shall chuse from them by Ballot the Vice President.

Clause 4: The Congress may determine the Time of chusing the Electors, and the Day on which they shall give their Votes; which Day shall be the same throughout the United States.

Clause 5: No Person except a natural born Citizen, or a Citizen of the United States, at the time of the Adoption of this Constitution, shall be eligible to the Office of President; neither shall any Person be eligible to that Office who shall not have attained to the Age of thirty five Years, and been fourteen Years a Resident within the United States.

Clause 6: In Case of the Removal of the President from Office, or of his Death, Resignation, or Inability to discharge the Powers and Duties of the said Office, the Same shall devolve on the Vice President, and the Congress may by Law provide for the Case of Removal, Death, Resignation or Inability, both of the President and Vice President, declaring what Officer shall then act as President, and such Officer shall act accordingly, until the Disability be removed, or a President shall be elected.

Clause 7: The President shall, at stated Times, receive for his Services, a Compensation, which shall neither be encreased nor diminished during the Period for which he shall have been elected, and he shall not receive within that Period any other Emolument from the United States, or any of them.

Clause 8: Before he enter on the Execution of his Office, he shall take the following Oath or Affirmation: — "I do solemnly swear (or affirm) that I will faithfully execute the Office of President of the United States, and will to the best of my Ability, preserve, protect and defend the Constitution of the United States."

Section 2.

Clause 1: The President shall be Commander in Chief of the Army and Navy of the United States, and of the Militia of the several States, when called into the actual Service of the United States; he may require the Opinion, in writing, of the principal Officer in each of the executive Departments, upon any Subject relating to the Duties of their respective Offices, and he shall have Power to grant Reprieves and Pardons for Offences against the United States, except in Cases of Impeachment.

Clause 2: He shall have Power, by and with the Advice and Consent of the Senate, to make Treaties, provided two thirds of the Senators present concur; and he shall nominate, and by and with the Advice and Consent of the Senate, shall appoint Ambassadors, other public Ministers and Consuls, Judges of the supreme Court, and all other Officers of the United States, whose Appointments are not herein otherwise provided for, and which shall be established by Law: but the Congress may by Law vest the Appointment of such inferior Officers, as they think proper, in the President alone, in the Courts of Law, or in the Heads of Departments.

Clause 3: The President shall have Power to fill up all Vacancies that may happen during the Recess of the Senate, by granting Commissions which shall expire at the End of their next Session.

Section 3.

He shall from time to time give to the Congress Information of the State of the Union, and recommend to their Consideration such Measures as he shall judge necessary and expedient; he may, on extraordinary Occasions, convene both Houses, or either of them, and in Case of Disagreement between them, with Respect to the Time of Adjournment, he may adjourn them to such Time as he shall think proper; he shall receive Ambassadors and other public Ministers; he shall take Care that the Laws be faithfully executed, and shall Commission all the Officers of the United States.

Section 4.

The President, Vice President and all civil Officers of the United States, shall be removed from Office on Impeachment for, and Conviction of, Treason, Bribery, or other high Crimes and Misdemeanors.

Article III.

Section 1.

The judicial Power of the United States, shall be vested in one supreme Court, and in such inferior Courts as the Congress may from time to time ordain and establish. The Judges, both of the supreme and inferior Courts, shall hold their Offices during good Behaviour, and shall, at stated Times, receive for their Services, a Compensation, which shall not be diminished during their Continuance in Office.

Section 2.

Clause 1: The judicial Power shall extend to all Cases, in Law and Equity, arising under this Constitution, the Laws of the United States, and Treaties made, or which shall be made, under their Authority; — to all Cases affecting Ambassadors, other public Ministers and Consuls; — to all Cases of admiralty and maritime Jurisdiction; — to Controversies to which the United States shall be a Party; — to Controversies between two or more States; — between a State and Citizens of another State; — between Citizens of different States, — between Citizens of the same State claiming Lands under Grants of different States, and between a State, or the Citizens thereof, and foreign States, Citizens or Subjects.

Clause 2: In all Cases affecting Ambassadors, other public Ministers and Consuls, and those in which a State shall be Party, the supreme Court shall have original Jurisdiction. In all the other Cases before mentioned, the supreme Court shall have appellate Jurisdiction, both as to Law and Fact, with such Exceptions, and under such Regulations as the Congress shall make.

Clause 3: The Trial of all Crimes, except in Cases of Impeachment, shall be by Jury; and such Trial shall be held in the State where the said Crimes shall have been committed; but when not committed within any State, the Trial shall be at such Place or Places as the Congress may by Law have directed.

Section 3.

Clause 1: Treason against the United States, shall consist only in levying War against them, or in adhering to their Enemies, giving them Aid and Comfort. No Person shall be convicted of Treason unless on the Testimony of two Witnesses to the same overt Act, or on Confession in open Court.

Clause 2: The Congress shall have Power to declare the Punishment of Treason, but no Attainder of Treason shall work Corruption of Blood, or Forfeiture except during the Life of the Person attainted.

Article IV.

Section 1.

Full Faith and Credit shall be given in each State to the public Acts, Records, and judicial Proceedings of every other State. And the Congress may by general Laws prescribe the Manner in which such Acts, Records and Proceedings shall be proved, and the Effect thereof.

Section 2.

Clause 1: The Citizens of each State shall be entitled to all Privileges and Immunities of Citizens in the several States.

Clause 2: A Person charged in any State with Treason, Felony, or other Crime, who shall flee from Justice, and be found in another State, shall on Demand of the executive Authority of the State from which he fled, be delivered up, to be removed to the State having Jurisdiction of the Crime.

Clause 3: No Person held to Service or Labour in one State, under the Laws thereof, escaping into another, shall, in Consequence of any Law or Regulation therein, be discharged from such Service or Labour, but shall be delivered up on Claim of the Party to whom such Service or Labour may be due.

Section 3.

Clause 1: New States may be admitted by the Congress into this Union; but no new State shall be formed or erected within the Jurisdiction of any other State; nor any State be formed by the Junction of two or more States, or Parts of States, without the Consent of the Legislatures of the States concerned as well as of the Congress.

Clause 2: The Congress shall have Power to dispose of and make all needful Rules and Regulations respecting the Territory or other Property belonging to the United States; and nothing in this Constitution shall be so construed as to Prejudice any Claims of the United States, or of any particular State.

Section 4.

The United States shall guarantee to every State in this Union a Republican Form of Government, and shall protect each of them against Invasion; and on Application of the Legislature, or of the Executive (when the Legislature cannot be convened) against domestic Violence.

Article V.

The Congress, whenever two thirds of both Houses shall deem it necessary, shall propose Amendments to this Constitution, or, on the Application of the Legislatures of two thirds of the several States, shall call a Convention for proposing Amendments, which, in either Case, shall be valid to all Intents and Purposes, as Part of this Constitution, when ratified by the Legislatures of three fourths of the several States, or by Conventions in three fourths thereof, as the one or the other Mode of Ratification may be proposed by the Congress; Provided that no Amendment which may be made prior to the Year One thousand eight hundred and eight shall in any Manner affect the first and fourth Clauses in the Ninth Section of the first Article; and that no State, without its Consent, shall be deprived of its equal Suffrage in the Senate.

Article VI.

Clause 1: All Debts contracted and Engagements entered into, before the Adoption of this Constitution, shall be as valid against the United States under this Constitution, as under the Confederation.

Clause 2: This Constitution, and the Laws of the United States which shall be made in Pursuance thereof; and all Treaties made, or which shall be made, under the

Authority of the United States, shall be the supreme Law of the Land; and the Judges in every State shall be bound thereby, any Thing in the Constitution or Laws of any State to the Contrary notwithstanding.

Clause 3: The Senators and Representatives before mentioned, and the Members of the several State Legislatures, and all executive and judicial Officers, both of the United States and of the several States, shall be bound by Oath or Affirmation, to support this Constitution; but no religious Test shall ever be required as a Qualification to any Office or public Trust under the United States.

Article VII.

The Ratification of the Conventions of nine States, shall be sufficient for the Establishment of this Constitution between the States so ratifying the Same.

Amendments to the Constitution

Amendment I.

Congress shall make no law respecting an establishment of religion, or prohibiting the free exercise thereof; or abridging the freedom of speech, or of the press; or the right of the people peaceably to assemble, and to petition the Government for a redress of grievances.

Amendment II.

A well regulated Militia, being necessary to the security of a free State, the right of the people to keep and bear Arms, shall not be infringed.

Amendment III.

No Soldier shall, in time of peace be quartered in any house, without the consent of the Owner, nor in time of war, but in a manner to be prescribed by law.

Amendment IV.

The right of the people to be secure in their persons, houses, papers, and effects, against unreasonable searches and seizures, shall not be violated, and no Warrants shall issue, but upon probable cause, supported by Oath or affirmation, and particularly describing the place to be searched, and the persons or things to be seized.

Amendment V.

No person shall be held to answer for a capital, or otherwise infamous crime, unless on a presentment or indictment of a Grand Jury, except in cases arising in the land or naval forces, or in the Militia, when in actual service in time of War or public danger; nor shall any person be subject for the same offence to be twice put in jeopardy of life or limb; nor shall be compelled in any criminal case to be a witness against himself, nor be deprived of life, liberty, or property, without due process of law; nor shall private property be taken for public use, without just compensation.

Amendment VI.

In all criminal prosecutions, the accused shall enjoy the right to a speedy and public trial, by an impartial jury of the State and district wherein the crime shall have been committed, which district shall have been previously ascertained by law, and to be informed of the nature and cause of the accusation; to be confronted with the witnesses against him; to have compulsory process for obtaining witnesses in his favor, and to have the Assistance of Counsel for his defence.

Amendment VII.

In Suits at common law, where the value in controversy shall exceed twenty dollars, the right of trial by jury shall be preserved, and no fact tried by a jury, shall be otherwise re-examined in any Court of the United States, than according to the rules of the common law.

Amendment VIII.

Excessive bail shall not be required, nor excessive fines imposed, nor cruel and unusual punishments inflicted.

Amendment IX.

The enumeration in the Constitution, of certain rights, shall not be construed to deny or disparage others retained by the people.

Amendment X.

The powers not delegated to the United States by the Constitution, nor prohibited by it to the States, are reserved to the States respectively, or to the people.

Amendment XI.

The Judicial power of the United States shall not be construed to extend to any suit in law or equity, commenced or prosecuted against one of the United States by Citizens of another State, or by Citizens or Subjects of any Foreign State.

Amendment XII.

The Electors shall meet in their respective states, and vote by ballot for President and Vice-President, one of whom, at least, shall not be an inhabitant of the same state with themselves; they shall name in their ballots the person voted for as President, and in distinct ballots the person voted for as Vice-President, and they shall make distinct lists of all persons voted for as President, and of all persons voted for as Vice-President, and of the number of votes for each, which lists they shall sign and certify, and transmit sealed to the seat of the government of the United States, directed to the President of the Senate;—The President of the Senate shall, in the presence of the Senate and House of Representatives, open all the certificates and the votes shall then be counted;—The person having the greatest number of votes for President, shall be the President, if such number be a majority of the whole number of Electors appointed; and if no person have such majority, then from the persons having the highest numbers not exceeding three on the list of those voted for as President, the House of Representatives shall choose immediately, by ballot, the President. But in choosing the President, the votes shall be taken by states, the representation from each state having one vote; a quorum for this purpose shall consist of a member or members from two-thirds of the states, and a majority of all the states shall be necessary to a choice. And if the House of Representatives shall not choose a President whenever the right of choice shall devolve upon them, before the fourth day of March next following, then the Vice-President shall act as President, as in the case of the death or other constitutional disability of the President. The person having the greatest number of votes as Vice-President, shall be the Vice-President, if such number be a majority of the whole number of Electors appointed, and if no person have a majority, then from the two highest numbers on the list, the Senate shall choose the Vice-President; a quorum for the purpose shall consist of two-thirds of the whole number of Senators, and a majority of the whole number shall be necessary to a choice. But no person constitutionally ineligible to the office of President shall be eligible to that of Vice-President of the United States.

Amendment XIII.

Section 1. Neither slavery nor involuntary servitude, except as a punishment for crime whereof the party shall have been duly convicted, shall exist within the United States, or any place subject to their jurisdiction.

Section 2. Congress shall have power to enforce this article by appropriate legislation.

Amendment XIV.

Section 1. All persons born or naturalized in the United States, and subject to the jurisdiction thereof, are citizens of the United States and of the State wherein they reside. No State shall make or enforce any law which shall abridge the privileges or immunities of citizens of the United States; nor shall any State deprive any person of life, liberty, or property, without due process of law; nor deny to any person within its jurisdiction the equal protection of the laws.

Section 2. Representatives shall be apportioned among the several States according to their respective numbers, counting the whole number of persons in each State, excluding Indians not taxed. But when the right to vote at any election for the choice of electors for President and Vice President of the United States, Representatives in Congress, the Executive and Judicial officers of a State, or the members of the Legislature thereof, is denied to any of the male inhabitants of such State, being twenty-one years of age, and citizens of the United States, or in any way abridged, except for participation in rebellion, or other crime, the basis of representation therein shall be reduced in the proportion which the number of such male citizens shall bear to the whole number of male citizens twenty-one years of age in such State.

Section 3. No person shall be a Senator or Representative in Congress, or elector of President and Vice President, or hold any office, civil or military, under the United States, or under any State, who, having previously taken an oath, as a member of Congress, or as an officer of the United States, or as a member of any State legislature, or as an executive or judicial officer of any State, to support the Constitution of the United States, shall have engaged in insurrection or rebellion against the same, or given aid or comfort to the enemies thereof. But Congress may by a vote of two-thirds of each House, remove such disability.

Section 4. The validity of the public debt of the United States, authorized by law, including debts incurred for payment of pensions and bounties for services in suppressing insurrection or rebellion, shall not be questioned. But neither the

United States nor any State shall assume or pay any debt or obligation incurred in aid of insurrection or rebellion against the United States, or any claim for the loss or emancipation of any slave; but all such debts, obligations and claims shall be held illegal and void.

Section 5. The Congress shall have power to enforce, by appropriate legislation, the provisions of this article.

Amendment XV.
Section 1. The right of citizens of the United States to vote shall not be denied or abridged by the United States or by any State on account of race, color, or previous condition of servitude.

Section 2. The Congress shall have power to enforce this article by appropriate legislation.

Amendment XVI.
The Congress shall have power to lay and collect taxes on incomes, from whatever source derived, without apportionment among the several States, and without regard to any census or enumeration.

[This amendment was proposed in 1909 and ratified on February 3,1913.]

Amendment XVII.
The Senate of the United States shall be composed of two Senators from each State, elected by the people thereof, for six years; and each Senator shall have one vote. The electors in each State shall have the qualifications requisite for electors of the most numerous branch of the State legislatures.

When vacancies happen in the representation of any State in the Senate, the executive authority of such State shall issue writs of election to fill such vacancies: Provided, That the legislature of any State may empower the executive thereof to make temporary appointments until the people fill the vacancies by election as the legislature may direct.

This amendment shall not be so construed as to affect the election or term of any Senator chosen before it becomes valid as part of the Constitution.

Amendment XVIII (later repealed)
Section 1. After one year from the ratification of this article the manufacture, sale, or transportation of intoxicating liquors within, the importation thereof into, or the exportation thereof from the United States and all territory subject to the jurisdiction thereof for beverage purposes is hereby prohibited.

Section 2. The Congress and the several States shall have concurrent power to enforce this article by appropriate legislation.

Section 3. This article shall be inoperative unless it shall have been ratified as an amendment to the Constitution by the legislatures of the several States, as provided in the Constitution, within seven years from the date of the submission hereof to the States by the Congress.

Amendment XIX.

The right of citizens of the United States to vote shall not be denied or abridged by the United States or by any State on account of sex.

Congress shall have power to enforce this article by appropriate legislation.

Amendment XX.

Section 1. The terms of the President and Vice President shall end at noon on the 20th day of January, and the terms of Senators and Representatives at noon on the 3d day of January, of the years in which such terms would have ended if this article had not been ratified; and the terms of their successors shall then begin.

Section 2. The Congress shall assemble at least once in every year, and such meeting shall begin at noon on the 3d day of January, unless they shall by law appoint a different day.

Section 3. If, at the time fixed for the beginning of the term of the President, the President elect shall have died, the Vice President elect shall become President. If a President shall not have been chosen before the time fixed for the beginning of his term, or if the President elect shall have failed to qualify, then the Vice President elect shall act as President until a President shall have qualified; and the Congress may by law provide for the case wherein neither a President elect nor a Vice President elect shall have qualified, declaring who shall then act as President, or the manner in which one who is to act shall be selected, and such person shall act accordingly until a President or Vice President shall have qualified.

Section 4. The Congress may by law provide for the case of the death of any of the persons from whom the House of Representatives may choose a President whenever the right of choice shall have devolved upon them, and for the case of the death of any of the persons from whom the Senate may choose a Vice President whenever the right of choice shall have devolved upon them.

Section 5. Sections 1 and 2 shall take effect on the 15th day of October following the ratification of this article.

Section 6. This article shall be inoperative unless it shall have been ratified as an amendment to the Constitution by the legislatures of three-fourths of the several States within seven years from the date of its submission.

Amendment XXI.

Section 1. The eighteenth article of amendment to the Constitution of the United States is hereby repealed.

Section 2. The transportation or importation into any State, Territory, or possession of the United States for delivery or use therein of intoxicating liquors, in violation of the laws thereof, is hereby prohibited.

Section 3. This article shall be inoperative unless it shall have been ratified as an amendment to the Constitution by conventions in the several States, as provided in the Constitution, within seven years from the date of the submission hereof to the States by the Congress.

Amendment XXII.

Section 1. No person shall be elected to the office of the President more than twice, and no person who has held the office of President, or acted as President, for more than two years of a term to which some other person was elected President shall be elected to the office of the President more than once. But this article shall not apply to any person holding the office of President when this article was proposed by the Congress, and shall not prevent any person who may be holding the office of President, or acting as President, during the term within which this article becomes operative from holding the office of President or acting as President during the remainder of such term.

Section 2. This article shall be inoperative unless it shall have been ratified as an amendment to the Constitution by the legislatures of three-fourths of the several states within seven years from the date of its submission to the states by the Congress.

Amendment XXIII.

Section 1. The District constituting the seat of government of the United States shall appoint in such manner as the Congress may direct:

A number of electors of President and Vice President equal to the whole number of Senators and Representatives in Congress to which the District would be entitled if it were a state, but in no event more than the least populous state; they shall be in addition to those appointed by the states, but they shall be considered, for the purposes of the election of President and Vice President, to be electors appointed by a state; and they shall meet in the District and perform such duties as provided by the twelfth article of amendment.

Section 2. The Congress shall have power to enforce this article by appropriate legislation.

Amendment XXIV.

Section 1. The right of citizens of the United States to vote in any primary or other election for President or Vice President, for electors for President or Vice President, or for Senator or Representative in Congress, shall not be denied or abridged by the United States or any state by reason of failure to pay any poll tax or other tax.

Section 2. The Congress shall have power to enforce this article by appropriate legislation.

Amendment XXV.

Section 1. In case of the removal of the President from office or of his death or resignation, the Vice President shall become President.

Section 2. Whenever there is a vacancy in the office of the Vice President, the President shall nominate a Vice President who shall take office upon confirmation by a majority vote of both Houses of Congress.

Section 3. Whenever the President transmits to the President pro tempore of the Senate and the Speaker of the House of Representatives his written declaration that he is unable to discharge the powers and duties of his office, and until he transmits to them a written declaration to the contrary, such powers and duties shall be discharged by the Vice President as Acting President.

Section 4. Whenever the Vice President and a majority of either the principal officers of the executive departments or of such other body as Congress may by law provide, transmit to the President pro tempore of the Senate and the Speaker of the House of Representatives their written declaration that the President is unable to discharge the powers and duties of his office, the Vice President shall immediately assume the powers and duties of the office as Acting President. Thereafter, when the President transmits to the President pro tempore of the Senate and the Speaker of the House of Representatives his written declaration that no inability exists, he shall resume the powers and duties of his office unless the Vice President and a majority of either the principal officers of the executive department or of such other body as Congress may by law provide, transmit within four days to the President pro tempore of the Senate and the Speaker of the House of Representatives their written declaration that the President is unable to discharge the powers and duties of his office. Thereupon Congress shall decide the issue, assembling within forty-eight hours for that purpose if not in session. If the Congress, within twenty-one days after receipt of the latter written declaration, or, if Congress is not in session, within twenty-one days after Congress is required to assemble, determines by two-thirds vote of both Houses that the President is unable to discharge the powers and duties of his office, the Vice President shall continue to discharge the same as Acting President; otherwise, the President shall resume the powers and duties of his office.

Amendment XXVI.

Section 1. The right of citizens of the United States, who are 18 years of age or older, to vote, shall not be denied or abridged by the United States or any state on account of age.

Section 2. The Congress shall have the power to enforce this article by appropriate legislation.

Amendment XXVII.

No law varying the compensation for the services of the Senators and Representatives shall take effect until an election of Representatives shall have intervened.

Glossary

Accessory   The person who assists a principal, but is not present when the crime occurs

Administrative law   A broad term encompassing the power of branches of government to delegate power to governmental agencies to perform specific areas of responsibility; also refers to the power of governmental agencies to regulate themselves, such as their ability to create their own rules and regulations

Admissible   Evidence that is relevant to the issues in the suit and helps prove or disprove a contention in the case

Adoption   A legal decree creating a parent-child relationship when one did not exist before

Affirm   The appellate court agrees with the verdict, or some ruling, entered in the lower court and votes to keep that decision in place

Agency   A governmental unit or department

Agent   One who acts on behalf of another, usually in a business context

Alimony   The monetary payment made by a former spouse to the other spouse to maintain that spouse in the standard of living to which that person has become accustomed

Answer   The defendant's response to the complaint, containing the defendant's denials and any counterclaims that the defendant may have against the plaintiff

Appeal   A request to an appellate court that it reverse or modify a decision made in a lower court

Appellant   The person bringing the current appeal from an adverse ruling in the court below

Appellee   The person who won in the lower court

Arbitration   The process of bringing both sides in a civil suit together to negotiate a resolution

Arraignment   A court appearance in which a person accused of a crime is given the opportunity to enter a plea of guilty or not guilty

Arrest   The detention of a person by the police

Assault   The defendant causes the plaintiff to have fear or apprehension of a harmful/offensive contact

Associates   Attorney-employees of a firm

Attorney-Client privilege   An evidentiary privilege that can be invoked by the attorney or the client to refuse to answer questions about confidential communications between them

Battery   The defendant causes harmful or offensive contact to the plaintiff

Beneficiary   The person who receives the benefits of the trust

Beyond a reasonable doubt   The proof required in a criminal case; not mere conjecture, but a doubt that would cause a reasonable person to have some hesitation in reaching a specific conclusion

Bilateral contract   A contract in which one promise is exchanged for another promise

Breach   The defendant fails to act according to a legal standard, or violates a duty

Burden of Proof   The requirement that the party bringing the suit prove the allegations against the other party

Calendar call   A mandatory court hearing in which the judge inquires about the readiness of the parties to go to trial; also known as a docket call

Capacity   The requirement that all parties to a contract have the mental, physical, and legal ability to understand the nature of the obligation assumed

Caption   The heading or title used in all legal pleadings

Case brief   The process of writing out key elements of the case so that you can refer to them later

Case law   The body of cases decided by judges who have interpreted statutes and prior cases

Causation   Also known as proximate cause; the requirement that the defendant's actions be the primary cause of the plaintiff's injuries

Cause of action   A claim that the law recognizes as actionable

Certification   When an individual meets the minimum requirements for admission into a professional body

Certiorari (Cert)   (Latin) "To make sure." The court's authority to decide which cases it will hear on appeal. A denial of certiorari means that the court has refused to hear the appeal

Challenge for cause   When a panel member is removed because she cannot sit on the jury

Checks and balances The right of one branch of government to oversee the actions of another branch of government. For instance, the U.S. Supreme Court is authorized to invalidate a statute created by the U.S. Congress

Circumstantial evidence Evidence that suggests a conclusion or proves a fact indirectly

Cloning The creation of a genetically identical person from the tissue of the donor

Code An organized, systematic collection of laws, rules, or regulations

Codify A systematic arrangement of the laws of a particular jurisdiction or area of law

Commingling Combining funds from different sources into one. The practice is unethical when the attorney does not have the right to use the funds entrusted to his keeping

Complaint The pleading filed by the plaintiff and later served on the defendant; it sets out the details of the wrong suffered by the plaintiff and the reasons why the defendant is liable for those wrongs

Confidentiality The ethical obligation of an attorney and staff to protect the secret information relayed to them by a client

Conflict letter A letter sent to the judge explaining that the attorney has several different appearances scheduled for the same date and detailing which courts the attorney will go to first

Consideration The requirement in a contract that all parties incur some form of legal detriment in binding themselves to the contractual terms

Contempt A ruling that a person is in violation of a court order

Contingency fee A legal fee calculated on the basis of the final amount awarded in a case

Contract A legally recognized agreement that can be enforced under the law

Conversion The act of removing property from the rightful owner and reducing it to the possession of the taker

Copyright The right granted to an author by the Federal Copyright Statute to reproduce, prepare derivative works, and distribute copies of the work created by the author

Copyright infringement When the holder of a copyright alleges that another has used the work without permission

Cross-examination The questioning of a witness to show bias, prejudice, or lack of knowledge

Custody The right to physical possession of the child; the parent with custody is entitled to make daily decisions about the child's clothing, education, and discipline. The child lives with this parent most of the time

Damages Monetary payments made in a civil case designed to compensate the plaintiff for an injury

Defendant The party who is sued in a civil case

Deposition Oral questions of a witness, taken under oath, by an attorney; this testimony is preserved in a transcript

Direct evidence Proof of a fact by presentation of specific evidence

Direct examination The questioning of a witness by the side who called the witness to the stand

Disbarment A temporary or permanent revocation of an attorney's license to practice law

Discovery The exchange of information between the sides involved in a suit

Domicile A person's legal residence

Duty An obligation to conform one's conduct in such a way as to avoid causing injury to another

Escheat The seizure of a person's estate when she has left no heirs

Executor The person appointed in the will to represent the testator's interests and to make dispositions according to the will's provisions

Fair use The right to use a copyrighted work without the author's permission; fair use must fall into the categories of criticism, comment, news reporting, teaching, or research

Fee simple absolute Absolute ownership interests in the property; all rights to the property are vested in a single owner or owners

Foreclosure The right of another to take legal action to auction off real estate to satisfy an outstanding indebtedness, such as a mortgage

Guilty/Not Guilty The verdict in a criminal case. Only authorized when the jury believes, beyond a reasonable doubt, that the defendant is guilty of the crime charged and that the government has proven that guilt

Habeas corpus (Latin) "You have the body"; an inquiry to determine whether a person who is incarcerated has received all constitutional guarantees

Holographic will A will that is in the testator's handwriting and bears the testator's signature

Hung jury A jury that is unable to reach a unanimous verdict

Information A document filed by the prosecution that accuses the defendant of a crime; commonly used by federal prosecutors. Also known as an accusation

Informed consent An agreement by a person to allow some type of action after having been fully informed and after making a knowing and intelligent decision to allow the action

Integrated bar A state that requires attorneys to be members before they are allowed to practice

Interrogatories Written questions posed by one side of a civil action to the other side

Intestate The term for a person who has died without preparing a will

Joint tenancy The right to real estate that exists in two or more owners who have the right of survivorship

Jurisdiction The power of a court to render a decision on issues and to impose that decision on the parties in the case

Jurors Those people who have been selected to sit on a jury; they will consider the evidence and reach a verdict in the case

Jury charge Oral instructions given by the judge to the jury about how they should deliberate and what law they should follow

Jury strike The removal of a jury panel member, also known as a Jury challenge

Law A rule or regulation that if not followed, subjects the rule breaker to some form of sanction

Legal malpractice Professional negligence committed by an attorney during the course of his representation of a client

Liable A determination that one party has some obligation to another party, usually in the form of monetary payments (damages)

Licensure Mandatory regulation required before a person may practice in a particular field

Life estate Creation of a temporary estate in which a person is given possession, use, and other rights to property, but only as long as he lives. On the possessor's death, the property reverts to another

Malice The intentional desire to harm a person

Malpractice The failure of a professional to exercise the degree of skill, expertise, and knowledge for the benefit of the client or patient, otherwise known as professional negligence

Mediation The process of submitting a claim to a neutral third party who then makes a determination about the ultimate liability and award in a civil case

Mistrial A judicial declaration that the trial is void and has no legal effect

Mortgage A pledge of real estate as collateral or security for a loan

Motion for directed verdict A motion by the defense that asks the court to enter a verdict in the defendant's favor because the plaintiff (or government) has failed to prove all material allegations against the defendant

Motion for new trial A motion filed at the end of the trial by the losing party requesting another trial

Motion in limine A motion made during the trial

Multiple Listing Service The advertisement of real property among real estate brokers, offering to share in a commission if a broker produces a buyer who is ready, willing, and able to purchase the real estate

Negligence The theory of tort law that gives the plaintiff a cause of action against a defendant who owed the plaintiff a duty not to injure him, who then breached that duty, such that there was proximate cause between the breach of duty and the plaintiff's resultant damages

Officer of the court A person who is either employed by a court or has an obligation to uphold ethical and moral standards. Attorneys are officers of the court

Opinion An appellate court's written explanation of the important facts and applicable law that justifies the court's decision and shows how the court followed the principle of *stare decisis*

Panel A group of people who have been called for jury duty; the final jury will be selected from this group; also known as venire

Parol evidence Oral testimony used to prove or interpret a written provision

Partners Attorney-owners of a law firm

Patent A U.S. government license recognizing that the inventor has created a new, useful, and non-obvious plant, product, or process

Per capita (Latin) "By the head." Each heir gets an equal share

Per stirpes (Latin) "By the root." Distributing property by classification or ranking of heirs

Peremptory jury strike The removal of a jury panel member for any legally permissible reason, also known as a peremptory jury challenge

Plaintiff The party who files suit through a complaint, seeking damages from a person who caused personal, financial, or emotional injuries

Plea bargain An offer made by the prosecution to a defendant in which the prosecution offers a reduced sentence or fine in exchange for the defendant's plea of guilty prior to trial

Premeditation An appreciable time period between forming the intent to kill and actually carrying out the murder

Prenuptial agreement An agreement between future spouses about division of property and other issues in the event that the marriage ends due to death or divorce

Preponderance of the evidence The proof required in a civil case; more likely than not to be true

Principal One who has an agency relationship with another who acts on his behalf

Principal The suspect directly involved in the commission of the crime

Probable cause Objective evidence that a crime has been or is about to be committed

Probation The portion of a criminal sentence that is served outside of prison; usually involves supervision and strict behavioral rules

Product liability Suits brought by consumers for defective products that cause injury to them; such suits can be brought even when the manufacturer is not at fault in designing, manufacturing, or marketing the product

Public domain A work that was never copyrighted, or whose copyright has expired

Real property Land and anything permanently attached to land, also commonly referred to as real estate

Reasonable doubt The standard of proof in criminal cases. It refers to the evidence that the government must prove before jurors are permitted to reach a verdict of guilty

Record The evidence, pleadings, motions, transcript of the trial, and any other documents relevant to the case

Recuse To disqualify, such as when a judge removes herself from considering a case or is removed by another judge

Remand The appellate court requires additional information or an evidentiary hearing; it cannot conduct such a hearing itself, so it sends the case back to the trial court for the hearing, and then considers the appeal based on that hearing

Reporter An annual edition containing all the published decisions of a particular court

Retainer A fee paid to an attorney to secure the attorney's services

Reverse To reverse a decision is to set it aside; an appellate court disagrees with the verdict, or some ruling, in the lower court, and overturns that decision

Right of survivorship The right of a surviving concurrent owner to take full title to the property on the death of the other concurrent owner

Sentence The prison term, probation/parole, and fine imposed on a defendant who has been found guilty

Separation agreement An agreement between a husband and wife who are considering divorce that sets out the details of their separation and makes provisions for temporary custody of children, allocations of assets, and other issues

Separation of powers A provision of the U.S. Constitution that mandates that specific branches enjoy certain powers and that these powers cannot be shared or usurped by another branch

Settlement A negotiated termination of a case prior to a trial or jury verdict

Settlor The person who originally has full title to property, who creates a trust

Standard of care The standard used by the law to determine negligence; the standard that a professional must act in the same manner as a reasonable, prudent member of the profession

Stare decisis (Latin) "Standing by the decision." The principle that previously decided cases stand as precedent for future cases

Statute A law that is enacted by the legislature and signed into existence by the executive branch

Surrogate mother A woman who agrees to bear a child and then surrender all parental rights to that child to another, sometimes in exchange for money

Tenancy by entirety The joint tenancy created by marriage; each spouse has the right of survivorship to the estate on the death of the other spouse

Tenants in common Concurrent owners who own unequal shares to real estate and have no right of survivorship

Testamentary intent The demonstrated intent of a person to create a disposition of her property after her death

Testate The term for a person who has died after preparing a will

Testator The person who distributes her property through a will

Title examination The process of examining the public records connected with a parcel of real estate to locate any encumbrances or other legal impediments

Tort A personal injury, often resulting from a breach of duty, that gives the injured party a cause of action

Trademark A symbol used by a company on its products; when registered under the Trademark Act, it gives the holder the exclusive rights to the symbol

Trial court The court that hears witness testimony, considers evidence and reaches a verdict in civil and criminal cases

Trustee The person responsible for managing and administering a trust

Unauthorized practice of law (UPL) When a person who is not an attorney gives legal advice or does any action traditionally reserved for members of the state bar

Unilateral contract A contract that exchanges a promise for an action

Verdict The jury's decision about the facts and responsibility in a case

Voir Dire (Fr) "To look; to speak." The process of questioning jurors about their potential biases in the case

Warranties An express or implied promise about the performance, manufacture, or use of a product

Will A written document, created by a person in anticipation of her death, that directs how her property will be devised and appoints a personal representative to act on her behalf

Index